# Taxation of Investment Partnerships and Hedge Funds

# Taxation of U.S. Investment Partnerships and Hedge Funds

## Accounting Policies, Tax Allocations, and Performance Presentation

**NAVENDU P. VASAVADA**

WILEY

John Wiley & Sons, Inc.

For general information on our other products and services, or technical support,
please contact our Customer Care Department within the United States at
800-762-2974, outside the United States at 317-572-3993, or fax 317-572-4002.

Wiley also publishes its books in a variety of electronic formats. Some content that
appears in print may not be available in electronic books.

For more information about Wiley products, visit our Web site at http://www.
wiley.com.

ISBN 978-0-470-60575-2 (cloth); ISBN 978-0-470-64256-6 (ebk);
ISBN 978-0-470-64257-3 (ebk); ISBN 978-0-470-64258-0 (ebk)

Printed in the United States of America.

10  9  8  7  6  5  4  3  2  1

*To Rupangi*
*with love and appreciation*

# Contents

# Preface

Over the last decade, I co-founded two U.S. investment partnerships as chief investment officer (CIO), undertaking direct responsibility for delivery of superior returns to partners. Investment partnerships that mainly trade in securities are loosely called hedge funds, or simply funds, irrespective of whether they actually hedge to reduce risks. While venture capital funds, such as venture funds in Silicon Valley, are basically U.S. investment partnerships, they are considered a distinct breed from hedge funds.

I embarked upon my hedge fund career believing that I would mostly focus on investment management strategy and securities trading. I engaged an accountant as a contractor to perform all the bookkeeping and take care of accounting issues. Over the years, I found that my role as managing partner required ongoing conversations with lawyers and accountants on the matters of securities law, disclosure documents, compliance requirements, offshore paperwork, critical tax matters pertaining to the hedge fund, making decisions on accounting policies, and implementing the details of Global Investment Performance Standards.

Initially, these tasks seemed overwhelming. Here I was, a novice, having to talk with expert lawyers and accountants. I had believed that engaging the best lawyers and accountants would enable me to comfortably delegate these relevant matters to professionals. Yet every discussion and decision taken in consultation with these serious professionals would eventually require me to make the critical decisions. During this process, my repertoire of relevant facts about partnership agreements, tax filings and compliance with tax laws, and accounting procedures and policies expanded greatly.

Over the years, I synthesized these facts into a knowledge base sufficient to make me reasonably well versed, if not a minor expert, on hedge fund structure, hedge fund accounting policies, and the taxation of hedge funds and investment partnerships. I have written this book to document my acquired knowledge and discoveries, without the pretense of posing as a subject matter expert, with a view to improving the lives of future generations of MBAs, CFAs, and hedge fund managers who may otherwise have to struggle and take several years to grapple with the multifaceted word of hedge fund structure, accounting policies, and taxation.

The first several chapters of this book focus on hedge fund structure. These are relevant at the time of forming the hedge fund and drawing up the investment partnership agreement, as well as in making future amendments as required to the original partnership agreement. The subsequent chapters, which constitute the middle to end sections of this book, unravel the nuances of accounting methodologies and policies for hedge funds. Once the nature of hedge fund accounting is clarified, the last part of this book covers taxation of hedge funds. The last chapters describe strategies as well as small matters of detail that would facilitate hedge funds in improving their tax efficiency. Whenever there is a complex and multifaceted taxation, the issue of optimal taxation and tax efficiency arises. This also applies to tax-exempt investors, who might search for mechanisms to recover some part of foreign taxes directly paid by their hedge fund.

This book does not require the reader to be an accountant, a tax expert, a tax lawyer, or a partnership contract lawyer. It is intended for the unwitting MBA and CFA who leads a hedge fund but gets drawn into an arcane world of legal, accounting, and tax matters, and despite delegation to accountants and lawyers is ultimately responsible to tax and regulatory authorities and to investors. Instead of presenting examples with hypothetical numbers, I mostly use the language of algebra. The book expects familiarity with algebraic notation of basic economics and math to follow the shorthand of algebra with subscripts and superscripts. Fortunately, the world of finance MBAs, particularly those versed in quantitative finance, comfortably deals with linear algebra, and for brevity we may sometimes use shorthand notation with vectors and matrices, though one might run into complex situations with nonlinearities that are mostly translations of verbally stated official rules and guidelines. Similarly, CFAs are intensely examined for quantitative finance knowledge and are keenly aware of solving for multiple unknowns. Accountants are usually comfortable with numerical examples; we believe that the abstract representation in algebra with only occasional use of numerical examples will not be daunting to them, particularly when it relieves the anguish of accurately translating loose, verbally stated regulations and procedures into distinct and unambiguous steps for hedge fund accounting and tax practice.

I am indebted to Jaime C. Dermody for providing spirited discussion and inspiration, as well as extensive constructive comments.

NAVENDU P. VASAVADA
December 2009

# Taxation of U.S. Investment Partnerships and Hedge Funds

# CHAPTER 1

# The Arcane World of Hedge Funds and Investment Partnerships

## What Is a "Hedge Fund"?

So, what is a hedge fund really? A "hedge fund" is an entity that offers "alternative" investments to investors, distinct from "traditional" investments in bonds and equities. A general counsel to the Securities and Exchange Commission (SEC) aptly simplified this as "The term *hedge fund* is not really descriptive, but just refers to a private pool of institutional capital."[1] One would have expected that in the freewheeling world of the Internet, wiki volunteers would have arrived at a concise definition, in place of a confusing opening attempt at definition: "A hedge fund is an investment fund open to a limited range of investors that is permitted by regulators to undertake a wider range of investment and trading activities than other investment funds, and that, in general, pays a performance fee to its investment manager."[2] In order to identify and decode the nature and character of hedge funds and their secretive "alternative" investment or trading strategies, we shall follow the U.S. SEC's attempt to corral and codify this popular object of perpetual regulatory concern.

---

[1] "The Future of Securities Regulation," Brian G. Cartwright, in a speech by SEC staff, University of Pennsylvania Law School Institute for Law and Economics, October 24, 2007.
[2] Wikipedia entry of "hedge fund" accessed on October 13, 2009, at http://en.wikipedia .org/wiki/Hedge_fund. Note that Wikipedia entries are dynamic.

In 2004, the U.S. SEC proposed hedge fund regulatory rules to bring most hedge funds into its regulatory net. These were published in the U.S. Federal Register in December 2004 and made effective February 2005, in 46 pages of fine print. The new rules lack both specificity and brevity, stating:

> There is no statutory or regulatory definition of hedge fund, although many have several characteristics in common. Hedge funds are organized by professional investment managers who frequently have a significant stake in the funds they manage and receive a management fee that includes a substantial share of the performance of the fund. Advisers organize and operate hedge funds in a manner that avoids regulation as mutual funds under the Investment Company Act of 1940, and they do not make public offerings of their securities. Hedge funds were originally designed to invest in equity securities and use leverage and short selling to "hedge" the portfolio's exposure to movements of the equity markets. Today, however, advisers to hedge funds utilize a wide variety of investment strategies and techniques designed to maximize the returns for investors in the hedge funds they sponsor. Many are very active traders of securities.

The 2005 SEC rules remained in force for barely one year. In June 2006, the U.S. Federal Court of Appeals in the District of Columbia struck down these 2005 SEC Hedge Fund regulatory rules.[4] During the remainder of the administration of George W. Bush's term through 2008, there was no further attempt to pass new legislation to regulate hedge funds.

The Federal Court of Appeals ruling that reversed and cancelled the SEC's hedge fund regulation provides interesting counterperspectives in its official court opinion. The very first line of the court opinion is "Hedge funds are notoriously difficult to define." The court then provided an interesting alternative definition by negation as "Hedge funds may be defined more precisely by reference to what they are *not*." In light of this federal appeals court reversal, new rules of the type that the SEC sought to enact under its own authority require higher legislative approval from U.S. lawmakers.

---

[3]The SEC rules entered into the Federal Register on December 10, 2004, are available to view in their entirety as a pdf file at the SEC Web page www.sec.gov/rules/final/ia-2333.pdf.

[4]The U.S. Court of Appeals for the District of Columbia has tabled it so opinion for the viewing public is in the form of a pdf file at http://pacer.cadc.uscourts.gov/docs/common/opinions/200606/04-1434a.pdf.

During the brief period when the new SEC rules were in force (before they were struck down in court), many large hedge fund managers registered with the SEC, even though they could have avoided such a registration by remaining exclusively offshore entities. This was because U.S. institutional investors indicated their preference to invest with hedge fund managers who registered with the SEC. Thus, SEC compliance was seen by U.S. institutional investors as a seal of good housekeeping, with the advantage of recourse to the U.S. legal system should disputes arise. Those hedge fund managers who operated as exclusively offshore entities risked losing the significant volume of their assets under management from U.S. institutional investors desirous of pursuing alternative investments.

At the time the proposed SEC rules were being actively debated, many neutral economists and policymakers warned that such SEC regulation of hedge funds would likely drive hedge funds to offshore locations without making any meaningful dent in their overall assets under management. Indeed, large European banks and offshore financial hubs might become beneficiaries of tightened U.S. regulation of hedge funds. The SEC regulations imposed meaningful reporting and compliance burdens on hedge fund managers that might have put small hedge fund managers at a cost disadvantage relative to large hedge funds.

## U.S. Venture Partnerships

Although hedge funds have obtained media limelight in the past two decades, their plain older cousins, venture-capital partnerships, also organized as U.S. limited partnerships with almost the same exact structure as hedge funds, including the structure of management and performance fees, but they have received less media attention. Contrary to hedge funds, typical Silicon Valley venture partnerships have been objects of admiration for achieving multibillion-dollar companies in a reasonably short time based on entrepreneurial seeds, mostly located in college dormitories and neglected academic university laboratories, mostly in their local geography vicinity, with Stanford University serving as an anchor showcase. The creation of Genentech out of a single molecular biology researcher's lab at the University of California at San Francisco based on an investment of less than $100,000 by Kleiner, Perkins, Caufield & Byers (Kleiner Perkins), and the more recent rapid growth of Google out of a personal project of Stanford University graduate students, also associated with early investment by Kleiner Perkins, would remain showcases.

Chapter 11 elaborates upon to the nuances and differences between hedge funds and venture funds, as well as primary aspects of pass-through taxation to taxable U.S. Investors, and concerns regarding Unrelated

Business Tax on Income (UBTI) for tax-exempt U.S. investors. Until then, much of the subsequent discussion on hedge funds almost exactly applies to U.S. Venture Funds (or, more appropriately, Silicon Valley venture funds).

We have not separately reviewed U.S. oil and gas partnerships, which were extremely popular in the 1980s. Their popularity was largely fueled by then-prevailing tax credits and deductions from intangible drilling costs and accelerated depreciation. Many investors believed that the tax benefits outweighed their investment cost, even if oil and gas were never found.

## Types of U.S. Hedge Fund Entities and the U.S. Tax Code

At origination, a U.S. investment fund makes a primeval choice by type-casting itself into one of the various molds of U.S. federal taxation: It is obliged to seek a U.S. taxpayer ID number as a subchapter C corporation, a subchapter S corporation, a SEC-regulated investment company, or partnership, following the creation of such an entity in a corporate entity-friendly state such as Delaware. Its physical place of business would most likely be a hedge-fund-friendly state, in terms of state securities laws, such as Connecticut.

A subchapter S entity is almost never chosen to structure an investment fund due to the limited number of investors that it can have (at most 100). Its investors/shareholders should be natural persons who are citizens or residents of the United States, which precludes the inclusion of institutional investors and foreigners. Similarly, a subchapter C entity is almost immediately banished from consideration due to its flat 35 percent U.S. corporate tax on all future profits (with the exception for reduced taxation on U.S. source dividends, called the "dividends reduced deduction").

Further, dividends and distributions to shareholders from such a subchapter C entity are double taxed (i.e., taxed once again) in the hands of the shareholders when remitted. The Bush administration softened the blow of double taxation by taxing dividends on holdings of more than 60 days at a reduced tax rate of 15 percent in the hands of the shareholders, under new rules that define such "qualified dividends." It is rare but not unusual to find a maverick fund manager operating what is largely an investment fund in the form of a subchapter C corporation. For instance, Warren Buffett's Berkshire Hathaway Corporation is only nominally an industrial company and is considered by many investors to be a grand mutual fund. Its subchapter C standing attracts double taxation. It remains a puzzle that this brilliantly managed pseudo industrial de facto financial and portfolio investment entity stands out alone as a subchapter C corporation, when every other fund manager is seeking to typecast their entity under the lowest possible tax regime with the lightest regime of regulation.

The SEC regulated investment company, more commonly called a mutual fund,[5] is also a tax pass-through entity. There is no U.S. corporate or state tax at entity level that applies to such a company. However, the constraints of operating a regulated mutual fund under the U.S. Investment Company Act limit the range of feasible and permissible investment strategies. The world of venture capital funds, private equity funds, illiquid-securities funds, and hedge funds is disjoint from the world of SEC-regulated mutual funds. The latter is organized mainly for the benefit of small investors.

The overwhelming majority of U.S. venture capital funds, private equity funds, illiquid securities funds, and hedge funds are formed as pass-through partnerships under the U.S. tax code. Most lawyers would use the expression "investment partnership" as formal representation for a hedge fund as well as its close cousin of Silicon Valley, a venture fund. The latter have become more colloquial terms.

The source income from U.S. investment partnerships is not subjected to paying two layers of tax, as is the case with a U.S. subchapter C entity, by organizing themselves as pass-through partnership entities for the purpose of taxation under U.S. tax law. A U.S. limited partnership or a U.S. limited liability company is permitted to file its tax returns as a partnership, paying no direct corporate tax as would a subchapter C corporation, passing through its taxable income to its partners, who in turn are taxed as individuals. Thus, the income and earnings of the hedge fund or investment partnership are taxed only once, at the relevant marginal tax rate of each partner. Tax-exempt U.S. partners would not be paying any tax. However, the investment partnership must avoid being classified as a U.S. "publicly traded partnership."[6] If such classification were to occur, the partnership would be treated as if it were a subchapter C corporation for federal tax purposes, and would have to pay corporate tax. Further, investment partners who receive cash flows that are considered to be dividends would be taxed once again on such cash flows. Nearly all U.S. investment partnerships, both hedge funds and venture funds, qualify not to be deemed publicly traded partnership due to not having an active secondary

---

[5]A mutual fund is a regulated investment company that is governed by the Investment Company Act of 1940, described in 15 U.S.C. Sections 80a-1 to 80a-64, available at www.law.cornell.edu/uscode/html/uscode15/usc_sup_01_15_10_2D_20_I.html.

[6]Section 7704 of the Internal Revenue Code defines a publicly traded partnership and provides exceptions to the definition: a partnership with 90 percent or more of its gross income consists of dividends, interest, rents, and capital gains, and its interests should not be readily tradable in a secondary market.

market in its partnership interests, and due to producing nearly all of its income comes from "qualifying" sources, that is, dividends, interest, rents, and capital gains.

Hedge funds that pursue computerized high-frequency trading strategies and decide to count the trading profits as operating income, as opposed to capital gains, would be trading partnerships. This is not a preferred form of structuring, except for trading partnerships that incur significant expenses and desire to offset these expenses directly with trading income.

## Organizing a Typical U.S. Hedge Fund

The hedge fund manager, formally the general partner to the hedge fund, a U.S. limited partnership (LP), is typically a U.S. limited liability company (LLC), which for U.S. tax purposes may elect to be taxed as a partnership. The most popular U.S. state for formation of the hedge fund general partner LLC and LP pass-through partnership entities is Delaware. This is primarily because the relatively small state of Delaware has positioned itself among the 50 states as a friendly regime for corporate domicile, with well-developed corporate laws and longstanding corporate case history in the state court system.

Delaware itself is a taxable state and imposes corporate tax on Delaware entities having a physical business presence in the state. For this reason, nearly all U.S. general partner entities establish a principal place of business in a U.S. state other than Delaware, which does not impose corporate taxes on LLC entities that are pass-through partnerships for U.S. federal tax purposes. Connecticut is one such popular state for Delaware entities setting up their principal place of business for hedge fund management and operations. Thus, such a general partner LLC pass-through entity does not pay either federal or state corporate tax on its income. All of the general partner entity's items of income are taxed only once, when passed through to its partners.

The hedge fund manager, that is, the general partner, charges fund management fees to its limited partners. The details of such fees, contractual provisions, as well as tax consequences both to the limited partners and the general partner are described later. The general partner is responsible for the day-to-day operations, administration, and overall management of the fund, and incurs management expenses.

Thus, a typical U.S. hedge fund structure is a *pair*. The hedge fund sponsor organizer sets up two entities, usually in the state of Delaware. The first is typically a Delaware LLC (limited liability company) that becomes the general partner of the second entity, a Delaware LP (limited partnership). The general partner entity is governed by a private operating agreement of the LLC signed by its members, who are its partners. LLC members are granted limited liability by the State of Delaware. At a minimum, the LLC agreement establishes the voting powers of members, designation of a manager (who could be a member), power of attorney and authority delegated to the manager, and profit sharing among members. The limited partnership entity is governed by its agreement of partnership. Delaware and other states do not require the operating agreement of the LLC or the partnership agreement of the LP to be filed, so they remain private documents in private domain. For a limited partnership, Delaware requires a sparse one-page formation document, "Certificate of Limited Partnership," provided on its Web site signed by an authorized representative of its general partner LLC entity, such as its manager or member. Similarly, the general partner entity, the LLC, files a sparse one-page formation document provided on the Delaware state Web site, "Limited Liability Company Certificate of Formation," signed by an authorized person who is either a member or simply an appointed or employed manager.

The GP/LP pair immediately obtain taxpayer identification numbers from the Internal Revenue Service (IRS) by filing the appropriate IRS Form SS-4, which requires clear identification of the type of entity in a check box. The LLC can elect to be either a subchapter C corporation or a partnership for the purposes of U.S. taxation. The LLC entity (which is general partner to the LP) wisely elects to be taxed as a pass-through U.S. partnership to avoid double taxation that a U.S. subchapter C corporation would face. The pair of entities is required to have nominal registered offices in the state of Delaware, which is really the physical address of its Delaware-registered agent named on the certificate of formation. The pair of entities appoints such a state agent prior to seeking entity formation, for which the agent charges a modest annual fee. The state of Delaware charges a modest initial filing fee, which at this time is $200 for an LP and $90 for an LLC. Subsequently, the LP and LLC that are formed in the State of Delaware are not required to file an annual report but are required to pay an annual flat tax of $250.

The pair subsequently establish a common physical place of business, which is typically in the state of Connecticut for hedge funds. For Silicon Valley venture partnerships, the physical place of business is in the state of California. (Silicon Valley venture partnerships have no particular affinity for Delaware and might elect to form their LP and LLC pair in Nevada or California.) They are required to make Delaware-like filings in their state of domicile and business presence, as a "foreign" out-of-state entity that is doing business in the state.

Delaware courts have well-established precedents that firmly protect the limited liability of partners in a limited partnership, as well as members in a limited liability company. The managers and members of the Delaware

LLC are shielded from personal liability that might arise from their actions conducted for the benefit of their LLC or LP. The manager of an LLC is presumed to be acting in the best interests of partners and shareholders. The general partner entity that runs the LP is an LLC, so it is automatically shielded from liability in excess of its assets. The manager and members of the general partner entity, which is an LLC, are similarly shielded from claims of personal liability. While this kind of protection from external liability claims upon individual managers and members of the LLC is offered practically in all other states, Delaware has the best established record of case law that demonstrates its seriousness as a business domicile. Large publicly traded subchapter C corporations particularly prefer Delaware, whose case law has favored companies and their directors in shareholder litigation relating to corporate takeovers.

Connecticut is a popular location for hedge fund operations. The most important reason is that its securities laws generally exempt those entities from state registration as an investment adviser as long as they are exempt from such SEC registration. Generally, a hedge fund that trades for its own account, with investors sharing common objectives in a limited partnership agreement, and all look-through investors being either U.S. "qualified purchasers" or suitable foreign purchasers, is exempt from registration as an investment adviser with the SEC and consequently from registration as an investment adviser with the state of Connecticut. A similar exemption is offered by the state of New York, which is why a large number of hedge funds maintain their operations in New York City.

The second important reason in favor of Connecticut as a business location for U.S. hedge fund is that, like many states, neither only state-resident partners of the general partner LLC entity nor the LP entity are subject to pass-through state income tax on investment income. Only resident partners of an LLC or LP in a particular state are required to pay that state's income taxes on taxable pass-through partnership income. Neither of the entities is subject to direct state taxation on income or assets. Similarly, a branch of an offshore hedge fund is not considered to be producing business income in the state and is not subjected to state tax on income or assets.

The general partner, which is the LLC entity, has no place of business in its state of formation (Delaware) and is not taxed (in Delaware) on any of its operating income as general partner. Likewise, the state of Connecticut where the LLC/LP pair maintains its physical place of business does not impose a blanket corporate tax on U.S. partnership entities. Only partners who are resident of the state of Connecticut have to pay personal tax on pass-through income arising from the LLC or LP.

The pair of entities is now ready for business. The fund organizers set up bank accounts for the LLC and LP, and securities brokerage accounts for the LP. This step requires passing the compliance standards and requirements of the banks and brokerage firms, whose compliance departments review both the LLC operating agreement and the LP agreement to determine the powers of attorney granted in the agreements and identify the relevant individuals who are the authorized signatories and traders.

The United States presents a simple procedural environment for forming pass-through limited liability entity-structures with no direct taxation. The hedge fund LLC/LP pair can be formed in Delaware and its IRS taxpayer ID obtained instantly, within one day. It may take a week or two to obtain a bank and securities brokerage account and begin trading, allowing time for review by compliance departments. That is the easy part. The thorny parts follow, of accounting, audit, tax filing, partner reporting, regulatory compliance, and, the most important challenge, of marketing the hedge fund to seek new fee-paying limited partners. A hedge fund appoints its legal counsel, organizes its accounting, seeks the engagement of an independent outside auditor, and prepares an information memorandum containing all pertinent information, including a description of the fund strategy, the people and investment decision makers in the fund, and its organization and governance. As the years go by, the information memorandum is updated with presentation of historical performance and risk measures, which is described in detail in Chapter 10.

The U.S. states under whose laws the LLC or LP were formed generally do not impose direct corporate income taxes on items of pass-through investment income. Their focus is on state corporate taxation of ordinary income from in-state business operations. Nearly all states charge an annual fee to their domiciled LLCs and LPs. This is usually a flat fee that is only nominally called an annual tax; yet there are some states that charge franchise fees that are linked to assets and income and are really state corporate taxes in disguise. Some states impose a de facto income tax on any partnership in the state, only it's not called an income tax but something else. The state of Illinois imposes a 1.5 percent "replacement tax" on taxable pass-through income of an Illinois partnership, to be paid by the LLC or LP entity. The state of Pennsylvania imposes "corporate capital stock tax" as a percentage of assets on LLCs (but not LPs) that are formed in that state or do business in that state, along with a complex formula that attempts to capitalize income according to a hypothetical statutory assets-to-earnings ratio. At the time of forming the core *pair* of entities (the LLC and LP) that constitute a U.S. hedge fund, the hedge fund organizers look carefully to selecting the state of formation so as to avoid or minimize fees and indirect taxes that are linked to income and assets. Conversely, states that are popular domiciles for partnerships that are LLCs and LPs tend to be states that have low flat annual fees and no direct or indirect taxes on assets and income. Delaware is one such state, which comes with the added advantage of a state court system with well-established legal precedents on entities formed in the state that clearly favor the entities.

Limited partner investors should recognize that the limited partnership agreement assigns power of attorney for banking and securities trading to the general partner entity, which in turn assigns its power of attorney for banking and securities trading to one or more individuals who are managers, members, or manager-members of the general partner LLC entity. Implicitly, a high-trust relationship is formed between the limited partner investors and the authorized signatories of the general partner entity.

In summary, a U.S. hedge fund is organized as a limited partnership by its organizer, who is also its fund manager as its general partner. Limited partners have limited liability and do not expect to lose any more than the amount of their capital investment. The general partner makes the legal appearance of absorbing all the residual liabilities of the hedge fund, in the unlikely event when liabilities exceed the value of the partnership. However, by simple legal construction, the general partner is organized as a limited liability entity and effectively bears negligible economic liability. The investment, trading, and administrative decision-makers for the hedge fund act in the capacity of managers to the general partner, and thus they do not personally absorb residual liabilities of the general partner entity under well-tested laws in states such as Delaware.

The general partner entity may itself contribute a portion of the capital of the hedge fund (i.e., into the limited partnership entity). However, instances of large holding by the general partner in the LP are rare. The general partner in a hedge fund typically contributes only a token amount of capital to the fund. The general partner usually does not pay any fees. The primary objective of the general partner is to earn fees on a larger base of capital that is raised from fee-paying limited partners. The fees are a source of cost to the limited partners that detract from their investment returns, and the sole source of revenue and profit to the general partner.

## Investor Clienteles in Hedge Funds

A hedge fund has to be careful in its choice of admitting appropriate limited partners. These clienteles of fee-paying investors whose inclusion and admittance would not trigger the regulation of the hedge fund by the SEC are described next.

**Accredited Investors.** These SEC limits appear to segment the income profile of typical professionals: It encompasses those individuals with at least $1 million in assets and $300,000 of family income.[7] This segment of investors is unlikely to raise the desired billions of dollars of capital for a mega hedge fund. Accredited investors are typically folded into hedge funds through "wrap accounts" offered by nearly all full-service brokerage firms, which in turn invest in a target hedge fund.

**Qualified Purchasers.** U.S. hedge funds typecast in the format of a U.S. investment partnership are typically targeted at limited partners who are considered "qualified purchasers" by the SEC, following their definition in the U.S. Investment Company Act, as a natural person who owns not less than $5 million dollars in investments, or an entity that invests at least $25 million.[8]

The hedge fund market largely draws from qualified purchasers, since a very small number of them might easily add up to orders of $100 million. Pre-existing SEC rules clearly exempt an investment adviser from registration with the SEC if all investors fall within this category. A large consortium of accredited investors joining a hedge fund through a brokerage firm wrap account would likely be considered by the SEC to have a surrogate single qualified purchaser. If the hedge fund organizers do not want to take chances of incurring the wrath of the SEC by admitting accredited investors into a large hedge fund, the recommended clean approach to keep the SEC at bay is to admit only qualified investors into a hedge fund. Note that all U.S. funds are *regulated* by the SEC, even those that are *exempt* from the SEC due to admitting qualified investors only. There is an immense benefit to hedge funds that are exempted from registration that the SEC, due to not having to comply with the ongoing burden of SEC registration and perpetual filings.

**Foreign Investors.** All of the SEC definitions of accredited and qualified investors apply only to U.S. persons or U.S. entities. The regulations are silent about financial wealth and standards for foreign investors admitted to a U.S. investment partnerships or hedge fund. A foreign investor to

---

[7]The SEC provides a clear definition of "accredited investors" at www.sec.gov/answers/accred.htm. The SEC is relaying a regulation that governs it, at 17 CFR part 230, section 501. The source is at http://edocket.access.gpo.gov/cfr_2006/aprqtr/17cfr230.501.htm. There is also a user-friendly Wikipedia entry at http://en.wikipedia.org/wiki/Accredited_investor.

[8]A complete formal and official definition of "Qualified Purchaser" is in Title 15 U.S.C. Chapter 2D, Subchapter I, Section 80a-2(a)(51). "U.S.C." stands for U.S. Code, which is published to the Internet in its entirety by the U.S. Government at www.gpoaccess.gov/uscode/browse.html.

whom adequate disclosure of the investment strategy and risks has been provided in an information memorandum, who appears to have sufficient wealth, and who demonstrates understanding and experience with risky investments could be viewed as a "suitable" investor and be duly admitted into a U.S.-domiciled hedge fund without reference to the formal accredited investor and qualified purchaser standards of the SEC that apply to U.S. investors. Many U.S. master hedge funds are based on admitting a foreign partner/investor who is actually an arm's-length-affiliated offshore feeder fund that is created by the hedge fund organizers.

**U.S. Investors, Tax-exempt and Taxable.**    In recent years, large numbers of U.S. institutional investors have sought participation in limited partners in hedge funds. These institutions, typically pension plans and nonprofit endowments or charities, are typically exempt from U.S. taxation. As a result, these large institutional tax-exempt investors in hedge funds mostly care about economic returns on their investment without regard to tax, except for perpetual fear of Unrelated Business Tax on Income (UBTI, also sometimes written as UBIT).[9] There are clear, legal precedents that establish borrowing or debt financing by tax-exempt entities, either directly or as a pass-through partner in an investment partnership, that would invite UBTI on all income flows attributable to the borrowing. Thus, hedge funds and venture funds that are U.S. entities and admit large institutional tax-exempt limited partners are effectively restricted from investment strategies that involve any direct form of debt. On the other hand, there are clear precedents that permit the same nonprofit entities to engage in forms of indirect borrowing such as forward and futures contracts or other derivatives such as options. Many hedge funds seek to establish private party swaps and notional principal contracts that contain embedded forward contracts and derivatives. After 2008, institutional investors are painfully aware that private swaps and notional principal contracts are subject to serious counterparty risk. The Lehman Brothers bankruptcy of 2008 was a grim reminder that private party swaps are not exactly safe from counterparty default, and that a new economic cost has been introduced, of insuring against default of private swap counterparty. Such default insurance is further subject to default by the insurer, as was highlighted by the recent collapse of AIG in September 2008.

A significant set of U.S. investors are taxable individuals and entities that are keenly sensitive to tax considerations surrounding cash flows from their investment in a hedge fund or venture fund. While taxable investors

---

[9]UBTI is described in the Internal Revenue Code Section 512(a)(3), which is available at www.law.cornell.edu/uscode/26/usc_sec_26_00006033----000-.html.

indeed primarily seek decent economic returns without regard to taxes, they also look at tax consequences and after-tax returns. Taxable investors often are obliged to make partial redemptions from a hedge fund to pay out tax obligations, some of which may be arising from their participation in the hedge fund. Most hedge funds and venture funds have strict clauses in their agreements to permit partners to make cash redemptions of all or some part of their partnership interest whenever there is any significant taxable cash flow or tax allocation. This is to ensure that the taxable partners have funds to pay tax liabilities arising from the present year tax allocations, which could be significant.

Foreign investors in U.S. hedge funds are usually domiciled in tax-free countries or regimes. The only relevant tax imposed on foreign investors by the U.S. government on foreign investors is a flat 30 percent withholding tax on U.S. source dividends. Generally, all other pass-through sources of partnership investment income and their tax allocations to foreign limited partners are not subject to U.S. withholding tax. Any ordinary income earned from business operations by a U.S. partnership is not considered "portfolio income" and is subject to 30 percent withholding tax to foreign limited partners.[10] The U.S. hedge fund becomes the withholding agent for the withholding tax on dividends and ordinary income. Typically, the amount of dividend tax payment by the foreign limited partner is funded by redemption of the tax amount from their partnership interest.

We should not ignore foreign investors in both U.S. and offshore hedge funds who are domiciled taxpayers in tax paying regimes, such as mature market countries in Europe and Asia. Nearly all countries that impose a personal tax have inter-country tax treaties. Thus, any withholding tax on U.S. source dividends held back for such a taxable foreign investor in either the U.S. entity or an offshore entity could be applied as credit toward their domestic home country taxes.

It should be noted that some hedge funds might report pass-through operating business income that arises from holdings in other operating businesses and partnerships, such as real estate operations and securities or commodities trading operations that report their income as ordinary operating income. A foreign partner's pass-through allocation share of such operating active net income would be considered as active U.S. source income that is subject to 30 percent withholding tax and not as passive U.S. "portfolio income" that is exempt from U.S. withholding tax.

---

[10]Rules for withholding tax of U.S. income of foreigners are stated in the Internal Revenue Code Sections 871 and 881. They are available at www.law.cornell.edu/uscode/26/usc_sec_26_00000871----000-.html, and www.law.cornell.edu/uscode/26/usc_sec_26_00000881----000-.html.

# Foreign Investors in a U.S. Hedge Fund

**Offshore Affiliate Feeder Fund.** A typical structure adopted by U.S. hedge funds for admitting foreign limited partners is to create an offshore affiliate that acts as a feeder fund. Such an offshore affiliate is organized in popular Caribbean colonies of the United Kingdom, such as the Cayman Islands, British Virgin Islands, and Bermuda, the Dutch colony of Netherlands Antilles, and so on. These regimes offer credible legal protection to investors by a court system and laws of their mother countries, the United Kingdom and the Netherlands, while at the same time offering the benefit of complete exemption from taxation as well as the benefit of participation in tax treaties between the U.S. and their mother countries. It is unlikely that independent sovereign countries that merely offer tax-free regimes would offer credible legal protection to investors. In the coming years, we may witness the rise of similar offshore locations in the Middle East (like Dubai) and in the Pacific (like Singapore), but these are unlikely to be viewed as regimes with the same legal protection to investors offered by the crown colony laws of the United Kingdom and the Netherlands.

The advantage of such a structure is that in its tax reporting, the U.S. hedge fund is required to report only the name of the feeder fund as the offshore entity to the IRS, and not the names of the individual foreign investors and shareholders of the offshore entity, in order to preserve their anonymity. If the same individual foreign investors are admitted as limited partners in the U.S. limited partnership, their names are reported to the U.S. IRS in the tax filing of the U.S. limited partnership.

# Offshore Funds

The expression "offshore fund" is a catchphrase that denotes a hedge fund located outside taxing jurisdictions and high-tax regimes, conveniently formed under the laws of a tax-free political regime that is friendly to nonresident shareholders and investors, but also belongs to the legal sovereign jurisdiction of solvent European countries with well-established legal systems to deter and punish fraud and protect investors.

A large number of foreign investors are alarmed by the fear of falling into the U.S. regulatory and tax enforcement net as direct foreign limited partners in a U.S. hedge fund. The last thing they want to receive is an IRS notice, however innocuous it might be. Their fears are often mitigated through participating in an offshore feeder fund that in turn purchases a partnership interest in a U.S. investment partnership. These investors usually seek comfort through investing in an entirely offshore fund with no tax enforcement connection with the U.S. government. Such an offshore fund might also directly invest in U.S. securities through a U.S. brokerage firm, which in turn acts as the U.S. dividend tax withholding agent. However, from the perspective of U.S. tax enforcement, there is a big difference to a non-U.S. investor between participating as a partner in a U.S. hedge fund versus participating in an offshore fund that in turn operates a brokerage account to trade U.S. securities. In the former case, the names of the foreign limited partners in the U.S. investment partnership are provided to the IRS. In the latter case, only the name of the foreign offshore feeder fund is provided to the IRS, not the names of its pass-through shareholders. Thus, for foreign investors desirous of investing in U.S. securities, participating in a U.S. domiciled hedge fund either directly into a U.S. master fund or indirectly by participating in an independent offshore fund, is a tradeoff. Direct participation in the U.S. partnership reveals their names to the IRS, while offering the benefit of the long arm of U.S. anti-fraud enforcement and the right to U.S. litigation. Indirect participation in a U.S. partnership (or, in general, in U.S. securities) through investment in an offshore fund or entity shields their names from the IRS but only offers light anti-fraud legal protection under the legal system in the offshore location.

What exactly is meant by a "U.S. security"? Generally, any security issued by a U.S. entity, particularly a publicly traded security in a stock exchange, securities exchange, or futures exchange, or a U.S. treasury bond, requires the issuer to record the name of the holder and pass on information about payments of dividends, interest, and security sales to the U.S. government. In a limited concession to the brokerage industry, brokerage firms retain the names of the foreign holders of U.S. securities on their own records and collect U.S. withholding taxes but do not have to submit the names of the foreign holders to the IRS. However, foreign investors do not take their chances. If they wish to invest in U.S. dollar denominated fixed income securities, they participate in the London Interbank Offered Rate (LIBOR) market rather than engage in direct holding of U.S. treasury bonds.

There is a large segment of independent offshore hedge funds that invest in non-U.S. securities. In the past several decades, when the United States housed the world's largest markets for bonds, equities, currencies, commodities, options and futures, credit derivatives, swaps, and other exotic forms of securities such as collateralized debt obligations, foreign investors needed access to these sophisticated U.S. markets. In future decades, with the rapid emergence of London, Paris, and Frankfurt as financial centers, followed by Dubai, Mumbai, Hong Kong, Singapore, Shanghai, and Tokyo, and the rapid economic growth in the developing countries, participation by non-U.S. investors in U.S. capital markets and hence in U.S. securities may not be as important as it might have been in the past. Similarly, the U.S. investors would likely increase their holding of non-U.S. securities in their portfolios.

**Organization of an Offshore Fund.**   Each offshore regime has different formats, definitions, and language for organizing tax-exempt hedge funds under their laws. In most of the popular offshore locations, such as the British crown colonies in the Caribbean, there are three forms of organization offered: as a company, a mutual fund, or a partnership. Companies and partnerships are loosely regulated, while mutual funds tend to have more controls and rules, though none as onerous as the enforcement and regulatory net of the U.S. government. The choice of organization primarily rests with the hedge fund managers and their clientele of investors. An offshore mutual fund or partnership best allows for contractual clauses for shareholders to pay management fees to the fund manager. A simple company is intended for distributing profits as dividends to shareholders according to their shareholding interest. Thus, it would be necessary to create corporate charters that are filed with the offshore government that permit two classes of shareholders, in which one class pays a management fee to another class. Generally, the simple company form of organization is best suited for small entities with a few investors intending to divide profits according to their shareholding. An offshore hedge fund is typically organized either as a limited partnership or as a mutual fund under the laws of the offshore government. The offshore governments usually do not require simple, small companies or partnerships to file annual audit reports of corporate financial statements. However, to offer a semblance of regulating an offering protection to investors, the offshore government usually requires an annual audit to be conducted by chartered accounting and audit firms in that country to sign an annual audit letter. The friendly tax and regulatory offshore regime collects annual filing fees, while local law and chartered accounting firms benefit from a nice stream of professional fees.

Thus, an independent offshore master fund that directly trades for itself, without having to affiliate itself with a U.S. hedge fund, offers some advantages. To the extent that the independent offshore fund trades in U.S. securities, a U.S. brokerage firm becomes the tax withholding agent. Since there is no direct filing to the U.S. tax and regulatory regime, the names of its shareholders are not filed with the U.S. authorities. The U.S. brokerage firm acts as a buffer between the offshore fund and the U.S. tax regime. From the perspective of the hedge fund manager, there is a great benefit of simplicity in administering such an offshore fund.

There are indeed some disadvantages to independent offshore hedge funds. Shareholders and limited partners of such funds are wary of the lack of strong protection from fraud that exists in the United States. Indeed, financial fraudsters in the United States and Europe are known to seek refuge in similar and ambivalent offshore political jurisdictions that might offer them some hope of not being extradited due to lack of extradition treaties. Offshore fund investors might find themselves only lightly protected from financial fraud. Indeed, the best protection for an investor against the risk of losses from financial fraud in an offshore fund, despite coming under the jurisdiction of the crown colony laws of the United Kingdom and the Netherlands, is to become a direct foreign limited partner in a U.S. hedge fund. Of course, such foreign investors must be willing to have their names reported to the IRS every year by the master U.S. hedge fund.

**Tax-Exempt U.S. Investors, UBTI, and Offshore "Blocker" Corporations.** As briefly mentioned before, a significant investment in a U.S. partnership by a tax-exempt institutional investor restricts on the investment strategy of the hedge fund or venture partnership by denying that the ability to borrow, issue debt, take on margin loans or any other form of collateralized loans, since such activity would trigger UBTI for these investors. A common fix is that the general partners or organizers of a U.S. investment partnership also organize an offshore feeder fund, which takes in the investment capital from tax-exempt U.S. investors. The objective is to block UBTI. Cash flows received from the offshore feeder fund by the tax-exempt U.S. investor are treated as dividends, which did not attract UBTI. The offshore feeder fund in turn purchases a limited partnership interest in the U.S. hedge fund or venture fund. The offshore feeder fund itself would be subject to 30 percent withholding taxes on dividends, ordinary income, or income that is not deemed to be portfolio income. As long as a U.S. partnership conducts its trading and investment activity and does not produce dividends and ordinary income, this may be a good arrangement.

Such an offshore blocker corporation structure would work for investment in trading strategies that are based on direct borrowing or taking any other form of collateralized loans. The tax-exempt U.S. institutional investor assumes a small risk that any dispute or impropriety conduct by the organizers relating to their investment in the offshore blocker corporation that is acting as the feeder fund would have to be resolved under the lighter and lesser tested justice systems in the offshore British and Dutch crown colony regimes. It is only logical that a U.S. tax-exempt investor of any meaningful size should establish captive offshore "blocker" corporations. However, most U.S. tax-exempt investors, whose financial statements and tax returns are public record, are hesitant to display direct nexus to captive offshore corporations due to fear of public censure.

# U.S. Investors in Offshore Funds

The U.S. tax code places serious burdens both on U.S. investors in foreign hedge funds and on offshore hedge funds that admit too many U.S.

shareholders or partners. If a foreign entity has majority ownership (i.e., more than 50 percent) by U.S. shareholders or investors, it may trigger the U.S. IRS rules that apply for "Controlled Foreign Corporations" (CFC).[11] It may be a stretch to consider a limited partnership interest or nonvoting shareholder interest in a foreign entity by U.S. investors as any kind of controlling interest. However, neither U.S. investors nor offshore hedge funds wish to get entangled with U.S. CFC classification, which effectively makes the foreign entity into a defacto U.S. entity. The more restrictive set of U.S. IRS regulations that apply to U.S. investors in foreign hedge funds that might be deemed as "foreign corporations" under U.S. tax law are the U.S. Passive Foreign Investment Corporation rules.[12] Broadly speaking, a foreign entity whose primary sources[13] of income and profit are dividends, interest, and capital gains could be deemed a PFIC. A U.S. investor in a PFIC is required to provide annual reporting of income from a PFIC, which could include accrued unrealized income, and pay a U.S. tax on it at the ordinary income rate of that investor. Furthermore, an offshore entity that is deemed to be a PFIC might be asked by the U.S. IRS to report PFIC income of U.S. investors. Most offshore hedge funds generally do not encourage the admittance of U.S. investors due to IRS compliance complexities associated with admitting them.

Most hedge funds are organized under a master-feeder structure that benefits from obtaining IRS classification of the offshore fund as a partnership or association for U.S. taxation purposes,[14] and thus *not be deemed a*

*the feeder*

---

[11] The formal IRS definition for a Controlled Foreign Corporation (CFC) appears at several IRS publication locations routinely, for example, in IRS Form 5471 Instructions at www.irs.gov/pub/irs-pdf/i5471.pdf. Section 956 of the Internal Revenue Code defines Controlled Foreign Corporations. This is available at www.law.cornell.edu/uscode/26/usc_sec_26_00000956----000-.html.

[12] The formal IRS definition for a Passive Foreign Investment Company is in Title 26, Section 1297 of the U.S. Internal Revenue Code (mirrored at the Cornell law library at www.law.cornell.edu/uscode/uscode26/usc_sec_26_00001297----000-.html), which further points to formal definition at Section 954 (mirrored at the Cornell law library at www.law.cornell.edu/uscode/uscode26/usc_sec_26_00000954----000-.html). This definition is routinely relayed in several IRS forms, such as the instructions to Form 8621 at www.irs.gov/instructions/i8621/ch01.html and www.irs.gov/pub/irs-pdf/i8621.pdf.

[13] Section 1297 regards a PFIC as a foreign entity with 75 percent of its income being "passive income" or 50 percent of its assets being "passive assets." Section 954 broadly defines passive income or assets as dividends, interest, capital gains, royalties, annuities, commodity trades, foreign currency gains, swaps (i.e., notional principal contracts), dividends claimed on short sales, etc.

[14] U.S. Code of Federal Regulations, Title 26, Part 301–Procedure and Administration, § 301.7701-3(b)(2) classification of certain business entities, foreign eligible entities.

*PFIC.* A U.S. investor in such a foreign fund that elects the IRS "check box" provision of its classification[15] is not subject to PFIC rules. Similarly, a tax-exempt U.S. investor in such a foreign fund is not subject to UBTI on cash flows received from such a fund. Several master offshore funds set up captive feeder entities solely for U.S. investors, which in turn own an interest in a master offshore hedge fund. Such a captive feeder entity, which is the U.S. entity, performs all the necessary compliance and paperwork that might be required for U.S. investors. The U.S. investors benefit from not having a difficult and draconian PFIC classification apply on their nexus to an offshore investment fund. Should the offshore fund the master fund and the U.S. fund be the feeder, or vice versa? A lot depends on the nature of the cash flows and investor clientele preferences. Note that it is possible for hedge fund organizers to set up multiple feeders into a single master according to client in preferences. In general, hedge fund organizers overwhelmingly prefer establishing the offshore fund as the master, and the U.S. fund as a feeder. The only thing holding them back are a limited number of large institutional investors who may be concerned during the process of their due diligence, that they bear risk of dispute and litigation of their potential future claims as investors and shareholders in an untested offshore non-U.S. jurisdiction.

Just as the U.S. has a vibrant supply of SEC regulated mutual funds, there is an equally healthy supply of foreign mutual funds that are similarly government registered or regulated. Would PFIC classification apply to investment in an offshore mutual fund by a U.S. person or entity? PFIC rules apply only to offshore entities that are corporations in the first place, which primarily produce income from interest, dividends and capital gain. An offshore mutual fund that that seeks classification as an association or partnership under U.S. tax regulations for the purposes of admitting U.S. investors is not a PFIC-rule triggering entity.

*↳ K1s instead*

## U.S. Investors in Swiss Bank Accounts

For comprehensiveness, we discuss the issue of U.S. taxable individual investors who maintain accounts in the secretive Swiss banks. The banking

---

This is accessible at the U.S. government's eCFR Web site at http://ecfr.gpoaccess .gov/cgi/t/text/text-idx?c=ecfr&sid=e02fe9b246c7f12f475bc874b923069c&rgn=div8 &view=text&node=26:18.0.1.1.2.20.69.4&idno=26.

[15] A foreign entity elects to be classified as an association or partnership for U.S. tax purposes by electing the appropriate checkbox in IRS Form 8832 Entity Classification Election. Once such an election is made, it cannot be changed for five years.

secrecy policy of the Swiss government and Swiss banks was partially penetrated by the IRS, which publicly announced its settlement with the Union Bank of Switzerland (UBS) on November 17, 2009, that UBS had agreed to turn over the names of 4,450 U.S. taxpayers whom the IRS suspected of evasion of U.S. taxes by using the bank's offshore services.[16] At one point, the 4,450 accounts held $18 billion, according to the IRS. The IRS had offered an amnesty, officially called a "voluntary disclosure program," to U.S. taxpayers, ending on October 22, 2009, to disclose their offshore accounts to mitigate stiff penalties. Subsequently, the IRS announced that more than 14,700 U.S. taxpayers disclosed their secret foreign bank accounts, including accounts held at foreign banks other than UBS, under its amnesty program. The IRS gave widespread publicity about its agreement of February 2007 with UBS to pay $780 million in fines and admit to criminal wrongdoing in facilitating offshore banking services to U.S. taxpayers that enabled the invasion of U.S. taxes. This may have motivated U.S. taxpayers holding secret Swiss banking accounts to participate in the IRS amnesty program.

A renewed challenge to the IRS-UBS settlement appeared in 2010. The Swiss federal administrative court ruled on January 22, 2010, that the account details of a U.S. depository client of UBS may not be disclosed. Earlier, on January 8, 2010, the Swiss federal administrative court ruled that the Swiss financial regulator broke the national banking secrecy law when it ordered UBS to provide client data to the U.S. government authorities. The Swiss government announced on March 30, 2010, that it did not support the court rulings and their reversal now available by vote in the Swiss parliament.[17]

The global hedge fund industry is indeed linked to European banking secrecy sector, since a good part of the asset base of offshore hedge funds is from these institutions. While a large number of U.S. taxable investors elect to keep their hidden assets in the form of nearly riskless interest-bearing bank deposits, a significant proportion diverts their Swiss bank holdings into hedge funds. Some of the Swiss banks invest in offshore hedge funds in the bank's beneficial name, while maintaining a record of

---

[16]This was widely reported in the global media. One such detailed media report is that of the *New York Times* on November 17, 2009, at www.nytimes.com/2009/11/18/business/global/18irs.html.
[17]These Swiss federal administrative court rulings were reported in the *New York Times* on January 9, 2010, at www.nytimes.com/2010/01/09/business/global/09ubs.html, and on February 23, 2010, at www.nytimes.com/2010/01/23/business/23tax.html. The reversal of the court rulings by the Swiss Federal Council and their pending approval by vote in the Swiss Parliament are reported at www.nytimes.com/2010/04/01/business/global/01ubs.html.

the underlying investors deeply guarded and hidden under Swiss banking secrecy laws. Thus, a considerable proportion of assets held in offshore hedge funds are indirect holdings by taxable U.S. investors who hitherto believed that, under Swiss banking secrecy, their names would not be known to the IRS. Another significant part of offshore hedge fund investment is indirect holdings of investors from countries other than United States, who wish to hide their assets from their respective governments and from the public eye.

We can appreciate why corrupt foreign officials or drug lords might want to hide their assets, which are acquired in violation of the laws of their own countries as well as the laws of other countries and international laws. Why would U.S. taxable investors want to hide assets from the U.S. government and the IRS? This could be partly because the United States taxes the global income of a U.S. citizen without regard to country of residency. Many other developed countries, like Canada and the United Kingdom, have a tradition of exempting their nonresident citizens from tax on income earned outside the home country. Income acquired by U.S. persons outside the United States might be part of hidden and underhanded deals, not visible as taxable income in any taxing regime, and eminently suitable for concealment in secret Swiss bank accounts. Further, there are U.S. persons who succeed in siphoning assets out of legitimate U.S. businesses through outright fraudulent means, and who seek a vehicle not just for hiding these assets under the shroud of offshore banking secrecy but also to earn tax-free investment income from such assets.

An interesting U.S. case is that of U.S. grocery store owner Stewart Leonard,[18] who was convicted in 1993 for skimming cash from his own grocery stores in Connecticut and smuggling it to the Caribbean, packed in suitcases or stuffed in baby gifts. Such U.S. tax evaders directly save at least 35 percent U.S. federal corporate tax and subsequent 36 percent on personal taxes for every pre-tax corporate dollar of their controlled corporation that is diverted for personal use. In addition to the incentive of reducing their U.S. corporate and personal income taxes, there is another serious incentive for wealthy U.S. persons to hide their assets from the IRS and the U.S. courts. Disclosed assets become part of hotly contested community property in lower court cases relating to divorce, paternity, and personal liability. If a divorce or liability settlement is viewed as a tax, though not imposed by the U.S. government but facilitated by the U.S.

---

[18]There is a Wiki on Stewart Leonard at http://en.wikipedia.org/wiki/Stew_Leonard, in addition to a large number of archived media reports on the case, such as that of the *New York Times* at www.nytimes.com/1993/07/23/nyregion/store-founder -pleads-guilty-in-fraud-case.html.

legal system, there is a significant saving, of as much as 50 percent of the assets, by hiding assets in an offshore bank account that is protected by banking secrecy.

Prior to the Bush administration, the U.S. gift and estate tax rate was 55 percent. The recent Bush administration reduced it according to a gradual schedule, from 55 percent in 2001 to 45 percent in 2009, and repealed it for only one calendar year, 2010. This repeal lasts only for one year! The estate tax rate reverts back to the top rate 55 percent in 2011. The Obama administration and U.S. Congress would have to vote in 2010 on whether to repeal the estate tax in 2011 and beyond. At this time, it seems unlikely that the repeal of estate taxes will prevail. The Obama administration is looking to all possible sources of tax revenue to fund its health care reform agenda and also to finance the deficits resulting from bailing out banks and brokerage firms in 2008. The Bush administration either did not have sufficient votes in the Senate and the Congress to enact a permanent repeal, and it may have acted to provide an incentive to wealthy U.S. taxpayers to support their party in the 2008 election. The one-year repeal, for calendar year 2010 only, at the tail of the Bush presidential term ending in 2008, does not appear to be serious tax reform policy. Without any new legislation, the estate tax automatically is reset to the top rate of 55 percent in 2011. United States legislators and the Obama administration would have to introduce new legislation to change U.S. estate tax policy.

By hiding assets in an offshore banking account that is protected by banking secrecy, a taxable super-wealthy U.S. person evades the looming 55 percent estate tax that would apply to hidden offshore assets passed on to successors. It might be a puzzle to a U.S. beneficiary of secret offshore assets: What to do with the secret inheritance? A beneficiary is not the perpetrator of estate tax evasion. Upon investigation of the source of such inheritance by the IRS, an estate might be further investigated and imposed an estate tax.

Thus, the combination of divorce and liability settlements being perceived as garnishment at a 50 percent rate, the hefty 55 percent U.S. gift and estate tax, layered on top of a U.S. personal tax rate of at least 35 percent on global income without regard to residency, and a corporate tax rate of 35 percent with double-taxation provides a strong incentive to U.S. taxpayers to hide their income and assets in offshore banking accounts. By these standards of direct taxes, estate taxes, and court enforcement of settlements, a super-wealthy U.S. citizen is perhaps the most taxed person on earth. It is not surprising that the wealthiest U.S. persons, Bill Gates and Warren Buffett, have pledged most of their wealth to charity, which is not only exempted from U.S. gift and estate tax but also is tax deductible from personal and corporate taxes.

# U.S. Investors in Madoff-Like Managed U.S. Trading Accounts

The recent scandal resulting in the conviction of Bernard Madoff,[19] on June 29, 2009, to 150 years in prison brought to light the colossal scale of onshore U.S. investment advisory schemes residing in securities trading accounts bearing trading authority delegated to an investment adviser. There were varying reports of amounts missing from clients' accounts, and the court-appointed trustee estimated actual losses at $18 billion. Prosecutors said that Madoff perpetuated the largest Ponzi scheme ever, exceeding $50 billion and involving 13,000 investors.

It is important to recognize that the Madoff scheme was not a hedge fund or investment partnership. On the contrary, it appealed to U.S. taxpayers who were uninterested in the evasion of U.S. taxes and therefore uninterested in offshore banking services that offer banking secrecy protection. Each investor would remit investment funds to a securities brokerage account at Madoff's SEC-regulated brokerage firm. All U.S. securities brokerage accounts have investor protection from the Securities Investor Protection Corporation (SIPC) to the extent of $0.5 million. Most U.S. securities brokerage firms offer excess-over-SIPC coverage from an independent insurance company, usually to the full extent of the assets. It is unclear whether investors paid attention to excess-over-SIPC coverage in a Madoff securities brokerage account, and Madoff probably did not buy such coverage. The subsequent Madoff litigation and SEC enforcement lacked the mention of claims upon an insurance underwriter for excess-over-SIPC coverage. Even if such an insurance policy existed, it may have had clear language clauses for denial of coverage in the event of fraud. In any case, the wealthy investors in the Madoff securities accounts ought to have conducted reviews with due diligence to examine the terms of excess-over-SIPC coverage, if any, and sought such insurance coverage (inclusive of securities firm fraud coverage) privately if the Madoff securities account would not provide it.

Subsequently, each account holder in a Madoff securities account delegated trading authority to the Madoff brokerage firm for conducting securities trades in their account, making them into managed securities accounts. Each account holder would get a typical securities brokerage statement every month, which turned out to be pure fiction[20] created

---

[19]The Madoff pyramid scheme provided huge media fodder. A good summary is in the Madoff Wiki, at http://en.wikipedia.org/wiki/Bernard_Madoff.

[20]A sample Madoff securities account statement presents a popular Web destination at www.scribd.com/doc/8976754/Madoff-Trading-Statement-November-2008.

by Madoff's computer programmers[21] who were arrested by the FBI on November 13, 2009.

The IRS made a special exception[22] to allow Madoff investors to claim theft loss equal to 95 percent of their net investment. Unfortunately, theft losses are itemized deductions on Schedule A of individual tax returns and are excluded from the calculation of alternative minimum tax, which is usually the binding tax structure that applies to high-income U.S. taxpayers. It is not surprising that the IRS was generous in making a special one-time exception to theft loss deductibility. The IRS stopped short of including this theft loss as a one-time deduction from alternative minimum taxable income, thus ensuring that the U.S. Treasury will not be subsidizing the theft losses.

In the meantime, Madoff investors are debating with the SEC and SIPC, while pressing lawsuits against the Madoff trustee. The SIPC has taken the view that investor losses should be the tax basis of their investment, that is, their initial cash investment, adjusted for any cash withdrawals. The SEC has suggested that the tax basis be adjusted for inflation. Most investors argue that their losses are to be derived from the final account statements that were delivered to them by the Madoff-managed brokerage account before the fraud was revealed. In either case, the SIPC compensation is limited to $0.5 million and would not offer any meaningful restitution to large investors in the Madoff-managed brokerage accounts.

What Madoff offered to U.S. investors were individualized managed securities brokerage accounts, with the appearance of an umbrella of strict U.S. regulations and enforcement tightly governed by the U.S. securities industry and securities brokerage firms within the industry. There was no hedge fund or limited partnership that kept the actual trades hidden from partners. All trades in holdings were reported monthly to each brokerage account holder. It appeared to be transparent, clean, and regulated outright by the U.S. government under strict securities laws in which investors placed their trust, as well as the self-regulatory compliance departments of the stock exchanges. Every U.S. securities brokerage firm is required to file IRS Form 1099 annually for each brokerage account, reporting on the gross proceeds of the sale of securities, interest, and dividends. A copy of this IRS Form 1099 is provided to the securities account holders, who are required to reconcile their schedule of realized capital gains,

---

[21] The Madoff computer programmers were reportedly given 25 percent pay increases and bonuses of about $60,000 to maintain their silence: www.nytimes.com/2009/11/14/business/14madoff.html.

[22] The IRS special rule for deductibility of Madoff theft losses is described at www.nytimes.com/2009/03/18/business/18madoff.html.

dividends, and interest on their personal tax return with the Form 1099 received from the brokerage firm. Madoff seems to have been a pioneer in providing fictional brokerage account statements and committing outright fraud under the much-feared watchful eyes of U.S. government regulatory agencies and self-regulatory compliance departments of the U.S. securities exchanges.

While the media and investors were focused on Madoff as the perpetrator of financial fiction and fraud, less attention has been paid to the weaknesses and lacunae in implementation and enforcement of securities law by regulatory agencies of the U.S. government. Although regulatory enforcement and court outcomes in British crown colony regimes such as the Cayman Islands are perceived as uncertain, Madoff pushed the envelope to establish the vulnerability of U.S. securities regulation and enforcement. At a minimum, the U.S. government ought to implement the same degree of regulatory enforcement and surveillance as it has for homeland security. The FBI and U.S. Treasury surveillance system was perhaps enhanced to watch for terrorist cash flows. It is now necessary to extend the same to SEC-regulated brokerage firms, to implement simple algorithms to test for implausibility, such as aggregating all Form 1099s submitted to the IRS across all capital accounts, and to check reported trading volumes at the regulated securities exchanges against aggregate trading volumes of customers reported by regulated securities firms. Until then, the U.S. regulatory and enforcement net is revealed to have gaping holes that can be exploited by scam artists, and investors are protected largely by the integrity and honesty of securities firms.

## Size of the Global Hedge Fund Industry

There are several hedge fund data-tracking services and companies that admit various hedge funds into their database universe to track returns and assets under management that are self-reported by the included hedge funds themselves. Notable hedge fund databases are Lipper-TASS, Hedge Fund Research (HFR), Barclay Hedge, and Morningstar-Altvest. For the last decade, the number of hedge funds in each of these database tracking and hedge fund reporting companies is of the order of 7,000 to 10,000 hedge funds. Compare this with 9,870 funds reported as having registered with the Cayman Islands Monetary Authority in 2008.[23] This exceeds the number of mutual funds in the U.S. There were 8,022 U.S. mutual funds in 2008.

---

[23]The Cayman Islands Monetary Authority provides statistics of Investment Funds regularly at its Web site, www.cimoney.com.ky/.

The number of U.S. mutual funds held steady at around 8,000 funds during the same decade of 2000–2009, as reported by the U.S. mutual fund industry organization the Investment Company Institute.[24] The latter also reports that assets of the U.S. mutual fund industry varied in the range of $7 and $12 trillion during the last decade. Considering that the Federal Reserve reported the aggregate financial assets (including bank deposits) of all U.S. households and nonprofit organizations combined as $42 trillion at the end of 2008,[25] the U.S. mutual fund industry's garnering of 20 to 25 percent of this aggregate is a significant achievement. This estimate is a reliable indicator of true wealth, or net asset savings, of mostly U.S. investors in U.S. mutual funds. This is because mutual funds do not take on leverage and do not take on short positions, which net out against long positions when aggregated across mutual funds.

Why are there so many hedge funds? In 1994, the Fidelity mutual fund manager Peter Lynch wrote:

> We've lately reached an important milestone in (mutual) fund making history: the number of funds now exceeds the number of individual stocks traded on the New York and American stock exchanges combined. This is even more remarkable when you consider that 328 of these individual stocks are actually funds in disguise.[26]

A similar situation has been reached with hedge funds. One distinction between the mutual fund and the hedge fund industry is that the survival rate of hedge funds is much lower than that of mutual funds. Hedge funds are constantly closing down due to poor performance and rapid investor redemptions, and at the same time, new hedge funds are constantly being formed. On aggregate, there appears to be a steady rise in the number of worldwide hedge funds every decade. Another important difference is that hedge funds do not have to disclose their portfolio holdings to their investors except voluntarily, and hence are able to apply a shroud of secrecy over their investment strategy. Mutual funds have to disclose their portfolio holdings, at a minimum in their annual reports, which has its own perverse consequence of year-end portfolio restructuring by active mutual funds for

---

[24] "2009 Investment Company Fact Book," Section 1: U.S. mutual fund totals, table 1. Investment Company Institute, 2009. This is accessible at www.icifactbook.org/fb _data.html#section1.

[25] Table B.100, Z.1, "Flow of Funds Accounts of the United States," Federal Reserve statistical release, Board of Governors of the Federal Reserve System, September 2009. The Table B.100 releases can be accessed at www.federalreserve.gov/releases/z1/current/accessible/b100e.htm.

[26] Peter Lynch, *Beating the Street* (New York: Simon & Schuster, 1994).

the purposes of window dressing and appearing good. The large universe of hedge funds has created business and career opportunities for hedge fund consultants and managers of "fund-of-funds" (FoF).

The corresponding net assets under management, or net investment or net liquidation value of partners by the hedge fund industry, is an elusive order of magnitude, indicated as about \$2.8 trillion at its peak in 2008 by one of the hedge fund industry's professional association, the Alternative Investment Management Institute.[27] One reason is a bookkeeping consideration: that the hedge fund industry numbers are not accurately checked for double counting under master-feeder structures, as well as fund-of-funds, which in turn invest in hedge funds. Another is that the secretive nature of this industry does not lend itself to reliable reporting, since all size and return numbers are self-reported voluntarily to database aggregator companies. Finally, unlike mutual funds, which are unleveraged and contain negligible short positions, if the holdings of hedge funds were aggregated, long and short positions would mostly cancel out. If combined with the books of swaps and derivatives traders, the grand aggregate position would be be zero, since *on an aggregate, forwards, futures, swaps, and options are in net zero supply.* For every long position in any kind of derivative, its supply is created by short sellers of the same position. Some of the short sellers might be natural hedgers, such as airlines wanting to hedge their fuel cost or farmers wanting to lock in prices from the next harvest.

Even though we might encounter reports stating that the gross assets of hedge funds are of the order of tens, or even hundreds, of trillions of dollars, gross of leverage, we should recognize that such aggregation of the absolute values of notional amounts present the hedge fund industry as being much larger than life. For every hedge fund that takes long positions in leveraged crude oil futures contracts, there is some hedge fund or futures trader out there who has exact corresponding short positions that net out to zero.

During the global financial meltdown of 2008, hedge funds are rounded up by the media and legislators as the usual suspects that might be responsible for intense market volatility arising from excessive leverage and hyper speculation. Indeed, several hedge funds collapsed or were seized by their banks as collateral against loans made out to them. It later became clear that that the financial meltdown was better attributable to banks who are

---

[27]"AIMA's Roadmap to Hedge Funds," commissioned by AIMA's investors steering committee, November 2008. The acronym AIMA stands for "Alternative Investment Management Association," which is one of the primary associations representing the hedge fund industry. Available at www.aima.org/en/knowledge_centre/education/aimas-roadmap-to-hedge-funds.cfm.

attempting to create net positive supply of complex asset backed securities, and not hedge funds. These complex securities were later termed "toxic assets" by the media and euphemistically labeled as "troubled assets" by Congress. Many hedge funds indeed became victims to these toxic assets that were manufactured in net positive supply by banks, which were not only internally leveraged but also further leveraged by collateralized borrowing. The hedge funds seem to have been a small force, perhaps a minor player, and perhaps even a target victim of the toxic assets that were originated by the banks.

At the time of this writing, Congress is debating measures to regulate hedge funds to find legal means to have them register with the SEC so as to facilitate better disclosure, and also considering measures to increase taxes on fees and profits that are earned by the organizers of the general partners of hedge funds and venture funds. Many of these fears of regulators seem to be overblown. Whatever may be the new legislative outcome that engulfs U.S. hedge funds and venture funds, most of the industry is already offshore, well outside U.S. jurisdiction. Further, from an economic perspective, hedge funds are broadly leveraged investors or short sellers. When combined with other derivatives traders, the net positions of forwards, futures, swaps, and other notional principal contracts aggregate of zero. The collapse of AIG and subsequent financial meltdown was triggered by the imprudent sale of credit default swaps by AIG at low prices. The tidal wave of the recent financial instability came from a source of net positive supply, of toxic assets with housing as collateral. Warren Buffett's popular saying that "derivatives are financial weapons of mass destruction"[28] needs modification to include complex asset-backed securities in net positive supply. Panic arising from financial failures of derivative counterparties may indeed amplify financial market volatility. The true source of underlying financial market volatility is the underlying assets, and their originators and issuers.

# Fund-of-Funds

The rise of fund-of-funds (FoF) within hedge fund industry is partly explained by a rarely mentioned but exceedingly common practice in the hedge fund industry, that the general partner entity is willing to pay 25 to 33 percent of its fees to an introducing broker or facilitator who brings limited partners into a hedge fund. Thus, as much as one-third of the 2

---

[28] "Buffett warns on investment time bomb," BBC News, March 4, 2003, available at http://news.bbc.co.uk/2/hi/business/2817995.stm.

percent fixed fee and 20 percent performance fee is shared with and introducing blocker or facilitator. An FoF organizer is usually successfully able to seek the same sharing of fees with each of the underlying hedge funds. Thus, without imposing a second layer of fees, they are able to offer their limited partner investors the same gross fee structure that they would face if they were to directly invest in a hedge fund. Many FoF investors also see value in obtaining a diversified exposure to 20 to 40 hedge funds, as against concentrated exposure in a limited number of hedge funds. Thus, through diversification, an FoF hedge fund indeed presents economic value to an investor.

The sharing of fees paid by limited partners to the general partners with introducing brokers and facilitators is the dark underbelly to the hedge fund industry. Indeed, many hedge funds jump-start themselves by finding their limited partner investors through paid fee-sharing intermediaries. When conducting due-diligence, limited partners ought to examine this issue. Are the general partners willing to disclose in writing that their general partner entity does not pay fees and commissions to outside brokers? If they do pay such fees, limited partner investors ought to seek a discount to the stated fee structure in the limited partnership agreement, representing a commission that would otherwise be paid to an introducing broker. Even though partners in a hedge fund share common objectives, the fees that each one pays to the general partner, and the proportion of their fees that are shared with introducing brokers, could be vastly different. The hedge fund manager's dark hour presents itself when an intermediary calls, saying, "I shall introduce this $100M investor client to you. What is in it for me?" It takes a determined hedge fund general partner sponsor to reply, "We have a policy not to share limited partner fees with third parties, and we do not pay commissions to agents for bringing clients to us."

In general, venture funds and private equity organizers in Silicon Valley, who typically invest in technologically driven venture projects, are not known to part with a share of limited partners' fees with commission agents. These funds have a long tradition of directly obtaining investments from limited partners, and would tend to be large U.S. nonprofit institutions. The venture fund organizers have multiple decade-long relationships with their limited partner investors. If they ever need to raise capital to finance a flurry of venture projects, they directly approach their long-standing limited partners.

In sharp contrast, the world of hedge funds is always in flux. New funds are constantly arriving to the market and searching for limited partner investors. A significant number of funds are imploding and falling apart due to sharp losses and investor redemptions. A substantial number of them start small and grow rapidly in size from internally generated profits attributable to stellar returns, which becomes a signal that attracts new investors. One fund's sharp losses becomes another fund's buying opportunity, due to an abundance of distressed securities that temporarily flood the capital markets.

## Incentives of the Hedge Fund Manager and Investors

**Incentives of Hedge Fund Investors.** The rapid evolution and steady growth of the global hedge fund market reveals the benefits and incentives to investors from investment strategies and investment vehicles that regulators do not ordinarily permit in standard mutual funds. Typically, hedge funds greatly benefit from obtaining a high degree of leverage; conducting short sales to benefit from overvalued securities; extracting returns from undervalued nonexchange traded securities; in liquid or lumpy securities; initiating leveraged speculative positions using both exchange traded and privately traded options, forwards, futures, swaps, and complex collateralized directives; or conducting high-frequency trading on exchanges to extract profits from becoming liquidity providers. Virtually none of these strategies or financial instruments are permitted in regulated U.S. mutual funds that are in turn governed by the Investment Companies Act. Net of the cost of management fees paid to the fund manager, hedge fund investors expect to earn superior risk-adjusted returns on their capital.

Many hedge funds are popular with investors due to that track record of earning steady investment returns with low volatility. Such hedge funds proudly present their superior "Sharpe ratio" (named after its inventor, William Sharpe, who shared the 1990 Nobel Prize in economics), which is the ratio of the hedge fund's excess return over the riskless rate to its volatility. The numerator of this ratio represents excess returns over the riskless rate, and the denominator seeks to quantify risk. There are a number of other risk-adjusted performance measures,[29] which are not described here but are detailed in later chapters. In summary, hedge investors seek superior risk-adjusted returns (net of management fees) through participation in innovative investment strategies that are not available through participation in standard regulated mutual funds.

**Incentives of The Hedge Fund Manager.** The hedge fund manager profits from collecting two types of management fees from the participating hedge fund

---

[29]The Treynor ratio is the excess return over riskless rate divided by the fund's beta relative to a benchmark index. The Sortino ratio is the excess return over riskless rate divided by variance of only those return observations with negative returns, sometimes called the "semi-variance."

investors. The first component is the fixed fee, much like with mutual funds, levied as a small percentage of the market value of the investor's capital balance in the hedge fund. The fixed fee ranges between 1 and 2 percent of assets and is very similar in order of magnitude to the fee structure of standard regulated mutual funds. Typically, the hedge fund manager makes only very marginal profit after deducting actual management expenses, including salaries, legal/accounting professional fees, and overheads. Just like with standard mutual funds, fixed fees can be a source of decent profit to the hedge fund manager when the fund manages large volumes with relatively lower costs. This is a benefit of scale economies.

The more important component is the performance fee paid to the hedge fund manager by the hedge fund investors according to preset contractual provisions in the partnership agreement. This performance fee in a typical hedge fund is about 20 percent of net new profits earned for investors in excess of a preset hurdle rate. The hurdle rate is typically set to the riskless Treasury bill rate within a return calculation period. In order to be fair to the investors, the hedge fund manager calculates new profits, so that previously achieved "high-water marks" on which performance fees have already been paid are not levied as a repeat performance fee. There could be situations where hedge fund investors who paid performance fees and subsequently are subjected to capital value drawdown due to market volatility. These investors are not levied any additional performance fees until the capital value recovers to the level, called a "high-water mark," at which they had paid performance fees. Investors entering and exiting the same hedge fund at different points in time are likely to have differing high-water marks.

## Valuation of a Hedge Fund Management Company

The publicly traded shares of investment management companies offer unusual insights into the world of hedge funds, also called "alternative" investment funds. While the shares of conventional investment managers trade at 0.4 percent to 0.5 percent of assets under management, those of "alternative" investment managers such as Blackstone Group, Och-Ziff Capital Management, and Fortress Investment Group trade at about 20 percent of assets under management in normal equity market conditions.

This glaring difference in the market valuation of investment management companies (as a percentage of assets under management) is directly attributable to the performance fee that exists in hedge funds, but that is absent in SEC-regulated mutual funds. The SEC attempt at defining hedge funds cited earlier stated, "(Hedge funds) receive a management fee that includes a substantial share of the performance of the fund." The SEC did not provide a quantitative estimate of the performance fee here. It is widely known that the performance fee of hedge funds is roughly 20 percent of profits, and some hedge funds are known to charge up to 25 percent of profits. Usually, "excess" profits are calculated in excess of a hurdle rate, equal to the U.S. Treasury bill rate, and in excess of a high-water mark. Thus, performance fees apply at a 20 percent rate on new profits generated during the calendar year (in excess of previously achieved profits engraved into a "high-water mark," and further, in excess of the hurdle rate for that year).

From an economic perspective, the performance fee is a call option granted by investors to the hedge fund manager, much like executive stock options. A performance fee can never be negative. Asymptotically, if the hedge fund consistently sustains positive excess returns over the hurdle rate, it is simply 20 percent, or one-fifth, of this excess return. Thus, if a hedge fund consistently earns 10 percent per year in excess of the Treasury bill hurdle rate, the performance fees would amount to 2 percent per year of hedge fund investors' capital (20 percent, or one-fifth, of 10 percent excess return is 2 percent). When such a hedge fund is scaled to a size of the order of $1 billion, cash flow from performance fees to the hedge fund manager is on the order of $20 million per year. This is nearly all pure profit, since the fixed fees paid to the hedge fund manager by the investors cover the operating costs and expenses of the hedge fund manager.

Despite the seemingly large absolute amounts of performance fees in this example of superior returns that are paid to the hedge fund manager, investors examine their net returns after all fees and evaluate associated risk. The enormous growth of the hedge fund market reveals the presence of a large number of hedge fund managers who deliver superior risk-adjusted returns. The mavericks among these hedge fund managers and their innovative strategies are keenly pursued by investors.

The valuation of alternative investment and hedge fund management companies at about 20 percent of assets under management almost directly reflects the markets' valuation of this upside call option granted to the fund management company by the limited partner investors, also combined with an expectation of the growth in assets under management. This stock market valuation also establishes the willingness of investors in limited partners to grant a call option on the upside of the hedge fund, as much as 20 percent of their initial investment, to the hedge fund management company. In an efficient market of rational institutional investors, this would suggest that investors expect superior risk-adjusted returns net of these enormous performance fees, and that the hedge fund management companies are privy to a secret sauce that would produce high returns from alternative investments that still remain attractive to investors after these high performance fees.

## Economies of Scale in Hedge Funds

Perhaps the most compelling feature of the hedge fund industry is the remarkable economies of scale. A relatively small fixed-cost operation is able to manage many billions of dollars. Typically, a single talented and experienced financial market trader with a few assistants and the support of a competent back-office that manages paperwork and IT (information technology) infrastructure can comfortably manage $2 billion to $5 billion. This could be considered the most profitable cottage industry to date. It is not surprising that various surveys estimate that there are 7,000 to 10,000 hedge funds today, which supposedly exert exposure to a significant portion of the global capital markets, amounting to several trillion dollars. Indeed, the tracking and reporting of performance of all these hedge funds has become a significant mini industry. In the United States, during the past decades, traditional institutional investors, such as pension plans, endowments, and insurance companies, dominated the U.S. capital markets. Today, U.S. and global hedge funds are at least as significant as traditional institutional investors in participating in the U.S. capital markets.

# CHAPTER 2

# The Structure of Hedge Funds

## Organizing a Typical Offshore Hedge Fund

There are barely a handful of offshore regimes that are considered sound for the purposes of establishing an offshore hedge fund. This is entirely based on British crown colony laws that apply to the British dominions of Bermuda, British Virgin Islands, and Cayman Islands. The Dutch government makes available Dutch dominions based on Dutch colony laws, notably the Netherlands Antilles. Although Britain has other sovereign dominions, such as the British Channel Islands, these aren't as popular with hedge funds. The British crown colony of Bermuda has taken a major lead in establishing intermediation between the U.S. and U.K. insurance sectors. The unambiguous exclusion of Bermuda insurance companies from either U.K. or U.S. taxation by treaty is the primary factor that propels the thriving business operations of Bermuda insurance and reinsurance companies. When the ambitious Internet global undersea cable telecom start-up Global Crossings took root during the dot-com boom (and soon went bankrupt), it selected Bermuda as its headquarters.

The higher administrative fees of corporate agents and other professional fees in Bermuda seem to have been the primary factor leading to the domicile of hedge funds in the British Virgin Islands and the Cayman Islands. Over time, the number of hedge funds and "special purpose vehicles" (SPVs) of U.S. corporations expanded sharply in the Cayman Islands, relative to the other British crown colonies. Although the Netherlands Antilles was a popular domicile for the early wave of hedge funds, it did not match the numbers and momentum of the British crown colonies, particularly the Cayman Islands.

What makes the Cayman Islands a haven for hedge funds and SPVs? As of 2009, there were 9,838 mutual funds and 806 insurance companies registered in the Cayman Islands.[1] This represents nearly a threefold increase relative to the 3,648 funds that existed in 2001. With a population of about 54,000, the Cayman Islands may contain the world's largest concentration of hedge funds per capita, only nearly all of these funds contain holdings of nonresidents. Apart from low administrative fees charged by agents and low ongoing registration fees to the local government, the biggest attraction is that a Cayman Islands entity is formed under the British legal system. These crown colonies are not independent republics like other countries in the Caribbean, but instead ruled under firm British law with British courts, governed by a British governor and a British colonial administration. Disputes, if any, are addressed and resolved in courts that are part of the British legal system. Britain has made one thing clear: Those entities formed under the laws of these crown colonies, complying with the ongoing requirement for registration and continuing approval, are completely exempt from any kind of taxation on income that is produced and sourced from outside these colonies. There is no corporate tax on the entities, nor is there any individual tax on foreign nonresident shareholders of these entities.

Why does Britain encourage the operation of tax havens so close to the shores of the United States that potentially contribute to a reduction in U.S. tax revenues? If Britain and the Netherlands were to impose corporate and individual taxes in their Caribbean crown colonies, it would bring about a sea change in location for hedge funds and SPVs. For one, Britain and the Netherlands are maintaining their old colonial tradition of not levying corporate and personal taxes on nonresidents doing business in their colonies. However, a decent economic benefit accrues to the residents of these British and Dutch colonies. The colonial government collects fees on hedge funds, SPV registrations, and annual renewals. Local law firms earn legal fees from U.S. and European clients. Local chartered accounting firms win engagements for bookkeeping and audits of hedge funds and SPVs. Local registered agents provide a physical address and thus earn decent fees. In one tiny office with two employees, a local registered agent can host hundreds and thousands of entities, none of which maintain any real physical presence in the islands. It is appropriate to say that the Cayman Islands entities are a legal fiction, and their official address is merely a virtual shell address hosted by an agent. We shouldn't be mark-edly critical of the Cayman Islands. The same practice in Delaware and all other states in the United States, that an entity's physical presence is its

---

[1] *Op. cit*, Chapter 1. The Cayman Islands Monetary Authority publishes statistics and names of all entities that are registered with it, accessible at www.cimoney.com .ky/Stats_Reg_Ent/default.aspx?id=300.

official address, which is that of its registered Delaware agent, is pure fiction. A professional Delaware registered agent houses hundreds and thousands of Delaware companies that conduct their business from almost everywhere but Delaware.

Having progressed this far, let us examine the specific steps that are taken by the organizer of an offshore hedge fund. We shall presume that the same organizer has already set up a U.S. Delaware LLC/LP pair primarily to admit U.S. taxable investors. The first step is to find a Cayman Islands agent. The next step is to decide which type of Cayman Islands entity is appropriate. There are three popular forms:

1. A Cayman Islands exempt company
2. A Cayman Islands mutual fund
3. A Cayman Islands limited partnership

Each of the three requires the preparation of an elaborate set of memoranda and articles of association that are retained by the Cayman Islands agent and not filed with the Cayman Islands government agencies. They are in the very formal language of the British tradition of forming companies. However, the primary objective is to establish a list of people who constitute the board of directors. These individuals have to provide proof of their identity and address in various forms that are considered acceptable under the local rules.

The first type of entity, the Cayman Islands exempt company (exempted from taxation), is not considered a fund or hedge fund. It is not expected to engage in frequent share issues and repurchases as if it were a mutual fund. It is not supposed to conduct any local business; it is organized solely to earn returns and income from sources that are outside the Islands. It is a traditional company, which issues shares to its shareholders. Generally, this structure is preferred for privately controlled entities that do not face the issue of routine entry of new shareholders and routine exit of previous shareholders through a share issuance and repurchase program. Even though it might establish a share repurchase program for redeeming investors and a share purchase program for new investors tied to the net asset value per share, and thus become a de facto hedge fund, the exempt offshore company structure works best when its shareholding is stable or its shareholders externally trade among each other without seeking redemption or repurchase of the shares directly from the company. For this reason, even if U.S. corporate taxes were magically removed from a U.S. subchapter C corporation, it would not be a popular vehicle for running a U.S. hedge fund. It is important to note that the setup fees and ongoing fees for a Cayman Islands exempt company are the lowest among the three types of entities.

The second type of entity, a Cayman Islands registered mutual fund, would work for implementing a hedge fund located outside U.S. shores, thus outside the taxation jurisdiction of the United States. The Cayman Islands Monetary Authority awards an annual mutual fund license that is based on a fee schedule linked to the asset levels of the fund. At inception, a governing document for the mutual fund is created and privately held by the Cayman Islands agent. The document identifies the directors of the mutual fund and describes the procedures and methodologies that are in place for the benefit of the mutual fund. Such a mutual fund is required to obtain an annual audit letter from a Cayman Islands accounting and audit firm, which is to be submitted to the Cayman Islands administration. The Cayman audit places a discipline upon the Cayman mutual fund to present a GAAP-compliant financial statement and satisfy the Cayman auditors that the procedures to establish the net asset value that are in place for taking in new investments and redeeming existing investments are in proper order. When the Cayman Islands mutual fund is a feeder into a U.S. master fund, the Cayman audit requirements are lighter, since the Cayman mutual fund's valuation is linked to its limited partnership interest in the U.S. master fund. The Cayman auditor honors the U.S. auditor's capital account audit for purposes of establishing the value of the Cayman Islands mutual fund.

The Cayman audit fees are likely to be lower for such a feeder fund, because less work is involved and there is less risk to the auditor on account of error or misrepresentation of the fund's value. The converse holds when the Cayman Islands fund is the master and the U.S. fund is the feeder. The hedge fund organizer would have to establish diligent accounting standards and procedures to establish the mark-to-market valuation of the Cayman Islands mutual fund. Generally, this Cayman Islands mutual fund entity is recommended by expert lawyers as suitable as an offshore feeder fund into a U.S. master fund, wherein the Cayman entity purchases a limited partnership interest in the U.S. master limited partnership fund. The feeder Cayman mutual fund itself does not charge fees to its investors. Instead, fees are applied by the U.S. master limited partnership fund.

There is one important IRS administrative issue of U.S. withholding taxes that arises with the U.S. master/Cayman Islands mutual fund feeder structure. The U.S. limited partnership, the master fund, becomes the withholding agent for collecting and remitting U.S. withholding taxes applicable to the Cayman Islands partner, the feeder fund. Note that there is a 30 percent withholding tax on U.S. source dividends that are allocated to the Cayman partner. The U.S. limited partnership is obliged to file Form 1042 annually with the IRS and remit appropriate withholding taxes for foreign partners, including its offshore feeder fund. The amount of such taxes withheld and paid to the IRS are taken out of the Cayman Islands feeder fund's partner account and treated as if it were a withdrawal. IRS penalties and recovery procedures apply to the U.S. withholding agent, not to the foreign partner, if withholding tax payments are not made to the IRS in the required time. Limited partners in the U.S. master fund should carefully examine whether their general partner absorbs IRS penalties and liabilities on behalf of the limited partnership acting as withholding agent for foreign partners. Slippage on the part of the general partner in the matter of the U.S. withholding tax can get the entire limited partnership subjected to IRS liability. It might be a hypothetical matter of contention whether the IRS would agree to a clause in the limited partnership agreement that passes on penalties and liabilities of withholding tax responsibility to the general partner.

The third type of entity, a Cayman Islands limited partnership, mirrors the U.S. LLC/LP pair. A similar pair is established in the Cayman Islands. The U.S. general partner entity creates an exempt Cayman Islands company (the first act of Cayman entity described earlier), which becomes the general partner. The Cayman company enjoys limited liability protection due to its very nature. A limited partnership agreement is drawn up, much like the limited partnership agreement that is created for the U.S. hedge fund. The limited partnership subsequently applies to the Cayman Islands government to seek approval of its formation and continuing operations. Though it is a limited partnership, it is considered to be a "fund" by the Cayman government, and it is subject to the same requirement for an annual Cayman audit as a Cayman registered mutual fund. Generally, the Cayman Islands limited partnership is operated as the master fund and the U.S. limited partnership as its feeder fund.

## Master-Feeder Structuring of Onshore/Offshore Arms: Organizing a Hedge Fund for Clienteles

From the previous discussion, we identify the following five distinct clienteles according to their tax regimes:

1. Nontaxable U.S. institutional entities, such as pension plans, college endowments, and nonprofit foundations.
2. Taxable U.S. individuals who face taxation according to individual tax schedules. This includes other pass-through partnerships, whose ultimate partners are taxable U.S. individuals.
3. Taxable U.S. entities such as taxable U.S. subchapter C corporations and taxable trusts.

**4.** Foreign individuals and entities who are domiciled in regimes or countries where no tax applies on their investment-related income.

**5.** Foreign individuals and entities who face taxation in their country of domicile, and their country of domicile may have a tax treaty with other countries, including the United States, to prevent double taxation of the same investment income in multiple countries.

Clearly, segments 1, 2, and 4 are most important since they account for practically all global hedge fund investment.

**Offshore Master/U.S. Feeder Versus U.S. Master/Offshore Feeder.**   What drives the master/feeder structuring of an offshore/offshore fund pair? A fund sponsor could set up independent side-by-side offshore and onshore funds with separate trading accounts and separate financial statements. However, both the investors and the hedge fund sponsor stand to benefit greatly from cost savings and trading efficiency from consolidating all assets into one single pool of capital through a master-feeder arrangement. One of the funds becomes a feeder into the other, which serves as the master. The feeder fund purchases a limited partnership interest in the master fund.

After an offshore fund entity has sought classification as an association or partnership for U.S. tax purposes by filing Form 8832, both taxable and tax-exempt U.S. investors could join it without fear of being subjected to passive foreign investment company (PFIC) rules and Unrelated Business Tax on Income (UBTI) (for tax-exempt investors). The fund sponsor may discourage taxable U.S. investors from joining the offshore entity, due to the likelihood of increased IRS vigilance and added U.S. compliance requirements, and reserve such entry to the offshore hedge fund only to nontaxable U.S. entities desirous of blocking UBTI and to non-U.S. investors. Similarly, the U.S. entity may admit U.S. taxable investors as well as non-U.S. investors. Tax-exempt U.S. entities would likely steer clear of the U.S. entity due to the possibility that some day it might engage in trades that trigger UBTI. As pointed out earlier, non-U.S. investors who are concerned about their names going to the IRS if they were to join the U.S. entity would prefer joining the offshore entity. Given this small degree of flexibility, the hedge fund sponsor has to decide which entity to make the master fund, and which the feeder.

The two key factors that sway the choice of which should be the master fund and which should be the feeder are the investor clientele and the nature of the trading and investment strategy.

Suppose a hedge fund sponsor has no tax-exempt U.S. investors (Type 1 on the list), has U.S. taxable investors (Types 2 and 3 on the list), and has some foreign investors (either Type 4 or Type 5 on the list). The simple master/feeder ordering is to make the U.S. hedge fund the master and the offshore fund its feeder. Foreign investors (Types 4 or 5) have a choice: Join the U.S. master fund as limited partners, or join the offshore feeder fund as mutual fund holders of partners as appropriate.

The problem arises when the hedge fund sponsor lands a large U.S. tax-exempt institutional investor (Type 1 on the list), whose officers have decided that they don't want to risk the imposition of UBTI that might occur if they joined the U.S. hedge fund as a limited partner. In such a situation, the U.S. tax-exempt entity joins the offshore hedge fund, which serves as a "blocker" to UBTI. Now consider a special situation where the trading strategy of this hedge fund sponsor is such that there are no U.S source dividends on its horizon, and therefore no withholding taxes due from foreign investors. In such a situation, the hedge fund sponsor generally elects to make the offshore fund the master and the U.S. fund its feeder.

Now suppose an asymmetry arises due to the hedge fund sponsor's trading strategy that contains elements that are subject to U.S. withholding tax to foreign investors, but not to U.S. investors. The hedge fund sponsors need to come up with an appropriate mechanism to shield U.S. tax-exempt investors in the offshore fund (serving as a "blocker" to UBTI) from U.S. withholding taxes, and also shield its U.S. feeder fund from being charged U.S. withholding taxes. Both structures would work, that is, the U.S. fund as master and the foreign fund as feeder, and vice versa, but with attention being paid to the detail of preventing U.S. tax withholding on U.S. investors in the offshore fund. In general, when the hedge fund sponsor's overall capital subscription base is mostly from tax-exempt U.S. investors and foreign investors, the preferred choice is to keep the offshore fund as the master and the U.S. fund as its feeder.

Now let us consider taxable U.S. investors joining the offshore fund, either directly or by joining as limited partners in a U.S. feeder fund. These U.S. taxable investors report capital gains on their U.S. tax returns on the proceeds of liquidation of their holdings of the offshore fund. Redemptions made of two holdings for more than one year qualify as long-term capital gains, which face the lowest tax rate and enjoy a high tax preference. Any involuntary cash flows that are received from the offshore fund in the interim are treated as dividends.

The offshore master hedge fund that accepts U.S. investors (including the U.S. feeder fund) faces a quandary. Suppose the offshore master hedge fund invests solely in plain fixed income securities, whose coupon income is taxable as interest income to U.S. taxable investors if they were to hold these fixed income securities themselves. The foreign master hedge fund seeks exemption from PFIC classification by filing Form 8832 and electing to be treated as an association for the purposes of U.S. tax law for U.S. investors. Suppose it does not distribute the fixed income coupon income to its U.S. taxable investors, but instead reinvests that income into more fixed income securities. Now suppose the U.S. taxable investors redeem their holdings in the foreign master hedge fund after holding them continuously for more than one year. What would have been interest income, had they directly purchased fixed income securities, is now transformed into long-term capital gains.

Most likely, to prevent this kind of tax arbitrage to U.S. taxable investors, of substituting interest income that is taxed at a higher rate of about 35 percent with long-term capital gains that is taxed at a lower rate of 15 percent, the offshore master hedge fund would have to take steps to distribute the fixed income coupon income to its U.S. partners. Thus, whenever there are taxable U.S. partners, it is preferable to make the U.S. hedge fund into a master and the foreign hedge fund into a feeder.

Suppose the U.S. master hedge fund engages in a trading strategy that involves the generation of dividends, and the hedge fund sponsors also have limited partner investors who are tax-exempt U.S. entities who have to be housed in the offshore feeder fund in order to block potential UBTI taxation. The hedge fund sponsor has to carefully organize a foreign tax withholding arrangement for the offshore feeder fund such that its U.S. tax-exempt partners are not subjected to the 30 percent dividend withholding tax.

The offshore master fund may establish a branch office and trade for its own account without being deemed to be producing U.S. source income. An important lesser-known provision of the Internal Revenue Code[2] makes it amply clear that an offshore hedge fund is considered to be trading for its own account, and hence any of the portfolio trading income that it produces does not constitute U.S. source trade or business. This exclusion applies, despite the offshore hedge fund maintaining a branch office within the United States with employees conducting its trades from within the United States on U.S. securities. This is a very powerful and serious provision in U.S. tax law. Most taxable regimes establish a taxation nexus by physical location within the regime. The United States magnanimously permits offshore entities to set up branch offices within the United States and still be exempt from U.S. tax on all securities trading and portfolio income–producing activities. The offshore entity's U.S. operations have to be considered to be effectively connected income to a U.S. trade or business for U.S. jurisdictional taxation to be triggered.

---

[2]U.S. Internal Revenue Code Section 864(b)(2)(A)(ii) exempts offshore entities for trading their own accounts in stocks and securities, and 864(B)(ii) exempts them for trading in their own accounts in commodities.

This lesser known provision of the Internal Revenue Code has produced a sweeping polarization in the physical location of trading operations of offshore hedge funds to the United States. The legal registration, domicile, and regulatory filings are routinely performed by lawyers and administrators in the offshore location. The economic decision making, operations, accounting, and trading of the offshore fund is mostly conducted from the U.S. branch office, usually located in New York City or Stamford, Connecticut.

From the perspective of the hedge fund sponsor, the biggest advantage of maintaining the offshore hedge fund as the master fund and a U.S. feeder fund for taxable U.S. investors is the elimination of filing the detailed U.S. tax return for the master fund. The feeder fund does indeed file U.S. partnership tax returns, but it is not required to report itemized capital gains on securities traded on the tax return, because there are no securities traded in the feeder fund. The offshore master fund can ignore this issue of itemization of items of realized income and capital gain, report long-term and short-term capital gain separately for the purpose of tax allocation, and engage in complex calculations to determine tax allocations. The offshore master fund can simply act to solely track the economics of the fund (i.e., its underlying net asset value) and each partner's economic capital account value.

Here are our summary recommendations:

As far as possible, the hedge fund should be structured such that the offshore fund is the master and the U.S. hedge fund is the feeder. If it is possible to persuade taxable U.S. investors to join the offshore hedge fund, the U.S. hedge fund as a feeder should be eliminated entirely. The offshore master hedge fund should make sure that it does not collect U.S. withholding taxes for U.S. taxable and tax-exempt investors, and acts as U.S. withholding agent only for its non-U.S. investors.

A U.S. master fund with the offshore fund as the feeder may be required if taxable U.S. investors are concerned about risk to taxation at the highest U.S. tax rate on cash flows from their holding of limited partnership interest or mutual fund shares in the foreign hedge fund.

*Disclaimer:* The analysis and recommendations provided here should not be considered an authoritative interpretation of whether taxable U.S. investors in an offshore entity that files Form 8832 with the IRS to be treated as an association or partnership are exempt from PFIC and controlled foreign corporation (CFC) rules, and how such investors should handle their own U.S. tax filings relating to such investment. An authoritative interpretation requires either direct clarification by the IRS in a private letter ruling or advice from tax attorneys who specialize in this area to determine clearly whether or not PFIC/CFC rules trump the Form 8832 election of an offshore entity.

# U.S. Withholding Agent for U.S. Withholding Taxes on Foreign Investors

**U.S. Master/Offshore Feeder.**  As described earlier, a Cayman Islands mutual fund is typically structured as a feeder fund into a U.S. master fund (a U.S. LP) when the offshore fund is established mainly for non-U.S. investors. The offshore fund does not maintain any securities accounts and does not conduct any trading. Its sole financial operation is the maintenance of a bank account to receive from and disburse funds to its non-U.S. investors. In a bare-bones feeder fund operation, the U.S. master fund can implement receipts and disbursement of funds to the investors of the feeder fund according to advance instructions from the feeder fund, though auditors would clearly prefer that remittances from the U.S. master fund's bank accounts be conducted only for its own partners. The U.S. master fund becomes the withholding agent for collecting U.S. withholding taxes levied upon foreign investors on U.S. source dividends by filing Form 1042. Only those hedge funds that trade in underlying U.S dividend-paying stocks need be concerned about this. U.S. withholding taxes generally do not apply to other distributive items of income, like interest and capital gains. Even though Form 1042 may have to be filed with the IRS by the U.S. master fund, the withholding tax entries would be blank.

The names of foreign investors in a U.S. partnership are conveyed to the IRS in its Form 1065 tax return and in Form 1042 filing for withholding taxes. When one of the limited partners of a U.S. master fund is the foreign feeder fund, the only name that goes to the IRS is that of the offshore feeder fund, along with its U.S. taxpayer ID number. (The offshore fund separately seeks a U.S. taxpayer ID number for banking and investment purposes.) The names of the partners and shareholders of the offshore feeder fund are not conveyed to the IRS, so their anonymity is preserved. Many non-U.S. investors strongly prefer such an arrangement, since they are deeply concerned about having anything relating to them being reported to the U.S. government.

On the other hand, there are indeed instances when foreign investors prefer to directly join as limited partners in a U.S. hedge fund. These investors are indifferent as to their names being reported to the IRS. If they are individuals, they do not have to seek a U.S. taxpayer ID number, but instead simply provide Form W8-BEN to the U.S. hedge fund. Since they are directly admitted as partners to the U.S. hedge fund, their names go to the IRS both in the hedge fund's tax return and in the hedge fund's withholding tax filing. These foreign limited partners of the U.S. hedge fund are either residents of other taxable European countries or have no particular reason to suppress their names from being recorded by the IRS. Indeed, under tax treaties, they can obtain a complete remission of U.S. withholding taxes or be able to seek credit for the U.S. withholding taxes paid from their home country taxes. However, they still are a significant set of foreign investors who are wary of their legal rights as shareholders, as mutual fund record holders, or as limited partners in a Cayman Islands or similar offshore entity. They perceive that the U.S. legal system is safer, and despite a British crown colony legal system that functions in the Cayman Islands and similar places, their investment is not as soundly protected as in the U.S.

Consider the case of a pure stand-alone offshore hedge fund. The offshore fund's U.S. securities brokerage firm would be willing to become the U.S. withholding agent for U.S. withholding taxes due from the offshore hedge fund. This is feasible because all investors of the offshore master hedge fund are symmetrical, that is, all of them face the same identical U.S. withholding tax structure. The securities brokerage firm would collect and remit the withholding taxes due, which is usually a 30 percent flat rate on U.S. source dividends.

Now consider the case where the offshore hedge fund becomes the master fund, and the U.S. hedge fund serves as its feeder. The offshore master fund has multiple clienteles from different tax regimes. The U.S. feeder fund (and its pass-through U.S. partners) is one such client, not subject to U.S. withholding taxes. The offshore master fund would have to perform the function of U.S. withholding agent. It would seek a U.S. taxpayer ID number and remit annual withholding taxes for its individual constituent non-U.S. partners only. There would be no withholding taxes for U.S. pass-through partners of the feeder fund and no withholding taxes for U.S. investors who join the offshore master fund. This is an important step because U.S. tax-exempt institutional investors become direct partners of the offshore master fund with the objective of blocking UBTI. They would not expect to be garnished for U.S. withholding taxes, which they are not otherwise required to pay. If the U.S. feeder fund has foreign investors, it files its own withholding tax return to collect and pay withholding taxes on behalf of its foreign partners.

All of this seems to be a tangle, but when examined closely, all that we are addressing is the establishment of routine mechanisms for collecting U.S. withholding taxes at the level of the U.S. hedge fund (if it has foreign partners) and at the level of the offshore hedge fund (particularly to ensure that U.S. partners are not subjected to U.S. withholding tax). To prevent the imposition of withholding tax on a U.S. tax-exempt entity that is a member of an offshore master fund, the offshore fund would arrange for U.S. withholding taxes on dividends to be remitted only for its non-U.S. investors. Even though accounting, bookkeeping, and withholding tax filing would be elaborate, the primary objective of sequestration of U.S. tax-exempt investors from non-U.S. investors in the offshore entity and the imposition of U.S. withholding taxes only on non-U.S. investors in the offshore fund is achieved.

**An Additional Offshore Feeder Fund May Be Required.**    An important exception occurs when the offshore master fund has the three clienteles: U.S. investors, either taxable or tax-exempt, and non-U.S. investors. If the offshore master fund serves as the withholding agent for U.S. withholding taxes due from non-U.S. partners, it would have to provide their names to the IRS on the annual U.S. withholding tax Form 1042. The primary economic purpose of the offshore master fund becoming the U.S. withholding agent is to ensure that its U.S. investors are not subjected to nonrecoverable U.S. withholding tax. Yet its non-U.S. investors desire anonymity and do not want their names to be sent to the IRS. But the offshore master fund would then have to sequester the names of its non-U.S. investors from the IRS by setting up an offshore feeder fund that solely admits non-U.S. investors. This offshore feeder fund purchases an interest in the offshore master fund, and the name of the offshore feeder fund, not the names of its investors and shareholders, is conveyed to the IRS in the U.S. withholding tax return of the offshore master fund. Thus, in this situation that adds an additional layer of complexity due to accommodating different clients, the hedge fund sponsor would have to create separate feeder vehicles to sequester its various clienteles with differing withholding tax and anonymity preferences. The administrative and accounting cost of the hedge fund sponsor increases because accounting and auditing have to be performed for each of the freestanding feeder entities. Yet the incremental cost is insignificant in relation to the assets of the entities, and even with zero assets in a feeder fund, the hedge fund sponsor usually keeps such entities alive and ready so that they can take in new fee-paying investors and limited partners without delays involved in setting up new entities with associated bank accounts.

# CHAPTER 3

# Hedge Fund Fees

## Starting Point: The Partnership Agreement

The starting point for every hedge fund is its key foundational document: its agreement of limited partnership. For offshore hedge funds, the equivalent foundational document is the memorandum and articles of association. U.S. hedge funds do not have to file a copy of the limited partnership agreement with any government agency. Most offshore regimes require the memorandum and articles of association to be filed with the regulatory regime, with the understanding that such a document would not be in the public domain.

The U.S. limited partnership agreement typically is a 10- to 20-page document with an elaborate set of definitions and clauses. Although the agreements appear to be customized, most of the clauses are likely to be boilerplate paragraphs assembled by lawyers to meet the specifications of the hedge fund manager. In order to facilitate opening a brokerage account and verifying the investment authority of the hedge fund manager, brokerage firms require the hedge fund's limited partnership agreement to be submitted to them for review and approval. The agreement itself is not directly signed by the limited partners, but instead by a hedge fund manager holding power of attorney granted by limited partners in the same agreement. The limited partners subsequently sign a separate agreement of admission. The same hedge fund manager, in the capacity of the general partner to the investment partnership, also signs the limited partnership agreement and the subsequent agreements of admission with limited partners.

This permits the master partnership agreement to remain invariant through the life of the hedge fund. Amendments are made only when absolutely necessary, since such amendments might cause concern to both existing limited partners and future new limited partners. Interestingly, the limited partnership agreement is signed twice by the same fund manager: once in the capacity of general partner, and once in the capacity of holding power of attorney for the limited partners. Each limited partner signs a subsequent agreement of admission into the limited partnership. Such agreements of admission become addenda to the master limited partnership agreement. In rare instances, compliance departments of banks and brokerage firms might want to examine the limited partners' agreements of admission.

## Fund Valuation at Discrete Opening Time Points

We shall apply a consistent and uniform algebraic notation throughout this book for clarity and brevity. Time points are denoted by with subscript $t$, starting $t = 0$ for the inception of the fund and $t = 12$ as the first calendar year anniversary of the fund. It is convenient to assume that $t = 0$ coincides with the beginning of the calendar year, so $t = 12$ denotes the end of the calendar year, and $t = 1, 2, 3 \ldots$ denote each month during the calendar year. Note that 13 time points $t = 0\ldots12$ are required to span 12 months of the calendar year.

Each time point has a fund closing value and a fund opening value. A fund is considered to be frozen in terms of changes in partnership ownership percentages between two time points. Deposits/withdrawals by existing partners, redemption by existing partners, and addition of new partners are permitted only at such discrete time points. An SEC-regulated mutual fund is a special case, where the discrete time points are the close of every business day. Hedge funds try to limit the closing/opening of their fund to deposits and redemptions at the end of every calendar quarter, rather than at the end of every month, and they require long notice periods, usually 45 days, from investors about their intention to redeem or make deposits.

We shall adopt the convention of monthly closing and opening of a hedge fund, due to a very valuable by-product that is quintessential to marketing to new investors: a monthly time series of hedge fund performance, which is amenable to more refined calculation of risk-adjusted return. Thus, for our purposes, the month-end time points $t = 0, 1, 2, 3, \ldots$ 12 represent the discrete closing/opening windows for the hedge fund. Our subscript $t$ is a monthly series, even though a hedge fund may practically allow closing/opening at quarter-end time points, which in our monthly frame of reference is the quarter-end subset $t = 0, 3, 6, 9, 12 \ldots$.

A hedge fund could adopt any consistent convention for determining month-end dates. Although most funds treat the end of the last business day of a month to be the month-end time point, some follow atypical conventions, such as the last business day that occurs on or before the last Friday of a month, except for December, which is the last business day on or before December 31.

A critical difference between a hedge fund and a Silicon Valley venture partnership is that the limited partners of a hedge fund are permitted under their partnership agreement to seek withdrawals or make deposits at the discrete time points, while a Silicon Valley venture partnership does not allow such discretion to limited partners. A venture partnership may make distributions of realized gains prior to the termination of the partnership and permit limited partners to withdraw a significant portion of such interim distributions so that they may pay their taxes, which are due on their tax allocations of realized gains. Similarly, a venture partnership may open a window for limited partners to make additions based on capital calls issued under the partnership agreement by the general partner. The primary difference between a hedge fund and a Silicon Valley venture partnership is that a hedge fund is generally supposed to be liquid and can be valued according to the market prices of its constituent holdings, and that partners may redeem their share of such interim market value of the hedge fund, while a Silicon Valley venture fund is not liquid at interim time points. The only time point when it is considered to be market-valued for purposes of redemption at its economic value by its limited partners is when all venture holdings are either written off or sold.

We shall focus our attention on hedge funds, which have the property that their interim fund value at market prices can be unambiguously determined at all the relevant discrete time points when their performance is measured, and that their limited partners are permitted under their partnership agreement to make withdrawals or deposits. Thus, at every time point $t = 0 \ldots 12$, withdrawals and deposits by investors (both the limited partners and the general partner) are permitted. Denote the *closing fund value before all fees* at time point $t$ by $W_t$. At inception time point $t = 0$, the closing fund value has to be zero, so $W_0 = 0$. This is the initial condition for every hedge fund.

At time point $t$, the hedge fund is "closed" according to market value, determined as $W_t$. Fees are calculated and charged to partners, reducing $W_t$ accordingly. Then, partners may initiate withdrawal or deposit. The hedge fund is then "opened" at its established "opening value," which is simply the closing fund value, less fees, plus deposits. In our subsequent discussion, we denote the opening fund value at time point $t$ as $V_t$. $W_t$ and $V_t$ are identical when there are no fees and no deposits or withdrawals at time point $t$.

## Calculation of Fixed Fees

Offshore hedge funds are blessed with simplicity in accounting and correctly calculating each partner's capital balance at any point in time. This is almost parallel to the methodology that is adopted by regulated mutual funds, with appropriate modifications for calculating the fund's fixed fees, also called management fees. There are a fixed number of valuation time points during the course of a year. For simplicity, these time points are calendar month-ends, or the last business day of every month, whichever is convenient to the fund manager from the perspective of valuation.

We shall presume that withdrawals and deposits by limited partners are permitted at each such month-end valuation time point. There are no withdrawals or deposits permitted in between, though there is no such hard-and-fast rule required. As long as the fund manager is able to properly value the fund at any time point, that becomes a feasible time point at which to permit withdrawals and deposits. The limited partnership agreement typically specifies the time points at which a limited partner may request withdrawals or deposits, and the hedge fund manager might accommodate the special needs of limited partners.

The closing fund value before all fees at time point $t$ is $W_t$ as defined earlier. The aggregate *fixed fees* paid by the fund at time point $t$ is denoted as $F_t$, a positive quantity. The aggregate (net) deposits at time point $t$ is denoted by $D_t$ (where negative $D_t$ denotes net withdrawals, positive denotes net deposits), so that the fund value at the same time point $t$ after fees and after net deposit is governed by the wealth conservation identity $W_t - F_t + D_t = V_t$. Here, $V_t$ denotes the *opening fund value* at time point $t$. We need to place a restriction on negative deposits (withdrawals): $D_t$ cannot be such that $V_t$ becomes negative because $V_t$, which is calculated at time point $t$ after deducting fees $F_t$ and after withdrawals/deposits $D_t$, must always be positive. If $V_t$ becomes negative, the hedge fund is bankrupt. Thus, $V_t \geq 0$ and $D_t$ are such that $V_t$ cannot be negative, that is, net deposits and withdrawals cannot drive down the fund value after fees to negative levels. Partners cannot withdraw more than the closing value of the fund before all fees, less the fees. Thus, $D_t$ has to satisfy $W_t - F_t + D_t \geq 0$.

We need the restriction, which may appear almost trivial, that either $W_t$ or $V_t$ at any time point $t$ cannot be negative, that is, the fund may not have a negative value. This requires that at any point in time $t$, we cannot have a situation where $W_t$, the closing hedge fund value, is negative. It is indeed possible that, due to risky leveraged investments, a hedge fund's value could abruptly become negative, due to the fund's borrowing obligations exceeding the value of its assets. In such a situation, the hedge fund seeks bankruptcy protection due to its formation as a limited liability entity. The negative fund value is transferred in bankruptcy court to lenders, after redeeming limited partners at zero value. The limited liability nature of the hedge fund as well as its constituent limited partners realistically allows us to place such a restriction on it. As described earlier, the general partner entity in a partnership is responsible for all liabilities of a limited partnership. However, by entity structuring of the hedge fund sponsors, the general partner is formed as limited liability entity, and thus has bankruptcy protection from liabilities in excess of its assets. The general partner entity rarely holds a significant partnership interest in a hedge fund or significant working capital, because those assets could be claimed in bankruptcy court by lenders to the hedge fund. Whenever the general partner entity receives large or significant profit-sharing allocations, it withdraws and distributes them to its own members, primarily to shield its assets from being attached in bankruptcy. Thus the general partner entity retains only a very little share in the hedge fund on an ongoing basis and barely sufficient working capital to maintain operations.

A hedge fund's general partner entity generally does not hold large surplus capital invested in excess of its working capital requirements, either as investment in its own hedge fund or as a cash "war chest" in a bank. Thus, most hedge fund general partners are likely to withdraw a significant part of their enlarged account value generated through fixed fees and performance fees and distribute the same back to their members, which subsequently might reinvest the proceeds of such withdrawal back into the same hedge fund that they manage in the capacity of individual limited partners protected by limited liability.

We need to track the $W_t$, $F_t$ and $D_t$ from which the closing fund value $V_t$ is derived. We need a second subscript $i$ to denote each unique *capital account* at time point $t$, where $i$ runs from 1 to $N_t$. The same limited partner may have multiple capital accounts in order to distinguish additions made to the fund by the same partner at different points in time. Multiple capital accounts for the same investor enable us to tackle the calculation of performance fees with ease and tractability. The number of capital accounts at time point $t$ could change depending on the entry or exit of disparate investors' capital accounts, hence the subscript $t$ is attached to $N_t$.

The empty nascent fund opens at inception time point $t = 0$ so that its closing value before fees and deposits at $t = 0$ is zero. We write the initial or starting condition as $W_0 = 0$. No fees are due at inception, so $F_0 = 0$. The fund is "funded" by deposits $D_0$ so that its opening value at $t = 0$, $V_0$ is the same as $D_0$. Thus, at the inception of the fund with the opening fund value $W_0$ at zero, aggregate positive deposits $D_0$ were added, and the closing fund value was $V_0 = W_0 + D_0 = D_0$. Applying the subscript $i$ to the list of investors at time point $t$, we denote the capital account constituents of the fund by $W_t^i$, $F_t^i$, $D_t^i$ and $V_t^i$ such that

$$\sum_{i=1}^{N_t} W_t^i = W_t$$

$$\sum_{i=1}^{N_t} F_t^i = F_t$$

$$\sum_{i=1}^{N_t} D_t^i = D_t$$

$$\sum_{i=1}^{N_t} V_t^i = V_t$$

Each capital account $i$ (where $i$ runs from 1 to $N_t$) is governed by the wealth conservation identity that applies:

$$W_t^i - F_t^i + D_t^i = V_t^i$$

Further, each opening capital account $V_t^i$ cannot become negative after withdrawals (negative deposits) $D_t^i$ at time point $t$. That is, $V_t^i \geq 0$, which requires $D_t^i$ to be such that $W_t^i - F_t^i + D_t^i \geq 0$. If it does ever become zero or negative, the fund is insolvent and bankrupt.

When aggregated across all capital accounts, the wealth conservation identity for the fund as a whole follows:

$$W_t - F_t + D_t = V_t$$

It becomes eminently handy to associate the dollar value $V_t^i$ representing the closing capital account (i.e., after deposits and fixed fees) time point $t$ for all capital accounts into fractional weights that add to 1 (or percentage weights that add to 100 percent) denoted by $\alpha_t^i$ as:

$$\alpha_t^i = \frac{V_t^i}{V_t}$$

$$\sum_{i=1}^{N_t} \alpha_t^i = 1$$

Partnership fractional weights added across all capital accounts must add up to 1, or alternately, partnership percentage shares across all capital accounts must add up to 100 percent.

Consider the investment time interval denoted by $[t - 1, t]$ where time point $t - 1$ is the beginning of the investment interval or period that ends at time point $t$. The absolute dollar economic investment profit for the fund as a whole, inclusive of all realized and unrealized gains and all investment cash flows like dividends and interest, during the investment time period $[t - 1, t]$ is:

$$\pi_t = W_t - V_{t-1} \text{ for } t = 1, 2, 3, \ldots$$

This represents the opening fund value at time point $t - 1$, $V_{t-1}$, growing to the closing fund value at time point $t$, $W_t$, before fixed fees or deposits made through the wise investment strategies deployed by the hedge fund manager. This profit made by the hedge fund before all fees, denoted by $\pi_t$, is simply the *opening fund value (before any fees or deposits)* $W_t$ at time point t, minus, the *closing fund value (after fees and deposits)* $V_{t-1}$ at time point $t - 1$.

Note that for an offshore fund in a tax-exempt regime, we do not care to track components of the hedge fund's profit before all fees $\pi_t$ that is, its breakdown by dividends, interest, and capital gains. This breakdown becomes extremely important for a U.S. hedge fund, which is analyzed in the subsequent chapters. By ignoring the components of absolute dollar profit within a reference framework of an offshore hedge fund, we are able to rapidly proceed in describing the process of tracking returns, capital accounts, and management fees—that is, a simple linear algebra framework for hedge fund accounting that can be implemented numerically in a spreadsheet. This is an economic accounting system, disregarding taxation. The economic accounting system also applies to a U.S. hedge fund, which has to subsequently implement a tax accounting system, described in detail in later chapters.

From the previous definition, we obtain the equivalent relationship:

$$(1 + r_t)V_{t-1} = W_t$$

where $r_t$ is the fractional return before all fees earned by the hedge fund for the time period $[t - 1, t]$.

As is the practice in most hedge funds, as well as in standard mutual funds, a periodic fixed fee is deducted from each capital account. The fixed fee is usually specified as an annual rate, which is denoted as $f_{annual}$. We have conveniently spaced the time points one month apart, thus the time point $t + 12$ is one year from the time point $t$. Thus, the fixed fee is transformed into a constant monthly rate $f$ according to the conventional formula for continuous compounding:

$$f = (1 + f_{annual})^{1/12} - 1$$

It is possible that a hedge fund partnership agreement specifies a periodic fee, such as a quarterly fee or a monthly fee, so $f$ is directly provided and no conversion from annual to monthly units is required.

The fixed fee $f$ is typically imposed on the capital account value (before fees) at the end of the period. Further, the fixed fee could vary across capital accounts. The general partner generally never pays fees, and this is usually stated in the partnership agreement. Even though a fixed fee rate applicable to all investors is stated in the hedge fund partnership master agreement, the subsequent agreement of admission might contain different fixed fee rates negotiated by a limited partner and fully permissible under the partnership agreement. Thus, the fixed fee has to be superscripted by $i$ for each capital account. The fixed fee rate could also vary for each capital account across different time periods, but we shall not pursue this extreme variation and not apply a second subscript $t$ to the fixed fee rate, now denoted by $f^i$.

With the application of fixed fees, the capital account identity is modified. We take the capital account of the general partner to be denoted by $i = 1$. The closing capital account value of each partner *before fixed fees and deposits* at time point $t$ denoted by $W_t^i$ is simply $[\alpha_{t-1}^i W_t]$. It is the aggregate fund value before fees at time point $t$, multiplied by the opening partnership fraction $\alpha_{t-1}^i$ that determines a partner's economic share for the investment subperiod $[t-1, t]$. Each partner is levied a fee dollar amount of $F_t^i = f^i[\alpha_{t-1}^i W_t]$ and thus, the capital account value *after fixed fees, but before deposits*, $V_t^i$ is:

$$V_t^i = (1 - f^i)[\alpha_{t-1}^i W_t] + D_t^i$$

The aggregate fixed fees collected from the capital accounts of the limited partners at time point $t$ are:

$$F_t = \sum_{i=1}^{N_t} F_t^i = \sum_{i=1}^{N_t} f^i[\alpha_{t-1}^i W_t] = W_t \sum_{i=1}^{N_t} f^i \alpha_{t-1}^i$$

For the general partner, $f^1 = 0$. The general partner pays no fees. Further, the summation of all fixed fees is taken out as an expense from the capital accounts of the limited partners of the hedge fund and remitted (at time point $t$) to the general partner entity, much as if it were a bank or brokerage expense incurred directly by the fund.

We denote it by the deposit of an amount equal to the aggregate fixed fees paid by limited partners and credited to the capital account of the general partner as $D_t^f$. In other words, the aggregate fixed fee amount is an additional deposit to the capital account of the general partner time point $t$, that is, $D_t^f = F_t$. Its tax treatment will be described in detail later. In summary, it is reported as taxable ordinary income to the general partner, irrespective of whether the general partner subsequently withdraws this amount.

The total deposit by the general partner at time point $t$ would be the aggregate fixed fees $D_t^f$ paid by the limited partners but not yet withdrawn by the general partner, plus any additional deposits or withdrawals made by the general partner, denoted by $D_t^1$. The aggregate fees do not reduce or increase the value of the hedge fund as a whole. That is because an amount equal to $D_t^f = F_t$ is *deducted* on an aggregate from the capital accounts of the limited partners; the value $D_t^f = F_t$ is *added* as a deposit to the capital account of the general partner.

The capital account wealth conservation identity for each capital account *after fixed fees* becomes:

$$W_t^i - F_t^i + D_t^i = V_t^i \text{ for limited partners } i = 2 \ldots N_t$$

For the general partner $i = 1$ for whom the fixed fee rate $f^1$ is typically zero,

$$W_t^1 + D_t^f + D_t^1 = V_t^1$$

When the preceding capital account conservation identities are aggregated across all capital accounts (including that of the general partner), we obtain the *opening fund value after fixed fees and deposits* at time point $t$:

$$W_t \sum_{i=1}^{N_t} (1 - f_i) \alpha_{t-1}^i + D_t^f + \sum_{i=1}^{N_t} D_t^i = \sum_{i=1}^{N_t} V_t^i$$

The previous equation reduces to the wealth conservation identity for the fund as a whole at time point $t$, $W_t - F_t + D_t = V_t$, since the fixed fees collected by deducting the capital accounts of the limited partners exactly cancel out against the same fees added as a deposit to the capital account of the general partner, representing income to the general partner. This is because, in our construction, we have $F_t = W_t \sum_{i=1}^{N_t} f^i \alpha_{t-1}^i$ and $D_t^f = F_t$.

If the general partner sets $D_t^1 = -D_t^f$, it means that the fixed fees paid by the limited partners at time point $t$ are immediately withdrawn in their entirety by the general partner at the same time point $t$. In reality, this is rarely possible in hedge funds, because their audit-quality valuation usually is concluded several business days after the closing time point $t$. SEC-regulated mutual funds take the art of management fee calculation and withdrawal to extremes, calculating fixed fees at the close of every business day, deducting them from the assets of the mutual fund, and remitting these daily fixed fees to the mutual fund management company.

Having created each opening capital account value $V_t^i$, in this situation where there are no performance fees imposed at time point $t$, we may proceed with the next investment period $[t, t + 1]$. Based on the values of each capital account after fees $V_t^i$, each capital account's fractional weight $\alpha_t^i = \dfrac{V_t^i}{V_t}$ is calculated corresponding to time $t$. This algebraic framework is now ready for managing and tracking the constituent capital accounts of a simple mutual fund based on periodic fixed fees in a tax-free regime, representing an economic accounting system that disregards tax consequences.

## Calculation of Performance Fees

Nearly all hedge funds calculate their performance fees at the end of every calendar year. The performance applies to capital accounts that participated for all or any portion of the calendar year. Thus, if a hedge fund commenced trading in July, capital accounts would be assessed a performance fee in December of the same year, based on their performance during a partial year. If a capital account is entirely redeemed prior to the end of the calendar year, say in July, it would be assessed a performance fee based on its performance over a partial calendar year, up to its point of departure in July.

**Partial Withdrawals.** The simplest way to deal with a partial withdrawal request from the capital account, whether during midyear or at calendar year-end, is to bifurcate the mother capital account into two daughter capital accounts simply by applying (linear) proportions (adding up to 100 percent) to the *closing capital account value after all fees,* such that one of the daughter capital accounts almost exactly meets the investors' partial redemption request and is withdrawn in entirety. The non-negativity restriction for a capital account ensures that such proportions cannot be negative, and thus a daughter capital account would not be negative. This type of bifurcation preserves linearity all along the way. Most hedge fund limited partnership agreements do not contain explicit language for proportional bifurcation of capital accounts requesting a partial redemption. However, such bifurcation is entirely consistent with the partnership agreement, which directly or indirectly permits an investor's interest in a hedge fund to be represented by several capital accounts.

We shall examine the base case where performance fees are levied on all capital accounts only on their calendar year anniversary, which is the time point $t = 12$, by arbitrarily selecting $t = 0$, the inception date, as a calendar year-end. We shall later examine the more general case where a limited partner makes a full or partial withdrawal prior to the calendar year anniversary time point $t = 12$.

We require an algorithm or procedure to calculate performance fees on each capital account separately, because every such capital account could have a different performance depending on the actual time point at which it started. However, to preserve linearity (and hence simplicity), we would like to have each capital account not include any positive deposits made in the middle of the calendar year. Such consolidation of net deposits within a capital account works well for a fund that is based on fixed fees alone, such as a standard mutual fund. Instead, we insist that each positive deposit made by a limited partner be treated as if it were a new capital account (belonging to the same partner).

So we place a new restriction on a capital account that is subject to performance fees: No positive deposits are permitted until the performance fee is calculated and applied. A midyear deposit by the limited partner is treated as if it were an entirely new capital account belonging to the same partner. Withdrawals in entirety are permitted both at mid-year and calendar year anniversary time points. Proportional bifurcation of a capital account is conducted to facilitate the entire withdrawal of a daughter capital account. An entire withdrawal of a capital account at mid-year, after applying midyear performance fees, is permitted.

Each such capital account indexed by the letter $i$ has an associated "high-water mark," which is simply the highest value of the capital account since its inception *after fixed fees.* The high-water mark is denoted by a pair $(H^i, T)$ where $H^i$ denotes the highest value achieved by the capital account after fixed fees since inception, or the last time point at which a performance fee was assessed. $T$ records the time point at which this high-water mark event occurred. The pair $(H^i, T)$ is tracked and recorded in memory and brought into consideration at the calendar year anniversary, at which time the performance fee calculation is conducted. Each capital account would be associated with its own unique high-water mark associated with its start date and fixed fee rate. Even if two capital accounts have the same inception date, they might have negotiated different fixed fee rates and have slightly different high-water marks associated with them.

We take the initial funding of the capital account $i$ to have occurred at time point $t = m$, where $m$ could be any time point between $t = 0$ and $t = 12$. Since there are no deposits to a capital account with performance fees, the series $\{V_t^i\}$ for $t = m \ldots 12$ denotes the evolution of the closing capital account value *after fixed fees* that was described earlier. A high-water mark is set at the last time point at which a performance fee was assessed, or its inception, thus $(H^i, T) = (V_m^i, m)$. This high-water mark pair $(V_m^i, m)$ is held constant until the next time point for calculation of the performance fee arrives, which for now is $t = 12$.

At that time point $t = 12$, the limited partnership agreement triggers the calculation of performance fees for every capital account according to the specific language contained in the limited partnership agreement. Typically, each capital account gives to the general partner a fraction, usually 20 percent, of profits in excess of the high-water mark, less a pre-defined "hurdle" amount.

We need an additional variable to differentiate between the value of a capital account after fixed fees but before performance fees, and the value of a capital account after both fixed fees and performance fees. $V_t^i$ for $i = 0$, 1, 2, 3, … denotes the value of the capital account at monthly intervals after fixed fees, derived exactly as in the case of a hedge fund with fixed fees only. The new variable $U_t^i$ for $t = 0, 12, 24, 36, 48, \ldots$ denotes the value of the capital account defined at 12-month intervals only after both fixed fees and performance fees. For now, the consideration of the case of withdrawal before year-end is removed from consideration. Thus, $\{V_t^i\}$, $\{W_t^i\}$, and $\{\alpha_t^i\}$ are monthly series, and $\{U_t^i\}$ is an annual series corresponding to the year-end time points when performance fees are applied.

The series $\{V_t^i\}$ is calculated exactly as developed earlier for the case of a simple hedge fund with fixed fees only:

$$V_t^i = (1 - f^i)[\alpha_{t-1}^i W_t]$$

for limited partners $i = 2 \ldots N_t$

$$V_t^1 = W_t^1 + D_t^f + D_t^1$$

for the general partner $i = 1$, where

$$D_t^f = \sum_{i=1}^{N_t} F_t^i = \sum_{i=1}^{N_t} f^i[\alpha_{t-1}^i W_t] = W_t \sum_{i=1}^{N_t} f^i \alpha_{t-1}^i$$

The general partner, with $f^1 = 0$, collects all fixed fees from limited partners and applies it as a deposit to its capital account. In the case with performance fees, $D_t^i = 0$ for limited partners $i = 2 \ldots N_t$ during the time interval $t = 1$ to $t = 12$.

The hurdle amount calculation is specified in the limited partnership agreement, usually according to the (riskless) short-term Treasury bill rate that otherwise would have been earned by investing the amount $V_m^i$ in Treasury bills starting at time point $t = m$ until time point $t = 12$. Setting $r_{m,12}$ as the deannualized return on short-term Treasury bills from $t = m$ to $t = 12$, which in turn is calculated from published annualized numbers, the hurdle amount for the capital account is simply $V_m^i(1 + r_{m,12})$.

We are provided with a capital account starting point at $t = m$ that does not have to be the inception date $t = 0$. This generalizes the performance fee calculation for capital accounts that could have started in the middle of the calendar year. However, it is best to consider that $m = 0$ for all capital accounts and new interim-year capital accounts do not exist. In such a case, the hurdle rate would be the annualized Treasury bill rate $r_{0,12}$. Strictly speaking, the riskless rate is determined *ex post* by looking back at the past 12 1-month rates or the past 4 quarterly rates and chain multiplying. We shall presume that the riskless rate that drives the hurdle amount is appropriately determined from the history of past riskless rates at time point $t = 12$ and represented as an annualized rate denoted by $r_{0,12}$, the riskless rate that would be earned between time point $t = 0$ and time point $t = 12$.

The linguistic representation of the performance fee calculation in the hedge fund partnership agreement that is applicable to all limited partners' capital accounts is algebraically translated here. In most limited partnership agreements, the performance fee applies on new profits in excess of the riskless hurdle rate. New profits are considered to occur only when the limited partner's account value rises to a level that is in excess of the previous high-water mark. The idea of new profits calculated relative to the high-water mark is to ensure that performance fees are not charged in situations where the account value declines and subsequently recovers to the previous high. $F_t^i$ denotes the fixed fees paid by capital accounts at time points $t = 1, 2, 3, \ldots$ The performance fee $P_t^i$ is paid by capital accounts at time points $t = 12, 24, 36, \ldots P_t^i$ and is contingent upon several variables. Here is $P_{12}^i$, the performance fee for the investor superscripted as $i$, on the hedge fund's first calendar year-end at time point $t = 12$, defined contingently as shown in the following equations:

$$P_{12}^i = \begin{cases} 0, V_{12}^i \leq H^i \\ 0, V_{12}^i > H^i \text{ and } V_{12}^i - V_m^i(1 + r_{m,12}) \leq 0 \\ = \delta^i\left[V_{12}^i - V_m^i(1 + r_{m,12})\right], V_{12}^i > H^i \text{ and } V_{12}^i - V_m^i(1 + r_{m,12}) > 0 \end{cases}$$

Note that we have provided for capital accounts that can start in the middle of the calendar year at time point $t = m$. However, both for simplicity and for clearer understanding, we replace $t = m$ by $t = 0$ and assume that there are no interim year capital accounts, so that the calendar year performance fees at time point $t = 12$ for a capital account that is indexed by the superscript $i$ is:

$$P_{12}^i = \begin{cases} 0, V_{12}^i \leq H^i \\ 0, V_{12}^i > H^i \text{ and } V_{12}^i - V_0^i(1 + r_{0,12}) \leq 0 \\ = \delta^i\left[V_{12}^i - V_0^i(1 + r_{0,12})\right], V_{12}^i > H^i \text{ and } V_{12}^i - V_0^i(1 + r_{0,12}) > 0 \end{cases}$$

$\delta^i$ is the performance fee fraction or rate that is specific to a capital account of a limited partner investor whose capital account is superscripted as $i$. Just as fixed fees may be negotiated by each limited partner such that the fees could vary across capital accounts, despite $\delta^i = 20$ percent that is usually specified in the master limited partnership agreement, each limited partner may negotiate a different performance fees rate. The general partner does not pay performance fees, so for the general partner represented by $i = 1$, $\delta^1 = 0$.

There is often debate as to whether performance fees should be levied according to changes in value of a capital account before fixed fees, or after fixed fees. Many hedge fund limited partnership agreements do not clarify this. We consider it appropriate to charge fixed fees first, then track the value of the capital account after fixed fees, and apply performance fees on the economic profits calculated according to the change in the capital account value *after fixed fees*. It is important not to leave this ambiguous and to specify the correct base on which the performance fee calculation applies clearly and accurately in the limited partnership agreement. If a hedge fund sponsor specifies calculation of fixed fees applying on the economic profits of a capital account before all fees (and before fixed fees), the previous algebraic expression for performance fees would have to be changed, replacing all instances of $V_t^i$ with $W_t^i$. (Of course, note that at time point $t = 0$, we defined the empty fund as having $W_0^i = 0$, so for the base starting point, we shall have to apply the starting capital account value $V_0^i$.) We shall continue our exposition based on the premise that performance fees are applied on economic profits calculated after fixed fees, that is, $V_t^i$.

Even though the payoffs at each of three contingent states are represented as linear payout functions, $P_{12}^i$ is not differentiable at the points of contingency. Indeed, the economic value of $P_{12}^i$ may be determined by applying option pricing formulae. The general partner is granted a call option on 20 percent of the upside payoff by each limited partner, at a strike price equal to the hurdle amount, contingent upon the value before fees exceeding the high-water mark.

The first contingency condition states that the performance fee for a capital account $P_{12}^i$ is zero if the value of the capital account after fixed fees at time point $t = 12$ is below the high-water mark that was established at time point $t = m$. $H^i$ is the first component of the high-water mark pair $(H^i, T = 12) = (V_m^i, m)$, so $H^i = V_m^i$. We are omitting $T = 12$ for compactness and writing $(H^i, T = 12)$ simply as $H^i$. For simplicity, we are also excluding capital accounts starting interim-year, so that the starting time point for all capital accounts is $m = 0$.

The second contingency condition states that a performance fee for a capital account $P_{12}^i$ is still zero, even if its value after fixed fees $V_{12}^i$ exceeds the high-water mark, if its value after fixed fees does not exceed the hurdle amount $V_m^i(1 + r_{m,12})$ that would be earned by investing the starting capital balance at time point $t = m$ in Treasury bills.

The third contingency condition states that a performance fee is positive if *both* its value after fixed fees $V_{12}^i$ exceeds the high-water mark, *and* its value after fixed fees exceeds the hurdle amount $V_m^i(1 + r_{m,12})$. If both of these conditions are not met, that is, the capital account value after fixed fees does not exceed both the high-water mark and the hurdle amount, no performance fee is to be paid by a capital account.

It is important to recognize that the third contingency triggers not only the imposition of the performance fee, but also the resetting of the new high-water mark, described later. We have presumed that the limited partnership agreement specifies a performance fee that is based on applying the sharing fraction $\delta^i = 20$ percent on the profits earned by a capital account in excess of a hurdle amount linked to the riskless rate. Many hedge funds entirely omit the consideration of a hurdle amount in their limited partnership agreement. In such a situation where the hedge fund has omitted the consideration of the hurdle amount linked to the riskless rate from the calculation of performance fees, the calculation becomes a three-step function as shown here:

$$P_{12}^i = \begin{cases} 0, V_{12}^i \le H^i \\ 0, V_{12}^i > H^i \text{ and } V_{12}^i - V_0^i \le 0 \\ = \delta^i[V_{12}^i - V_0^i], V_{12}^i > H^i \text{ and } V_{12}^i - V_0^i > 0 \end{cases}$$

The omission of the hurdle amount linked to the riskless rate from a limited partnership agreement results in a peculiar situation where the hedge fund might invest entirely in riskless Treasury bills and charge a performance fee that is effectively $\delta^i = 20$ percent of the riskless rate.

However, we are unlikely to find hedge funds that do not provide for a high-water mark. Even if there did exist a hedge fund that applied performance fees without a high-water mark, we would consider this an error and an omission in the design of the limited partnership agreement. This is because the high-water mark mechanism is designed to prevent the general partner from charging performance fees to limited partners many times over solely driven by the volatility of the underlying assets. In such a situation where the hedge fund has omitted the consideration of both the hurdle amount linked to the riskless rate and the high-water mark from the calculation of performance fees, the calculation becomes the much simpler two-step function shown here:

$$P_{12}^i = \begin{cases} 0, V_{12}^i - V_0^i \leq 0 \\ \delta^i [V_{12}^i - V_0^i], V_{12}^i - V_0^i > 0 \end{cases}$$

A high-water mark mechanism ensures that only new profits are subjected to performance fees. In its absence, performance fees would apply for any increase in the capital account value over the calendar year, even if it were a recovery from disastrous losses in a previous year. If the underlying assets of the hedge fund were to follow a whipsaw path of crashes followed by a recovery, performance fees levied in periods of recovery would eventually drive down limited partners' capital accounts to zero.

If a performance fee is due, that is, $P_{12}^i > 0$, the amount $P_{12}^i$ has to be deducted from the capital account of the limited partner and added to the capital account of the general partner as if it were a new deposit occurring at $t = 12$. To enable such a partial withdrawal of the amount $P_{12}^i$ we have to apply the proportional bifurcation procedure, described earlier in words and now implemented in algebra. We calculate the *bifurcation proportion* for each capital account denoted by $\beta^i = \dfrac{P_{12}^i}{V_{12}^i}$. $\beta^i$ may also be given a subscript $t = 12$ which we omit.

Why do have we to go through this seriously cumbersome procedure of calculating the performance fee for each capital account and bifurcating it into two parts, a proportion $\beta^i$ being transferred from the capital account superscripted by $i$ of a limited partner, and the remainder $(1 - \beta^i)$ being retained in the same capital account? Why can't we simply withdraw cash equal to the performance fee fraction $\beta^i$ and pay the cash to the general partner? This is for a very important reason: tax efficiency from the perspective of the general partner as well as the limited partners. Under U.S. tax law for U.S. partnerships, such a contingent fee that is transferred in kind in accordance with the limited partnership agreement is taxed to the members of the general partner entity according to the nature of the gains that are transferred. Thus, if most of the economic profits of the hedge fund are realized long-term capital gains, the members of the general partner entity would be receiving their performance fees as tax-preferred items, with long-term capital gains being taxed to U.S. individuals at 15 percent. During 2009, a bill[1] was introduced in the U.S. Congress to specifically amend the Internal Revenue Code to tax performance fees collected by the general partner of a U.S. partnership at the highest ordinary income tax rates to the pass-through members of the general partner entity.

How is this allocation of performance fees calculated on profits, and transferred to the general partner according to the nature of gain, tax efficient from the perspective of the limited partners? Actually, this is *extremely* important from the perspective of the limited partners. If the performance fees were treated as if they were in the same category as fixed fees, limited partners would have to seek itemized deductions for performance fees in addition to fixed fees on their personal tax returns. Unfortunately, for most U.S. taxpayers who fall into the alternative minimum tax, this itemized deduction for investment management fees vanishes. Limited partner investors would have to pay taxes on gross taxable income items allocated by the hedge fund, inclusive of performance fees, but effectively could not deduct either the fixed fee or the performance fee as a tax-deductible expense due to the exclusion of the latter from the calculation of alternative minimum tax, which typically applies to high-income U.S. taxpayers.

Under this current practice of transferring a fraction $\beta^i$ of taxable economic gains from a U.S. limited partner to the general partner, the limited partner is effectively subjected to taxation on income allocations net of performance fees, thereby effectively deducting performance fees from taxable investment income at the source. Of course, the taxable members of the general partner who receive the profit-sharing allocation pay taxes according to the nature of gain, but we note that U.S. taxes have been applied on the fraction $\beta^i$ of economic profits only once. If limited partners were unable to deduct performance fees in their tax calculation under any future revision to the Internal Revenue Code, U.S. taxes on the fraction $\beta^i$ of taxable economic income would be taxed twice: once to the members of the general partner entity who receive that income, and once to the limited partners who cannot deduct the performance fee fraction $\beta^i$ from their taxable income due to U.S. rules of the alternative minimum tax. It has been the tradition in U.S. tax legislation to preserve symmetry and

---

[1] Bill sponsored by Rep. Sander Levin on April 2, 2009, H.R.1935, "To amend the Internal Revenue Code of 1986 to provide for the treatment of partnership interests held by partners providing services." Its status can be tracked at http://thomas.loc.gov/cgi-bin/bdquery/z?d111:h.r.1935.

prevent double taxation. We hope that the proposed 2009 bill or similar future bills, which largely attempted to remove the tax preference of profit-sharing allocations of a general partner, does not disturb the tax deductibility of performance fees paid by limited partners.

The capital account with value $V_{12}^i$ is bifurcated into two separate capital accounts, one with value at $t = 12$ equal to $(1 - \beta^i)V_{12}^i$ and the other with value at $t = 12$ equal to $\beta^i V_{12}^i$. The sum total of these proportionally bifurcated capital accounts is $V_{12}^i$. The latter is withdrawn in entirety so that $D_{12}^i = -\beta^i V_{12}^i$ so that the opening capital balance of the surviving daughter capital account after fixed fees and performance fees at $t = 12$ is $W_{12}^i = (1 - \beta^i)V_{12}^i$. It is this surviving daughter capital account that continues through the subsequent time points $t = 13, 14, 15$, and would be subject to a performance fee at time point $t = 24$ (or earlier if it is withdrawn before time point $t = 24$).

At time point $t = 12$, the wealth conservation identity for each capital account requires a definition of a new variable $U_{12}^i$: This is the surviving daughter capital account value of a limited partner after paying both the fixed fee and the performance fee, plus the deposit or withdrawal $D_{12}^i$ made from the daughter capital account at time point $t = 12$. This is written as $U_{12}^i = V_{12}^i - P_{12}^i + D_{12}^i$. Clearly, the capital account cannot become negative after withdrawals, so we must have $U_{12}^i = V_{12}^i - P_{12}^i + D_{12}^i \geq 0$, that is, if $D_{12}^i$ is a negative number due to withdrawals at time point $t = 12$, we must have $V_{12}^i - P_{12}^i \geq -D_{12}^i$.

The capital account wealth conservation identity at $t = 12$ for each capital account other than the general partner *after fixed fees and performance fees*, therefore, is:

$$U_{12}^i = V_{12}^i - P_{12}^i + D_{12}^i$$

We bifurcate $V_{12}^i$ as $V_{12}^i = (1 - \beta^i)V_{12}^i + \beta^i V_{12}^i$ so that:

$$U_{12}^i = [(1 - \beta^i)V_{12}^i + \beta^i V_{12}^i] - P_{12}^i + D_{12}^i$$

Since the bifurcation fraction is set so that $\beta^i V_{12}^i = P_{12}^i$, and we earlier had defined $W_{12}^i = (1 - \beta^i)V_{12}^i$, we obtain:

$$U_{12}^i = W_{12}^i + D_{12}^i$$

In words, the starting value of the surviving capital account, which we continue to index by the superscript $i$, is the account value after fixed and performance fees, plus deposits at time point $t = 12$.

The preceding applies only to limited partners, so that $i = 2 \ldots N_t$ where $t = 12$.

Just as the fixed fees at time points $t = 1, 2, 3, \ldots 12$ when aggregated across limited partners becomes a deposit $D_t^f$ to the capital account of the general partner, the performance fees at time point $t = 12$ that accrue to the general partner, denoted by $D_{12}^p$, is the aggregation:

$$D_{12}^p = \sum_{i=2}^{N_{12}} P_{12}^i$$

For the general partner $i = 1$ for whom $P_{12}^1$ the performance fee at $t = 12$ is zero due to $\delta^1 = 0$, we include the performance fees $D_{12}^p$ collected from limited partners as if it were an extra deposit:

$$U_{12}^1 = W_{12}^1 + D_{12}^p + D_{12}^f + D_{12}^1$$

What this means is that, for the general partner denoted by superscript $i = 1$, the opening capital account at time point $t = 12$ is the closing capital account, plus performance fees collected from limited partners, plus fixed fees collected from limited partners, plus deposits (or withdrawals) made by the general partner.

It is important to initialize $U_0^i = V_0^i$ to ensure that its time series acquiring its initial value $U_0^i$ is meaningful.

When we aggregate all the capital accounts at $t = 12$ after performance fees are paid by the limited partners to the general partner, we may verify that the fund value as a whole, after fixed and performance fees, is conserved so that $\sum_{i=1}^{N_t} U_t^i = V_t$. If the general partner decides to withdraw the entire performance fee amount at time point $t = 12$, then $-D_{12}^1 = D_{12}^p$, that is, the withdrawal at time point $t = 12$ by the general partner is set equal to the performance fees collected by the general partner at time point $t = 12$.

At $t = 12$, we take a look at the high-water mark and decide whether it has to be reset. Note that $H^i = V_m^i$ for this situation. As long as $V_{12}^i > V_m^i$, the previous high-water mark (that was set at inception of the capital account $t = m$) $H^i = V_m^i$ has been surpassed. The previous high-water mark, after having been surpassed by a new high-water mark, no longer has to be retained in memory. We set the new high-water mark according to the pair $(H^i, T) = (U_{12}^i, 12)$. Note that $H^i$ is pegged to the surviving *daughter capital account* value $U_{12}^i$.

We represent the *resetting of the high-water-mark* at calendar year anniversary time point $T = 12$, for reckoning performance fees at time point $T = 24$, as:

$$\left(H^i, T = 24\right) = \begin{cases} \left(H^i, T = 12\right), V_{12}^i \leq \left(H^i, T = 12\right) \\ U_{12}^i, V_{12}^i > \left(H^i, T = 12\right) \end{cases}$$

The resetting of a high-water mark $\left(H^i, T\right) = \left(U_{12}^i, 12\right)$ occurs as long as $V_{12}^i > V_m^i$ even if no performance fee was due in the situation where the terminal value $V_{12}^i$ did not exceed the accumulated value at $t = 12$ of investing the starting amount $V_m^i$ at time $t = m$ in Treasury bills.

Linearity has been maintained in this framework all the way until the point of calculation of the performance fee, which is based on contingencies. The resulting complexity is the bare minimum required to implement the legal and contractual language contained in a hedge fund partnership agreement. Almost all limited partnership agreements do not specify the procedure for bifurcating capital accounts to withdraw performance fees, and more importantly, do not mention the pegging of the hurdle amount to the surviving daughter capital account after performance fees are paid by limited partners.

In order to continue this procedure through the time points beyond $t = 12$ if a nonzero performance fee was paid, just as we recognized the need to reset the high-water mark $(H^i, T) = U_{12}^i$, we require establishing a base on which the subsequent $\{V_t^i\}$ series will propagate. We can no longer use the value $V_{12}^i$ as the base for calculating the economic profits at time point $t = 13$, since its value has been reduced to $U_{12}^i$ after bifurcating it to pay for the performance fee. Thus, in subsequent calculations of all series, wherever $V_{12}^i$ appears, we replace it with $U_{12}^i$. Thus, the profit before fees at $t = 13$ would be, according to a modification:

$$\pi_t = W_t - V_{t-1} \text{ whenever } t-1 \text{ is not zero or is not a multiple of 12}$$

$$\pi_t = W_t - U_{t-1} \text{ whenever } t-1 \text{ is zero or is a multiple of 12}$$

Thus, all of the formulas developed earlier for a fund without performance fees apply by initially calculating $V_t$ before performance fees, then calculating $U_t$ after the application of performance fees, and then for the purposes of moving forward in time, replacing $V_t$ with $U_t$ at $t = 12, 24, 36, \dots$.

It is also important to recognize that the $\{\alpha_t^i\}$ series is calculated according to $U_t$ at $t = 12, 24, 36, \dots$

$$\alpha_t^i = \frac{V_t^i}{V_t} \text{ whenever } t \text{ is not zero or is not a multiple of 12}$$

$$\alpha_t^i = \frac{U_t^i}{U_t} \text{ whenever } t \text{ is zero or is a multiple of 12}$$

$$\sum_{i=1}^{N_t} \alpha_t^i = 1 \text{ at all time points } t$$

Thus, at $T = 12$, $\alpha_t^i$ is based on $U_t$. When $t$ is not a multiple of 12, $\alpha_t^i$ is based on $V_t$. $U_t$ is valid only at $T = 12$ and multiples of 12.

Consolidation of multiple capital accounts of distinct limited partners is possible when the freshly computed and reset high-water marks after deduction of performance fees coincide. Thus, when the condition for reset of the high-water mark is triggered by calculation of the performance fee, we would have $(H^i, T) = U_{12}^i$ for each capital account. If two or more capital accounts belonging to the same limited partner are reset such that $T = 12$ (or multiples of 12) for the time periods going forward, all these capital accounts can be consolidated for simplicity into a single capital account.

For example, suppose a limited partner index owns the set $\{J\}$ of capital accounts in the hedge fund during at the time point $t = 12$. We can consolidate all $U_{12}^i$ belonging to set $\{J\}$ according to $\hat{U}_{12}^j = \sum_{i \in J} U_{12}^i$. Going forward at $t = 13$, the limited partner owns only one capital account with starting value time point $t = 12$ of $\hat{U}_{12}^j$. At $t = 13$, the capital accounts are indexed by $i = 1 \ldots N_{13}$ and the consolidated capital account superscript $j$ belongs to this new list $i = 1 \ldots N_{13}$.

It is extremely important to consolidate capital accounts whose high-water mark is established according to the calendar year-end after performance fees are applied. This is to reduce complexity. Such inclusion into consolidation cannot apply at a calendar year-end when the conditions triggering a performance fee and resetting the high-water mark did not occur, that is, $V_{12}^i \leq H^i$, for a capital account belonging to the same partner. The remaining capital accounts belonging to the same partner where the high-water mark was reset should be consolidated. Multiple capital accounts associated with different high-water marks would continue through the next calendar year and would be consolidated only when a high-water mark is set at the same time point for all of them.

# Claw-Back Provision: Performance Fee Returned to Limited Partners

In large hedge funds containing major investment by institutional investors, the partnership agreement might include "claw-back" provisions that effectively restore past performance fees to limited partners if the value of the hedge fund declines in subsequent years, after performance fees are paid in preceding years. Its algebraic representation would depend on the specific language of how such provisions are expressed verbally. At a minimum, the performance fees paid to the general partner by the limited partners have to be restricted so that they are accessible for claw-back. In general, the implementation of such a claw-back provision would simply require reversing all the steps conducted to implement a performance fee and recalculating the relevant parameters such as the high-water mark according to the provisions. Such a restoration by reversal is feasible only when the restricted performance fees are retained by the general partner in the hedge fund and only withdrawn after contributor limited partners eventually redeem their partnership interest in its entirety.

In order to attract limited partners to assemble a very large-scale hedge fund on the order of $10 billion to $15 billion at inception, the general partners approach very sophisticated institutional investors with deep investment pockets and the capability to invest in chunks of $100 million to $500 million. These mega-institutional investors have the bargaining power to demand greater concessions or some form of reduced fees from the general partner. Typically, the fixed fee of 1 percent to 2 percent is not considered to be negotiable, nor of a meaningful order of magnitude, since it is supposed to represent the actual operating costs of the general partner. Thus, the object of bargaining becomes the hefty annual performance fee, which is usually 20 percent of the economic profits in excess of a hurdle rate, the latter usually tied to the U.S. Treasury bill rate.

Institutional investors in these bargaining situations are able to win a concession that is typically called the claw-back provision. In principle, what is achieved is that the performance fee is averaged over a longer term holding period, and not just over a period of one year. Thus, the annual performance fees could be considered provisional. The legal contract in the limited partnership agreement may prevent the general partner from withdrawing any part of such a provisional performance fee (which is sometimes called performance "allocation"). If the hedge fund produces a negative return in the subsequent year or years, the provisional performance fee allocation of the general partner is returned partly or fully to the limited partners. This is very similar to the income averaging provisions that exist in the U.S. tax code for subchapter C corporate entities. In any given year, such a U.S. corporate entity is permitted to calculate its tax liability based on averaging income over three years and claim a tax refund if it had paid huge taxes based on a spike in income in previous years. This is a calculation that CFOs and tax accountants of all U.S. corporate entities routinely conduct in order to claim a refund against higher taxes paid in past years. The "look-back" window for calculating average income and consequently average corporate tax is confined to three years. If a U.S. subchapter C corporate entity had windfall profits in prior years and only losses in the subsequent three years, it cannot claim a refund, since the tax paid for years prior is outside the three-year look-back window.

The exact nature of the claw-back provision and its legal language would determine its specific mathematical representation. We derive a mathematical representation here for a claw-back provision based on the minimum features that it has to be associated with. For instance, a claw-back provision must have a look-back window, such as a period of three years, or be customized for each limited partner according to its date of inception of the capital account. Clearly, the general partner would prefer that a look-back window be confined to a fixed retrospective time period, while heavyweight limited partners would seek a look-back window going as far back as the inception of their capital account. What finally is written on the limited partnership agreement depends on each party's bargaining power. The limited partner would obviously recognize that restricting the withdrawal of annual performance fees by the general partner indefinitely is not a good business idea. What is more, once such a withdrawal of performance fees by the general partner has taken place, it is impractical to make the general partner pay back a negative fee, fee reimbursement, or fee claw-back into the partnership.

Unless the general partner is an entity located within the jurisdiction, often entirely a tax-free offshore regime, there are many uncertain tax and accounting issues that arise from a claw-back provision, as well as ambiguity under Global Investment Performance Standards (GIPS, described in detail in a later chapter) performance reporting standards, which have not even remotely addressed the idea of negative performance fees or a negative adjustment to prior performance fees. Like Long-Term Capital Management (LTCM), if the general partner is a U.S. Delaware entity and accounts for annual provisional non-negative performance fees without reducing claw-back liability from taxable income in a given year, its pass-through partners or members would be liable for taxes in that year.

The IRS never refunds personal taxes paid by pass-through members of the general partner LLC entity. The only circumstance where the IRS would refund prior taxes paid in a look-back window of three years is when the general partner entity is organized as a U.S. subchapter C corporation (which pays 35 percent corporate tax at entity level). Only a U.S. subchapter C entity is eligible for a tax refund (without interest) against negative fees earned in a window of the next two years (the total income-averaging window is three years). Most U.S. general partner entities are organized for tax purposes as partnerships in order to mitigate the burden of double taxation that would apply if they were organized as subchapter C entities (once on corporate profits and then on corporate dividends).

A myriad of tax and accounting ambiguities arise: Who pays tax on the current year's contingent performance fee allocations? Suppose the heavyweight limited partners with claw-back provision are taxable entities. They would have to pay tax distributive items of income relating to the current year's contingent performance fees. The general partner treats annual contingent performance fees as tentative memorandum allocations that are not recognized as income, and only recognizes income and withdraws corresponding funds when the claw-back liability goes away. The general partner would pay taxes on claw-back–free performance fees, while the limited partners would get a corresponding tax benefit in the form of an adjustment against capital gain only when they withdrew from the partnership. Such partners have had to pay tax on tentative performance fees in early years and obtain a tax deduction only in later years to such fees paid as an adjustment to capital gain reported on their individual tax returns upon withdrawing from the partnership.

The issues are simpler and manageable when the limited partners are nontaxable limited partner entities, such as U.S. tax-exempt institutional pension plans or tax-exempt foreign investors. Such investors do not care for tax consequences or the intertemporal profile of taxable cash flows from partnership allocations, though this is not strictly true for foreign investors subject to the nonrecoverable 30 percent U.S. dividend withholding tax on U.S. source dividend allocations, and for U.S. tax-exempt institutional investors subject to nonrecoverable foreign tax on foreign dividend tax allocations.

From the general partner's perspective, the tax tangle due to claw-back allocations simplifies only if the claw-back look-back window spans three years and the general partner entity is a subchapter C U.S. entity that can recover prior U.S. taxes, being automatically eligible for income averaging (or loss carry-back) over a look-back period of three years. It is extremely rare to find a general partner entity that elects to organize itself as a subchapter C entity, which faces a flat corporate tax of 35 percent. In contrast, pass-through long-term capital gains of the general partner entity are taxed in the hands of its individual partners and owners at 15 percent.

Irrespective of the intertemporal tax liabilities facing both limited partners and the general partner that may arise from implementing annual contingent performance fees subject to claw-back or income averaging, we must recognize that the contingent performance fees remain in the hedge fund and experience the performance increases and decreases in subsequent years. Thus, a claw-back provision should not be expressed in terms of an absolute amount (say, 100 million absolute dollars to be recovered from the general partner), but indexed according to the hedge fund's performance in the years following the year in which the non-negative contingent performance fee was calculated.

We shall establish a mathematical framework of expressing returns and capital account values for the limited partners and the general partner based on a fix to look-back period of, say, five years. Depending on the specific bargaining situation, it could be shorter, like three years, or span the entire history of a particular capital account going back to its inception date. Under GIPS, only the GIPS-compliant performance number would span this look-back time period. Since annual returns after the contingent performance fee are subject to claw-back liability of the general partner, they do not represent the total return to a fund investor net of *all* fees. Only the performance number calculated over a time horizon that is net of the claw-back liability of the general partner would be GIPS compliant under the strict standards of GIPS. Thus, a hedge fund may report three series of numbers: (1) monthly return series after fixed fees but before contingent performance fees and before contingent claw-back reimbursement by the general partner, (2) annual return series after fixed fees and after contingent performance fees, but before contingent claw-back and reimbursement by the general partner, and (3) *annualized* return over the look-back time span after fixed fees and performance fees net of claw-back reimbursement by the general partner. The first and second series are appropriately described to prospective investors as indicative return series that exclude their corresponding contingent adjustments. Only the third is strictly GIPS compliant. Investors must recognize that GIPS standards are defined in such strict and broad terms to mandate inclusion of all fees, and that the contingent performance fees and claw-back provisions require complex calculations requiring longer time spans according to the partnership agreement of the hedge fund.

In the previous section, we have provided an exact algebraic representation for the calculation of the annual performance fees for a hedge fund under the assumption that the limited partnership agreement does not have a claw-back provision. In this section, we first provide a robust linguistic description or definition of a claw-back provision that is likely to be written in the limited partnership agreement, and then provide its exact algebraic representation.

"Claw-back" is another way of describing carry-back of a current year's loss to past years, just as the "high-water mark" is another way of describing carry-forward of a current year's loss to future years. A claw-back provision must contain clear language to define a time span or time horizon over which a current year's loss can be applied to offset previous years' performance fees due to previous years' gains. The claw-back time span has to be set at some fixed number of years, such as three or five years. If the time span is left unspecified, the general partner cannot withdraw performance fees until the limited partner fully withdraws and adjusts for claw-back. The claw-back time span could be the interval starting at time point $T = 0$, the inception of a limited partner capital account assumed to be a strict calendar year beginning and ending at time point $T = 60$ (60 months or 5 years), to be specified in the limited partnership agreement.

First, the performance fees calculated at $T = 12, 24, 36, 48, 60$ are treated as provisional allocations to the general partner and aggregated over the claw-back time span of 60 months:

$$P^i_{0-60, provisional} = P^i_{12} + P^i_{24} + P^i_{36} + P^i_{48} + P^i_{60}$$

where $P^i_{12}$ and so on are the annual performance fees defined earlier, now considered a provisional fee subject to claw-back. Note that some of the annual performance fees could be zero in years when there is a loss.

A new calculation of performance fees net of claw-back is conducted at time point $T = 60$:

$$P^i_{0-60, final} = \begin{cases} 0, V^i_{60} \leq H^i \\ 0, V^i_{60} > H^i \text{ and } V^i_{60} - V^i_0(1 + r_{0,60}) \leq 0 \\ = \delta^i[V^i_{60} - V^i_0(1 + r_{0,60})], V^i_{60} > H^i \text{ and } V^i_{60} - V^i_0(1 + r_{0,60}) > 0 \end{cases}$$

In the above calculation, the high-water mark $H^i = V_0$, the initial investment, and $r_{0,60}$ is the cumulative nonannualized *ex post* riskless rate calculated at time point $T = 60$.

The claw-back rebate amount to be reduced from provisional fees and transferred back to the capital accounts of the respective limited partners (indexed by superscript $i$) is:

$$C^i_{0-60} = P^i_{0-60, provisional} - P^i_{0-60, final}$$

provided that $P^i_{0-60, provisional} - P^i_{0-60, final} \geq 0$, otherwise $C^i_{0-60} = 0$.

Due to nonlinearity, we cannot rule out the quirky situation that $P^i_{0-60, provisional} - P^i_{0-60, final}$ could be negative, however slightly.

In the above derivation, is assumed that the claw-back horizon is five years, so the computation is made at time point $T = 60$ months for the limited partner's investment made at time point $T = 0$. It is appropriately modified according to the time span that is exactly specified in a given limited partnership agreement.

On the whole, despite achieving the implementation of the idea of claw-back of performance fees over some specified time horizon, the main drawback is that throughout the claw-back horizon, the limited partners pay nonrecoverable taxes on interim tentative performance fees. Even though the cumulative gain is reduced by possible losses in the hedge fund in later years of the claw-back horizon, the pass-through capital losses (net of claw-back adjusted performance fees) of the limited partners in these later years cannot be carried back. The primary purpose of the claw-back provision is to establish incentives for the general partner to obtain performance fees from the limited partner calculated over a longer time horizon. However, it ends up costing taxable limited partners nonrecoverable tax payments on interim (provisional) performance fees. Of course, this is an economic cost if it is imposed on taxable limited partners. For tax-exempt limited partners, any form of interim nonrecoverable tax cost on interim (provisional) performance fees does not arise. Thus, it is not surprising that claw-back provisions are sought by large institutional tax-exempt investors. This puts the organizers of the hedge fund in a quandary. The limited partnership agreement is common across all investors. Thus, a claw-back provision along with all its drawbacks of possible interim nonrecoverable taxation of provisional performance fees would impose economic costs on taxable investors.

# Representation of a Fund's Net Asset Value (NAV) per Share

The algebraic frameworks thus far have provided for multiple capital accounts accommodating different fee rates for different limited partners. A fund's net asset value (NAV) is well recognized by market participants as the price per share in the fund in mutual fund terminology.

In order to meaningfully define NAV per share for a fund, we require homogeneity of fees across all participants. We shall provide a concrete example of an offshore hedge fund, the Carlyle Capital Corporation (CCC) based in the Channel Islands, United Kingdom, which was seized by its lenders in March 2008 due to having defaulted on $16.6 billion of debt. This fund was offered to investors as Class B shares in the "company" CCC, which was formed in August 2006 as a closed-end fund listed as a stock (or equity shares) on the exchange Euronext Amsterdam NV (under the symbol CCC, or CCC:NA after appending the code for the Euronext exchange).

From the data of the listed companies displayed at Euronext, as of March 2008, when it was seized by its creditors, CCC:NA had about 51 million Class B shares outstanding and had made its initial public offering (IPO) in April 2007. It traded on Euronext for about $20 shortly after its IPO, then traded in a range of $8–$10 until its sudden collapse, with reasonable trading volume.

Clearly, CCC:NA shares are homogenous, that is, every share in CCC Class B is subject to the same fee structure. It is as if they represent one single capital account of the CCC hedge fund entity. It would be safe to assume that CCC Class A shares represent a different capital account with different privileges of voting and likely fee waivers. Traders of CCC:NA discover a price that presumably tracks its NAV per share, either based on shareholder information disclosed by CCC, or by constructing their own models and applying their own conjectures for valuation.

Our objective is to take such a homogenous capital account of a hedge fund, such as the aggregated value of CCC:NA shares, and calculate its NAV per share from our algebraic framework, which so far is based on representing every homogenous or distinct capital account in terms of value (say, in dollars). The regulatory, auditing, and accounting procedures in some offshore regimes might require the representation of capital accounts in terms of a certain number of shares and associated price per share (NAV per share).

The linear transformations required to meet this requirement are simple. An arbitrary number of shares of one single homogenous capital account denoted by $n_0^b$ is offered at inception to represent the aggregate hedge capital account at its inception (IPO), denoted by $V_0^b$. This initial value $V_0^b$ is one of the many capital accounts in the hedge fund, and $b$ belongs to the set of capital accounts indexed by $i = 2...N$.

In the case of CCC:NA, if about $1 billion of initial value of a homogenous capital account was offered to shareholders for 50 million shares, the NAV at the inception $p_0^b$, also called the "par value" of the shares, is simply the value of the hedge fund $V_0^b$ divided by the number of shares $n_0^b$ that is, $p_0^b = \dfrac{V_0^b}{n_0^b}$, which in this example is \$20 per share.

It is useful to maintain the number of shares $n_0^b$ to be constant, and changes made only when there is a shift desired in the fund's capital structure. This is possible in a closed-end fund like CCC. Within an open-end fund, or at times when a closed-end fund wants to take in more capital to be amalgamated with the homogenous capital account, the number of shares change at the relevant time points. For example, with U.S. SEC-regulated mutual funds, investors are allowed to redeem their shares or purchase additional shares at the NAV per share calculated at the close of every business day.

The change in NAV per share tracks changes in the aggregate value of the hedge fund *before any withdrawals and deposits*. Subsequent redemptions (or withdrawals) are treated as buy-back or repurchase of the shares from shareholders at a price equal to the hedge fund's NAV per share. New share purchases (or deposits) are treated as issuance of new shares at the same price as for redemption (i.e., the hedge fund's NAV). For each such homogenous aggregated capital account that is subdivided into shares (indexed by the superscript $b$), there are always three associated numbers at time point $t$: the quantity of shares $n_t^b$, the total value of the shares $V_t^b$, and the hedge fund's NAV $p_t^b$.

At inception $t = 0$, the issue of fees does not arise. At all subsequent points in time $t$, the total value of the shares $V_t^b$ is the opening value of the homogenous aggregated capital account *after all fees*. The interpretation of $V_t^b$ is simple in a regime of only fixed fees that are applied at short intervals, which could be daily or monthly. For example, all U.S. SEC-regulated mutual funds apply fixed fees at the close of every business day. The interpretation of $V_t^b$ is troublesome for hedge funds that always apply performance fees at discrete year-end intervals. Since performance fees apply only at calendar year-end, the value of the homogenous capital account $V_t^b$ *after all fees* is defined for a hedge fund only at $t = 0, 12, 24, 36, \dots$ , that is, when $t$ is a multiple of 12.

Thus, traders in shares of a closed-end "company" such as CCC:NA, who trade on all business days during the year, have to make their own judgments about the interim value of $V_t^b$ and the performance fees that might apply at $t = 12$ based on all information available to them. It would indeed be helpful to traders if the hedge fund "company" released interim data $V_t^b$ with the explicit qualification that this data series did not include the performance fees that would be applied at time point $t = 12$, and only at that time point would $V_{12}^b$ reflect the true value of the homogenous capital account after all fees.

The economic valuation at time point $t = \tau < 12$ of performance fees that would apply at time point $t = 12$ requires sophisticated stochastic dynamic modeling or complex option pricing formulas to value the embedded call option given by the shareholders to the fund manager for $\delta^b = 20$ percent of the upside performance in excess of the riskless rate (subject to the high-water mark). We now address the deconstruction and approach to valuation of this embedded call option given by the investors to the fund manager (as a fraction of their investment).

A simple "liquation" valuation approach could be applied at any interim time point $t = \tau < 12$ for performance fees in the same manner as the contingent calculation for $P_{12}^b$, only that $t = 12$ is replaced by $t = \tau < 12$. $P_{12}^b$ and $P_\tau^b$ converges to the annual performance fee at time point $\tau = 12$. This is the payoff to the embedded call option maturing at $t = 12$ if exercised early at $t = \tau < 12$. The value of the homogenous capital account at time point $t = \tau < 12$ is calculated as $U_\tau^b = V_\tau^b - P_\tau^b$. The interim NAV is now calculated according to $U_\tau^b$, thus $p_\tau^b = \dfrac{V_\tau^b - P_\tau^b}{n_0^b} = \dfrac{U_\tau^b}{n_0^b}$. Traders could use this "interim liquidation value as a benchmark for valuing closed-end hedge fund shares like those of CCC:NA on any given business day.

## Black-Scholes Formula Valuation of Performance Fees

We provide an options pricing approach to valuation of the contingent upside payment by limited partners $\beta^b V_{12}^b$ at time point $t = 0$ to the general partner. This is modeled as a call option granted by the limited partners to the general partner, funded by dilution of the interest of the limited partners, much like executive stock options or equity warrants.

This call option is detachable, i.e. may be valued as a stand-alone call option the fund as underlying asset. From the perspective of the general partner, it is an American option which may be exercised prior to maturity by liquidating the fund and redeeming capital to investors. Early exercise of an American call option is less valuable than not exercising and holding the call option to maturity. We may apply the Black-Scholes formula[2] to value this as a European call option exercised at maturity.

---

[2] The Black Scholes call option valuation formula is $BS(S,X,\sigma,r,T) = SN(y) -$ $Xexp(-rT)N\left(y - \sigma\sqrt{T}\right)$ where $y = \dfrac{\log(S/(Xexp(-rT)))}{\sigma\sqrt{T}} + \dfrac{1}{2}\sigma\sqrt{T}$. The parameters $S,X,\sigma,r,T$ represent stock price, exercise price, volatility, riskless rate and time to maturity. The riskless rate is in continuously compounded units, so that $r$ is the log of one plus the annualized percentage interest rate. The Black-Scholes formula has the property that $BS(S,X,\sigma,r,T)/S = BS(1,X/S,\sigma,r,T)$. When a stock pays a continuously compounded dividend $d$, the stock price parameter in Black-Scholes formula is replaced by $S' = S(1 + d)^{-T}$.

At time point $t = 0$, the limited partners have granted a call option corresponding to initial stock price $S_0 = V_0^b$, which is the high water-mark. The time to maturity is $(T - 0)$ which is 1 year, denoted as $T = 1$. The annual riskless rate earlier written as $r_{0,12}$ is abbreviated without a subscript as $r$. The exercise price $X = V_0^b(1+r)^T$, which is the high water-mark $V_0^b$ at inception compounded by the riskless rate $(1 + r)^r$. The constant dividend yield for options pricing purposes is the fixed fee rate $f_{annual}$, written here without its subscript as $f$, so the adjusted stock price for option pricing is $S_0' = V_0^b(1 + f)^{-T}$. The annualized volatility of the stock price $S_t$ (equal to fund's value $V_t^b$) is $\sigma$.

The limited partners who granted the call option, and thus hold a short position in a call option, hold the right to cancel the remainder life of the option by redeeming early from the fund. On the start date, they have the right to instantly cancel the option and not pay any exercise settlement. Instead,in their wisdom, they elect to grant the call option to the general partner, based on motives that are analyzed at the end of this section. We may therefore view this as a detachable (stand-alone) non-cancellable call option granted by the limited partners and value it according to the Black Sholes formula as:

$$C_0 = \delta^b BS(S_0', X, \sigma, r, T)$$

where $BS(\ )$ is the Black-Scholes call option valuation formula. We divide both sides by $V_0^b$ to obtain:

$$c_0 = \delta^b BS\left[(1+f)^{-T}, (1+r)^T, \sigma, r, T\right]$$

This is the value of the call option as a percentage of the starting fund value, which is also the high-water mark, is determined by 2 internal parameters of the fund, the fixed fee rate $f$ and the performance fee share $\delta^b$. The riskless rate $r$ and time to maturity $T$ of 1 year are fixed. The Black-Scholes formula has the property that that $c_0$ increases with volatility $\sigma$. The general partner has an incentive to deploy investment strategies with higher volatility. The limited partner owns the remaining portion of the fund $1 - c_0$ after dilution through granting the call option to the general partner. The Black-Scholes formula provides $c_0 V_0^b$ as the economic value of the future contingent payment $\beta^b V_{12}^b$.

The performance fee appears large based on $\delta^b = 20$ percent. However, $c_0$ is has an order of magnitude that most investors would consider reasonable. Applying the parameters $\delta^b = 20$ percent, $f = 1$ percent, $\sigma = 12$ percent, $r = 0.33$ percent, and $T = 1$ year, we obtain $c_0 = 0.85$ percent. Over a one year horizon, $c_0$ is not much. Even if the hedge fund volatility was as high as $\sigma = 25$ percent, $c_0$ is 1.88 percent. Over a multiple year horizon, when the sequence of annual $c_0$ is added up, we would obtain a larger total value that is roughly equal to $c_0$ times the number of years.

The Black-Scholes formula depends on volatility $\sigma$ only, and not on the mean or expected return $\mu$ that the general partner is expected to deliver to the fund. Suppose limited partners only care about the Sharpe ratio measure of risk-adjusted return, which is described in more detail in later chapters. Their Sharpe ratio is $\dfrac{(1-c_0)\mu - r}{\sigma}$. If this exceeds the Sharpe ratio of their relevant investment benchmarks, such as broad equity or bond market indices, it is worth granting a call option valued at $c_0$ to the general partner. This decision requires the limited partners to make assumptions and forecasts of $\mu$ and $\sigma$ for a given hedge fund or venture partnership.

A venture fund has only one call option $c_0$ with time to maturity of $T = 12$ years. Assuming that the volatility of underlying venture portfolio is as high as $\sigma = 25$ percent, the hurdle rate is zero, $\delta^b = 20$ percent, $f = 1$ percent and $r = 3.70$ percent according to the 10 year Treasury rate, $c_0$ for such a venture fund is about 7.91 percent. Due to the one-time nature of $c_0$ in a venture fund, $c_0$ is also the Black-Scholes valuation of the venture fund management company.

It was noted in Chapter 1 that listed shares of "alternative" investment managers such as Blackstone Group, Och-Ziff Capital Management and Fortress Investment Group trade at about 20% of assets under management in normal equity market conditions. This is about 3 times the Black-Scholes valuation. In the Black-Scholes formula, we would require $\sigma = 200$ percent to achieve this order of $c_0 = 20$ percent.

The Black-Scholes formula is based on the expected return $\mu$ becoming redundant, so the call option value is driven by volatility $\sigma$ only. An alternate explanation to the high market valuation of publicly traded venture funds is that the Black-Scholes formula may work well for short maturity options, but the market disregards its validity in situations with long maturity, such as 12 years in a venture fund, and in situations with high expected return. Investors take the expected return $\mu$ of the venture fund assets into consideration and estimate the expected value of the call option granted to the general partner, denoted by $c_o^E$, which easily exceeds 20 percent of assets.[3]

Consider the earlier example of the Black-Scholes valuation of a venture partnership, for which $c_0 = 7.91\%$ when the hurdle rate is zero, $\sigma = 25$ percent, $\delta^b = 20$ percent, $f = 1$ percent, and $r = 3.70$ percent according to

---

[3]The expected value of a call option is $E[C(S,X,\mu,\sigma,r,T)] = Sexp[(\mu + 0.5\sigma^2)]N(y) - Xexp(-rT)N(y - \sigma\sqrt{T})$ where $y = \dfrac{\log(S/X) + (\mu + \sigma^2)T}{\sigma\sqrt{T}} + \dfrac{1}{2}\sigma\sqrt{T}$. This reduces to the Black-Scholes call option formula $BS(S,X,\sigma,r,T)$ when $\mu + 0.5\sigma^2 = r$. $E[C(S,X,\mu,\sigma,r,T)]$ exceeds $BS(S,X,\sigma,r,T)$ when $\mu + 0.5\sigma^2$ exceeds $r$ and when $T$ is large.

the 10 year Treasury rate. Taking into account $\mu = 15$ percent, the expected value of the call option $c_o^E$ is 87.47 percent. This is the expected value of the venture capital management company as percentage of assets. By this measure, the shares of Blackstone Group that trade for a value of about 20 percent of assets in normal market conditions are greatly undervalued.

A high expected return $\mu$ in the numerator of the Sharp ratio makes the investment prospect appear attractive. However, when the expected value of the call option $c_o^E$ is calculated based on $\mu$ after disregarding the Black-Scholes formula, $c_o^E$ is an increasing function of $\mu$ and acts to dampen the Sharpe ratio. A limited partner investor is not daunted by $c_o^E$ being as high as 87%, because this has to be annualized over 12 years. Limited partners evaluate their Sharpe ratio in annualized units as $\dfrac{\left(1 - c_o^E\right)^{1/T} \mu - r}{\sigma}$. With $T = 12$, $\left(1 - c_o^E\right)^{1/T}$ evaluates to 0.84. Investors would achieve 0.84 or 84 percent of the annualized expected return $\mu$.

# CHAPTER 4

# Hedge Fund Accounting and Tax Filing

## Partnership Accounting for U.S. Funds

A hedge fund located in a taxable regime is obliged to comply with requirements of tax collectors and regulators, much like any other taxable entity. Most hedge funds seek the support of consultants, accountants, fund administrators, and lawyers to deal with these matters.

A U.S. hedge fund that is typically organized as a limited partnership has to file a U.S. partnership tax return. The hedge fund itself is not taxed as an entity, but is required to report all components of pass-through income to its partners in its tax filing. Each partner of the hedge fund pays taxes according to its own individual or entity tax procedures and is relieved from double taxation of the income earned by the hedge fund. In contrast, a U.S. subchapter C entity, like Warren Buffett's Berkshire Hathaway, is obliged to pay corporate tax at the entity level, and dividends paid to its shareholders from the entity's post-tax income are taxed again for a second time as they arrive in the hands of its shareholders.

Even though the federal government does not impose an entity tax on a U.S. hedge fund organized as a partnership, individual states might impose an entity tax if such a hedge fund's office is located within their borders. An example is the state of Illinois, which imposes an entity tax of 1.5 percent of income on pass-through U.S. partnerships located in Illinois. It is not surprising that a significant majority of U.S. hedge funds are located in the state of Connecticut, which like many states does not levy an entity tax on U.S. partnerships. Connecticut offers the added advantage of uncomplicated compliance under its state securities law for U.S. hedge funds and similar simple exemptions to branch offices of foreign hedge funds located in that state. As mentioned earlier, Delaware is the state of choice where

U.S. hedge funds are formed. Subsequently, these Delaware partnerships do not keep any physical presence in Delaware, but instead plant themselves physically in Connecticut.

The framework that was established in the previous chapter for a hedge fund in a tax-free regime is now adapted specifically to U.S. taxation of partnership interests. Every U.S. partnership is required to file Form 1065, U.S. Return of Partnership Income, annually to the Internal Revenue Service (IRS). The partnership entity, that is, the hedge fund itself, does not pay any direct entity tax. On this particular tax return, the partnership reports its balance sheet, income statement, and breakdown of income under various categories. Further, the breakdown of all income items by partner is to be reported. Each of these income items flows through each limited partner's U.S. tax return. Limited partners that are U.S. entities or persons are obliged to factor in the pass-through income under the various categories into their own tax returns. Non-U.S. limited partners, that is, foreign investors who do not file annual U.S. tax returns, may interpret the information provided by the partnership on its U.S. tax return for meeting their tax obligations in their home countries. Some foreign investors, such as those who are connected with ongoing U.S. trade and business or those who are ordinarily resident in the United States for the purpose of U.S. taxation, would have to factor in the taxable pass-through items of income from their U.S. limited partnership interest into their personal or entity U.S. tax return.

If the U.S. hedge fund has foreign limited partners, it becomes the withholding agent for U.S. withholding taxes applicable to each foreign limited partner. The hedge fund is required to file IRS Form 1042, Annual Withholding Tax Return for U.S. Source Income of Foreign Persons, along with timely remittance of the withholding taxes due from foreign partners. Typically, each foreign limited partner's withholding tax is funded by a withdrawal at the end of the calendar year capital account balance after fixed fees and performance fees. Generally, foreign limited partners are exempt from U.S. withholding tax on pass-through interest income and capital gains (both long term and short term). U.S. source dividends are subjected to 30 percent withholding tax. Foreign source dividends are exempt from U.S. dividend withholding tax. Depending on tax treaties between their home country and the United States, foreign investors may be able to recover all or some of the U.S. dividend withholding tax in the form of a tax credit elsewhere.

# IRS Tax Return Filings for U.S. Hedge Funds

In the setup for administering a hedge fund in a tax-exempt regime, we had defined the monthly profit before all fees as $\pi_t$. This can be viewed as the economic profit generated by the fund. Clearly, investors desire that the average economic profit over some reasonable period of time should be positive. The IRS wants a tally of the total of all profits earned during the calendar year, further broken down by the pass-through allocation to every limited partner. Based on the primary variables that were defined under a tax-exempt regime, we are required to aggregate and provide breakdowns by subcomponents, leading to more definitions.

For the partnership as a whole, we need the aggregate net deposits of each individual capital account by adding up their monthly deposits:

$$D^i = \sum_{t=1}^{12} D_t^i$$

Note that we run the time subscript according to $t = 1\ldots12$. The inception of the fund is represented by $t = 0$, which must satisfy $V_0 = W_0 + D_0 = D_0 = \sum_{i=1}^{N_0} D_0^i$. (That is because $W_0 = 0$.)

Aggregate deposits across all partners during the year (i.e., the time period spanning time points $t = 1$ to $t = 12$, but excluding the inception time point $t = 0$) is $D_{1,12} = \sum_{i=1}^{N} D_i$ , where $i = 1\ldots N$ represents each distinct capital account in the hedge fund for all or any part of the year. For monthly lists of capital accounts, the subscript $i$ in any given month $t$ previously ranged according to $i = 1\ldots N_t$. The latter is a more complex double summation notation, first across capital accounts, and then across time. Also, the subscript $i$ denotes distinct capital accounts, and the same limited partner may have multiple capital accounts. Recall that multiple capital accounts for the same limited partner were then introduced to track different performance fees that are applicable at year-end according to different points in time of entry during the year. Multiple capital accounts are not needed for the general partner, since the general partner typically never pays either fixed fees or performance fees.

For simplicity in implementation, it is a good idea to fix the capital accounts to $i = 1\ldots N$, expanding $N$ if new capital accounts are added mid-year. These new mid-year capital accounts would have zero amount entries in the months preceding their inception. Likewise, if capital accounts are fully withdrawn from the hedge fund during mid-year, they would have zero amount entries in the months following until year-end. Thus, it is not particularly important to track $N_t$, the number of capital accounts in month $t$, since we can find a larger fixed number $N$ with zero entries denoting empty capital accounts. This is merely a computation and database programming issue of using a fixed-sized array to track $N$ capital accounts, with many empty dummy capital accounts to make room for new capital accounts that might be added during mid-year, versus a data structure of length $N_t$ that might vary at different points in time, and not containing dummy or empty capital accounts. Thus, for the remainder of this analysis, the number of capital accounts during a particular year is taken to be fixed as $N$, independent of $t$. We will no longer need that formal double summation to track varying $N_t$ for different $t$. We could subsequently restore generality and reintroduce varying $N_t$, accompanied by appropriate tracking and summation across $N_t$ varying number of capital accounts at different points in time denoted by the subscript $t$.

In the terminology of the IRS, deposits are "capital contributions." In all of the tax reporting to the IRS, pass-through income for a given limited partner is aggregated across all its capital accounts. Note that this expression includes a component for $i = 1$ representing the general partner, which would be making negative deposits (withdrawals) from its capital account, which keeps increasing due to positive deposits to its capital account from fixed fees and annual performance fees. If no deposits of new external money occur during the calendar year, $D_{1,12} = \sum_{t=1}^{12} D_t = 0$. This is a special case where all of the fixed fees and performance fees are negative deposits to the limited partners' capital accounts, aggregated and transferred as a positive deposit to the general partner's capital account.

The aggregate economic profit before any fees for the full calendar year of the U.S. hedge fund's tax return is simply: $\Pi_{1,12} = \sum_{t=1}^{12} \pi_t$. The opening balance sheet of the hedge fund, at inception $t = 0$, to be reported on its tax return is: Assets $A_0$ as cash in bank $= D_0$, Liabilities as partners' capital $V_0 = D_0$. This is the quantity (or stock) of capital at inception, and no fees are charged at the instant $t = 0$, so partners' capital is $V_0$. There are no debt or margin loans that are assumed to be in existence at inception $t = 0$.

The income statement for the first calendar year spanning $t = 1...12$ is simply $\Pi_{1,12}$, broken down by its components. This will be elaborated upon later. This represents the total flow of income to the hedge fund. Thus, $\Pi_{1,12}$ includes fixed fees as an expense aggregated across limited partners, but does not include performance fees. This is because the performance fees are deducted from the capital accounts of limited partners and are added to the capital account of the general partner. This is an internal transfer of wealth among partners, whose tax treatment will be described later.

The balance sheet of the hedge fund at time point $t = 12$ is based on reporting aggregate debt $B_{12}$. Assets $A_{12}$, which are *inclusive* of deposits at time point $t = 12$, *must* add up to $B_{12} + D_0 + D_{1,12} + \Pi_{1,12}$. Liabilities and partners' equity *must* add up to the same. If $D_{1,12} = 0$, that is, there was no net money coming into the fund and no money has left the fund, the fund's assets must increase by $B_{12} + \Pi_{1,12}$. If $D_{1,12} \neq 0$, the fund's assets must increase by $B_{12} + D_{1,12} + \Pi_{1,12}$. Partners' aggregate capital at time point $t = 0$ is $D_0$. Partners' aggregate capital at time point $t = 12$ is $D_0 + D_{1,12} + \Pi_{1,12}$.

Many partnerships prefer to exclude the deposits $D_{12}$ made at time point $t = 12$ from the fund's assets and factor them into the opening fund assets in their next period. In this situation, the balance sheet of the hedge fund at time point $t = 12$ is assets $(A_{12} - D_{12})$, which *exclude* deposits at time point $t = 12$, *must* add up to $B_{12} + D_0 + D_{1,11} + \Pi_{1,12}$ This is achieved by noting that $D_{1,12} = D_{1,11} + D_{12}$. Partners' aggregate capital excluding deposits $D_{12}$ at time point $t = 12$ is $D_0 + D_{1,11} + \Pi_{1,12}$.

The IRS partnership tax return requires the fund's balance sheet to be filled into Form 1065, Schedule L, broken down by various components of assets and liabilities. The specific breakdown can be provided according to data available. Whatever number is reported for debt (or liabilities other than partners' capital) is multiplied by each partner's percentage ownership share at the end of the year after all fee calculations $\alpha_{12}^i$ and reported as an item named "nonrecourse partner's share of liabilities" under that partner's Schedule K-1, Partner Share of Income, Deductions and Credits. We are dealing with a hedge fund formed as a limited partnership, so that partners have no obligation to pay any more money beyond their investment.

Through the reporting of the partnership's debt $B_{12}$ and its year-end allocations $\alpha_{12}^i B_{12}$, the IRS has full knowledge of the extent to which the partnership as well as individual partners are leveraged. This is a year-end snapshot. The levels of margin loans and debts may vary at all points in time.

Due to unfavorable market turmoil, cumulative aggregated profit $\Pi_{1,12}$ (individual period profits aggregated across all time points $1...t$) could become such a large negative number that partners' equity $A_t - B_t$ becomes negative. Partners have limited liability and hence are not obliged to make additional deposits to bring equity to positive levels. Banks and financial institutions, which have lent the amount $B_t$, would seek a fresh infusion of new deposits by the hedge fund's partners to back up the debt, or margin calls, failing which the hedge fund is economically bankrupt. The lenders would likely seize the fund's assets and liquidate them in order to repay as much of the debt $B_t$ as possible. On March 7, 2007, the *New York Times* reported that "London-Carlyle Capital, the investment fund linked to the private equity firm Carlyle Group, said that it was 'considering all available options' after it received further margin calls, prompting some analysts to warn that more funds could struggle to meet increasingly tighter margin requirements." The same *New York Times* report stated, "The fund, which invests mostly in triple-A rated mortgage debt and whose investors include Carlyle Group managers, issued the statement after some of its lenders called in loans and then liquidated the collateral. Shares in the fund were suspended from trading on the Amsterdam stock exchange on Friday after dropping 58 percent the day before."

The sudden demise of this offshore fund seems to be attributable to very high leverage. Its ratio of debt $B_t$ to partners' equity $A_t - B_t$ was reported to be of the order of 32 before the fund ran into bankruptcy troubles. Thus, the hedge fund's debt/equity ratio, or leverage, is $\dfrac{B_t}{A_t - B_t}$ and the fund is technically bankrupt when the denominator becomes zero or negative. An alternate representation of leverage is the ratio of assets to equity, $\dfrac{A_t}{A_t - B_t}$.

When we loosely say that "a hedge fund is 10 times leveraged," we usually mean that for every \$1 of partners' equity, the fund has purchased \$10 of asset exposure, and we implicitly mean that the fund has achieved its leverage by borrowing \$9 against \$10 of assets placed as collateral and \$1 of partners' equity. Since $\dfrac{A_t}{A_t - B_t} - \dfrac{B_t}{A_t - B_t} = 1$, that is, the asset-to-equity ratio, minus the debt/equity ratio adds up to 1, it has to be the case that the asset/equity ratio is simply 1 plus the debt/equity ratio. This idea and definition has meaning only when the denominator, partners' equity, is positive. It is absurd and undefined when partners' equity is zero or negative, just as in the case of stock price valuation, where a stock's price-earnings ratio is meaningless for zero or negative earnings. Lenders get extremely worried and may issue margin calls when the denominator approaches their threshold of critical debt/equity ratio, and they may seize the hedge fund's assets for liquidation if the denominator becomes negative. The same *New York Times* article previously excerpted added, "Some analysts said that the fund, based in Guernsey, the Channel Islands, may have been more vulnerable because of its slightly higher leverage level of 32 times the amount of its equity, but that the margin calls are mostly related to the deteriorating market environment."

Most lenders are regulated financial institutions, which in turn are required to comply with strict regulatory guidelines and regulations on collateral, risk, and lending standards. For instance, collateralized borrowing against listed exchange-traded stocks in the United States is governed by the strict margin requirements of the Federal Reserve Bank. Similarly, collateralized borrowing against government and agency bonds, as well as collateral quality and term requirements of bank loans, are also strictly defined. Should mark-to-market revaluation of the collateral result in inadequate equity backing the loans, the regulated financial institutions are required to issue margin calls to restore equity level, failing which the lenders are required to call in their loans.

A hedge fund with no explicit debt, $B_t = 0$, could also cross the threshold of bankruptcy. The fund's aggregate cumulative profit $\Pi$ (aggregated across time points $1...t$) could become hugely negative, so that equity $A_t - B_t$ becomes close to zero or negative. The fund actually owes money at time point $t$ to pay for its cumulative net losses. Instruments of indirect leverage, such as swaps and forwards contracts, could result in large losses. Such a situation is unlikely if the unleveraged hedge fund owns assets that can never be negative in value (for example, if it owns unleveraged exchange-traded equity or private equity only, and does not own instruments of indirect leverage). Yet, there are indeed situations that can create enormous liabilities in excess of equity capital without explicit leverage, such as short selling, unexpected litigation outcomes, and so on.

We established definitions above for leverage and bankruptcy for hedge funds. We proceed to expand the algebraic framework developed thus far for preparing the partnership tax return, with the consequence of pass-through taxation to limited partners.

## Financial Statements for Hedge Funds and Venture Funds

It is important to resolve polemic but trivial positions taken by partnerships on presenting the financial statements of a hedge fund (whether onshore or offshore) or a venture fund. One camp of accountants insist that the net assets or net value of a fund be reported at year-end time point $t = 12$ after all fees, but before year-end deposits or withdrawals. Thus, instead of basing the fund valuation according to $V_t$ in our terminology, which for $V_{12}$ is the value of the fund *after* deposits or withdrawals at time point $t = 12$, they prefer to report $V_{12} - D_{12}$, which is the fund value after all fees but before deposits at time point $t = 12$. Under this approach, $D_{12}$ is counted as a deposit occurring at time point $t = 12$, but under the period $t = [12, 13]$. It is unimportant which approach is taken, but important to remain consistent.

Most partnerships exclude $D_{12}$ (or $D_t$) when they report the net value of the fund at time point $t$. In order to stay with the majority, we define a new variable $X_t = V_t - D_t$ and create the financial statements according to $X_t$. In this world, the opening value of a hedge fund changes at the beginning time point. It requires recognition of $X_t = V_t - D_t$, as the fund value *before* deposits at time point $t$, and $V_t$ as the fund value *after* deposits at time point $t$.

To clarify, we could consider any discrete time point $t$ to represent three time points, which are nanoseconds apart. If $n$ denotes one nanosecond, we follow three steps at the close of every time point in the following sequence: (1) at the time point $t - n$, we determine $W_t$, the value of the fund before all fees and before deposits; (2) at the time point $t$, we calculate $X_t = V_t - D_t$, the value of the fund *after* all fixed and performance fees, but excluding deposits and withdrawals $D_t$; and finally, (3) at time point $t + n$, we calculate $V_t = X_t + D_t$, the opening value of the fund after fees and deposits. For consistency and ease of understanding, we record the fund's financial statements according to $X_t = V_t - D_t$.

The fixed fees calculated at time point $t$ are set aside as an amount payable by the fund to the general partner. It is excluded from the net value of the fund. At time point t + $n$, the payable fixed fees are applied as a credit or deposit to the capital account of the general partner, who may choose to withdraw them instantly.

Performance fees that are calculated at time point $t$ are extracted from the capital accounts of the limited partners and instantly credited at that same time point $t$ to the capital account of the general partner.

It would be useful to examine the simple identities that generate the hedge fund's balance sheet and to establish the condition for the hedge fund's bankruptcy. The subscript $t$ is a time point when we aggregate debt, cumulative deposits, and cumulative profit for the fund, but exclude the deposits at the exact time point $t$. The time point $t$ does not have to coincide with the particular year-end.

At any point in time $t$ before $t = 12$, the hedge fund's assets are $A_t = D_0 + B_t + D_{1,t-1} + \Pi_{1,t}$. It is important to note that $A_t$ and $B_t$ are quantity or stock of debt and total assets at time point $t$, while $D_0$ is the initial inflow of deposits at time point $t = 0$, $\Pi_{1,t}$ is the *cumulative* net profit respectively between time points $(1...t)$, and $D_{1,t-1}$ is the cumulative net deposit from time point $t = 1$ to $t - 1$, excluding deposits $D_t$ at the time point $t$. Cash flows, if any, due to deposits at time point $t$ $D_t$ are not included in the fund's assets $A_t$.

This identity can be rewritten as $A_t - B_t = D_0 + D_{1,t-1} + \Pi_{1,t}$ where the left-hand side $A_t - B_t$ is the partner's equity or net worth at time point $t$ excluding pending deposits $D_t$, which should equal the right-hand side, the aggregate cumulative deposits (net of withdrawals), plus aggregate cumulative net profits ($\Pi_{1,t}$ may be interpreted as retained earnings when there are no withdrawals). $A_t - B_t$ is also the value of the hedge fund after all fees at time point $t$, which we had denoted earlier as $X_t$. (Note that $X_t = V_t - D_t$.) Thus, we have the identity for partner's equity at time point $t$, also called the value of the hedge fund at time point $t$, as $A_t - B_t = X_t$. The left-hand side constitutes the net assets of the hedge fund at market value, and the right side constitutes partner's equity, without counting pending deposits or withdrawals $D_t$. In accounting terminology, this identity is the *balance sheet* of the hedge fund and is better recognized when it is rewritten as $A_t = B_t + X_t$. The left-hand side is gross assets excluding borrowing, and the right-hand side is debt plus partners' equity.

The income statement of the hedge fund for the subperiod $[t - 1, t]$ is simply $\Pi_{t-1,t} = \Pi_{1,t} - \Pi_{1,t-1}$. We also represent it in shorthand as $\pi_t$. This is further reported as a sum of its individual income subcomponents $\pi_{k,t}$.

Note that we had earlier defined $\pi_t = \sum_{k \in K} \pi_{k,t}$ where K denotes the set of components of income, K={4, 5, 6a, 8, 9a, 13b, 13d, 16l, M1L6}.

The flow of funds statement of the hedge fund for the subperiod $[t - 1, t]$ is the identity:

$$X_{t-1} + D_{t-1} + \pi_t = X_t$$

Since $A_t - B_t = X_t$ we can also write this as:

$$(A_{t-1} - B_{t-1}) + D_{t-1} + \pi_t = A_t - B_t$$

The above rewritten form of funds flow statement reads as: opening net assets at time point $t - 1$, plus net deposits made at time point $t$, plus profits earned during the period $[t - 1, t]$ must equal the net assets at time point $t$.

The identity states that partners' equity at time point $t - 1$, plus deposits/withdrawals made at the very beginning of subperiod $[t - 1, t]$, plus profits earned during the subperiod $[t - 1, t]$ should add up to partners' equity at time point $t$ (without, of course, counting pending deposits $D_t$ at time point $t$).

The entire sequence of financial statements at discrete points in time $t = 1, 2, 3, 4, \ldots$ are bootstrapped by the closing balance sheet at time point $t = 0$, defined simply as $A_0 = B_0 + X_0 = 0$. The left side is assets, the right side is partners' equity, debt at inception $B_0$ is zero, and partners' equity at inception $X_0$ is the initial zero net equity, since we are not counting non-negative deposits $D_0$ that are made by investors at time point $t = 0$. Thus, we have the hedge fund's financial statement at every discrete point at $t = 0$ and subsequently at $t = 1, 2, 3, \ldots$ consisting of the following:

(1) The income statement for the period $[t - 1, t]$ is simply $\pi_t$, where the income is broken down according to its components $\pi_t = \sum_{k \in K} \pi_{k,t}$, where K denotes the set of components of income.
(2) The funds flow statement, which links partners' equity at time point $t$ to the same at time point $t - 1$, is $X_{t-1}\ D_{t-1} + \pi_t = X_t$.
(3) The balance sheet at time points $t = 1, 2, 3, 4 \ldots$ consists of two parts: the opening balance sheet at time point $(t - 1)$ according to $A_{t-1} = B_{t-1} + X_{t-1}$ and the closing balance sheet at time point $t$ according to $A_t = B_t + X_t$.

We have $t = 0, 1, 2, 3, \ldots$ which is a monthly sequence. Thus, we would have 12 monthly income statements, 12 monthly funds flow statements, and 12 monthly closing balance sheets. How would we construct an annual audit-quality financial statement for a hedge fund for a period spanning a calendar year, starting at $t = 0$ and ending at $t = 12$? We need an annual income statement and an annual funds flow statement. The balance sheets at the open and close of the calendar year are already determined, so no new work is required. We obtain the annual statements as follows:

(1A) The annual income statement is $\Pi_{1,12} = \sum_{t=1}^{12} \pi_t$, which is broken down according to its components $\sum_{k \in K} \sum_{t=1}^{12} \pi_{k,t}$.

(2A) The annual funds flow statement is $X_0 + D_{1,11} + \Pi_{1,12} = X_{12}$. Note our earlier definition for aggregate deposit/withdrawal is $D_{1,11} = \sum_{t=1}^{11} D_t$, where $D_t$ is the aggregate deposit/withdrawal across all capital accounts at time point $t$. Deposits $D_{12}$ at time point $t = 12$ are not included.

(3A) The balance sheet consists of two parts: opening balance sheet at time point $t - 12 = 0$ as $A_{t-12} = B_{t-12} + X_{t-12}$ and closing balance sheet at time point $t = 12$ according to $A_t = B_t + X_t$.

**Venture Funds.** Assets of a venture partnership consist of investment in venture portfolio companies, which have no discernible market value. The only occasion when an adjustment occurs to the asset value $A_t$ is when the income statement due $\Pi_{1,12}$ reports nonzero income due to write-off, liquidation, or exit. The assets $A_t$ are reported at initial cost $A_0$, plus cumulative adjustment according to income received from portfolio venture companies every year. Thus, the remaining assets of a venture fund are at book value. The only assets that were transformed into tangible market value (in the form of cash or write-off) were those of venture portfolio companies, which were either written off or produced cash upon exit. Thus, the partners' equity reported on the financial statement does not reflect the economic profits that might be earned on venture portfolio investments. The income statement only reports realized gains. But due to the inability to determine the market value of venture portfolio companies, the income statement reports only realized gains from that portion of the venture portfolio that has been successfully liquidated for gains or written off as an unrecoverable permanent loss.

**Hedge Funds.** Unlike venture funds, hedge funds mostly invest in securities whose market value can be determined, and it is indeed such determination that permits hedge funds to redeem existing partners or add new partners, according to the economic market value of the security that is contained in the hedge fund at the specific time point of entry or exit by a partner. Consequently, it has to track assets $A_t$, borrowing $B_t$ according to mark-to-market values. The profit in every subperiod $\pi_t$ includes not just realized gains and realized cash flows from dividends and interest, but also the new unrealized gains based on mark-to-market prices (i.e., the change in unrealized gains) on securities. This results in the determination of partners' equity $V_t$ that is driven by the mark-to-market valuation of the securities contained in the hedge fund.

It is extremely important for a hedge fund not to just value its assets and liabilities at their true market value, but also to adopt the practice of valuation based on factoring in accrued interest and dividends. This requires more work for the bookkeeping accountants of the hedge fund to adjust their valuation reports received from securities firms for accrued interest and dividends. This requires maintaining a list of actual cash interest and dividend payments received during the month, excluding them from the hedge fund's account value, then calculating the appropriate accrued interest and tracking accrued dividends during the month, and adding these accrued interest and dividend amounts back to determine the hedge fund's account value. This is a well-recognized accounting principle, and IRS Form 1065 (U.S. partnership tax return) requires a checkbox to indicate whether the method of accounting for the partnership is cash or accrual. U.S. generally accepted accounting principles (GAAP) requires the accrual method of accounting. Even though the IRS permits cash-based accounting, that is, reporting dividends and income as they are received, as opposed to reporting them as they are accrued, it is not a good policy for a hedge fund to adopt the cash method of accounting and ignore the accrual method. A U.S. hedge fund seeking an audit report on its annual financial statement would be pressed by its auditor to report its financial statements based on accrued interest and dividends. But the more important reason for the adoption of accrual-based valuation is not the preference of accountants or the IRS, but to ensure that equitable economic allocations are maintained among partners in a situation when there is a change in percentage ownership due to entry or exit of some partners.

Failure to adopt the accrual method of accounting would result in distortions and wealth transfers among partners. For instance, if a partnership does not correctly accrue interest and departs before the lumpy semiannual bond coupon interest is received in cash, the economic share of the partnership at the time of redemption is underestimated. An economic wealth transfer occurs from the departing partner to the remaining partners.

Limited partners who are examining the fine print of a limited partnership agreement should look carefully at the partnership's stated accounting methodology and seek verification that the accrual method of accounting would be followed for valuation of the hedge fund every time there is a change in percentage ownership among partners. This ought to be incorporated into the limited partnership agreement, so that the general partner may be held responsible.

In general, the tracking of accrued interest and dividends is labor intensive and cumbersome. Securities brokerage firms do not always provide valuation of a securities account based on accrued interest and dividends. Each income security held in a hedge fund portfolio has to be correctly modeled, a convention established for calculating accrued interest, and a manual formula implemented. Zero-coupon bonds present an additional challenge, since the hedge fund has to calculate originally issued discount (OID) interest on such a bond held at year-end and report it as taxable interest income (even though no cash interest was received), and further accrue the OID interest monthly for purposes of monthly account valuation. A cumbersome process would be in place to track the accretion of the zero-coupon bond to its par value at maturity along its accrued OID path. As OID interest is accrued and treated as if it were taxable cash interest, the cost basis of the zero-coupon bond is raised by an equivalent amount. This is to prevent self-imposed double taxation of OID interest, once as interest and again as capital gain upon sale of the zero-coupon bond.

The actual market value of the zero-coupon bond would deviate from that path according to the prevailing market interest rates, resulting in the recognition of unrealized gain or loss according to the difference between the market price and the accreted OID path value. At maturity, since the market price and OID path must converge, there is no capital gain. However, if such a bond is sold prior to maturity, there is a realized capital gain according to the market price, less the accreted OID path value.

The tracking of OID interest may be straightforward with default-free zero-coupon or discount bonds. However, with risky bonds, OID tracking is linked to tracking capital gains, principal repayment, and recognition of defaults. A high-yield risky bond generally invites recognition of OID interest income according to the high-yield rates, which becomes taxable pass-through income to limited partners. When a high-yield bond experiences prepayments or defaults, the partnership has to recognize capital gain or losses. Taxable U.S. partners might experience an adverse situation where high-taxable OID yields are experienced in the initial years and a later default leads to a capital loss. Such capital loss cannot be offset against past taxable high yields. Offshore hedge funds experience the relief of not having to track OID interest. For efficiency in tracking and accounting, a large fixed-income hedge fund that participates in diverse risky fixed-income securities is better structured as an offshore master fund with a U.S. feeder fund, as was the case with the large LTCM fund that was described earlier.

Although there are no specific regulations and language for calculating OID interest on short positions, a U.S. hedge fund may successfully prevail with calculating OID interest on short positions in high-yield bonds (that trade at a deep discount to the par value) and report such OID interest legitimately as interest expense that would pass through to taxable U.S. limited partners. As discussed later, interest expense is a preferred tax item, since it is allowable as a deduction against any form of investment income to U.S. individual taxpayers. This interest expense is mirrored to reduce the basis of the short position, so that when it is closed, the capital gain is calculated as short sale opening price, minus short sale closing price, plus the OID interest.

The issue of accrual accounting and bookkeeping of securities in a hedge fund portfolio presents a thorny, labor-intensive problem. This accrual bookkeeping and truing-up of cumulative accrued and realized amounts of interest and dividends should be maintained in audit-quality standards and should be considered as part of the grand account books of the hedge fund, rather than private spreadsheets resident on some hedge fund general partner employee's computer.

It is important to note that bond market trade settlements are made according to the bond price plus accrued interest. Thus, the calculation of accrued interest is not just an accounting issue, but also part of calculating the market value of bonds.

It is not surprising that the global investment performance standards (GIPS) of the CFA Institute, which are described in more detail later in the context of the presentation of hedge fund performance, require the adoption of the accrual method of accounting for dividends and interest income. Although GIPS is voluntary and does not purport to reflect any statutory accounting standard, it is interesting to observe its choice of words on the adoption of accrual accounting for dividends and interest:

**1.A Input Data—Requirements ...**
*1.A.2 PORTFOLIO valuations MUST be based on MARKET VALUES (not cost basis or book values).*
*1.A.6 ACCRUAL ACCOUNTING MUST be used for fixed-income securities and all other assets that accrue interest income. Market values of fixed-income securities must include accrued income.*

**1.B Input Data—Recommendations ...**
*1.B.1 ACCRUAL ACCOUNTING SHOULD be used for dividends (as of the ex-dividend date).*[1]

The uppercase emphasis is reproduced according to the relevant text excerpts of GIPS. Clearly, the CFA Institute, which publishes the voluntary GIPS, considers accrual accounting to be mandatory in the context of accurate investment performance reporting. The adoption of accrual accounting for interest and dividends also has the pleasant consequence that partnership percentages are calculated equitably without distortion at the times when there is a change in partnership percentages due to withdrawals and deposits. Indeed, venture partnerships would have trouble

---

[1] *Global Investment Performance Standards Handbook*, 2nd ed. (Charlottesville, VA: Center for Financial Market Integrity, CFA Institute, 2007).

with section 1.A.2 of GIPS, because the market value of the underlying venture portfolio investments cannot generally be determined. GIPS has a separate section on guidelines for private equity, which we describe in more detail later.

Do hedge funds routinely implement accrual accounting for interest and dividends? Given that hedge funds are secretive, it would be a practical problem to conduct an exhaustive survey to determine what practice really is adopted. In general, the limited partner investor could look to whether the U.S. hedge fund provides an annual capital account audit that verifies the limited partners' economic values of holding in the fund. Due to the requirements of GAAP, an auditor would insist that the annual financial statement of the hedge fund should include accrued interest and dividends at calendar year-ends. A natural corollary to an auditor signing a capital account audit report for individual limited partners suggests that the auditor ought to have verified that the partner share in the hedge fund has been correctly and equitably calculated at interim time points of withdrawals and deposits by other partners, for which accrual accounting should have been implemented by the hedge fund. In reality, this is a subtle issue that auditors tend to ignore, and many auditors release capital account audit reports individually for limited partners based on whatever partner level data is provided by the hedge fund, without actually verifying or insisting that all securities should be valued inclusive of accrued dividends and interest any time there is a withdrawal or deposit by a partner, subject only to materiality provision that instances of tiny or inconsequential withdrawals and deposits may be excused.

This is what typically happens in a hedge fund, whether onshore or offshore. At year-end, valuation is conducted after adjusting for accrued interest and dividends. In the interim months of the year, valuation inclusive of accrued dividends and interest is ignored and the cash valuation methodology is adopted, which is traceable to securities brokerage and bank account statements for audit verification. Withdrawals and deposits routinely occur at interim-year time points, such as every quarter ending, according to cash valuations. Such practice is at odds with the spirit and the letter of the partnership agreement.

In the absence of verifiable assurance provided by the general partner of the hedge fund that the accrual method of accounting is adopted not just at year-end, but at all times when partnership proportions change, the limited partners should recognize that their capital account values, though numerically detailed to the last penny, are error-laden estimates of their true economic participation, and that wealth transfers could occur between partners in situations where the hedge fund experiences lumpy distributions of interest and dividend income shortly after a closing date for withdrawals and deposits. The magnitude of such error could be large, considering that the general partner's allocation performance fee is typically 20 percent, which leads to significant withdrawals out of the general partner's capital account. In contrast, the mutual fund industry publishes a daily net asset value (NAV) per share for every mutual fund at the close of every business day and permits mutual fund shareholders to withdraw and deposit according to this published NAV. It is mandatory to calculate NAV based on the GIPS principle of accrual valuation. There is no room for ambiguity and no excuse for labor-intensive bookkeeping for truing up daily accrued dividends and interest with subsequent cash receipts of dividends and interest. The hedge fund industry ought to rise to this challenge of implementing accrued accounting at the relevant discrete points in time of valuation of a hedge fund. Professional accountants who serve as auditors to hedge funds ought to alert their clients that valuation according to market prices inclusive of accrued dividends and interest at all relevant points in time is expected of them.

## Interim Valuation: The Core of a Hedge Fund's Accounting Operation

The establishment at discrete time points denoted by $t$ of the closing value of a hedge fund $W_t$ (according to market prices and accrual accounting of interest and dividends), the calculation of fixed fees and performance fees for each capital account, and the reckoning of withdrawals and deposits to each capital account (including that of the general partner), leading to the ultimate establishment of the opening value of the hedge fund, $V_t$ may be considered to be core of the hedge fund's accounting operation.

For an offshore fund, whether master or feeder, this could be seen as a relatively simple task, because the closing value of the offshore hedge fund at time point $t$ could be linked to account statements and market valuation reports that are received from banks and securities brokerage firms, with appropriate manual adjustment for accrued interest and dividends (to the extent that these statements of securities firms do not precisely establish valuation inclusive of accrued interest and dividends). The offshore fund's income for the period $[t - 1, t]$ is simply $\pi_t = W_t - V_{t-1}$. The individual complements of the period's income $\pi_t$ that are readily available from the bank brokerage account statements are dividends, interest, taxes paid, and expenses paid. The offshore fund does not have to conduct detailed month-by-month analysis and reconsideration of realized and unrealized gains, and a further breakdown of realized gains by long term and short term, because the offshore regulatory regime does not require the reporting of such breakdown. The financial statements of an offshore fund may report the aggregate sum of realized and unrealized gains in the income statement and still remain in compliance with accounting, audit, and regulatory standards in the offshore regime. Indeed, core accounting and preparation of interim and annual financial statements for an offshore hedge fund is a straightforward task.

However, for a U.S. hedge fund, the core accounting process requires the dedicated tracking of long-term and short-term realized gains, which are required to be reported to the IRS as a Schedule D attachment to the Form 1065 tax return. Along with all other taxable components of income, the reported long-term and short-term realized gains are to be further allocated to partners. The U.S. hedge fund is required to report the complete breakdown of components of income, including a further breakdown of realized short-term and long-term gains by individual security, showing trade dates, purchase cost, and sales proceeds.

The major accounting challenge to a U.S. hedge fund is the reconciliation of aggregate income with its components. Most hedge funds set up a parallel tracking and accounting system based on manual input to take trade data that is reported in monthly brokerage account statements and transcribed properly into realized long-term and short-term gains by individual trade according to the IRS Schedule D format.

There are a few minor but painstaking accounting adjustments required, such as the exclusion of wash sales and tracking of such wash sale securities. The IRS considers any security that is repurchased within 30 days of a loss-making sale as a wash sale and requires such loss to be factored into the cost of the repurchased securities. The wash sale exclusion and tracking is important, since the U.S. securities brokerage firm reports the gross proceeds of all securities sold during a calendar year to the IRS on Form 1099-B. The IRS is likely to spot large deviations between gross securities sales reported by securities brokerage firms and gross sales reported in Schedule D and to initiate an examination of the tax return. It is implicit that a U.S. hedge fund should track any wash sales and provide an explanatory statement on Schedule D.

Other such minor but necessary tracking that a U.S. hedge fund's accountants are implicitly expected to conduct are short positions at calendar year-end that are not closed. A short position has the sales proceeds received first and cost paid next at the time of closing. U.S. securities brokerage firms would report proceeds from short sales as part of Form 1099-B. It is therefore important for the hedge fund to provide an explanatory statement on Schedule D, reconciling the gross securities sales reported to the IRS versus that part of gross sales that are excluded in Schedule D because they correspond to short positions that are not yet closed at year-end. Similarly, since cash dividends and interest are reported by U.S. securities firms to the IRS, it is important for a U.S. hedge fund to maintain a supplemental schedule for the IRS that is derived from the accrual accounting system for dividends and interest, where cumulative accrued amounts are reconciled with cash receipts.

Thus, U.S. hedge funds are faced with a higher order of requirements for reconciliation and accounting compared to offshore hedge funds. Can this process be automated? With the significant advances made in information technology and computing, this ought to be a straightforward computer automation task. The hurdle to automation is that the mark-to-market valuation of securities and reports for realized trades come in the form of diverse electronic and paper reports from securities brokerage firms that require parsing scripts to convert into an automated data feed stored in a database system for the hedge fund. Many securities firms realize the accounting burdens faced by their hedge fund clients and offer so-called "prime brokerage" services that include reporting that is consistent with both economic valuation of a hedge fund, as well as for IRS reporting on the hedge fund's tax return. However, most hedge funds have multiple bank and securities accounts at different institutions, not just based in the United States but also at overseas locations. No two securities firms follow the same formats and standards for reporting mark-to-market valuation and realized or closed trades, even though their reports are outputs from sophisticated computing systems. The back office of a U.S. hedge fund ends up becoming a labor-intensive task, where the job description of such back-office employees is that they largely take numbers that come out of one computer system and put them into another computer system. (In the financial industry, the "front office" is the trading and investment decision-making operation, and the "back office" is the tracking, reporting, monitoring, and accounting operation.) Indeed, that description might apply to back-office operations of the global financial industry of banks, securities firms, insurance companies, investment management firms, and hedge funds. The global financial industry is one of the largest users of business computing and information technology.

It is amply evident that the accounting operation of a U.S. hedge fund is a vexing source of labor-intensive tracking, analysis, reporting, and tax filing with the IRS. This is due to having to file a detailed statement of realized gains and losses for each and every individual security or tax lot that is traded by the hedge fund, and having to track its reconciliation with other data being directly reported to the IRS by U.S. securities brokerage firms. A hedge fund organizer virtually eliminates this reliance on a heavy-duty accounting operation by organizing the hedge fund as an offshore master fund with a U.S. feeder fund. The offshore master fund files Form 8832 with the IRS and elects treatment as an association for the purposes of U.S. tax law for U.S. investors, which in this case is the U.S. feeder fund with its pass-through U.S. investors. The offshore master fund, say, a Cayman Islands mutual fund or a Cayman Islands partnership, is not required to provide a breakdown of long-term and short-term realized gains in their country of domicile. From the perspective of the U.S. feeder fund, cash flows received from the master fund are recognized either as dividends and distributions when received involuntarily, and capital gains when voluntary redemptions are sought. Despite the offshore hedge fund not falling under U.S. jurisdiction and therefore not being required to file reports to the IRS, it is in the best interests of the offshore hedge fund to distribute portfolio annual cash flows of dividends and interest to its partners, including its U.S. partners. This will ensure that portfolio interest and interest income from fixed-income securities does not become a tax-preference item at the lower capital gains tax rate of 15 percent to U.S. investors. Until such time that the IRS comes up with a specific ruling on the U.S. reporting obligations of an offshore entity containing U.S. shareholders and partners that files Form 8832, the hedge fund organizers have valuable grounds for applying discretion in accounting and reporting, as well as maintaining a simplistic barebones accounting operation whose primary function is to delineate the economic value of the hedge fund and the economic allocations to its partners.

## Books of Account and Financial Statements for Hedge Funds

Our algebraic framework is already set up for maintaining the books of account of a U.S. partnership. We provide the steps that constitute the core of an accounting database system that provides audit-quality books of account for presentation to an auditor, as well as economic performance measurement according to recommended GIPS standards. We shall use the structure and format of the U.S. partnership tax return, Form 1065, to represent the financial statements of the U.S. hedge fund. An offshore hedge fund could use the same exact procedure and track more detailed constituents' income, even though they are not required to be tracked or reported in tax-free offshore regimes.

To simplify matters, we shall presume that the hedge fund is not an operating business, not in commercial real estate with nuances of rental income, rental expenses, and depreciation, or an oil and gas or energy partnership, which is intensive on depreciation, intangible drilling costs, and such aspects. Thus, the U.S. hedge fund has no ordinary income or deductions and no physical inventory of goods that requires inventory valuation. Thus, line 22 of Form 1065, Ordinary Business Income, is blank, and so also is Schedule A, Cost of Goods Sold.

Our objective is to maintain just one book of accounts, which tracks the economic value of the partnership and each partner's capital account.

Schedule L of Form 1065, Balance Sheet per Books, thus refers to only one set of books, the economic books of the partnership. At this point, we need to clarify that a hedge fund which admits new partners and allows interim redemptions according to the economic mark-to-market value of the partnership and limited partners' holdings therein, is eminently amenable to this assumption, that the sole books of account that are being maintained represent their true economic (market) value at all points in time. For a venture partnership, this is assumption is untenable. The interim market value of portfolio venture investments cannot be meaningfully measured. The only adjustments to the initial assets at cost are markdowns and write-offs from recognizing failed venture projects, and additions to cash or marketable securities due to realized gains, hopefully windfall realized gains, from exit, monetization, or liquidation of successful venture projects. Thus, even though the same exact algebraic representation and implementation of the books of account holds for venture funds, the biggest difference between a venture fund and a hedge fund is that the latter tracks the mark-to-market value of unrealized gains on securities, while the former treats unrealized gains on venture projects as if they are always zero.

We return to our focus on U.S. hedge funds that invest in liquid securities and have audit-quality procedures in place to establish the market value of the holdings, particularly at a time point when limited partners are entering or exiting the fund according to the economic value of the partnership.

The income statement on Form 1065 is somewhat abstracted, appearing only as a confusing schedule to reconcile the partnership's book income with taxable realized income, called Schedule M-1. There is only one line to represent the partnership's book income: Schedule M-1, line 1, which reappears in the partnership's cash flow statement for the year, Schedule M-2, as the entry for partnership book income in schedule M-2, line 3. However, Schedule K, which requires reporting of all taxable items of realized income and other items of realized income such as tax-exempt interest income, provides more than adequate detail for presentation in a GAAP-compliant financial statement.

## Audit of an Offshore Fund

An offshore fund audit is a much simpler procedure in instances where the offshore fund is a feeder fund to a U.S. master fund. The auditor in the offshore regime places great importance and weight on the U.S. master fund's inability to obtain a clean audit letter from a reputable U.S. audit firm. Indeed, many audit firms in offshore regimes are affiliates of the major global accounting and auditing firms. The offshore fund's auditor, comfortable with the fund's values coming from clean audited entities, now has to simply look at the financials, shareholding, entry, and exit for the offshore feeder fund only.

There being no obligation to make adjustments according to U.S. GAAP accounting standards, the auditors of an offshore fund have wider latitude in examining its financial statements. The accounting standards applied by an offshore fund's auditors correspond to those of the U.K. and Dutch accounting professions. In the case of an offshore Cayman Islands mutual fund, the Cayman audit letter is to be submitted to the government regulatory agency during the annual renewal of the fund's business license.

## Audit of a U.S. Fund

The audit of a U.S. hedge fund by a U.S. accounting firm becomes a serious matter. U.S. auditors have to conform to standards and regulations of the U.S. accounting profession and accounting rules and standards established by the U.S. Financial Accounting Standards Board (FASB).[2] The audit firm is sensitive to the risk of liability from partner lawsuits in the event of dispute or fraud by the general partner of the hedge fund. Audit fees vary greatly according to the reputation of the audit firm and the size of assets of the hedge fund. The audit firm's risk from partner lawsuits is proportional to the size of the fund, as well as to the risky nature of the hedge fund's investment strategy.

The auditor expects the hedge fund manager to provide financial statements of the fund as a whole and a breakdown of capital accounts by partners. Under U.S. GAAP accounting to standards, the fund's valuation has to be conducted at relevant periodic intervals using credible mark-to-market external sources of reference, as well as factoring in accrued interest, dividends, and expenses. Many hedge funds struggle to present financial statements that are acceptable to the auditor without change or restatement. Typically, the hedge fund provides economic, financial, and valuation spreadsheets containing relevant numbers, from which the audit firm prepares a financial statement according to its own simple standard format. If a hedge fund were to follow the valuation and accounting procedures for establishing financial statements and partner capital accounts according to the description and procedures provided in this book, and summary financial statements as well as capital accounts presented to the auditor, we are confident that the audit firm would likely issue a clean

---

[2]AICPA, "Investment Companies—Audit and Accounting Guide," 2009.

audit report and would mostly focus on testing and cross-checking mark-to-market valuation.

Even if an audit report is not required by the limited partnership agreement, it is a good idea to obtain such an audit report for the fund, including capital account audit reports. If the hedge fund does not want to pay large fees to name-recognized audit firms, a low-cost independent auditor might be appointed. The audited financial statements of the fund and individual audited partner capital account statements not only provide an assurance to partners, but also persuade the fund to adopt discipline in accounting. It also facilitates rapid completion of tax filings to the IRS by a tax accountant. If the IRS ever initiates an examination of a hedge fund's tax returns, that the fund has been audited is a positive consideration.

## Capital Account Audit for Both Offshore and U.S Funds

When a limited partnership agreement establishes the requirement of an annual audit, it usually does not mention the requirement for a capital account audit. Partners assume that their capital accounts must be in proper order when a fund obtains an audit letter. It is usually possible for a hedge fund's auditor to provide a capital account audit letter to each partner or shareholder. This is a small incremental effort in the auditor's examination of the financial and partner capital structure, which is part of the auditor's work. It provides a great degree of comfort to partners that their own account values embedded within a larger commingled fund were audited.

# CHAPTER 5

# Partner Tax Allocations in U.S. Partnerships

## U.S. Tax Allocation Rules Governing U.S. Partnerships

The taxation of U.S. partnerships is governed by the U.S. Code, Title 26 (Internal Revenue Code, often abbreviated as IRC), Subtitle A (Income Taxes), Chapter 1 (Normal Taxes and Surtaxes), Subchapter K (Partners and Partnerships), Part I (Determination of Tax Liability). This tree has nine further branches, sections 701 to 709, of which Section 704 (Partners' Distributive Share) holds the key to tax allocations to partners.

Section 704(a) innocuously suggests that the partnership agreement governs the distribution by stating "A partner's distributive share of income, gain, loss, deduction, or credit shall, except as otherwise provided in this chapter, be determined by the partnership agreement."

Section 704(b) states, "A partner's distributive share of income, gain, loss, deduction, or credit (or item thereof) shall be determined in accordance with the partner's interest in the partnership (determined by taking into account all facts and circumstances), if—

(1) the partnership agreement does not provide as to the partner's distributive share of income, gain, loss, deduction, or credit (or item thereof), or
(2) the allocation to a partner under the agreement of income, gain, loss, deduction, or credit (or item thereof) does not have substantial economic effect.

Section 704(b)(1) provides a default method for allocating items to partners according to their percentage ownership share. This would apply to partnerships that have not explicitly established their own specific customized rules for allocation items.

Section 704(b)(2) has the power to override the allocation rules provided in a partnership agreement if such allocations have "substantial economic effect." What exactly is meant by "substantial economic effect"? This is a matter of much debate among lawyers and accountants. Most would agree to a conservative interpretation, that whatever tax allocation rule is applied (to determine distribution of shares of income and expense items), it should correspond with the partnership's rule for economic allocations to partners' capital accounts. Many professionals believe that if tax allocation across partners substantially diverges from their respective economic allocations, the IRS may deem such inconsistency to have a "substantial economic effect" and require the tax allocations to be made consistent with the economic allocations.

The IRS provided an official interpretation of this key phrase, stating, "*1.704-1(b)(ii) Economic Effect-(a) Fundamental Principles.* For an allocation to have economic effect, it must be consistent with the underlying economic arrangement of the partners. This means that, in the event that there is an economic benefit or burden that corresponds to the allocation, the partner to whom the allocation is made must receive such economic benefit or bear such economic burden."[1] Lawyers and accountants typically paraphrase this principle in stating that "tax allocations should follow economic allocations in a partnership."

A simple test example provides meaningful insight into this issue. Consider a U.S. partnership that has two partners: one that is taxable, and one that is tax-exempt (such as a charitable organization). The partnership produces a taxable interest income only. Suppose the partnership agreement allocates the economic gain due to interest income to partners' accounts according to their percentage ownership. Now suppose the partnership allocates all the taxable interest income for tax purposes to the tax-exempt partner and none to the taxable partner. There is no tax consequence to the tax-exempt partner. The taxable partner does not pay tax on pass-through interest income and receives an equal amount in the form of long-term capital gain when it withdraws from the partnership. Interest income is taxed to the partner at the higher ordinary income rate, while long-term capital gains are taxed at a lower rate. This partnership agreement effectively postpones tax on interest income for a taxable partner until that partner fully withdraws from the partnership. Most likely, upon audit or examination, the IRS might consider this to be a "substantial economic effect" and direct the partnership to allocate taxable interest income

---

[1]26 C.F.R. Section 1.704-1(b)(2)(ii)(a), which is accessible at http://edocket.access
.gpo.gov/cfr_2009/aprqtr/pdf/26cfr1.704-1.pdf, also repeated in the Federal Register,
November 18, 2005 (Volume 70, Number 222), accessible at http://edocket.access
.gpo.gov/2005/05-22281.htm.

to a taxable partner according to its percentage ownership as provided in Section 704(b). There could be other alternative interpretations to this simple example, and hence this topic of tax allocations deviating from economic allocations is a popular subject for interpretation and debate among lawyers and accountants.

Most U.S. hedge funds and investment partnerships do not want to get involved in interpretation and argument with the IRS, and hence they do not specify customized rules for tax allocations in the partnership agreement that could deviate from the procedure for economic allocations in their limited partnership agreement by the standards of Section 704(b)(2). It is therefore practical to consider making tax allocations to partners being made exactly according to their partnership ownership fractions, which is automatically consistent with the provisions of Section 704(b).

## Tax Components of U.S. Investment Partnership Income

The simplicity of locating a hedge fund in a tax-exempt regime is striking. The breakdown of components of income and items on the balance sheet are provided entirely to suit accounting standards and investors' desire for details. A hedge fund manager in the tax-exempt regime may focus entirely on producing economic gains for the investors. In contrast, a U.S. hedge fund has to set up an accounting operation to provide all of the information relating to the subcomponents of its income and the pass-through allocation to its partners.

Schedule K of the U.S. hedge fund's partnership tax return, with the title "Partners' Distributive Share Items," is the reporting of the pass-through taxable components of the aggregate annual income at time point $t = 12$, defined earlier as $\Pi = \sum_{t=1}^{12} \pi_t$. The taxable components of $P$ require additional subscripts. We shall utilize the line items of Schedule K as the relevant subscript. For instance, line 4 of Schedule K is "Guaranteed Payments," which we shall denote as $\pi_{4,t}$ in month t, and its aggregate as $\Pi_4 = \sum_{t=1}^{12} \pi_{4,t}$. The most pertinent line items of income for a U.S. hedge fund are guaranteed payments (line 4), which will be described later, interest income (line 5), ordinary dividends (line 6a), net short-term capital gain (line 8), and net long-term capital gain. Qualified dividends (line 6b) are a subset of ordinary dividends (line 6a) that meet IRS criteria of arising from securities held for longer than 60 days and are subject to a lower tax rate. For now, the other line items for breakdown of hedge fund income are ignored, based on the simplifying assumption that dividends, interest, and realized capital gains are the only items of realized income of the hedge fund.

The next breakdowns are critical items of pass-through expense incurred by the hedge fund, of which investment interest expense (line

13b) and other investment expense deductions (line 13d) have paramount importance.

Dividends reported under line 6a are gross dividends before any application of foreign withholding taxes on foreign source dividends earned by the U.S. hedge fund. In order to enable pass-through partners to claim credit against their pass-through share of foreign taxes paid, the hedge fund reports passive foreign gross income (which is the subset of foreign source dividends included under total dividends in line 6a) on line 16d, and total foreign taxes paid by the hedge fund on line 16l.

Schedule K has a block for "other information" where aggregate distribution (i.e., withdrawals or negative deposits) are reported in line 19a and line 19b. Line 20a reports aggregate investment income excluding capital gains, which for the hedge fund is a sum of dividends and interest. Line 20b reports aggregate investment expenses excluding interest expense, which for the hedge fund is "other deductions" reported in line 13d.

A hedge fund may have other items of realized income such as tax-exempt interest income arising from investment in U.S. municipal bonds. Line 18a reports tax-exempt interest income for the partnership.

In order to complete a mathematical representation, we need to define one component of income that is not reported on Schedule K: the unrealized capital gains on securities, which is not considered to be a component of pass-through taxable income. There is a place on Form 1065, U.S. Return of Partnership Income, in Schedule M-1, line 6 as "income recorded on books this year but not included on Schedule K, lines 1 through 11." This item also permits us to record items like tax-exempt interest, which increase book or economic income, but are not reported on Schedule K since they are not taxable. Since Schedule K includes only items of realized income, it has no place for unrealized gains (or losses) of the U.S. hedge fund. The entry in Schedule M-1, line 6 permits us to enter and track unrealized gains. We shall index unrealized gains of the hedge fund by the unwieldy subscript "M1L6."

The U.S. partnership tax return, Form 1065, has a field in Schedule M-1, line 7, to enter "deductions included on schedule K, but not charged against book income during this year." This item provides for tracking items like depreciation, which are expensed on Schedule K, but not reduced from unrealized income.

To summarize, we denote subscripts for our algebraic expressions to stand for the respective line items in Schedule K:

Subscript 4: guaranteed payments (to be described and clarified later)
Subscript 5: taxable interest income
Subscript 6a: total ordinary dividends

Subscript 6b: qualified dividends included in total ordinary dividends (subscript 6a)

Subscript 16d: foreign gross dividends included in total ordinary dividends (subscript 6a)

(Note that 6b and 16d are subcomponents of 6a.)

Subscript 8: net short-term capital gain

Subscript 9a: net long-term capital gain

Subscript 13b: investment interest expense

Subscript 13d: other investment expense deductions (management fixed fees)

Subscript 16: foreign taxes paid

Subscript 18a: tax-exempt interest income

For now, we shall ignore depreciation under Schedule M-1, line 7 and consider Schedule M-1, line 6, to represent the *change in unrealized gains* on securities, or alternately, that portion of economic profits that are made by the partnership during the year but not taxed according to taxable line items. Schedule M-1, line 8, reports the net of the inclusion of a tax-exempt interest income under Schedule M-1, line 6 and line 7. Thus, Schedule M-1, line 8 is the sum of the *change in unrealized gains* and *nontaxable items of income*. It is important to recognize that Schedule M-1, line 6 is not the absolute unrealized gains on the portfolio of mark-to-market securities, but the *change*, or *increase*, in unrealized gains on securities from the beginning of the year to the end of the year. When tax-exempt interest income is added to this, we derive the total economic income of the partnership during the year that was not taxed. Thus, Schedule M-1, line 8 represents new unrealized gains that are obtained during the year, plus tax-exempt interest income during the year. Note that the change in unrealized gains number could well be negative, that is, the partnership could have new unrealized losses during the year.

It is also important to recognize that only when the unrealized gains on securities are zero at the year beginning do we have a situation where the change in unrealized gains is the same as the year-end level of unrealized gains. This is guaranteed to happen at the end of the first year of operation of a hedge fund, because there are no securities in the hedge fund's portfolio and consequently no unrealized gains at the beginning of the year, which was the inception of the fund. Similarly, if a hedge fund liquidates all securities and begins a year with only cash, the change in unrealized gains at the end of the year is same as the level of unrealized gains at the end of the year.

We shall index the net unrealized gains portion of the economic income of a U.S. hedge fund by the equally unwieldy subscript "*M1I6*."

In summary, a U.S. investment partnership is obliged to track its *aggregate economic profit* at every sub time period as:

$$\pi_t = \pi_{4,t} + \pi_{5,t} + \pi_{6a,t} + \pi_{8,t} + \pi_{9a,t} - (\pi_{13b,t} + \pi_{13d,t} + \pi_{16l,t}) + \pi_{18a,t} + \pi_{M1L6,t}$$

This may be simplified as:

$$\pi_t = \sum_{k \in K} \pi_{k,t}$$

where $K$ denotes the set of components of income, $K = \{4, 5, 6a, 8, 9a, 13b, 13d, 16l, 18a, M1L6\}$.

The symbol $\in$ is shorthand for "belongs to," so the subscript $k \in K$ means income component indexed by $k$, belonging to the larger set $K$ of income components. As noted earlier, tax-exempt interest that is under line 18a is included under Schedule M, line 8 (M1L8), so we did not need to track tax M1L8 separately. M1L8 would equal M1L6 plus 18a.

We are ignoring and excluding other taxable line items or categories of income and expense for now, by assuming that they are zero in a typical U.S. hedge fund or investment partnership:

$$KX = \{1, 2, 3c, 7, 9a, 9c, 10, 11, 12, 13c, 14a, 14b, 14c\}$$

These line items, while necessary for partnerships that are involved in real estate or in operational business, might be ignored for the time being without any loss of generality. Our focus is the universe of hedge funds and venture partnerships, which primarily earn their income from dividends, interest, and capital gains. We could later include all of these line items to represent a generalized U.S. investment partnership.

The negative sign surrounding the term $(\pi_{13b,t} + \pi_{13b,t} + \pi_{16l,t})$ is due to the convention that these are reported as positive numbers on Schedule K, even though they are actually expenses, which reduce profit.

The hedge fund must also track the detail of $\pi_{6a,t}$, $\pi_{6b,t}$, and $\pi_{16d,t}$ and maintain a report of their breakdown and summary.

Based on tracking the subperiod breakdown of income, a hedge fund reports its aggregate profits and its components as:

$$\Pi = \Pi_4 + \Pi_5 + \Pi_{6a} + \Pi_8 + \Pi_{9a} - (\Pi_{13b} + \Pi_{13d} + \Pi_{16l}) + \Pi_{18a} + \Pi_{M1L6}$$

where for each subcomponent $k$, $\Pi_k = \sum_{t=1}^{12} \pi_{k,t}$.

Accounting professionals in the United States are eternally busy in fulfilling the IRS requirement that aggregate partnership (or fund)-level income by subcategory that is reported in Schedule K has to be further broken down by partners and reported for each partner in a similarly ordered and line item numbered in Schedule K-1. Thus, each subcomponent of aggregate profit $\Pi_k$ must be further broken down for each partner $i = 1 \ldots N$ as $\Pi_k^i$. Further, the breakdown by partners cannot deviate from the aggregate, so that for each component of income $k$, it must be the case that $\Pi_k = \sum_{i=1}^{N} \Pi_k^i$. This satisfies the condition that a U.S. partnership is a pass-through entity, whose components of income are fully transferred to its partners, who subsequently pay U.S. taxes as individuals on their transferred shares of partnership income allocations.

## Fixed Fees: Income to the General Partner and Expense to the Limited Partners

The fixed fee paid to the capital account of the general partner is deemed to be a "guaranteed payment" (with subscript 4). The amount withdrawn from the capital accounts of the limited partners to pay the fixed fee is considered an "investment expense" that gets included in the category "other investment expense deductions" (with subscript 13d).

We had already set up the definitions for the fixed fees, so it is going to be simple to calculate and report these two items.

Earlier, we had calculated the aggregate fixed fees paid by limited partners as:

$$D_t^f = \sum_{i=1}^{N_t} F_t^i = \sum_{i=1}^{N_t} f^i[\alpha_{t-1}^i W_t] = W_t \sum_{i=1}^{N_t} f^i \alpha_{t-1}^i$$

To simplify notation, we no longer use the index $N_t$ signifying varying number of capital accounts during time period $[t - 1, t]$. Instead, unique capital accounts that are extant during all or any part of the year are assigned the range $1...N$. The $N$ is fixed for one year and may be changed at the beginning of the next year. Note that the general partner $i = 1$ does not pay any fixed fee so that $f^1 = 0$. The limited partners may have multiple capital accounts. The set of capital accounts represented by the range $1...N$.

When summed up for the full year, $\sum_{t=1}^{12} D_f^t$ is the total fixed fees paid to the general partner, to be reported as $\Pi_4$ for the aggregate fund in Schedule K, line 4. The components of $P_4$ by partner are $\Pi_4^1 = \Pi_4$ for the general partner and $\Pi_4^1 = 0$ for the limited partners $i = 2...N$.

The general partner in turn would absorb the guaranteed payment $\Pi_4^1$ in its partner Schedule K-1 and record it as ordinary income in its own U.S. entity tax return. So far, performance fees are not deemed to be guaranteed payments due to their contingent nature, and hence they are excluded from this subcategory of "guaranteed payments" that are treated as ordinary income for the general partner.

The fixed fee payments aggregated for each limited partner are arrived at in two steps. The fixed fees for the full year for every capital account indexed by $i$ are represented as $F^i = \sum_{t=1}^{12} F_t^i$. The same limited partner may have multiple capital accounts represented by the set $\{J\}$, so the fixed fees are further aggregated across all capital accounts in the set $\{J\}$ as $\Pi_{13d}^j = \sum_{i \in J} F^i$ and reported as their investment expense. The same unique limited partner who owns the set $\{J\}$ of capital accounts is indexed by the superscript $j$.

Thus, the set of capital accounts indexed as $i = 1...N$ is further aggregated by unique limited partners if $j = 1...M$ where $M \leq N$. Thus, there are $N$ capital accounts during the year, and $M \leq N$ unique investors during the year. The IRS requires the breakdown of taxable income components by unique partners, thus requiring $M$ filled-in pages of Schedule K-1, one for each unique partner. In the previous sections, such a distinction of unique partners was not necessary, and hence all of the analysis was based on unique capital accounts, which are indeed required to correctly calculate performance fees. The only time we needed aggregation across capital accounts of unique partners was to facilitate merging such multiple capital accounts into one single capital account at the beginning of the next year, provided all of these multiple accounts' high-water marks were reset at the same time point $T = 12$ after the implementation of the performance fee. A U.S. pass-through taxable hedge fund therefore would have to track lists of capital accounts linked to their unique owners.

To summarize, we have identified that for the general partner $i = 1$, $\Pi_4^1 = \Pi_4 = \sum_{t=1}^{12} D_f^t$ and $\Pi_{13d}^1 = 0$. Similarly, for each unique limited partner $j=1...M, \Pi_4^j = 0$, and $\Pi_{13d}^j = \sum_{i \in J} F^i = \sum_{i \in J, t=1}^{12} F_t^i$. The definitions $D_t^f = \sum_{i=1}^{N_t} F_t^i$ and $F_t^i$ come from the earlier framework set up for modeling a hedge fund in a tax-exempt regime. Further, each term for capital account fixed fees in turn is derived according to $F_t^i = f^i [\alpha_{t-1}^i W_t]$.

As we shall see in the subsequent sections, the calculations of breakdowns of other item of partnership income are slightly more complex due to having to factor in the performance fee that is allocated to the general partner.

## Generalizing the Allocation Formula to Other Components of Income

We may generalize the formula for allocation of taxable interest income to all other categories of income that are to be allocated in the same manner as a taxable interest income. This general formula is obtained by simply replacing the subscript 5 for taxable interest income with subscript $k$, where $k$ belongs to the set $K' = \{4, 5, 6a, 13b, 13d, 16l\}$, a subset of $K$, which are items of *taxable* interest income, dividends, and expenses. As we shall see later, we require different treatment for the set of capital gains components $K'' = \{8, 9a, M1L6\}$. Thus we have our general allocation formula for all items other than realized long-term and short-term capital gain, and realized capital gain.

For the general partner denoted by $j = 1$, we have:

$$\Pi_k^1 = \sum_{t=1}^{12} \alpha_{t-1}^1 \pi_{k,t} + \sum_{j=2}^{M} \sum_{i \in J, t=1}^{12} (1 - \beta^i) \alpha_{t-1}^i \pi_{k,t}$$

For each unique limited partner denoted by $j = 2 \ldots M$, we have:

$$\Pi_k^j = \sum_{i \in J, t=1}^{12} \beta^i \alpha_{t-1}^i \pi_{k,t}$$

It has to be the case that the partner allocations add up to the amount for the partnership as a whole:

$$\Pi_k^1 + \sum_{j=2}^{M} \Pi_k^j = \Pi_k$$

The subscripts $k$ are members of the set $K' = \{4, 5, 6a, 13b, 13d, 16l, 18a\}$, that is, 4: guaranteed payments, 5: taxable interest, 6a: gross dividends, 13b: investment interest expense, 13d: other investment expense, 16l: foreign tax paid, and 18a: tax-exempt interest.

## Tax Basis of Partner's Investment in a U.S Partnership

Every partner who invests in a U.S. partnership is expected to track their "basis," also sometimes called the "tax basis." This is not provided readily on any part of the U.S. partnership tax return or Schedule K-1 that is provided to partners, but is implied by all of the numbers reported in the partnership tax return and partners' Schedule K-1. There is no ambiguity regarding how the tax basis of partners' interest is defined and determined.[2] Translated to algebraic notation, the tax basis for a partner is denoted by $K_t^j$ (withdrawals are considered negative deposits) made by the partner superscripted as $j$, plus all allocations of *realized taxable* income[3] called "tax allocations," plus all allocations of tax-exempt income made to the partner, from inception until the time point $t$. Note that withdrawals are simply negative deposits represented by negative numbers in this framework. Further, reporting to the IRS is done at time points $t = 0, 12, 24, 36, \ldots$ calendar

---

[2]The definition of partners' basis with numerical examples is provided in the U.S. Code of Federal Regulations (C.F.R.) under 26 C.F.R. Section 1.705-1, accessible at http://ecfr.gpoaccess.gov/cgi/t/text/text-idx?c=ecfr&sid=dbae86a86b48352b1b6ed1 bc345ac5c7&rgn=div8&view=text&node=26:8.0.1.1.1.0.13.240&idno=26.

[3]Section 703 (a) of the Internal Revenue Code provides a blanket definition of taxable income of a partnership being the same as in the case of an individual with appropriate exclusions for items such as personal exemption, foreign taxes paid, charitable contributions, etc. The U.S. Code, specifically Title 26, which is the Internal Revenue Code, is found at the Web portal GPO Access, a service of the U.S. Government Printing Office.

year-end, so the tax basis $K_t^j$ is defined for all partners $j = 1...M$ only at time points $t = 0, 12, 24, 36, ...$ .

At the inception $t = 0$, the partner's basis is simply $K_0^j = D_0^j$. From the perspective of the IRS, this is the cost basis of the partners' investment into the partnership at their time of entry, $t = 0$.

The IRS interpretation of tax basis as a running total representing a partner's cost of investment in the partnership is based on viewing a partnership as if it were distributing all of its realized allocations to a partner, who pays tax according to the nature of each subitem of realized allocation. In reality, such a distribution is not made, so the implicit assumption is that the partner reinvests these taxable distributions back into the partnership. Thus, the initial deposit (or contribution) *adds* to the partner's tax basis. Subsequent positive deposits *add* to the tax basis, and negative deposits (or withdrawals) *reduce* the tax basis. The items of realized taxable income that are always positive (guaranteed payments, interest income, dividend income) *add* to the tax basis. Tax-exempt interest income, if any, even though not taxed to the partner, is a form of realized income and hence *adds* to the tax basis. Realized capital gains (whether short term or long term) *add* to the tax basis when they are positive and *reduce* the tax basis when they are negative. The items of (realized) expenses (interest expense, management fixed fee expense, foreign taxes paid) *reduce* the tax basis.

Allocations of unrealized income have no impact on the tax basis. Thus, unrealized capital gains, whether negative or positive, are disregarded in the reckoning of the tax basis. This is the source of variation between a partner's capital account value (which includes unrealized capital gains) and the tax basis (which excludes unrealized capital gains). When a partner entirely withdraws from a U.S. partnership, the partnership distributes cash or securities equal to the capital account value. In the calendar year of entire withdrawal from the partnership, the partner is obliged to report the deviation between redemption and the tax basis as a capital gain on the individual or entity tax return. Thus, if the terminal redemption distribution exceeds the tax basis, the partner records a realized capital gain on the individual tax return. If the terminal redemption is less than the tax basis, the partner records the realized capital loss on the individual tax return.

It is almost inevitable that the capital account value would deviate from the tax basis for a partner at any point in time, due to unrealized gains on securities held in the partnership. A U.S. partnership would most likely be holding securities bearing unrealized capital gain (positive or negative) at the year-end time point of its tax filing. Let us consider a simple example where the U.S. partnership holds only one single nondividend-paying equity security, which steadily only increases. The partnership does not sell any stock, except for raising cash to fund withdrawals by partners. One could imagine an extreme situation where the cash required to fund the withdrawals of one partner comes from the cash deposited by a new or existing partner. Thus, there are minimal realized gains, and hence the tax basis would be less than the capital account value. The difference between the two is the partner's cumulative allocations of unrealized capital gain (less any allocations of realized capital gain). At the time of entire withdrawal from the partnership, the IRS requires the withdrawing partner to transform the embedded cumulative *unrealized capital gain* into *realized capital gain* and report the latter on the individual tax return for this same year. In the end, the partner reports the same capital gain amount, whether the equity security is directly held by the partner or indirectly held in a limited partnership that invests solely in that same equity security.

The inclusion of tax-exempt income in calculating the tax basis ensures that it is excluded in the calculation of realized capital gain attributable to the entire disposition of the partnership interest that is required to be reported by partners on their individual tax returns.

Returning to our algebraic framework, we need an extra subscript to track each tax allocation subitem indexed by $k$ as $\Pi_k^j$, which was defined earlier for time point = 12, to all of the calendar year-end time points $t = (12, 24, 36, \ldots T)$. We sum up all subitems $k$ belonging to the set $K' = \{4, 5, 6a, 13b, 13d, 16l, 18a\}$ and denote this as as $\Pi_{k,\in K',T}^j$, where $t = (12, 24, 36, \ldots T)$.

$$\Pi_{k,\in K',T}^j = \sum_{k \in K'} \Pi_{k,T}^j = \sum_{k \in K'} \sum_{t=12,24,36,\ldots}^{T} \Pi_{k,t}^j$$

The cumulative net deposits of a partner indexed by $j$ is the sum of all deposits at time moved points $t = 0, 1, 2, 3, \ldots T$. This is written as:

$$D_T^j = \sum_{t=0,1,2,3,\ldots}^{T} D_t^j$$

The tax basis of a partner at calendar year-end $T$ is:

$$K_T^j = D_T^j + \Pi_{k \in K',T}^j$$

The first term on the right-hand side is simply the sum of all deposits (including negative deposits). The second term on the right-hand side is the sum of all realized tax allocation subitems contained in the set $K' = \{4, 5, 6a, 13b, 13d, 16l, 18a\}$. For the general partner $j = 1$, $D_t^1$ is inclusive of the total fixed fee collected from limited partners $D_f^t$ and credited to the capital account of the general partner.

The above procedure is based on laboriously aggregating each and every item of realized tax allocations along with each and every deposit until the point in time $t = T$. There is a simpler way to achieve the same result: We simply aggregate only the *change in unrealized gain* allocated to the partner at every calendar year-end.

$$\boldsymbol{\Pi}_{M1L6,T}^{j} = \sum_{t=12,24,36,\,\dots}^{T} \Pi_{M1L6,t}^{j}$$

Denoted in boldface, $\boldsymbol{\Pi}_{M1L6,T}^{j}$ is the *cumulative* unrealized gain for partner $j$ since inception. Without boldface, $\Pi_{M1L6,T}^{j}$ is the *change* in unrealized gain for partner $j$ for the calendar year ending at time point $T$. It is also calculated at any time point $t$ as $\boldsymbol{\Pi}_{M1L6,t}^{j} = \sum_{t} \Pi_{M1L6,t}^{j}$, that is, the sum of all changes in unrealized gains for $[t-1,\ t]$. This definition is equivalent to stating that $\Pi_{M1L6,t}^{j} = \boldsymbol{\Pi}_{M1L6,t}^{j} - \boldsymbol{\Pi}_{M1L6,t-1}^{j}$.

The capital account value after all fees at time point $t = T$ was defined earlier as $U_T^j$. This is what is due to a partner at time point $t = T$ who seeks redemption in entirety ($T$ need not be calendar year-end and should really be $t = \tau$, but it makes it simpler for now to assume that $T$ is a calendar year-end).

Note that the definition of $U_T^j$ was based on including deposits $D_T^j$ at the calendar year-end time point $T$. Many accountants prefer to exclude the take time point deposit $D_T^j$ and consider $\left(U_T^j - D_T^j\right)$ to be the relevant capital account value. In our framework, this is irrelevant since we clarify whether $D_T^j$ is included or excluded.

The tax basis of a partner *inclusive* of the tail deposit $D_T^j$ is simply:

$$K_T^j = U_T^j - \boldsymbol{\Pi}_{M1L6,T}^{j}$$

The difference between the capital account value and the tax basis is simply the cumulative *change in unrealized capital gain* allocation since inception, which is simply the cumulative unrealized capital gain since inception, $\boldsymbol{\Pi}_{M1L6,T}^{j}$. This can be rewritten as:

$$\boldsymbol{\Pi}_{M1L6,T}^{j} = U_T^j - K_T^j$$

The tax basis of a partner *excluding* the tail deposit $D_T^j$ at tail time point $T$ is simply:

$$\left(K_T^j - D_T^j\right) = \left(U_T^j - D_T^j\right) - \boldsymbol{\Pi}_{M1L6,T}^{j}$$

The withdrawing partner is required to report a capital gain of $U_T^j - K_T^j = \boldsymbol{\Pi}_{M1L6,T}^{j}$ on the individual tax return corresponding to time point $T$. The deposit $D_T^j$ at time point $T$ would be a negative number representing a withdrawal equal to $-U_T^j$, so that the economic capital account value in the partnership becomes zero. The capital gain reporting entry on the individual tax return would look like this:

*Security description:* Entire disposition of partnership interest in XYZ
   partnership

*Sales proceeds:* $U_T^j$

*Cost basis:* $K_T^j$

*Capital gain:* $U_T^j - K_T^j = \mathit{\Pi}_{M1L6,T}^j$

The capital gain could be positive (a gain) or negative (a loss). For
example, a hedge fund may be hanging on to unrealized losses due to
securities having deteriorated in value in the hope of recovery. The redemption amount $U_T^j$ is less than the tax basis $K_T^j$, resulting in recognition of a
capital loss on the partner's individual tax return.

## Accountants' Terminology

The U.S. accounting profession and the IRS commonly refer to the partner's
economic liquidation value (after all fees) $U_T^j$ as a partner's "book capital
account value." The tax basis of the partner $K_T^j$ in our definition, consistent
with the definition of the IRS, is called by some accountants the "tax capital
account value." The cumulative unrealized capital gains $\mathit{\Pi}_{M1L6,T}^j$ since inception, which equals $U_T^j - K_T^j$ under our terminology, is called by some
accountants the "memorandum capital account value"[4] and is presented as
a balancing entry to reconcile a partner's book capital account value with
tax capital account value. Though each capital account is considered as
distinct and separate, superscripted as *i* in our terminology, we are aggregating the numbers corresponding to multiple capital accounts owned by
the same investor, because this is what is expected to be reported to the
IRS on the U.S. partnership tax return. When a partner entirely redeems its
capital accounts and partnership interest, the redeeming partner is required
to report to the IRS the redemption amount (which equals the book capital
value) *minus* the tax basis or tax capital value as a capital gain on its
individual tax return. The redemption amount is reported as sales proceeds
and the tax basis is reported as the cost basis on the redeeming partner's
individual tax return.

## Tax Allocations of Realized and Unrealized Income to Partners

Allocation of realized capital gain is a nonissue for hedge funds and investment partnerships that are domiciled in tax-exempt offshore locations.

---

[4]Chris Bellamy, "Tax Allocations for Securities Partnerships," *The Tax Adviser,*
August 1, 2003, pp. 472–476. This article is also online at www.aicpa.org/pubs/
taxadv/online/aug2003/clinic7.htm.

Partners' capital accounts at time point $T$ are redeemed for economic value $U_T^j$. Even though securities may have to be sold to generate cash for the redemption, the offshore fund (in a tax-exempt regime) is not required to make any distinction of realized vs. unrealized gains allocated to partners.

However, in the case of a U.S. partnership, the allocation of realized capital gains is a thorny issue. If this is not well understood or addressed up front, there could be enormous drainage of management attention away from the primary objective of generating superior returns.

It may appear that partnership tax allocation methodologies are inherently complex. However, their complexity would be manageable and greatly reduced if not for their vital need to perform the functions of both tracking economic profit sharing to partners and making associated tax allocations to the limited partners and the general partner. Despite many of the formulas provided here for the implementation of tax allocations seeming to be grotesque, unseemly, and unwieldy, they are extensions and developments that build upon our methodology and notation derived earlier for calculating performance fees and profit sharing of the general partner. We present methodologies and approaches to derive tax allocations to partners driven by the economic allocation procedures we have already identified and established. We are primarily focused on providing these methodologies for a U.S. hedge fund, which is required to report both aggregate items of realized and unrealized components income for the hedge fund as a whole, and a breakdown by each individual partner. This tax reporting triggers an obligation to the U.S. partners to properly account for distributive items of taxable components of income from the partnership and pay U.S. taxes accordingly.

There are two methodologies that have been adopted by U.S. accountants over the past few decades. The first is called the method of layering. The second is called the method of aggregation. The latter is further implemented in the form of two distinct (though arbitrary) schemes known as "full netting" or simply aggregation and "partial netting." We describe these methodologies in sufficient detail so as to remove any ambiguity on how U.S. partnership tax allocations should be implemented. We have noted several times that the IRS provides only broad verbal guidelines on how tax allocations should be implemented in Section 704(b) of the Internal Revenue Code. Restated in simpler language, the IRS expects tax allocations to partners to follow economic allocations. Upon examination, if the IRS determines that some tax allocation scheme has a "substantial economic effect," it is empowered to dismiss such a scheme. In other words, if the tax allocation scheme egregiously assigns taxable items with tax preference (i.e., lower tax payments) to partners that do not correspond to economic allocations made to them, the IRS might intervene and force the general partner to implement a scheme to meet the requirements of Section 704(b).

Although disputes between U.S. partnerships and the IRS on the matter of tax allocations to U.S. partners have almost never claimed any media headlines, hedge fund organizers, general partners, and the accounting profession are wary of implementing tax allocation schemes that are obviously egregious. Instead, a separate market of sophisticated trades and entity structures are created in an entirely different marketplace: that of tax shelters created by U.S accountants, accounting firms, and tax attorneys expert at pushing the envelope of ambiguity in the Internal Revenue Code for the benefit of participating taxable U.S. investors. Hedge funds are not in the marketplace as tax shelter structures and do not want to be censured by the IRS for appearing to operate such structures. Though hedge funds and their partners are indeed concerned about the tax efficiency of their investment strategies, their focus is on the economic nature of the trades and investment strategies, rather than complex structuring that is solely targeted at reducing taxes for investors.

## The Tax Allocation Method of Layering

No discussion on tax allocations is complete without addressing and understanding the tax allocation method of layering, over which there is much debate and little clarity on what exactly it represents and how exactly it is implemented. Our objective is to cut through this confusion and provide an unequivocal and simple explanation. Many U.S. accountants are committed to this method, believing it to be the only sound method of making tax allocations to partners that are entirely consistent with their economic allocations, and hence guaranteed to comply with Section 704(b) of the Internal Revenue Code. Some accountants seem to recommend this method because it is also time intensive, requiring customized or dedicated software, thus leading to higher billing and a lock on their hedge fund clients, who would face high switching costs if they were to switch to other independent accountants, or examination by the IRS if they were to make errors during such a transition or were to change their tax allocation methodology from layering to aggregation (full or partial netting, described later), which might require filing Form 3115, Application for Change in Accounting Method, with the IRS.

Yet the method of layering has obvious merits. The central idea in this methodology, despite its complexity, is that for every subperiod where economic allocations are made to partners according to their partnership percentages, their taxable and nontaxable components are also allocated according to the *same partnership percentages during the same subperiod.*

The implementation of this idea is straightforward for allocating the taxable income components of accrued interest, accrued dividends, management fixed fees, investment expenses, foreign taxes paid, and so on. Just as the economic gains made by a partnership during the subperiod are allocated to partners according to their partnership percentages for the subperiod (that were established at the opening of the subperiod and remained in force through the closing of the same subperiod), these taxable components of partnership income, with the exception of realized capital gains, are made to partners according to the same partnership percentages for the subperiod.

This appears simple. The exception arises in applying the principle of tax allocations following economic allocations for realized capital gains, which are usually the prime source of profits and the primary economic engine of both hedge funds and venture funds. Realized capital gains that occur during a subperiod relate to a history of prior investing and the entry/exit of partners from the hedge fund based on valuing unrealized capital gains at mark-to-market prices. Thus, if we were to allocate the realized gains that occurred in, say, the month of June to partners according to their percentage ownership in the month of June, we would ignore the previous history of ownership and economic participation in the specific trades that produced realized capital gains in June.

In order to strike a resonance with Section 704(b) of the Internal Revenue Code, accountants have followed the guidelines and examples provided in Title 26 of the U.S. Code of Federal Regulations (26 C.F.R.), which govern the IRS. While the Internal Revenue Code only provides broad language for tax allocation, 26 C.F.R in Section 1.704-1 elaborates upon what is considered to be consistent with Section 704(b) of the Internal Revenue Code and provides 30 specific numerical hypothetical examples of how tax allocations of realized capital gains to partners should be made. Each of the 30 examples has 4 to 10 subexamples, where a variation to the base facts and data is made to the base example. These 26 C.F.R examples have led accountants to formulate procedures and algorithms over the years for allocation of realized capital gains to partners.

The method of layering is the implementation of 26 C.F.R 1.704-1(b) (5), Example 13, with five variations 13(i) to 13(v), based on partners who invest in marketable securities. Even though the word "layering" is not explicitly used anywhere, accountants recognize this as a simple instance of what they commonly considered to be layering. Example 13(iv) is the clear-cut case, where the sole traded security owned by the partnership has risen to an interim high. At that time, one partner sells part of his or her interest in the partnership to a new entrant partner without the underlying securities being sold in the partnership's portfolio. Subsequently, the security held by the partnership falls in value, and the underlying securities are sold. This is a three time point (two-period) example, with no realized gains during the first period due to no securities sales, and realized gains occurring in the second period. The tax allocations are made to partners at the end of the second period based on their economic participation over two periods, and not merely based on the partnership percentages at the time of the realized gain in the second period.

Let us try to paraphrase this example of layering in clear and concise language, instead of the elaborate example with situational twists provided in the Treasury Regulations. A hedge fund has successive time periods, and partners are allowed to exit or enter partially or fully at every interregnum time point. The partnership ownership percentages are frozen during a period, and changes are allowed only at the interregnum time point. Economic profits for a period are calculated irrespective of whether they are realized or unrealized and allocated to partners according to their partnership percentages. Tax allocations are made to partners for realized income items such as accrued interest and dividends according to their partnership percentages during the period. However, realized capital gains are allocated to partners according to a methodology that reflects their participation across multiple periods. The implicit algorithm indicated by the example in the Treasury Regulations calls for calculating unrealized gains for every security tax lot contained in the partnership portfolio and allocating them to partners according to their varying partnership percentages in every distinct. When a security tax lot is sold in some subsequent period, all of the past unrealized gains by partners relating to this tax lot are summed up and allocated as realized gains to each partner. Under this allocation method, if there is volatility in the underlying security mark-to-market prices, there could be situations where some partners might be allocated capital losses even though a particular tax lot was sold for an overall realized gain.

Since neither the Internal Revenue Code nor the Treasury Regulations say anything about interpreting the nature of the gain, and the example provided in the Treasury Regulations indicates a situation where all securities are sold, there are two ambiguities that arise:

**Layering Ambiguity 1.** How should the conversion of unrealized gains into realized gains (that is, triggered by the entire disposition of a particular securities tax lot) be further broken down into long-term gains and short-term gains for the partner and the fund as a whole? Consider a situation where a security was held for slightly more than one year. The overall gain it produced upon disposition is reported as a long-term gain in Schedule D of tax return of the U.S. partnership. However, some partners who are allocated unrealized gains corresponding to this tax lot were in the partnership for less than one year. The presenting ambiguity is: Should the unrealized gains that are being converted into realized gains for the partner who belonged to the partnership for less than a year be allocated as short-term capital gains to that partner? In such a situation, long-term gains reported for the partnership would not add up to the long-term gain allocations made to partners. To this date, the Treasury Regulations do not shed any light, and nobody has yet sought a private letter ruling from the IRS to clarify this matter. Indeed, if such a procedure is adopted, to report long-term and short-term nature of gain according to the tenure of partners in the partnership, the tax return of the aggregate partnership may have to provide an additional explanation to reconcile the sum total of long-term and short-term capital gain allocations across partners in Schedule K-1, versus short-term and long-term gains reported for the partnership in Schedule K. The IRS expects that the sum total of taxable items of income at the level of the partnership in Schedule K should equal the sum across partners of the same taxable items of income in Schedule K-1.

**Layering Ambiguity 2.** What if a particular securities tax lot is not sold by the partnership and is held after at least one partner, who previously shared an economic interest in it, redeems the capital account for its economic value, financed by reducing cash held in the partnership? Even though such a partner has no economic interest and hence no economic allocations upon redemption, a final K-1 to such a partner can be issued only after all tax lots containing historical economic participation and consequent allocations of capital gains are sold. The IRS may be concerned that tax allocations are being made to a partner with zero economic interest, hence likely triggering an examination of the partnership's tax allocation methodology. To prevent this, an explanatory note or schedule may be provided with details of such tax allocations. We consider this to be a serious flaw, almost a fatal flaw, with the layering methodology for several reasons. Departing partners expect to receive a final K-1 so that they may close their own tax records relating to their participation in the fund. Hedge fund managers may act to trade tax lots for accounting and administrative convenience, rather than for economic reasons. The IRS is nagged by observing that a departed partner is receiving tax allocations of capital gains.

# Tax Allocation of Interest

Accrued interest income, which measures the time value of money, is readily represented as an income flow that is directly proportional to capital invested in fixed-income instruments. The (accrued) interest income recorded for the partnership as a whole for the subperiod $[t - 1, t]$ is $\pi_{5,t}$. It is appropriate to allocate the aggregate interest income that is earned by the hedge fund during the period $[t - 1, t]$ according to ownership fractions $\alpha_{t-1}^i$ that were recorded for each capital account at time point $t - 1$.

If there were no performance fees applicable at time point $t = 12$, the interest income allocated to each capital account indexed by $i$ at time points $t = 1\ldots12$ is simply $\alpha_{t-1}^i \pi_{5,t}$. The tax allocation of interest income to a capital account is determined only by their percentage economic ownership during the time period $[t - 1, t]$ represented by $\alpha_{t-1}^i$. The history of percentage economic ownership in previous time periods is not relevant in calculation of the tax allocation for a particular time period.

We have to provide for the generalized case where a performance fee is applied ex-post at time point $t = 12$, for which each capital account was bifurcated, so that the fraction $(1 - \beta^i)$ of the capital account value was retained for the limited partner for the subsequent year, and the fraction $\beta^i$ of its value was assigned to the general partner towards performance fee. This process of bifurcation of every capital account to pay for the performance fees was described earlier.

Recall that $\beta^i = \dfrac{P_{12}^i}{V_{12}^i}$ is the performance fee per unit of capital account value before performance fees. It is the economic value sharing fraction applying to the capital account value. We scale $\beta^i$ by $\dfrac{V_{12}^i}{V_{12}^i - V_0^i}$ to obtain a profit sharing fraction that applies on economic profits to be shared according to the limited partnership agreement, as $\hat{\beta}^i = \beta^i \, \dfrac{V_{12}^i}{V_{12}^i - V_0^i} = \dfrac{P_{12}^i}{V_{12}^i} \dfrac{V_{12}^i}{V_{12}^i - V_0^i} = \dfrac{P_{12}^i}{V_{12}^i - V_0^i}$. Thus, $\hat{\beta}^i = \dfrac{P_{12}^i}{V_{12}^i - V_0^i}$ is the performance fee per unit of economic profit. Note that the denominator in this expression for $\hat{\beta}^i$ is the economic profit calculated without regard to the high watermark and the hurdle rate.

This profit sharing fraction $\hat{\beta}^i$ applies to all subitems of economic income or profit, and also extends itself naturally to calculate the sharing of all subitems of tax allocations (other than capital gains). The year-end allocation of pass-through taxable interest income (after performance fees) for every *unique limited partner* $j = 2\ldots M$ is:

$$\Pi_5^j = \sum_{i \in J, t=1}^{12} \hat{\beta}^i \alpha_{t-1}^i \pi_{5,t}$$

The notation $i \in J$ needs clarification. The general partner is denoted by $j = 1$. There are $j = 2\ldots M$ unique limited partners. Each unique limited partner is indexed by $j$ and owns the subset $\{J\}$ of capital accounts. The capital accounts are indexed by $i = 1\ldots N$, and $M$ is no bigger than $N$. The purpose of this notation is to aggregate tax allocations of distinct partners from their multiple capital accounts, if any.

The general partner $j = 1$ has two sources of interest income. The first source is attributed to its own investment partnership share $\alpha_{t-1}^1$ at time points $t = 1\ldots12$. The second is the interest income attributed to a performance fee that is paid by bifurcating each limited partner's capital account to transfer the proportion $\beta^i$ of its value to the general partner. Thus, the year-end allocation of pass-through taxable interest income to the general partner is:

$$\Pi_5^1 = \sum_{t=1}^{12} \alpha_{t-1}^1 \pi_{5,t} + \sum_{j=2}^{M} \sum_{i \in J, t=1}^{12} \hat{\beta}^i \alpha_{t-1}^i \pi_{5,t}$$

The above expression has an interesting interpretation. The full-year allocation of interest income to the general partner is a sum of the interest income attributable to its own partnership ownership percentage, plus the interest income attributable to the bifurcated capital accounts of limited partners diverted to the general partner as performance fees at time point $t = 12$.

Note that $\Pi_5^1 + \sum_{j=2}^{M} \Pi_5^j = \Pi_5$. This ensures that $\Pi_5$, which is reported as interest income for the partnership as a whole in its Schedule K, is the sum total of the interest income allocated to the general partner and limited partners in Schedule K-1.

It is important to verify that the above identity indeed holds. This type of breakdown of aggregate partnership income components into pass-through allocations to limited partners has to be repeated for all line items on Schedule K. This verification is provided here.

$$
\begin{aligned}
\Pi_5^1 + \sum_{j=2}^{M} \Pi_5^j &= \left\{ \sum_{t=1}^{12} \alpha_{t-1}^1 \pi_{5,t} + \sum_{j=2}^{M} \sum_{i \in J, t=1}^{12} \hat{\beta}^i \alpha_{t-1}^i \pi_{5,t} \right\} \\
&\quad + \left\{ \sum_{j=2}^{M} \sum_{i \in J, t=1}^{12} \left(1 - \hat{\beta}^i\right) \alpha_{t-1}^i \pi_{5,t} \right\} \\
&= \sum_{t=1}^{12} \alpha_{t-1}^1 \pi_{5,t} + \sum_{j=2}^{M} \sum_{i \in J, t=1}^{12} \alpha_{t-1}^i \pi_{5,t} \\
&= \sum_{t=1}^{12} \pi_{5,t} \left[ \alpha_{t-1}^1 + \sum_{j=2}^{M} \sum_{i \in J, t=1}^{12} \alpha_{t-1}^i \right] \\
&= \sum_{t=1}^{12} \pi_{5,t} \\
&= \Pi_5
\end{aligned}
$$

This is because by the definition of partnership fractions,

$$\left[ \alpha_{t-1}^1 + \sum_{j=2}^{M} \sum_{i \in J, t=1}^{12} \alpha_{t-1}^i \right] = 1$$

That is, the sum total of all partnership fractions across all capital accounts at the same time point must add up to 1.

# Tax-Exempt Interest Income, Line 18a

Interest income arising from investment by the hedge fund in municipal bonds is exempt from U.S. taxation to the pass-through partners. The partnership is required to report this on line 18a. The breakdown of tax-exempt interest income is calculated exactly as for taxable interest income (line 5). To obtain a formula for allocation of the aggregate tax-exempt interest income to unique individual partners, we simply replace the subscript 5 in the formulas for taxable interest income with the subscript 18a.

## Similar Calculation for Tax Allocation of Dividends, Investment Expense, Foreign Tax Paid

The calculation for tax allocations under the layering methodology for accrued dividends is identical. We replace the subscript 5 representing accrued interest (line 5) with subscript 6a representing accrued dividends (line 6a). Similarly, the component of accrued dividends that are the tax preference item (inviting a lower tax rate of 15 percent) is tracked based on replacing the subscript as 6b (line 6b, qualified dividends). Similarly, by replacing the appropriate subscript, we get the tax allocations to partners for all other categories of taxable income and expense. Subscript 16d would be for foreign gross dividends included in total ordinary dividends (subscript 6a). The items 6b and 16d are subcomponents of 6a. Subscript 13b would be for investment interest expense. Subscript 16 would be for foreign taxes paid.

## Tax Allocation of Fixed Fees Paid by Limited Partners

The only exception to the generalized tax allocation formula for interest income, dividends, interest expense, and foreign taxes under the layering methodology does not apply to subscript 13d, which is the investment expense deduction to limited partners' fixed fees. Fixed fees are paid only by the limited partners and not by the general partner. Further, as we had described earlier, each capital account may have a distinct and different fixed fee rate that is negotiated privately and recorded in limited partners' agreement of admission to the partnership. Performance allocations to the general partner are made after fixed fees are paid by limited partners. So the fixed fees paid by limited partners are not bifurcated and reallocated back to the general partner, as is the case with interest income, dividends, interest expense, and foreign taxes. We had previously denoted the fixed fee for every capital account $i$ as $F_t^i = f^i\left[\alpha_{t-1}^i W_t\right]$. Thus, fixed fees also share the property of layering tax allocations for dividends and interest, so that they are driven by the current period partnership ownership percentages and do not depend on their history. However, there is no bifurcation and reassignment of a portion of the fixed fees from limited partners to the general partner at the calendar year at anniversary when performance fees are calculated. Thus, for each capital account, under subscript 13d, we have for each limited partner $j$:

$$\Pi_{13d}^{j} = \sum_{i \in J, t=1}^{12} F_t^i = \sum_{i \in J, t=1}^{12} f^i \left[ \alpha_{t-1}^i W_t \right]$$

$\Pi_{13d}^{j} = 0$ for the general partner $j = 1$ since the general partner's fixed fee rate $f^1 = 0$.

## Tax Allocation of Guaranteed Payments (of Fixed Fees) to the General Partner

Subscript 4, guaranteed payments, applies only to the general partner. It is the sum of all fixed fees paid by the capital accounts of limited partners to the general partner. Thus, $\Pi_4^1 = \sum_{j=2}^{M} \Pi_{13d}^j$.

$\Pi_4^j = 0$ for all limited partners $j = 2 \ldots M$, since they do not receive any fixed fees or compensation from the partnership.

For the partnership as a whole, guaranteed payments are $\Pi_4 = \Pi_4^1$ and the identity $\Pi_4^1 = \sum_{j=2}^{M} \Pi_{13d}^j$ must hold. At the level of the partnership, the sum total of the fixed fee expenses paid by the limited partners is reported as ordinary income to the general partner as guaranteed payment. The general partner subsequently reports the amount $\Pi_4^1$ as gross income on its own entity tax return.

## Reporting Subcomponents of Interest Income and Dividends

Federal interest income from investment in U.S. Treasury bonds by the partnership is exempt from state interest income taxation to the pass-through partners. Even though there is no specific line item in the U.S. partnership tax return to report the subcomponent of federal interest income, the partnership could report it in a separate note attached to its tax return. We could create a new subcomponent item, which could be labeled as component 5g, to be understood as a subset of component 5. Thus, $\Pi_{5g}^1$ and $\Pi_{5g}^j$ are reported, such that $\Pi_{5g}^1 + \sum_{j=2}^{M} \Pi_{5g}^j = \Pi_{5g}$ with the understanding that $\Pi_{5g}$ is already contained in $\Pi_5$.

"Qualified dividends" are corporate ordinary dividends received on securities that are held by the partnership for at least 60 days. This subcomponent of dividend income is taxed at a lower rate of 15 percent to its partners. Line 6b on Schedule K is provided for reporting this item $\Pi_{6b}$. The breakdown of $\Pi_{6b}$ by partners $\Pi_{6b}^j$ is obtained by applying the same general formula above, with subscript $k = 6b$. It is to be understood that $\Pi_{6b}$ is a subset already contained in $\Pi_{6b}$.

# Tax Consequences of Shorting

Since many hedge funds distinguish themselves from mutual funds primarily through deploying investment strategies that involve short sales in traded equities and fixed-income securities, we describe the tax consequences to such short positions in a U.S. hedge fund. An equity short position is based on borrowing shares of a traded equity security, selling that security instantly at the current market price, holding onto the liability of returning the borrowed shares, and compensating the securities lender for dividends. The short position is closed by purchasing the same number of shares of the same security in the open market, and delivering them back to the securities lender.

The proceeds of short sale are not made available to the short seller (the hedge fund in this case), but instead held as interest-bearing escrow, to be paid to the short seller only when the liability of returning the borrowed shares is fulfilled. The rate of interest paid on the proceeds of short sale held in escrow, called "short credit," is usually lower than the prevailing market interest rate, reflecting a fee or profit to the securities lender and a mirroring expense to the short seller. The economic gain in a short sale transaction from the perspective of the short seller is the sales proceeds, plus interest received as "short credit," minus dividends claimed by the securities lender, minus the cost of repurchase in the shares to return to the securities lender. The economic cost of shorting to the short seller and mirroring the economic profit to the securities lender is the difference between the market interest rate and the "short credit" rate applied on the proceeds of short sale held in escrow.

A fixed-income short position follows the same exact steps as equity short selling. The short seller is obliged to meet claims of the fixed-income securities lender of all coupon payments until such time as the short position is closed.

## Short Positions: Tax Treatment of Equity Dividends or Bond Coupons Claimed as Interest Expense

Hedge funds that engage in short sales of securities are required to make payments to the securities lender in lieu of equity dividends and bond coupons, to compensate for such dividends and coupons that the securities lender would have otherwise received. These amounts that are claimed from the short seller by its brokerage firm exactly mirror the positive dividend that is due to the securities lender. The IRS guidelines on short sales allow such payments of dividends claimed to be counted as part of capital gain. However, if a particular short position is held for more than 45 days, the short seller may elect to treat such payments as if they were interest expense incurred by the partnership.

Thus, a hedge fund that engages in short sales would track its dividends claimed and break it down into two components: The first corresponding short positions held for 45 days or less is absorbed into the capital gain of the respective securities, and the second corresponding to short positions held for more than 45 days is considered to be an interest expense.

When calculating and reporting that total interest expense (as a positive number), $\Pi_{13b}$ is the interest paid by the hedge fund on borrowings and debt *plus* the dividends and coupons claimed on short positions held for more than 45 days. Likewise, when calculating the net short-term capital gain $\Pi_{6b}$, the negative number representing expense of dividends and coupons claimed on short positions held for 45 days or less is combined with the gain/loss resulting from change in the security price. This step is important and holds great value for taxable U.S. partners in a U.S. hedge fund. Pass-through interest expense may be considered a tax preferred item, since the deduction of interest expense from any form of investment income is permitted. In contrast, when such dividends and coupons claimed are applied as an expense to capital gains, they can only be offset by a positive capital gain and not other forms of investment income. In the case of short positions on fixed-income securities held for more than 45 days, the advantage can be significant, because the entire coupon income that is paid to the securities lender becomes an interest expense, much like borrowing.

There appears to be no direct ruling by the IRS that pass-through allocations to partners of interest expense attributable to shorting in a U.S. hedge fund is deemed to be a form of borrowing for U.S. tax-exempt partners. However, there is a risk that shorting activity of a U.S. hedge fund could lead to UBTI taxes imposed on U.S. tax-exempt partners. This makes it critical for hedge funds that have significant U.S. tax-exempt partners to establish an offshore UBTI "blocker" fund, as feeder or master as appropriate.

## Distributions from Partnerships Owned

A hedge fund may invest some part of its assets into another hedge fund partnership. A feeder fund would invest all of its assets into a master hedge fund. A foreign hedge fund in a tax-exempt regime may account for ownership of partnership interests in any manner consistent with its overall accounting policy. A U.S. hedge fund ends up having to track its tax basis in partnerships owned, exactly according to the formulas established earlier that define tax basis for a partner in a U.S. partnership. The tax basis of each partnership investment is the original investment amount, plus additional investment amounts, plus all tax allocations received, less all distributions received. The motivation for tracking the tax basis is to ensure that the pass-through partners of the hedge fund do not pay more capital gains tax than is actually due upon redemption or liquidation of the partnership holdings. What is being suggested here is that a U.S. partnership that in turn invests in other partnerships should set up tracking of the tax basis of its investments (in other partnerships), so that its pass-through partners do not end up paying more capital gains tax than is necessary when these investments (in other partnerships) are liquidated.

# CHAPTER 6

# Tax Allocations of Realized Gains by Layering

## Tax Allocation of Unrealized and Realized Capital Gains Using the Method of Layering

The tax allocation of unrealized and realized capital gains to partners, which are the three items $\Pi^j_{M1L6,T}$ (unrealized gains), realized short-term gains $\Pi^j_{8,T}$, and realized long-term gains $\Pi^j_{9a,T}$, is reviewed in this chapter and further elaborated in the next chapter.

The one-period procedure for calculation of tax allocations of dividends, interest, and foreign taxes paid is not applicable to the following components of taxable income:

Subscript 8: net short-term capital gain
Subscript 9a: net long-term capital gain

The method of layering is intricately linked to simultaneously tracking and calculating the residual subcomponent of income, which is:

Subscript M1L6, the change or increase in unrealized gain

This method of layering is considered to be a gold standard from the perspective of meeting the requirements of Section 704(b)(2) of the U.S. Internal Revenue Code. It ensures that an allegation by the IRS of tax allocations having a "substantial economic effect" is unlikely, by adopting steps consistent with example 13(iv) of the related Treasury Regulations 26 C.F.R 1.704-1(b)(5). This is achieved by ensuring that at the time point of redemption $t = T$, $\Pi^j_{M1L6,T} = 0$ so that the capital account value $U^j_T$ is identical to the tax basis $K^j_T$. An accountant could safely declare that tax allocations exactly follow economic allocations at all points in time, until the time of redemption.

The redeeming capital partner would still have to show a zero capital gain entry on the individual tax return to record the entire disposition of the partnership interest as:

Sales proceeds: $U_T^j$

Cost basis: $K_T^j$, which happens to be identical to $U_T^j$

Capital gain: $U_T^j - K_T^j = \Pi_{M1L6,T}^j = 0$ under the method of layering, provided that $\Pi_{M1L6,T}^j$ does not contain economic value on account of a tax-exempt interest and thus solely represents unrealized capital gains. To keep matters simple, we have decided to suppress economic value arising from tax-exempt interest and depreciation by considering them to be zero, so that $\Pi_{M1L6,T}^j$ represents *only the cumulative change or increase in unrealized capital gains on securities*. We can generalize $\Pi_{M1L6,T}^j$ to track its nontaxable subcomponents: the change in unrealized gains on securities, tax-exempt interest income, and depreciation. Our analysis is focused on tax allocations of realized long-term and short-term capital gain and the associated tracking of the change in unrealized gains, which is why we dispel the distracting consideration of other nontaxable items.

This "capital gain" required to be reported by partners on their individual tax returns upon the entire disposition of their partnership interest is different from capital gain tax allocations to partners by the partnership at every year-end. Upon redemption at time point $t = T$, the taxable U.S. investor (superscripted as $j$) has to report capital gain on the personal return attributable to the entire disposition of the capital account (partnership interest) as the difference between the reported sales proceeds of redemption value and the cost basis of acquiring the partnership interest. The sales proceeds reported on the investor's capital gains schedule on the personal tax return is the economic value $U_T^j$ received in cash at time point $t = T$. The cost basis, or tax basis, is $K_T^j$. It is the sum of the initial investment $D_0^j$, plus all cumulative net deposits $D_T^j = \sum_{t=0,1,2,3,\ldots}^{T} D_t^j$ since inception, plus all cumulative tax allocations since inception, for investor $j$.

*The method of layering ensures that the terminal capital gain to be reported for the entire redemption of the partnership interest is zero, because the cost basis (or tax basis) exactly equals the economic value redeemed.* (We are assuming that other nontaxable items of income, that is, tax-exempt interest and depreciation, are zero. Even if they are nonzero, they are easily adjusted for by not counting the tax-exempt income under reported capital gain.)

*The method of layering works only when the investment partnership sells all tax lots of its securities that contain any unrealized capital gain allocation attributable to the redeeming capital account.* Ignoring this impractical constraint by assuming that it holds at the time when the capital account indexed by the subscript *j* is redeemed, let us examine what it involves and how it works. We will later provide an in-depth critique of this assumption and discuss what may be practically implemented.

Let us assume that a U.S. partnership admits partners at monthly time points $t = 0, 1, 2, 3, \ldots$. There are no redemptions until a point in time $t = T$, at which point the entire portfolio of securities owned by the partnership is sold, even if only one partner redeems his or her capital account.

A partnership engages in a giant database operation, which tracks the unrealized gains on every distinct "tax lot" of securities from that point in time when it was purchased until the point in time $t <= T$ when it is sold. (The same security purchased at two different times constitutes two distinct tax lots.) The change or increase in unrealized gains is computed until the eve of the sale of the tax lot, broken down by month. The sum total of the sequence of these incremental changes to unrealized gains in every subperiod must add up to the realized gain for a tax lot.

Each partner is allocated the change or increase unrealized gains for each tax lot according to his or her monthly partnership percentage ownership. When that security tax lot is sold, all of its sequence of unrealized gains become realized, so each partner's allocation of this sequence of unrealized gains is allocated in the form of realized gain to the partner. The time point for such conversion of cumulative unrealized gain allocations for a specific tax lot into realized gain allocation is the time point at which the tax lot was sold.

We recast this in algebra for a tax lot indexed by the additional subscript *m* to denote a particular tax lot. For simplicity, the presumed tax lot is to be purchased at $t = 0$ and sold at $t = T$.

On the eve of the sale of this tax lot at time point $t = T$, the cumulative unrealized gain (since inception of the tax lot) for this tax lot *m* is:

$$\Pi_{M1L6,T,m} = \sum_{t=1}^{T} \pi_{M1L6,t,m}$$

where $\pi_{M1L6,t,m}$ is the change or increase in unrealized gain on the tax lot *m* earned over the period $[t - 1, t]$.

For each partner capital account indexed by *j*, the ownership share fraction at time point $t - 1$ is denoted by $\alpha_{t-1}^{j}$ under the further simplifying assumption that each partner is only one capital account. (This is easily generalized to one partner having multiple capital accounts, and avoided because it would require the additional step of summation of capital accounts across distinct partners.)

The ownership share fractions at any point in time $(t - 1)$ have the property that:

$$\sum_{j}^{M} \alpha_{t-1}^{j} = 1$$

Each partner's allocation of the change or increase in unrealized gain corresponding to tax lot $m$ at time point $t$ is simply $\alpha_{t-1}^{j}\pi_{M1L6,t,m}$.

*This is the core foundation, the first step, of the layering methodology: that each partner is allocated the change or increase in unrealized gains in every subperiod according to the partner's economic ownership percentages of the partnership. This step does not yet involve tax allocations, which happen only after the tax lot is sold at some later date.*

Each partner's cumulative allocation of unrealized capital gain for tax lot $m$ at time point $T$ is its summation:

$$\sum\nolimits_{t=1}^{T}\alpha_{t-1}^{j}\pi_{M1L6,t,m}$$

Thus, cumulative unrealized gain for this tax lot $m$ (since its inception) on the eve of its sale at time point $T$ is:

$$\Pi_{M1L6,T,m} = \sum\nolimits_{t=1}^{T}\pi_{M1L6,t,m} = \sum\nolimits_{j=1}^{M}\sum\nolimits_{t=1}^{T}\alpha_{t-1}^{j}\pi_{M1L6,t,m}$$

When the security tax lot $m$ is sold at time point $t = T$, its cumulative unrealized gain becomes realized, so that for the partnership as a whole, the realized capital gain reported in Schedule K would be:

$$\Pi_{k,T,m} = \Pi_{M1L6,T,m}$$

where the subscript $k = 8$ if the holding period of the tax lot $m$ exceeds one year, that is, $T - 0$ exceeds one year (long-term capital gain, line 8 in Schedule K), or $k = 9a$ if the holding period of the tax lot $m$ is less than one year, that is, $T - 0$ is one year or less (short-term capital gain, line 9a in Schedule K).

After converting all of the cumulative unrealized gains, $\Pi_{M1L6,T,m}$ is reinitialized to zero.

Under the layering methodology, upon sale of the tax lot $m$, a partner's cumulative unrealized capital gain allocation for tax lot $m$ until the eve of sale becomes the realized capital gain allocation:

$$\Pi_{k,T,m}^{j} = \Pi_{M1L6,T,m}^{j} = \sum\nolimits_{t=1}^{T}\alpha_{t-1}^{j}\pi_{M1L6,t,m}$$

where the subscript $k$ and $T$ were described above. That subscript $k = 8$ if $T - 0$ exceeds one year, and $k = 9a$ if $T - 0$ is less than one year.

*This is the closure step, the second step, for calculating realized gains tax allocations based on the layering methodology: that all previous allocations of changes or increases in unrealized gains corresponding to a particular tax lot are transformed into tax allocation of realized gains upon sale of that tax lot.*

The realized capital gain summed up across partners for a given tax lot $m$ must add up to the realized capital gain for that tax lot in the partnership as a whole, thus:

$$\Pi_{k,T,m} = \sum_{j=1}^{M} \Pi_{8,T,m}^{j} = \sum_{j=1}^{M} \sum_{t=1}^{T} \alpha_{t-1}^{j} \pi_{M1L6,t,m}$$

where $k = 8$ if $T - 0 > 1$, and $k = 9a$ if $T - 0 < 1$.

At time point $T$, the long-term capital gain and short-term capital gain are separately summed up across respective tax lots to arrive at the aggregate long-term/short-term capital gain numbers reported in each partner's Schedule K-1. Thus,

$$\Pi_{8,T}^{j} = \sum_{m \in LT} \Pi_{8,T,m}^{j}$$

where tax lots m $\in$ $LT$ belong to the set of tax lots denoted by $LT$ that produce long-term capital gain, and

$$\Pi_{9a,T}^{j} = \sum_{m \in ST} \Pi_{9a,T,m}^{j}$$

where tax lots m $\in$ $ST$ belong to the set of tax lots denoted by $ST$ that produce short-term capital gain,

The above algebraic representation is easily generalized for tax lots purchased at different points in time and sold at different points in time, provided all tax lots are sold on or before time point $t = T$.

Since all tax lots have been sold at $t = T$, and all of their unrealized gain until the eve of its sale have been converted to realized gain, there is no more unrealized gain remaining, so $\Pi_{M1L6,T,m}^{j}$ is reset to zero and its aggregation across all tax lots $\Pi_{M1L6,T}^{j} = \sum_{m \in LT,ST} \Pi_{M1L6,T,m}^{j}$ is also reset to zero.

As we can see, there is no residual unrealized gain upon sale of all tax lots at time point $T - t$, that is, after transfer of cumulative unrealized gains on the eve of sale to realized gains, $\Pi_{M1L6,T,m} = 0$ for the partnership as a whole reported on Schedule K, and $\Pi_{M1L6,T,m}^{j} = 0$ for each individual partner reported on Schedule K-1.

This looks neat: Tax allocations follow economic allocations, and there are no hanging residual capital gains or losses to be separately recorded on their individual tax returns by partners.

Many observers note that there can be situations where $\Pi_{8,T}$ (or $\Pi_{9a,T}$) could be zero or close to zero, but each partner's $\Pi_{T}^{j}$ could vary widely, driven by market price volatility of the underlying securities held in the partnership and different points of entry by different partners. It is possible to have $\Pi_{T}^{j}$ be hugely positive for some partners and hugely negative for other partners, with all of their $\Pi_{T}^{j}$ summing up to nearly zero $\Pi_{8,T}$. If the IRS becomes concerned that such variation (where positive and negative partner allocations add up to nearly zero) might be due to wayward tax allocations bearing a "substantial economic effect," the partnership would have to provide justification for its calculation.

A major flaw, which causes this neat method of layering to nearly collapse, is that every tax lot that contains the slightest allocation of unrealized capital gain on the eve of redemption or withdrawal by a partner has to be sold. This is because a partnership ideally would not want to attribute realized capital gains to a partner or capital account that has departed. Further, even if a partnership were to sell all securities when one partner withdraws, if any of those securities bearing cumulative unrealized losses at the time of sale are repurchased within 30 days, that would be considered a wash sale according to IRS regulations and the realized gain would not be recognized. Should the partnership intend to hold the same loss-making securities for the benefit of the remaining partners, a 30-day wait is required.

The complexity in implementation of this methodology of layering are the accompanying drain on management time in ensuring that the calculations are error free, combined with these flaws, has resulted in an exodus from its widespread adoption. In spite of these factors, there are many "die-hard" fund administrators, accountants, and fund manager CFOs who implement their investment partnership accounting and operations on complex software systems based on the layering methodology.

Unless the IRS comes up with strict rules mandating the implementation of the layering methodology, a U.S. investment partnership would greatly benefit from the simplicity and the practicality of the alternate methodology of "aggregation" or "netting," described in the next chapter.[1]

## Ignoring Ambiguity #1 with Layering

A good database structure and design can track whether partners shared changes to unrealized gains in a tax lot for less than one year until the tax lot was sold, even though the tax lot was sold after more than one year. In other words, after implementing closure or the completion step for tax allocations according to the layering methodology, should the long-term gains for a specific tax lot at the level of the partnership be allocated to partners as short-term gains if they participated in that tax lot for less than one year? If we implement this, the long-term gains at the partnership level would not add up to the long-term gains across partners. An explanatory schedule would have to be filed along with the tax return of the partnership reconciling why this happened. What we are economically considering is whether a strict interpretation of Section 704(b) of the Internal Revenue Code requires such treatment. The answer lies in interpreting whether the

---

[1]Bellamy, *op. cit.*, provides a simple numerical example of tax allocations of capital gains under layering, partial aggregation, and full aggregation approaches. See note 4 in Chapter 5.

involuntary reduction in partnership percentages of existing partners triggered by the entry of a new partner constitutes a sale of economic interest by existing partners on the new partner's entry date, and a mirroring purchase of economic interest by the new partner only on the entry date. A strict interpretation likely would consider the time duration of economic participation in a partnership to be the relevant driver for declaring tax allocations to be classified as long-term or short-term in nature.

Until the IRS provides pinpointed clarification on this matter, hedge funds that implement the layering methodology generally ignore this finer point of distinction and follow the practice of allocating realized long-term gains from a tax lot to partners as tax allocation of long-term gains to all partners, notwithstanding that some partners may not have participated economically in that tax lot for more than one year. Thus, the new limited partner joining a hedge fund mid-year, having only a part-year of economic participation in the partnership, may be assigned long-term capital gains attributable to its part-year participation in a tax lot that was held for more than a year by the partnership and that produced long-term gains.

At some later time, if the IRS does issue clarification on this matter, it would be simple to modify the database algorithms accordingly to implement the required procedure.

## Work-Around to Fix Ambiguity #2, the Fatal Flaw with Layering

As we have described earlier, the methodology of layering works only when all tax lots containing even the slightest ownership by a departing partner are sold and fully liquidated. It may not be practical to do so, since a partnership has common objectives across all partners, and thus each and every tax lot would contain a representation of their participation and interest.

We provide a work-around to make the layering work. This work-around "fix" requires clear communication to partners that, in order to prevent loss of integrity and consistency in making tax allocations, a partner may be permitted to withdraw the economic value of its interest and draw its capital account to zero (or practically zero, like $0.01), but the partner would not be permitted to exit from the partnership, and a Final K-1 would not be issued to the partner until each and every unsold tax lot that bears some part of its past economic interest in that tax lot is entirely liquidated. In the year of liquidation of such tax lots, the partner would get additional tax allocations. It may appear that such partners would have to pay additional tax if such tax allocations are positive. However, the tax liability from new tax allocations of capital gains is offset by the increase in the tax basis of the partnership interest, which reduces the capital gain (or produces a capital loss) that the partner reports on the individual tax return relating to the entire disposition of interest in the partnership.

The departing partner makes its own choice of various alternatives to report capital gain on account of the entire disposition of the partnership interest. One simple method would be to postpone its reporting until the Final K-1 is issued by the partnership after all tax lots bearing their unrealized gain allocations are fully sold. Though this may appear to be a case of tax deferral and postponement being implemented by a partner, the IRS would be satisfied upon examination that the partner is reporting all tax allocations on the tax returns, and even though the economic capital account balance is drawn down to nearly zero, the partnership still has future tax allocations to be made pending the sale of tax lots containing their economic participation. The IRS would be appeased that even if there seems to be a postponement of tax on withdrawal of economic interest, the postponement is due to unsold tax lots bearing the economic participation of the partner and still held in the form of unrealized gains.

One other simple method for a departing partner would be to recognize a capital gain on the individual tax return when the capital account is redeemed. The Final K-1 signifying entire dissociation with the partnership is not yet on hand, due to unsold tax lots bearing their past economic participation. Subsequently, such tax lots are sold and a tax allocation is made to the departed partner along with a Final K-1. The departed partner presents two entries on the individual tax return under capital gains. One entry is the capital gains corresponding to tax allocation received from the partnership. It is exactly offset by one other entry, which is the mirror image with opposite sign corresponding to reduced capital gain due to increasing cost basis from the tax allocation. To facilitate the processing of the individual tax return by the IRS, an explanatory note may be provided, stating that a capital gain was recognized upon redemption of partnership interest in a previous year, and that subsequently a new tax allocation was received, which is reported as capital gain, and the same new tax allocation increased the cost basis of the partnership interest and is hence being reported as a reduction to capital gain. The two entries cancel out, and there is no net individual tax liability to the departed partner.

Note that under layering, when there are no longer any tax lots containing an allocation of unrealized gains to a particular partner, and at the same time, the partner no longer has any remaining economic interest in the partnership, there are no allocations of income flows attributable to new tax lots that are purchased in the partnership. That is, there are no new allocations that are made, of either tax allocations or unrealized gain allocations attributable to tax lots that are purchased after a withdrawing partner's economic participation is drawn down to zero.

What could be frustrating to departing partners or their accountants is that the Final K-1 from the partnership might extend indefinitely until all tax lots are sold. Even though they have economically withdrawn from the partnership, they are required to hold on to it and account for future tax allocations from unsold tax lots bearing their former economic participation in the partnership.

This work-around of salvaging the methodology of layering effectively lifts a perceived constraint by fund sponsors and general partner entities that departing partners should not be subjected to future tax allocations. Most fund sponsors prefer that a Final K-1 should be issued upon the withdrawal of limited partners from the partnership. Effectively, the work-around ties down partners into a partnership until each and every tax lot bearing unrealized capital gains allocations attributable to them has been sold.

Most fund sponsors and hedge funds prefer to apply simpler methods of allocating dividends, interest, and bond coupon income. Even though we have identified a working fix to salvage the methodology of layering for actual implementation, we discover that at every stage along the way, the methodology is fraught with complexity. Even though in the era of modern computation and information technology we would be able to successfully and accurately implement the methodology of layering, bearing no computational errors, the complexity of the methodology is its principal weakness. Imagine the daunting task faced by a tax examiner or tax preparation accountant to verify that all of the calculations and allocations have been done correctly.

It should be emphasized that any hedge fund that implements the methodology of layering should do so by automated computing within a database system with appropriate mechanical queries and scripts. At its heart, the automated computerized system would be tracking partner tax allocations of ownership of every tax lot at every point in time. This is not a project to be implemented on a spreadsheet, where even the slightest human error could introduce a cascade of errors and cause it to collapse completely.

# CHAPTER 7

# Partial and Full Netting Methods

## The Methods of Aggregation or Netting

The various methods of aggregation or netting follow a simple principle: to aggregate realized gains for a full calendar year, and then allocate to each partner based on some measure of their history of economic ownership. All allocation methods including layering methods will have deviations between the economic (or "book") capital value and the tax basis (or "tax" capital value) due to unrealized gains that are contained in the economic value but are excluded from the tax basis. These deviations would be reported as capital gain to the IRS on individual tax returns only when (1) a partner redeems entirely from the partnership, (2) the partnership undergoes a technical termination under Section 708(b)(1)(B) due to the exit or sale of 50 percent or more of the partnership interest and restarts immediately, forcing all remaining partners to report the deviations as capital gains to the IRS on their individual tax returns, or (3) the partnership sells all securities at year-end and holds a different set of securities for at least 30 days so that none of the realized gains are wash sales, and so that the partnership does not contain any unrealized gains.

Let us examine the origin of the methodologies of aggregation in the tax code. We haven't so far referred to Section 704(c) of the Internal Revenue Code, which governs in-kind contributions of property made by a partner to a partnership. This is not particularly important for hedge funds, which are largely based on cash contributions by partners and cash redemptions to partners. In rare instances, partners may contribute a portfolio of securities to a partnership in lieu of cash, and the general partner combines these securities into the portfolio of the partnership when the securities are compatible with the investment strategy of the partnership.

The motivation for in-kind property contributions by partners into a partnership is that such partners are not required to recognize gains embedded in the property contributed, but instead record their original basis, that is, the original cost incurred by them to acquire the property, as their cost basis of acquisition of the partnership interest in the new partnership into which they have contributed property. Accountants usually call this the "outside basis" or "outside tax basis" to distinguish it from the "inside basis" or "inside tax basis," where the latter is based on the market value of the property contributed, without regard to the cost of acquisition of the contributing partner. Generally, the tracking of the outside basis and reporting of capital gains on individual tax returns relative to this outside basis is the responsibility of the property-contributing partner, though the partnership might assist such a partner in such tracking.

The U.S Treasury Regulations have provided explanations of alternative methodologies to the methodology of layering in the context of contributed property and tax allocations to partners, which are explicitly named "full netting" and "partial netting."[1] Since contribution of cash by partners is a special case of a contribution of property, where the unrealized gain in contributor properties is zero, the definitions and explanations provided for these two approaches are perfectly valid for implementation in a U.S. hedge fund. Let us visit these specific definitions and explanations.

## Partial Netting

**Step 1p:** 26 C.F.R. 1.704-3(e)(3)(iv)(A) states, *"(The partnership) nets its book gains and book losses from qualified financial assets since the last capital account restatement and allocates the net amount to its partners."* In this context, "book gains" and "book losses" are the economic gain and losses. The partnership does not have to track tax lots and assign gains to partners within each tax lot for every period. Instead, the partnership aggregates all economic gains made by the partnership during a full year, whether realized or unrealized, and allocates them to partners according to their economic interest. The economic or book capital account values

---

[1]26 C.F.R. Section 1.704-3 provides principles, definitions, and operating rules for tax allocations in the context of contributed property. Paragraph 1.704-3(e)(3)(iv) describes the partial netting approach, which is illustrated in Example 1 contained in paragraph 1.704-3(e)(3)(ix). Paragraph 1.704-3(e)(3)(v) describes the full netting approach, which is illustrated in Example 2 contained in paragraph 1.704-3(e)(3) (ix). This relevant section of the U.S. Code of Federal Regulations is accessible at http://ecfr.gpoaccess.gov/cgi/t/text/text-idx?c=ecfr&sid=0bad37fd91f398951df96016 726ab7cb&rgn=div8&view=text&node=26:8.0.1.1.1.0.13.238&idno=26.

at every point in time under this method are the same as we derived earlier, denoted as $U_T^j$ at every calendar year-end. There is no change to the numerical value of $U_T^j$ under this method, other than dispensing with tracing its origin to every single tax lot.

**Step 2p:** 26 C.F.R. 1.704-3(e)(3)(iv)(B) states, *"(The partnership) separately aggregates all tax gains and all tax losses from qualified financial assets since the last capital account restatement."* Here is the big relief to accounting burden that is offered to U.S. hedge funds. Instead of tracking the unrealized and realized gains of each tax lot as we did before for the method of layering, the partnership aggregates all positive realized gains into one aggregate quantity for the full year and aggregates all negative realized gains (i.e., losses) into a second aggregate quantity for the full year.

**Step 3p:** 26 C.F.R. 1.704-3(e)(3)(iv)(C) states, *"(The partnership) separately allocates the aggregate tax gain and aggregate tax loss to the partners in a manner that reduces the disparity between the book capital account balances and the tax capital account balances (book-tax disparities) of the individual partners."* Here is the big relief to U.S. hedge funds and accounting professionals who are dedicated to their service. This procedure for allocation of realized capital gains stated lightly, providing wide latitude to accountants to follow one of thousands of ways to allocate the two quantities, aggregate realized gains and aggregate realized losses, all of which could be considered to be reducing the tax-book disparity.

Steps 1p, 2p, and 3p must be done separately for long-term gains and short-term gains. This is made explicit in the Treasury Regulations. Section 26 C.F.R. 1.704-3(e)(3)(vi)(C) states, *"Type of tax gain or loss.* The character and other tax attributes of gain or loss allocated to the partners under this paragraph (e)(3) must: (A) Preserve the tax attributes of each item of gain or loss realized by the partnership." This settles a debate on whether all realized gains and losses, whether long-term or short-term, may be aggregated into one single quantity. Aggregate long-term gains (and losses) are considered as distinct from aggregate short-term gains (and losses). We have to apply the above Steps 1p, 2p, and 3p twice over: first for allocating long-term gains, and again for allocating short-term gains.

As with many U.S. Treasury Regulations, it is important to clarify the scope of the "preserve nature of gain" clause. U.S. partnerships and their accountants have generally interpreted this as a requirement to ensure that the sum total of partner allocations of short-term realized gains must equal the overall short-term realized gains at the partnership level, and likewise for long-term gains. It is the imposition of two simple constraints, $\sum_j \Pi_{8,T}^j = \Pi_{8,T}$ and $\sum_j \Pi_{9a,T}^j = \Pi_{9a,T}$. The language of this particular Treasury Regulation does not suggest that the expression "preserve nature of gain" extends to other mathematically expressed constraints, such as requiring all partners to be allocated short-term and long-term realized gains such that the ratio $\dfrac{\Pi_{8,T}^{j}}{\Pi_{8,T}^{j} + \Pi_{9a,T}^{j}}$ across all partners should be identical and should equal the ratio at the partnership level, $\dfrac{\Pi_{8,T}}{\Pi_{8,T} + \Pi_{9a,T}}$.

We need new variables and subscripts at this stage to represent these new quantities. We already have the *aggregate* realized gains for the partnership as $\Pi_{8,T}$ for short-term realized gains (line 8), and $\Pi_{9a,T}$ for long-term realized gains (line 9a) at calendar year-end time point $T$. We decompose each of these two aggregate realized capital gains further into two subsets each. For short-term capital gains $\Pi_{8,T}$, we create one subset based on combining the short-term realized gains on all securities tax lots that made realized capital loss, denoted by $\Pi_{8,T,L}$, and another subset of all securities that made realized capital gains denoted by $\Pi_{8,T,G}$. The additional subscript $L$ denotes aggregation across loss-making tax lots, and the additional subscript $G$ denotes aggregation across gain-making tax lots. A similar regrouping of realized gain tax lots is conducted for long-term gains and one subset of all securities that made realized capital gains, denoted by $\Pi_{9a,T}$, into two subsets $\Pi_{9a,T,L}$ and $\Pi_{9a,T,G}$. In our notation, the loss-making subsets $\Pi_{8,T,L}$ and $\Pi_{9a,T,L}$ are negative quantities (i.e., negative numbers) and the gain-making subsets $\Pi_{8,T,G}$ and $\Pi_{9a,T,G}$ are positive quantities (i.e., positive numbers).

It must be the case that $\Pi_{8,T} = \Pi_{8,T,L} + \Pi_{8,T,G}$ and $\Pi_{9a,T} = \Pi_{9a,T,L} + \Pi_{9a,T,G}$. The sum total of all realized gains across all tax lots $\Pi_{8,T}$ and $\Pi_{9a,T}$ could be negative or positive quantities.

We should note that we might need a database system to track the individual tax lots that contribute to each of these realized gain and loss aggregates. But it is eminently clear that the methodology of aggregation (or "netting" in IRS phraseology) no longer requires allocation of the change or increase in unrealized gains of each tax lot to each partner in each subperiod that is required by the methodology of layering. This is indeed a great relief.

In our algebraic framework, the expression "tax-book disparity" in U.S. Treasury Regulations terminology was clearly defined as $U_T^{j} - K_T^{j}$, where $U_T^{j}$ is the book or economic capital account value, and $K_T^{j}$ is the tax basis for partner $j$ at calendar year time point $T$ (after all fixed and performance fees). When aggregated across all partners superscripted as $j$, at the level of the partnership, we must have $U_T - K_T = \Pi_{Mn16}$. That is, the difference between the aggregate economic value of the partnership $U_T = \sum_{j} U_T^{j}$ and the aggregate tax basis of partners $K_T = \sum_{j} K_T^{j}$ must equal the cumulative unrealized gains on securities since inception, which is denoted by $\Pi_{Mn16}$. This is an identity that must be satisfied under all methodologies of tax allocation to partners, failing which the accounting numbers are out of order. "Tax-book" disparity at partner level is simply $\Pi_{M1L6,T}^{j} = U_T^{j} - K_T^{j}$. The magnitude of $K_T^{j}$, and consequently that of $\Pi^j_{M1L6,T}$, would be different when calculated under the layering methodology versus the aggregation or netting methodologies. Only the economic or book value of a partner's capital account $U^j_T$ would be invariant to the choice of tax allocation methodology.

Let us examine the pivotal Step 3 closely. The partnership's allocation procedure is to simultaneously determine for each partner $j$, who belonged to the partnership at any time point during the subperiod $[T-12, T]$ (where $T$ is a calendar year-end time point), their partner allocations $\Pi^j_{8,T,G}$ and $\Pi^j_{8,T,L}$, which on an aggregate must add up as $\sum_j \Pi^j_{8,T,G} = \Pi_{8,T,G}$ and $\sum_j \Pi^j_{8,T,G} = \Pi_{8,T,G}$, in such a manner as to reduce the tax-book disparity of the partners, that is, some composite measure of $\Pi^j_{M1L6,T} = U^j_T - K^j_T$ across partners should demonstrate an effort to reduce its disparity across partners. Each of the partner allocations $\Pi^j_{8,T,G}$ must be positive quantities, while each of the $\Pi^j_{8,T,L}$ must be negative quantities. We shall interpret the tax regulation term "disparity" and discuss procedures for reducing the same after describing the method of full netting.

# Full Netting

As with the definition and description of partial netting, the Treasury Regulations provide a three-step procedure to define and describe the full netting approach. This is simpler and easier than the partial netting approach, since it does not involve building subsets of realized long-term and short-term gains.

**Step 1f:** 26 C.F.R. 1.704-3(e)(3)(v)(A) for full netting is identical to partial netting Step 1p: 26 C.F.R. 1.704-3(e)(3)(iv)(A), word for word. We repeat it here:, *"(The Partnership) nets its book gains and book losses from qualified financial assets since the last capital account restatement and allocates the net amount to its partners."*

**Step 2f:** 26 C.F.R. 1.704-3(e)(3)(v)(B): *"The partnership nets tax gains and tax losses from qualified financial assets since the last capital account restatement."* This step is much simpler than with partial netting. The partnership calculates one grand quantity for net realized gains, combining all realized net taxable capital gains and net taxable capital losses.

**Step 3f:** 26 C.F.R. 1.704-3(e)(3)(v)(C): *"The partnership allocates the net tax gain (or net tax loss) to the partners in a manner that reduces the book-tax disparities of the individual partners."* The previous method of partial netting required the allocation of two grand numbers to partners: of net gains (from tax lots that produced realized gains) and net losses (from tax lots that produced realized losses). This method of full netting is substantially simpler, requiring that the single grand number of realized net gains from all securities is to be allocated to partners.

We do not need new variables to represent these quantities of really short-term and long-term capital gains. We already have the aggregate realized gains for the partnership as $\varPi_{8,T}$ for short-term realized gains (line 8), and $\varPi_{9a,T}$ for long-term realized gains (line 9a) at calendar year-end time point $T$. The method of full netting permits us to allocate these partnership-level aggregates to individual partners as $\varPi_{8,L}^{j}$ and $\varPi_{9a,T}^{j}$ to each partner $j$ in a manner that reduces the book-tax disparities of the partners.

The pivotal Step 3f of full netting requires us to simultaneously determine allocations $\varPi_{8,T}^{j}$ and $\varPi_{9a,T}^{j}$ so that a measure of the book-tax disparity, which is some composite measure derived from $\varPi_{M1L6,T}^{j} = U_T^j - K_T^j$ across partners.

## Measures of Book-Tax Disparity across Partners

The book-tax difference for a partner (superscripted as $j$) is that partner's allocation of *cumulative* unrealized gains on securities, $\varPi_{M1L6,T}^{j} = U_T^j - K_T^j$. We have a new idea presented in the Treasury Regulations: that of disparity across partners. We could consider the aggregate $\sum_j \left| \varPi_{M1L6,T}^{j} \right|$, the sum of absolute book-tax difference of partners, to be one of the many possible measures of disparity between the economic value of partners' capital accounts from their tax basis. The larger this number, the greater the disparity across partners. In the terminology of some accountants, who sometimes call the book-tax difference of partners their "memorandum capital account," we could state that the methods of partial netting and full netting attempt to bring partners' memorandum capital accounts as close to zero as is feasible.

Another measure of disparity across partners that is more tractable than the sum-of-absolute-values measure is the sum-of-squares measure, which is a popular approach in statistics and economics: $\sum_j \left[ \varPi_{M1L6,T}^{j} \right]^2$.

The method of partial netting is a rule to allocate the grand total $\varPi_{8,T,L}$, $\varPi_{8,T,G}$, $\varPi_{9a,T,L}$, and $\varPi_{9a,T,G}$ across partners such that, after allocation, a measure of book-tax disparity across all partners is minimized, that is, $\sum_j \left| \varPi_{M1L6,T}^{j} \right|$ or $\sum_j \left[ \varPi_{M1L6,T}^{j} \right]^2$ is a minimum, and ideally, every instance of $\varPi_{M1L6,T}^{j}$ across all partners is zero when all tax lots are sold. The method of full netting is a simpler rule to allocate $\varPi_{8,T}$ and $\varPi_{9a,T}$ across all partners such that disparity across all partners is minimized, that is, $\sum_j \left| \varPi_{M1L6,T}^{j} \right|$ or $\sum_j \left[ \varPi_{M1L6,T}^{j} \right]^2$ is a minimum. Note that $\varPi_{M1L6,T}^{j}$ includes the most recent period tax allocations $\varPi_{8,T}^{j}$ and $\varPi_{9a,T}^{j}$ to partners.

Consider the simpler case of tax allocations under full netting. We have to be careful about the relevant sign of the allocation across partners $\varPi_{8,T}^{j}$ and $\varPi_{9a,T}^{j}$. If the aggregate net short-term gain at the level of the partnership $\varPi_{8,T}$ is a negative quantity (denoting aggregate short-term loss), then each of the partner allocations $\Pi_{8,T}^j$ have to be negative quantities. We cannot have a situation where some partners are assigned positive quantities and some partners are assigned negative quantities of short-term gains. Thus, the sign of partner allocations of gains $\Pi_{8,T}^j$ and $\Pi_{9a,T}^j$ have the same signs as the sign of aggregate gains $\Pi_{8,T}$ and $\Pi_{9a,T}$.

## Formulating the Problem for Optimal Partner Tax Allocations under Full Netting

Full netting is simpler than partial netting, since there are only two quantities at calendar year-end time point $T$, aggregate short-term gains $\Pi_{8,T}$ and long-term net gains $\Pi_{9a,T}$, to be allocated to partners. For each partner, we are required to assign partner allocations $\Pi_{8,T}^j$ and $\Pi_{9a,T}^j$, respectively. The input data are the book-tax difference at time point $T$ for each partner *before* their realized capital gains allocations $\Pi_{8,T}^j$ and $\Pi_{9a,T}^j$. are determined. The book-tax difference *after (or inclusive of)* realized capital gains allocations is $\Pi_{M1L6,T}^j = U_T^j - K_T^j$. We need an additional symbol to denote the book-tax difference *before* realized capital gains allocations, such as $\rho_T^j = U_T^j - \kappa_T^j$, where $\kappa_T^j$ are the cumulative tax allocations and deposits of partner $j$ from inception until time point $T$, *excluding* the allocations of realized capital gains $\Pi_{8,T}^j$ and $\Pi_{9a,T}^j$, which we're attempting to determine. Thus, $\kappa_T^j$ includes *all* the components of $K_T^j$ *except* realized capital gains $\Pi_{8,T}^j$ and $\Pi_{9a,T}^j$, which are to be determined. To summarize, at time point $T$, we have on hand data (which may be considered as constants) for each partner of $\mu_T^j$. We are given aggregate short-term and long-term capital gains for the partnership, $\Pi_{8a,T}$ and $\Pi_{9a,T}$, respectively. These two quantities may also be considered constants. Based on these data on hand of fixed number parameters, the problem is to determine partner allocations of capital gains $\Pi_{8,T}^j$ and $\Pi_{9a,T}^j$. Once this is achieved, the tax basis after allocation of capital gains to partners is $K_T^j = \kappa_T^j + \Pi_{8,T}^j + \Pi_{9a,T}^j$, and the book-tax difference is $\Pi_{M1L6,T}^j = U_T^j - K_T^j = U_T^j - \kappa_T^j - \Pi_{8,T}^j - \Pi_{9a,T}^j = \rho_T^j - \Pi_{8,T}^j - \Pi_{9a,T}^j$.

Can we construct a self-contained solution procedure that takes fixed numbers $\{\rho_T^j, \Pi_{8,T}, \Pi_{9a,T}\}$ as input and obtains $\{\Pi_{8,T}^j, \Pi_{9a,T}^j\}$ as output? The U.S. Treasury has presented the U.S. hedge fund and accounting community with the following constrained nonlinear optimization problem:

Given fixed data $\{\rho_T^j, \Pi_{8,T}, \Pi_{9a,T}\}$ for partners $j = 1$ to $M$ as input, we seek to minimize by choice of tax allocations $\{\Pi_{8,T}^j, \Pi_{9a,T}^j\}$ a metric of "disparity" of book-tax disparities across partners, such as the sum of their squared deviations: $\sum_j \left[\Pi_{M1L6,T}^j\right]^2 = \sum_j \left[\rho_T^j - \Pi_{8,T}^j - \Pi_{9a,T}^j\right]^2$,

Subject to the *feasibility constraints*, that for all partner allocations $\Pi_{8,T}^j$ and $\Pi_{9a,T}^j$,

$$\Pi_{8,T} \le \Pi_{8,T}^j \le 0 \text{ when } \Pi_{8,T} \le 0, \text{ or}$$

$\Pi_{8,T} > \Pi^j_{8,T} > 0$ when $\Pi_{8,T} > 0$.
$\Pi_{9a,T} \leq \Pi^j_{9a,T} \leq 0$ when $\Pi_{9a,T} \leq 0$, or
$\Pi_{9a,T} > \Pi^j_{9a,T} > 0$ when $\Pi_{9a,T} > 0$.

These constraints apply because we cannot permit a (negative) realized loss allocation to a partner when the aggregate partnership realized gain is positive, and vice versa. If a partnership makes a net short-term loss on an aggregate, then tax allocations to all partners must also be losses. We cannot have a situation where some partners have allocated net short-term realized gains and others allocated net short-term realized losses, which add up to the partnership's aggregate short-term realized gain. Further, no partner may be allocated a realized gain that exceeds that of the overall partnership or be allocated a loss that is larger than that of the overall partnership.

Further, the realized gain tax allocations are subject to the two aggregation constraints:

$$\sum_{j=1}^{M} \Pi^j_{8,T} = \Pi_{8,T}, \text{ and}$$

$$\sum_{j=1}^{M} \Pi^j_{9a,T} = \Pi_{9,T}.$$

The above aggregation constraints simply state that the short-term realized gain tax allocations must add up to the total short-term gains for the partnership, and likewise for long-term gains. These two constraints are the algebraic implementations of the requirement in the Treasury Regulations described earlier to preserve the nature of gains when making allocations under full netting and partial netting.

The two aggregation constraints eliminate the need for an upper bound to gain allocations and a lower bound to loss allocations constraints. Take the case of allocation of long-term gains that must add up to $\Pi_{9a,T}$. The feasibility constraints require that partner allocation should be non-negative, that is, $\Pi^j_{9a,T} > 0$. This forces each partner allocation to be less than the overall gain at the partnership level, so that the constraint $\Pi_{9a,T} > \Pi^j_{9a,T}$ is implicit and we can eliminate it from formal consideration. A simple numerical example will demonstrate this point. Consider a partnership with two partners and an aggregate partnership-level long-term realized gain of 100. The allocations to the two partners must add up to 100. None of these allocations can be negative. That implies that the allocations to each partner have to be less than 100. Suppose it were otherwise, and one partner were allocated gains of 110. The other partner would have to be allocated −10, so that the total allocations add up to 100. But that is not allowed, since both partners have to be allocated gains that are positive numbers. This partner example can be easily extended to multiple partners with the same result.

We therefore restate our optimization problem as:

*Full netting:*

$$\min_{\Pi_{8,T}^{j}, \Pi_{9a,T}^{j}} \sum_{j=1}^{M} \left[ \rho_T^j - \Pi_{8,T}^j - \Pi_{9a,T}^j \right]^2$$

subject to *feasibility constraints* that:

$\Pi_{8,T}^j \leq 0$ when $\Pi_{8,T} \leq 0$, or $\Pi_{8,T}^j > 0$ when $\Pi_{8,T} > 0$ ($M$ such constraints);
$\Pi_{9a,T}^j \leq 0$ when $\Pi_{9a,T} \leq 0$, or $\Pi_{9a,T}^j > 0$ when $\Pi_{9a,T} > 0$ ($M$ such constraints);
$\sum_{j=1}^{M} \Pi_{8,T}^j = \Pi_{8,T}$, and $\sum_{j=1}^{M} \Pi_{9a,T}^j = \Pi_{9,T}$ (2 constraints)

We have $2M$ unknowns, $\{\Pi_{8,T}^j, \Pi_{9a,T}^j\}$ for $j = 1 \ldots M$, that we have to solve for, subject to $2M + 2$ constraints. This is a classic convex optimization problem to which there is no closed-form direct formula solution. The domain, that is, the 2M choice variables $\{\Pi_{8,T}^j, \Pi_{9a,T}^j\}$, constitute a convex set.[2] The objective function $\sum_{j=1}^{M} \left[ \rho_T^j - \Pi_{8,T}^j - \Pi_{9a,T}^j \right]^2$ is also strictly convex.[3] It is a quadratic function, interpreted geometrically as the graph of the objective function $\sum_{j=1}^{M} \left[ \rho_T^j - \Pi_{8,T}^j - \Pi_{9a,T}^j \right]^2$ always having upward positive curvature, shaped like a U at any given tax allocation $\{\Pi_{8,T}^j, \Pi_{9a,T}^j\}$. The constraint set of $2M$ linear inequalities and two linear equalities is also convex, because all linear functions are convex. We are guaranteed a unique solution to this

---

[2]The domain of a convex optimization problem must be a convex set. If the vectors $x_1$ and $x_2$ are two tax allocation vectors, then any linear combination $\theta x_1 + (1 - \theta)x_2$, where $0 \leq \theta \leq 1$, must also be an allowable tax allocation. The domain of the tax allocation is the real number hyperspace in $2M$ dimensions, $R^{2M}$, a convex set.

[3]Let a tax allocation vector be $x = \{\Pi_{8,T}^j, \Pi_{9a,T}^j\}$ for $j = 1 \ldots M$, and f(x) be the objective function $f(x) = \sum_{j=1}^{M} \left[ \rho_T^j - \Pi_{8,T}^j - \Pi_{9a,T}^j \right]^2$. Strict convexity requires that the domain of $f(x)$, that is, the tax allocation set $x$, be convex, and the Hessian matrix associated with $f(x)$ is positive semidefinite for all $x$ in its domain, that is, $\nabla^2 f(x) \geq 0$. Geometrically, what this means is that if $x_1$ and $x_2$ are two tax allocation vectors, then $f(\theta x_1 + (1 - \theta)x_2) \leq f(\theta x_1) + (1 - \theta)f(x_2)$ where $0 \leq \theta \leq 1$. This is also called Jensen's inequality, which holds for convex functions. We have verified this to hold for our specific quadratic objective function $f(x)$. The Hessian matrix associated with our function $f(x)$ turns out to be a positive semidefinite matrix with a sparse structure of

the form: $H = 2 \begin{bmatrix} E & \cdots & Z \\ \vdots & \ddots & \vdots \\ Z & \cdots & E \end{bmatrix}$ where $E$ is a $2 \times 2$ matrix of ones along the diagonal, and

$Z$ is a $2 \times 2$ matrix of zeros at all other off-diagonal positions. In the case of partial netting, discussed in the next section, $E$ and $Z$ become $4 \times 4$ matrices.

convex optimization problem. This unique solution has to be uncovered by a computerized numerical algorithmic search, which requires the application of a mathematically sound search algorithm.[4] Practical computer methods to solve this convex optimization problem are described later, after we formulate the convex optimization problem for tax allocation under partial netting.

## Formulating the Problem for Optimal Partner Tax Allocations under Partial Netting

In the previous section, we developed a framework for tax allocations under full netting, which was quite elaborate. We shall pursue the same steps for solving for tax allocations of realized gains under partial netting. Full netting takes fixed numbers $\{\rho_T^j, \Pi_{8,T,L}, \Pi_{9a,T,L}\}$ as input and obtains $\{\Pi_{8,T}^j, \Pi_{9a,T,L}^j\}$ as output. Partial netting takes fixed numbers $\{\rho_T^j, \Pi_{8,T,L}, \Pi_{9a,T,L}, \Pi_{8,T,G}, \Pi_{9a,T,G}\}$ as input and obtains $\{\Pi_{8,T,L}^j, \Pi_{9a,T,L}^j, \Pi_{8,T,G}^j, \Pi_{9a,T,G}^j\}$ as output.

The principal advantage offered by partial netting, despite its increased complexity, is that a partnership is likely to have tax lots that are made realized losses, which can be allocated to the loss-making partners, that is, partners with negative $\rho_T^j$, so as to reduce their book-tax disparity. Under full netting, both short-term and long-term realized gains for the partnership could be in net positive numbers, and any allocation of net positive realized gains to loss-making partners would increase their book-tax disparity. Partial netting would produce much reduced book-tax disparity compared to full netting for the same partnership.

The optimization problem setup for partial netting is similar to that of full netting, with more terms leading to the appearance of greater complexity. The formulation of the convex optimization problem is similar to that under full netting. The only major difference is in the feasibility constraints, which are different. Under full netting, the sign of the tax allocations of short-term realized gains should be the same as the sign of the partnership's aggregate realized short-term gains. Similarly, under full netting, long-term gain allocation to partners must have the same sign as the partnership's aggregate long-term gains. Under partial netting, tax allocations of realized

---

[4]Stephen Boyd and Lieven Vandenberghe, *Convex Optimization* (Cambridge, University Press, U.K.; 2004) is an undergraduate engineering textbook on the subject. On pages 561–571, an algorithm called the barrier method is provided for an optimization problem with a convex objective function and linear inequality constraints. This algorithm converges to the unique optimum. Chapters 2 and 3 of this book provide an exposition of convex sets and convex functions.

capital losses, both short-term and long-term have to be negative numbers, representing loss allocations. Similarly, allocations of realized capital gains have to be positive numbers, representing gain allocations.

We describe the optimization problem setup for partial netting here, for determining the tax allocation for $M$ partners and the partnership.

*Partial netting:*

$$\min\nolimits_{\Pi^j_{8,T,L}, \Pi^j_{9a,T,L}, \Pi^j_{8,T,L}, \Pi^j_{9a,T,L}} \sum\nolimits_{j=1}^{M} \left[ \rho^j_T - \Pi^j_{8,T,L} - \Pi^j_{9a,T,L} - \Pi^j_{8,T,G} - \Pi^j_{9a,T,G} \right]^2$$

subject to the *feasibility constraints* that:

$\Pi^j_{8,T,L} \leq 0$ ($M$ such constraints)
$\Pi^j_{9a,T,L} \leq 0$ ($M$ such constraints)
$\Pi^j_{8,T,G} \geq 0$ ($M$ such constraints)
$\Pi^j_{9a,T,G} \geq 0$ ($M$ such constraints)

and subject to the four aggregation constraints that:

$$\sum\nolimits_{j=1}^{M} \Pi^j_{8,T,G} = \Pi_{8,T,G}$$
$$\sum\nolimits_{j=1}^{M} \Pi^j_{8,T,L} = \Pi_{8,T,L}$$
$$\sum\nolimits_{j=1}^{M} \Pi^j_{9a,T,G} = \Pi_{9a,T,G}$$
$$\sum\nolimits_{j=1}^{M} \Pi^j_{9a,T,L} = \Pi_{9a,T,L}$$

We have $4M$ unknowns to be solved for, subject to $4M + 4$ constraints.

As with full netting, we do not have to state the lower bounds to individual partner capital loss allocations and upper bounds to partner capital gain allocations, since the four aggregation equality constraints combined with the $4M$ inequalities constraints make these lower/upper bounds implicit. Together, these $4M + 4$ constraints ensure that the partial aggregate short-term losses allocated to any partner cannot be larger than the partnership's partial aggregate short-term losses. An analogous condition applies to partial short-term gains, long-term losses, and long-term gains. We therefore do not need to specify the implicit $4M$ additional constraints, which are:

$$\Pi_{8,T,G} \leq \Pi^j_{8,T,L}$$

$$\Pi_{9a,T,L} \leq \Pi^j_{9a,T,L}$$

$$\Pi_{8,T,G} \geq \Pi^j_{8,T,G}$$

$$\Pi_{9a,T,G} \geq \Pi^j_{9a,T,G}$$

The $4M$ inequality constraints merely state that realized loss allocations to partners have all got to be negative quantities, and that realized gain allocations to partners have all got to be positive quantities. Under partial netting, when partial aggregate short-term losses (of tax lots that each produce such losses) $\Pi_{8,T,L}$ are being allocated to partners, each of the partner allocations $\Pi_{8,T,L}^{j}$ are negative quantities. We cannot have a situation where some partners are being allocated profit (positive sign) and other partners are allocated loss (negative sign). All partners have to be allocated losses with the appropriate negative sign.

The four equality constraints ensure that partner allocations add up to the aggregate quantity of partial gains or losses for the partnership as a whole. Further, the equality constraints together with the inequality constraints ensure that the partial aggregate short-term losses allocated to any partner cannot be larger than the partnership's partial aggregate short-term losses. An analogous condition applies to partial short-term gains, long-term losses, and long-term gains.

## Solving the Convex Optimization Problem of Tax Allocation

To find a partner tax allocation solution under either full netting or partial netting by convex optimization, we have to resort to constrained nonlinear convex optimization models that are available in a number of software operations research (OR) packages. One such package is the SAS/OR module of SAS.[5] The nonlinear optimization module of the popular open-source free statistical computing software named R[6] is a relevant alternative. Matlab,[7] which is popular with scientists and engineers, has modules for nonlinear and convex optimization.

Best of all, the ubiquitous software program Microsoft Excel has an add-in module called Solver on its installation disk, which miraculously works and nicely solves small-size convex optimization under linear inequality and equality constraints. We tested instances of full netting and partial netting for a 10-partner tax allocation convex optimization problem using the Microsoft Excel 2007 Solver add-in and found that it produced

---

[5]SAS/OR is an optional software module within the SAS data analysis software of SAS Institute Inc., Cary, NC.

[6]The open source software for statistical computing named R is accessible at www.r-project.org/. It contains modules for solving constrained nonlinear optimization problems in R, described at http://r-forge.r-project.org/projects/rino/.

[7]Matlab analytical software, offered by Mathworks, Natick, MA, has a software module, Optimization Toolbox, for large-scale optimization, including the relevant category of convex (quadratic) optimization that is of particular relevance to us.

nearly instantaneous results. The only problem with the Excel Solver add-in is that it requires manual setup of the objective function and constraints as Excel cells. The exact nature of the algorithm used behind the scenes is not documented, so we cannot be sure that the solution provided, though meeting the feasibility constraints, is the guaranteed optimum that exists. It turns out that Excel Solver is not directly produced by Microsoft, but by a Microsoft vendor named Frontline Systems.[8] Given such a large installed user base of Excel with its included Solver add-in, on the order of 500 million, it is unlikely that Microsoft would provide documentation beyond what it already has put out.

The Microsoft Excel Solver add-in does solve for optimal partner tax allocations, which certainly meet the feasibility constraints. At some point, Excel Solver may refuse to take on additional constraints as the number of partners in a partnership increases. We recommend trying out Excel Solver first, since it certainly works for solving for a small number of partners, and it certainly produces a better solution than arbitrary tax allocations made manually. For a partnership with a large number of partners, and given the large dollar magnitudes involved, we recommend the large-scale convex optimization software platforms and modules that are used by scientists and engineers. At an extreme, we might design and implement large-scale stand-alone dedicated optimization software based on a published engineering textbook algorithm[9] that is guaranteed to locate the optimum partner tax allocation, and that also graphically displays its search path and visualizes the optimum. All of the paraphernalia of loading the

---

[8] Frontline Systems reveals itself as the source of Microsoft's Solver add-in engine at www.profitpt.com/excel_solver.asp.

[9] Such as, the barrier method algorithm published in Boyd and Vandenberghe, *op. cit.,* pages 561–571. The Matlab documentation on solving quadratic programming problems, accessible at www.mathworks.com/access/helpdesk/help/toolbox/optim/ug/quadprog.html, provides two algorithms on which the Matlab quadratic programming solver is based: T.F. Coleman. and Y. Li, "A Reflective Newton Method for Minimizing a Quadratic Function Subject to Bounds of Some of the Variables," *SIAM Journal of Optimization,* Vol. 6, no. 4 (1996): 1040–1058; and P.E. Gill, W. Murray, and M.H. Wright, *Practical Optimization* (London: Academic Press, 1981). The open source software R (the R Project) documents at http://cran.r-project.org/web/packages/quadprog/quadprog.pdf the implementation of the dual method for solving quadratic programming problems expressed in canonical form according to the algorithms in D. Goldfarb and A. Idnani, "Dual and Primal-Dual Methods for Solving Strictly Convex Quadratic Programs," in J.P. Hennart (ed.), *Numerical Analysis* (Berlin: Springer-Verlag), 1982, pages 226–239; and D. Goldfarb and A. Idnani, "A numerically stable dual method for solving strictly convex quadratic programs," *Mathematical Programming,* Vol. 27 (1983): 1–33.

convex optimization problem into the format of SAS, R, Matlab, or Excel is eliminated.

The popular scientific software program Matlab has a built-in module quadprog within its "optimization toolbox." Similarly, the open source statistical package R has a module that is also named quadprog. Both of these packages take the convex quadratic programming problem in its canonical form as input (i.e., according to a standard format described in their documentation) and produce the output of the optimum solution, along with the certificate that the solution provided is indeed optimal, in the form of the optimal solution to the dual problem. A small inconvenience with these scientific software programs is that our original optimization problem must be expanded by longhand multiplication and condensed into the canonical form expressed in the form of matrices and vectors.[10] The output is returned in an abstract, old-school, mainframe-era format and has to be mapped back to the tax allocation decision variables that we are attempting to solve for in the first place. Despite these inconveniences and the lack of Excel-like familiarity and ease of use, the advantage of deploying these supported scientific and engineering packages is that we obtain a thoroughly researched, documented, and tested optimal solution to the tax allocation quadratic programming problem, along with a mathematically sound certificate that the solution provided is indeed optimal.

---

[10] Our objective function for full netting, $f(x) = \sum_{j=1}^{M} \left[ \rho_T^j - \Pi_{8,T}^j - \Pi_{9a,T}^j \right]^2$, where the $2M$ row vector $x = \left\{ \Pi_{8,T}^j, \Pi_{9a,T}^j \right\}$ for $j = 1 \ldots M$, is expressed in Matlab's canonical matrix form as $1/2\, x'Hx + g'x$, where $x'$ is the transpose of $x$, and $g'$ is 2 times the transpose of the $2M$ length row vector $\{\rho_T^i, \rho_T^j\}$ for $j = 1 \ldots M$. It consists of two repeated elements, $M$ times in a row, making it of length $2M$. Our longhand expansion of $f(x)$ includes the constant term $\sum_j \left( \rho_T^i \right)^2$, which is omitted from the canonical form objective function in Matlab and R. This is because the optimal solution is invariant to the addition of a constant term to the objective function. The matrix
$$H = 2 \begin{bmatrix} E & \cdots & Z \\ \vdots & \ddots & \vdots \\ Z & \cdots & E \end{bmatrix}$$
is the same Hessian matrix that we encountered before. It is the positive semidefinite sparse block diagonal matrix of size $2M \times 2M$, where $E$ is a $2 \times 2$ matrix of ones along the diagonal and $Z$ is a $2 \times 2$ matrix of zeros at all other off-diagonal positions. We are required by Matlab to provide the matrix $H$ and vector $g$ as input, in addition to the inequality and equality constraints in matrix form. The same exact canonical form is implemented in the open source software R (R Project). The matrices and vectors for partial netting in canonical form have a similar structure of size $4M$.

A convex (quadratic) programming problem subject to linear inequality and linear equality constraints is guaranteed to have an optimal solution. This required certificate is the solution to its equivalent dual problem.[11] The optional reports produced by Excel Solver do provide this certificate, expected by scientists and engineers, that the solution is indeed optimal.[12] We benchmarked a simple documented test problem in Matlab and Excel Solver and obtained the same solution with the same certificate of optimality.[13]

Appendix 2 presents the formulation of the tax allocation of realized gains by full netting, then translates it as inputs and structure for software, and finally solves a large-scale test problem with 100 partners. The methodology provided in this chapter is extended to identify a unique and robust solution from among multiple solutions that achieve the same optimum. Appendix 3 implements the same large-scale test problem for

---

[11] The basic idea in duality is that the objective function is augmented by a weighted sum of the constraint functions to create a Lagrangian dual that is associated with the primal problem. The weights are called Lagrangian multipliers or dual variables associated with the inequality or equality constraints. A proposed optimal solution of a primal problem is certified as optimal only if the value of the minimized objective function of the primal problem coincides with the value of the objective function evaluated at the optimum of the dual problem. Thus, the optimal solution of the dual problem acts as a certificate that the primal problem solution provided is indeed optimal. This is because the primal and dual optimal points act as a pair that must satisfy the Karush-Kuhn-Tucker conditions. The solution to the dual problem is in itself of interest, since it directly reveals which of the constraints are binding and which are nonbinding. See Boyd and Vandenberghe, *op. cit.*, page 215.

[12] The optional reports provided by Excel Solver are the Answer Report, the Sensitivity Report, and the Limits Report. The Answer Report provides the (proposed) optimal solution, along with an indicator for all constraints on whether a particular constraint is either binding or nonbinding. The Sensitivity Report provides the Lagrange multiplier corresponding to each constraint. The required certificate of optimality automatically results when the Lagrange multiplier (provided in the Sensitivity Report), times the constraint evaluated at the proposed optimal solution (provided in the Answer Report), summed over all constraints, is zero. What this means is that binding constraints may have a nonzero Lagrange multiplier, and nonbinding constraints *must* have a zero Lagrange multiplier. A constraint is binding if it evaluates to zero at the proposed optimal solution, and this evaluation is also provided in the Answer Report. The Limits Report is not of any particular significance.

[13] We tested the small-size sample problem provided in the documentation of quadprog in Matlab. The code problem in the Matlab documentation, when fed to Matlab, produced the results shown in the documentation. We implemented the same problem in Excel Solver and obtained the same results and the same certificate as produced by Matlab.

the allocation of capital gains under partial netting. Appendix 4 takes into account the tax preferences of partners and solves the same large-scale test problem in a manner that is consistent with the treasury regulations for full partial netting. Appendix 5 formulates the methodology to allocate all items of taxable income, including dividends, interest, investment expense, and capital gains, and solves the same large-scale test problem according to partial netting.

# CHAPTER 8

# Comparative Tax Consequences of Layering and Netting Methods

## Which Is the Better Method for Allocation of Realized Gains: Layering, Full Netting, or Partial Netting?

These are three of many methods that we could apply, each with their advantages and limitations. What we would like to have is a procedure that is fully consistent with the Treasury Regulations that aim to reduce partners' book-tax disparities, but that is also simple in implementation and has the property of producing unique unambiguous solutions to partner tax allocations of realized gains. So far, this has been elusive, and the only method on hand that guarantees a unique solution to tax allocations of realized gains is the method of layering, which collapses and becomes impractical due to intense complexity and requires the fixing of ambiguities and flaws that were discussed earlier. We have discovered that, while the method of layering is pure linear algebra, attempts to replace it with simpler methods with the objective of reducing the tax-book disparities of partners ends up with the unintended consequence of becoming a degenerate nonlinear optimization problem in the realm of management science and operations research.

We have described methodologies for tax allocation to limited partners in their exact algebraic formulation: that of layering, and that of netting. The methodology of aggregation or netting has two forks permitted by the IRS: full netting and partial netting.

As we described earlier when developing the details of the layering methodology, it has several weaknesses. Its implementation entails:

1. Significant complexity of tracking the time-varying ownership of each and every tax lot.
2. Ambiguities arising from illiquid nontradable securities that remain in a portfolio after a limited partner has departed and exited from the fund.
3. Conversion of memorandum gains into realized gains in the year when any tax lot is sold or liquidated. To partners who are allocated net positive gains in any year prior to entire liquidation, this would trigger interim tax payments that might not be recoverable in subsequent years against allocated capital losses.
4. Most important, and the strongest ground for disqualifying this methodology from consideration, is that when a partner exits, all tax lots containing that exiting partner's memorandum gains must be sold. This is simply not practical for a hedge fund that trades a large portfolio of securities.

Item 3 above needs clarification since is the first time we've introduced this idea. The term "interim" is applied here in the sense that these are tax allocations in the years prior to a partner's exit from the hedge fund. This potentially unrecoverable payment of tax arises due to the very definition of layering, where the unrealized gains on every tax lot are transferred across partners according to their entry and exit dates and considered to be memorandum realized gains for preexisting partners, as if that particular tax lot was bifurcated and considered as being sold to the new entering partners at the time of entry of the new partners.

## Layering Examples Showing Earlier Tax Payment

Layering: Example A.    This idea may appear confusing, so we need a simple example to make this clear. A hedge fund has only one limited partner and invests 100 in only one security. Its interim value rises from 100 to 200 due to unrealized gains in its portfolio. A second limited partner joins and contributes 100, taking the fund value to 300. The additional 100 is held as cash by the fund, so the fund now has 200 in securities by market value and 100 in cash. Under the layering methodology, as of the new partner's entry date of interim valuation, the initial charter partner is supposed to have realized a gain of 33, which is held on record as a memorandum but not allocated until the security is actually sold. Suppose a few months later, within the same tax year, the security that peaked at 200 deflated on the date of interim valuation and entry of the new partner, and it later fell to its original price, 100, and was sold. The value of the fund falls to 200, of which 100 is in the security and 100 is in cash. The initial charter partner owns 67 percent of the fund, and the subsequent entrant partner owns 33 percent of the fund based on ownership percentages that are determined on the entry date of the new partner. The partnership as a whole would report zero realized loss, because the security was purchased for 100 and sold at 100. The value of the fund is now 200, all held in cash. For now, we assume that the fund is not liquidated and cash is held for one more complete tax year.

Under the layering methodology, in Year 1, the charter initial partner would be allocated +33 of capital gain and the second partner would be allocated −33. Across the partners, when tax allocations are aggregated, +33 and −33 add up to zero, which is the realized gain achieved upon liquidation of the underlying security. In this example, the charter partner who is allocated gains of +33 in the year of entry of new partners would have to pay capital gains taxes on this amount. It would increase the tax basis of the charter partner's investment in the hedge fund from 100 to 133. At the end of Year 1, the value of this ownership is 133 (67 percent of 200).

The mirror image happens to the new partner. A realized capital loss of −33 is allocated and flows through the tax return in Year 1. At the end of Year 1, the value of this ownership is 67 (33 percent of 200).

Let us move on to Year 2. The fund holds only cash and produces no income. At the end of Year 2, it liquidates and remits the capital account balances to its investors. The charter investor receives 133. The tax basis of the charter investor is 133. The capital gain or loss for the charter investor on account of the entire disposition of the partnership interest in Year 2 is 133 liquidation value minus 133 tax basis = zero. There is no tax due in Year 2. All of the taxes for the economic activity were allocated in Year 1, and the tax basis of the partnership interest was adjusted accordingly at the end of Year 1.

Similarly, the new partner receives 67 at the end of Year 2 toward the entire disposition of the partnership interest. The new partner's tax basis at the end of Year 1 is 67. The capital gain or loss for the new partner on account of the entire disposition of the partnership interest in Year 2 is 67 liquidation value minus 67 tax basis = zero. There is no tax due in Year 2. All of the tax losses for the economic activity of the partnership in Year 1 were allocated to the second partner in Year 1, and the tax basis of the partnership interest adjusted accordingly at the end of Year 1.

Note in this example that volatility of the underlying security has translated to a form of volatility in tax allocations. In a situation of unrealized capital gains in the underlying portfolio, preexisting partners are deemed to have involuntarily realized those gains as if the partnership had sold the underlying portfolio in the market. New partners are deemed to have purchased a mirror image amount of the underlying securities in the market.

This hypothetical transaction is held in memory, as a memorandum number on record. When that specific tax lot is sold or closed, realized gains attributable to this implicit transaction are allocated to the respective partners.

This particular methodology of layering appears to follow the principle of Section 704(b) of the Internal Revenue Code that tax allocations should follow economics. However, it seems to be more an unintended consequence of forcing this interpretation onto the layering methodology, because it triggers an involuntary hypothetical liquidation of assets whenever there is a withdrawal or deposit into a hedge fund. The most troubling aspect of layering is that despite its elegance in adhering to the principle of Section 704(b) partnership tax allocations, its strict adherence requires the liquidation of all tax lots containing memorandum gains of a departing partner.

Thus, if a partnership were to strictly follow the layering methodology, we would reach an intractable and impractical situation, when a partner wants to exit and liquidate ownership interest, but the underlying portfolio is carrying several tax lots containing memorandum numbers for gains to be allocated to them for tax purposes when the tax lot is liquidated.

Illiquid and nontradable tax lots add to the impracticality of the layering methodology. Even though nontraded tax lots could be written off and marked down to zero for accounting purposes, it would likely be a breach of fiduciary duty of the general partner. An amicable solution would be to mark down the illiquid tax lot to zero for all partners and distribute the withdrawing partners' share to them in kind. Thus, withdrawing partners would get cash for their share of liquid and tradable tax lots held in the partnership's asset portfolio, as well as an in-kind distribution of their share of illiquid and nontradable tax lots held in the portfolio at the time of their exit. This same equitable solution applies under any other alternate tax allocation methodology.

Summary: In this arbitrary simple two-period (two-year) example, which we shall call Example A, we have demonstrated that under the method of layering, differential tax allocations are made to partners as soon as an underlying tax lot in the fund is sold or closed. In this particular example, partners are allocated capital gains in Year 1 and are not subject to capital gains tax upon entire redemption in Year 2. Indeed, tax allocations are following the economics, subject to this primary condition that we have met: that all tax lots containing memorandum capital gains allocated to a partner are liquidated before the withdrawal and exit by the same partner. Partners are differentially assigned allocations of realized gains and losses that are involuntarily triggered by the entry of new partners.

**Layering: Example B.**   Having grappled with this two-period Example A, let us make a change in Year 2. At the beginning of Year 2, the partnership takes its previous year's closing value of 200, which is all in cash, and purchases another single security for 200. The partnership no longer holds cash. Toward the end of Year 2, the partnership discovers that its single security has declined to 120 and sells it. That tax lot made a loss, −80. The resulting proceeds of the sale of 120 are held as cash into Year 3. Let us follow through with the tax allocations in Year 2 under the methodology of layering. The partners do not liquidate their holdings at the end of Year 2, but instead remain in the partnership into the third year, Year 3. The partnership simply holds its value of 120 as cash. No new securities are purchased or sold in Year 3.

Under this extended and modified example, which we shall call Example B, new tax allocations have to be made at the end of Year 2. The total loss on the liquidated sole tax lot of Year 2 is −80 (due to the purchase price of 200 and sale price of 120). The charter partner owns 67 percent of the partnership. Under the layering methodology, the charter partner would be allocated a tax loss of −80 times 67 percent, equal to −53. The second partner, the one who joined later, midstream during Year 1, would be allocated a tax loss of −80 times 33 percent, equal to −27. The tax basis of the charter partner, which was 133 at the end of Year 1, is now 80. The tax basis of the second partner, which was 67 at the end of Year 1, is now 40. The capital account value of the charter partner is the total partnership value of 120 times 67 percent, which is 80. Similarly, the capital account value of the second partner is 120 times 33 percent, which is 40.

Now let us assume that both partners withdraw at the end of Year 3. The charter partner reports zero capital gain attributable to the disposition of their entire partnership interest at the end of Year 3, because the proceeds of redemption are 80 (67 percent of 120) and the tax basis of their partnership interest is also 80. The second partner also reports zero capital gain attributable to the disposition of their entire partnership interest at the end of Year 3, because the proceeds of redemption are 40 (33 percent of 120) and the tax basis of their partnership interest is also 40.

We have introduced Example B to highlight the tax case of the charter partner, whose tax allocation in Year 1 was +33, in Year 2 was −53, and in Year 3 was zero. Assuming that this charter partner did not have other capital gain and loss offsets in Year 1, there would have been a tax liability and consequently taxes paid for pass-through capital gain of +33 at the end of Year 1. These taxes paid in Year 1 are completely unrecoverable against the Year 2 capital loss allocation of −53.

For the second partner, who was allocated capital loss of −33 at the end of Year 1, no taxes were due. To the contrary, the second partner may have been able to offset capital gains taxes from other sources against this capital loss of −33 and obtain a tax benefit. At the end of Year 2, the second partner is allocated an additional capital loss of −27. Unlike the charter partner, the second partner was never allocated any capital gains, and as a result did not face tax liability in Year 1 or Year 2.

Under a taxation regime where taxpayers could carry back capital losses in Year 2 to offset capital gains in the prior year, Year 1, the charter partner would only be concerned to the extent of timing or time value of money. Unfortunately, in the United States, this privilege of carrying back capital losses to offset the prior year's capital gains is permitted only to subchapter C entities. Every other form of taxable entity or individual faces an asymmetry: Capital losses can be carried forward to offset capital gains in future years, but not the other way around.

Thus, under Example B, we have established that under the methodology of layering, some partners might be subjected to nonrecoverable taxes from tax allocations made in early years prior to complete exit and withdrawal from the partnership. We shall repeat this analysis of tax allocations under the alternate methodology of aggregation, full netting, and compare the differences.

## Full Netting Examples Showing Tax Postponement

Aggregation with Full Netting: Example A2.   We now apply the methodology of aggregation with full netting to our simple Example A with layering methodology and call it Example A2. The only tax lot that was owned by the partnership in Year 1 was sold and closed for zero capital gain. Indeed, the time span of the tax lot straddled the charter partner and the new partner. The percentage ownership of each partner was calculated at any interim time point of mark-to-market valuation of this tax lot. In Year 1, after the sale of this tax lot, the aggregated or fully netted capital gain at the partnership level was zero. As a result, each partner is allocated zero capital gain during Year 1.

Note the immediate advantage to the charter partner. Due to there being no capital gain allocation as in Example A with the layering methodology (which allocated +33 of capital gain to the charter partner), the charter partner has no tax liability and pays no tax in Year 1. This particular charter partner obtained the benefit of mean reversion in the valuation of the risky asset tax lot.

The second partner, who joined the partnership in the middle of Year 1, would also be allocated zero capital gain. Recall that with the layering methodology of Example A, the same partner would have been allocated a capital loss of −33.

Since the aggregate capital gain was zero and no capital gain allocations were made to either partner in Year 1, their respective tax basis in the partnership remains unchanged from their inception date in the partnership: The charter partner's tax basis remains at 100, and the second partner's tax basis also remains at 100.

The total value of the partnership at the end of Year 1 in Example A is 200. Due to interim mark-to-market valuation and recalculation of partnership percentage at the time of entry of the second partner during the middle of Year 1, the charter partner owns 67 percent of the partnership at the end of Year 1, valued at 133. The new second partner owns the remainder, 37 percent of the partnership at the end of Year 1, valued at 67.

As in Example A, the fund holds 200 in cash through the end of Year 2, and both partners exit and withdraw from the partnership at the end of Year 2. There has been no new capital gain during Year 2, so there is no capital gain tax allocation to the partners. The charter partner would have to recognize a capital gain of +33 on account of the entire redemption of their partnership interest, calculated as the redemption proceeds of 133, minus their tax basis of their partnership interest of 100. Similarly, the second partner would have to recognize a capital loss of −33 on account of the entire redemption of their partnership interest, calculated as the redemption proceeds of 67, minus their tax basis of 100.

Let us now compare tax outcomes of Example A under the layering methodology with Example A2 under the aggregation with full netting methodology. Over a period spanning two tax years, Year 1 and Year 2, the charter partner obtained a capital gain of +33 and the second partner a capital loss of −33 under both methodologies. If this did not happen, we would legitimately have to be concerned. However, the timing of tax allocations in this specific example under the layering methodology, compared to the methodology of aggregation, is that some taxpayers might have tax liabilities imposed on them early (i.e., before entire redemption). This arises from capital gains allocations made to them early, and because the early tax payments most likely would not be recoverable against potential future realized capital losses or future capital loss allocations. There is always a mirror image to such an event: other partners who have capital loss allocations made to them early under the layering methodology.

Example A2 clearly establishes that the aggregation methodology offers a tax benefit to all partners of postponing (for early partners) early taxation arising from implicit involuntary transfer and sale of appreciated mark-to-market securities in the partnership portfolio to new partners.

Example A2 was created to demonstrate the benefit of tax deferral on involuntary mark-to-market gains for the charter partner. We did not have to calculate the proportion of realized capital gains to be allocated to each partner according to their economic participation in the partnership, because the aggregate realized capital gain was deliberately constructed as zero.

**Aggregation with Full Netting: Example B2.** We shall extend Example A2 to Example B2 to address the issue of allocating a nonzero capital gain among the partners. Under Example B2, as with Example B, the aggregate realized capital gain during Year 2 is −80. This has to be equitably allocated to each of the partners, consistent with a principle of Section 704(b).

Once again, Example B2 is constructed to be easy. Capital gain of −80 in Year 2 is a short-term capital loss incurred on the sole security tax lot held in the partnership for less than a full year during Year 2. Since this is the case of short-term capital loss, we do not have to look at partnership ownership percentages prior to Year 2. During Year 2, the partnership ownership percentages held steady and did not change, at 67 percent for the charter partner and 33 percent for the second partner. Thus, the capital gain of −80 is allocated according to 67/33, that is, −53 to the charter partner and −27 to the new partner.

In this Example B2, at the end of Year 2, the tax basis of the charter partner would be their original 100 at inception, plus zero for tax allocations in Year 1, plus −53 for tax allocations in Year 2, totaling 47. At the end of Year 3, upon redemption of their entire partnership interest, the charter partner would report capital gains of −33, which is their redemption proceeds of 80 (67 percent of 120) minus the tax basis of 37.

Similarly, in this Example B2, at the end of Year 2, the tax basis of the second partner would be their original 100 at inception, plus zero for tax allocations in Year 1, plus −27 for tax allocations in Year 2, totaling 73. At the end of Year 3, upon redemption of their entire partnership interest, the second partner would report capital gains of −33, which is their redemption proceeds of 40 (33 percent of 120) minus the tax basis of 73.

Example B2 under aggregation with full netting starkly displays the benefit of tax deferral to partners under aggregation, compared to Example A2 under layering. Under both methodologies, the cumulative capital gain after combining tax allocations and capital gain triggered by entire disposition of the partnership interest is the same. However, under the methodology of aggregation of Example B2, early tax allocations are deflected and deferred.

It should be emphasized that tax deferral to partners under the method of aggregation (relative to the method of layering) is unintended, and not part of any grand objective of tax optimization or deferral. It is simply a consequence of recognition of the event of implicit transfer and sale of tax lots by existing partners to new partners at interim mark-to-market prices at the time of the entire disposition of partnership interest, rather than at the time of entire disposition of the relevant tax lots in the method of layering.

# CHAPTER 9

# Tax Efficiency of Hedge Funds

## Tax Efficiency Considerations for Offshore Hedge Funds

The organizers of offshore funds, whether master or feeder, generally take the view that taxation and tax efficiency considerations are immaterial due to exemption from all taxes in the offshore regime (such as the Cayman Islands). Investors are expected to deal with their own tax regimes and factor in their own tax efficiency considerations. However, offshore funds might be subjected to withholding taxes in various countries according to the nature of the securities that they trade and their own investment strategies. Generally, offshore funds do not take steps to investigate whether some of the withholding taxes imposed by securities trading jurisdictions are recoverable for some of their investors, or whether they could help their investors to pursue such recovery.

Many offshore funds elect to file Form 8832 with the IRS so that their U.S. investors, whether taxable or tax-exempt, are not subjected to harsh PFIC rules. Such offshore funds effectively are treated as associations or partnerships that are not PFICs. Having already taken proactive steps to make IRS filings for the benefit of U.S. investors, such offshore funds could go the extra mile and implement steps so that U.S. withholding taxes on dividends are waived for their U.S. investors, or are reported in such a manner that they are recoverable by their U.S. investors in the form of tax credits or tax refunds. Similarly, offshore funds ought to investigate whether withholding taxes of various European governments arising from securities traded under their regimes could be waived or recovered for their U.S. and European investors.

As mentioned before, it is unclear whether an offshore fund that is organized as a Cayman Islands partnership and files Form 8832 with the IRS leads to pass-through taxation according to the nature of pass-through gains for taxable U.S. investors, as if it were a U.S. partnership. This question should be investigated by engaging expert U.S. tax lawyers and obtaining a private letter ruling from the IRS. Ordinarily, the offshore entities are not under the jurisdiction of the IRS, despite filing Form 8832, and thus taxable U.S. investors might report any involuntary cash flows from interim distributions as dividends and recognize capital gains upon the entire disposition of their holding, which would be tax-preferred long-term capital gains taxed at 15 percent if the offshore partnership interest is held for more than one year. This is indeed a form of tax arbitrage, since a U.S. partnership would have to report a breakdown of really short-term and long-term capital gains, and the short-term gains component is taxed at the maximum individual rate of about 35 percent. It remains unclear how this apparent tax arbitrage would be permitted to persist for offshore partnership entities that elect to file Form 8832 with the IRS.

Large offshore hedge funds that have significant holding by U.S. investors might implicitly contain protection from the U.S. banking and regulatory regime. The enormous $4 billion hedge fund, Long Term Capital Management (LTCM), which collapsed and was bailed out by the Federal Reserve Bank, had organized itself as a U.S. (Delaware) partnership located in Connecticut as a feeder fund, and that U.S. entity was the general partner, which operated the offshore master fund Long Term Capital Portfolio L.P. as a Cayman Islands partnership. Most of its investors were U.S. entities, both taxable and nontaxable. Being a partnership and not a foreign corporation, it would have been eligible not to be deemed a PFIC entity for taxable U.S. investors. However, LTCM's main U.S. clientele was tax-exempt U.S. investors, so partnership status was not particularly relevant as much as being considered a "blocker" entity that prevents UBTI taxation to its tax-exempt U.S. investors. For taxable pass-through U.S. investors, the enormous interest expense resulting from enormous leverage likely would have been available to them in the form of tax-deductible interest expense. For tax-exempt U.S. investors, participating directly or indirectly through a U.S. feeder fund into the Cayman Islands master partnership, the thorn of UBTI that would arise from any U.S. domestic partnership pass-through borrowing would have been unambiguously and clearly eclipsed. One of the principal factors that seem to have led to the quick rescue of LTCM by the Federal Reserve Bank, at the time when Alan Greenspan was the chair of its board of governors, was that should LTCM file for bankruptcy in the Cayman Islands courts, the judicial outcome and time frame of court proceedings under Cayman Islands laws might have been unpredictable, with Cayman courts' jurisdiction prevailing over that of U.S. courts, leading to greater market panic and deepening financial crisis.[1]

The U.S. Treasury has indeed established at least one benefit of organizing the master fund as a limited partnership at an offshore location, and the feeder fund as well as the general partner entity to the offshore limited partnership as a U.S. Delaware partnership based in Connecticut. Under bankruptcy, the Fed is obliged to organize a rescue if the collapsed fund happens to be sufficiently large so as to melt down global financial markets. LTCM was spared the expenses of bankruptcy court litigation. What is left unstated, but is amply clear for this form of hedge fund structure organization, is that taxable U.S. investors in LTCM would likely record taxable pass-through cash flows according to their nature. Tax-preferred items reported by the master offshore fund, such as tax-deductible interest expense, U.S. tax credit for foreign taxes paid, and so on would likely be available to taxable U.S. investors and partners.

## Tax Preference Ordering for U.S. Investors

It is useful to evaluate and rank the distributive line items of income to partners, so that both the limited partners (investors) and the general partners (the hedge fund managers) carefully factor in taxes for calculating their after-tax return.

To begin with, for tax-exempt U.S. investors, taxes arise only if there is UBTI triggered by any kind of direct borrowing by the hedge fund, manifested by the distributive item of interest expense. If the hedge fund's investment strategy involves any form of direct borrowing that leaves

---

[1]Robert E. Rubin, Alan Greenspan, Arthur Levitt, and Brooksley Born, "Hedge Funds, Leverage, and the Lessons of Long Term Capital Management," Report of the President's Working Group on Financial Markets, presented on April 28, 1999, to the U.S. House of Representatives and the U.S. Senate. This is posted for public view by the U.S. Treasury at www.ustreas.gov/press/releases/reports/hedgfund.pdf. On page 27, the report says, "... it is believed that the Fund itself would have sought bankruptcy protection in the Cayman Islands courts, under Cayman law. Had that been the case, any U.S. bankruptcy proceeding would likely have been ancillary to the main Cayman Islands proceeding." Further, on page 28, the Fed's rescue action is justified: "If LTCM had declared bankruptcy in the Cayman Islands, its Cayman receiver could have sought a Section 304 Injunction prohibiting at least temporarily the liquidation of U.S. collateral pledged by LTCM to its counterparties. Even a temporary delay in the liquidation of collateral could have had detrimental financial consequences for those parties holding that collateral." Section 304 here refers to Section 304 of the U.S. Bankruptcy Code.

behind a trail of interest expense, as well as any form of direct short selling of securities where dividends claimed could count as interest expense, it immediately imposes a 35 percent UBTI tax upon tax-exempt U.S. investors attributable to income associated with the borrowing. Thus, hedge funds would do well to prevent this possibility by organizing an offshore blocker corporation for the benefit of tax-exempt U.S. investors. Those tax-exempt U.S. investors who hesitate to become a partner or member in an offshore entity may be encouraged to set up their own captive offshore blocker entity.

Having thus deflected the imposition of UBTI, we proceed to rank order the broad distributive line items of income and expense to taxable investors. Tax-exempt investors are indifferent to these subcategories of income and expense and are mostly concerned about aggregate economic returns without the consideration of taxes. Given that almost no hedge fund is isolated from taxable investors and solely invests for the benefit of tax-exempt U.S. limited partners, such a tax preference ordering is indeed relevant. At a minimum, the general partner entity has pass-through partners and members who are themselves taxable entities or individuals.

Long-term capital gains in net positive quantity are the highest preferred form of distributive income, since they are subjected to a maximum tax rate of 15 percent for U.S. individuals. The Obama administration has other economic priorities and for the time being is unlikely to return to the previous regime when long-term capital gains for U.S. individuals were subject to 28 percent tax.

The next equally preferred item of distributive income to limited partners who are taxable U.S. individuals are qualified U.S. source dividends, which are taxed at 15 percent. It is therefore important for the hedge fund to track the portion of its dividend income that counts as qualified U.S. source dividends under U.S. tax law. Generally, dividends of U.S. subchapter C companies held by the hedge fund for more than 60 days within a 120-day window around an ex-dividend date count as qualified U.S. source dividends eligible for taxation at this preferred rate. The qualified dividend classification ends on December 31, 2010. It seems likely that the Obama administration will renew and continue this provision enacted during the administration of George W. Bush.

All other items of distributive income are taxed to U.S. individuals at the ordinary income rate, including interest income, nonqualified dividends, and short-term capital gains (i.e., gains on trade holding periods of less than one year).

Exchange-traded futures contracts offer a unique tax treatment to taxable U.S. investors. Capital gains or losses made on any U.S. exchange-traded futures contracts are bifurcated. Sixty percent of the gain is considered to be long-term, and 40 percent of the gain is considered to be short-term, irrespective of the holding period of the futures contract. This was an early tax benefit given to the U.S. futures industry at the time of its foundation and growth. The economic argument behind treating 60 percent of gain from exchange-traded futures contracts as long-term capital gain is that futures hedgers and traders roll over a sequence of short-maturity futures contracts in order to achieve their investment objectives, which are actually based on longer time horizons. Short-maturity futures contracts attract the greatest liquidity and are traded efficiently with small-market impact and bid-ask spread. The U.S. exchange-traded futures contract industry has been unable to attract sufficient liquidity and market depth into long-maturity futures contracts. There are proposals in the Obama administration to repeal this long-standing tax advantage to traders in exchange-traded futures contracts. However, it is unlikely that the administration would pursue radical change from historical precedent when its economic priorities lie elsewhere.

Not all hedge funds engage in investment strategies that are based intensively on exchange-traded futures contracts. Hedge funds indeed resort to exchange-traded futures contracts to offset risk elsewhere in their holdings. With the exception of trading strategies in energy and crude oil, where exchange-traded futures contracts are the primary market for trading and speculation, hedge funds do not exclusively rely on exchange-traded futures contracts.

Indeed, private notional principal contracts, that is, private forwards, futures, swaps, and options with private counterparties, mainly banks and investment firms, are more common in the hedge fund industry. Rare are instances when private notional principal contracts become popular vehicles for the hedge fund industry, such as credit default swaps during 2006–2008. Gains or losses on these are considered to be capital gains, depending on the holding period, thus no different from capital gains from trading securities. Similarly, any appropriate interim cash flows relating to such contracts, such as interest income, are interest payments, and are treated no differently from interest income on fixed-income instruments and interest payments on borrowing.

Short-term capital gains in net positive quantity have the lowest tax preference, since the taxes to U.S. individuals add their maximum marginal tax rate, which is about 36 percent.

Interest expense is a serious tax preference item, since it is counted as investment interest for a taxable U.S. individual. Investment interest can be applied to offset other taxable investment income, including interest income, dividend income, and long-term or short-term capital gains. It is important to note that dividends claimed on short positions held for more than 45 days are permitted by the IRS to be counted as interest expense. (By default, or if the short positions were held for 45 days or less, any dividends claimed are combined with the basis of the short position and therefore become equivalent to short-term capital loss.)

Foreign taxes paid are fully or partly recoverable against the U.S. tax liability of taxable U.S. investors.

Management fees, or equivalent fixed fees that are paid to general partners by limited partners, have the least tax preference. That is because they are mostly not tax deductible, due to a large threshold of 2 percent of aggregate gross income being first excluded from the management fees, and subsequently, the net amount being counted as an itemized deduction, which is neutralized under the alternative minimum tax. Effectively, taxable U.S. investors have hardly any economic reduction in their tax liability due to management fees. This asymmetry is astounding, since all gross capital gains and other income flows are subject to tax for taxable U.S. investors. The mirror image applies to the general partner, who collects fixed management fees from the limited partners. These fixed management fees are counted as ordinary income for the general partner and attract the highest U.S. ordinary income tax rate. The general partner is permitted to deduct expenses relating to its activity of earning management fees, and only then net positive income, if any, is taxed to its pass-through partners and members at the highest ordinary income tax rate.

The same lack of tax preference applies to other pass-through items of investment expense, such as out-of-pocket expenses for data feeds and investment newsletter subscriptions. It is therefore not surprising that practically all investment funds, not just hedge funds, engage in "soft dollar" arrangements with the brokerage industry, wherein they pay slightly exaggerated brokerage commissions, which are applied as kickbacks to pay for data feeds and data terminals at the fund manager's trading location. Safe harbor provisions in the Securities and Exchange Act prevent abuse of soft dollar arrangements. However, so far, fund managers' data terminals subscriptions being paid for by brokerage firms indirectly from brokerage commissions are considered to be within the safe harbor provisions. Effectively, the cost of data terminals and data subscriptions is embedded as an item of capital loss, which is a higher tax preference, rather than an item of investment expense, which is the lowest tax preference.

Both net negative long-term capital gains and short-term capital gains (i.e., net short-term and long-term capital losses) are mild items of tax preference. This is because capital losses can be carried forward indefinitely and can be applied to offset future capital gains. Unfortunately, they cannot be carried back to offset past capital gains, with the exception only for a three-year carry-back window for any kind of net losses incurred by a subchapter C corporation. It is in the interest of investors to carry a war chest of capital losses to offset future unexpected capital gains, particularly future short-term capital gains upon which the highest tax rate is applied.

To summarize, the order of tax preference of distributive line items of income in a U.S. partnership are in the following order:

Items of income:

1. Net positive long-term capital gains (most preferred)
2. Qualified dividends
3. Net positive short-term capital gains
4. Nonqualified dividends
5. Interest income (least preferred)
6. UBTI (unrelated business taxes on income) for tax-exempt limited partners

Items of expense:

1. Interest expense (most preferred)
2. Net negative long-term and short-term capital gains (i.e., net losses)
3. Foreign taxes paid
4. Management fees
5. Investment expense (least preferred)

We now proceed to identify tax preferences according to specific elements of the U.S. partnership tax return. Recall that each item of tax allocation to partners by a U.S.-domiciled hedge fund was carefully defined and associated with symbols, subscripts, and superscripts. We shall utilize the same notation and symbols in this section.

It was noted earlier that a U.S. hedge fund reports its aggregate profits for the calendar year and its components to the IRS on its tax return as:

$$\Pi = \Pi_4 + \Pi_5 + \Pi_{6a} + \Pi_8 + \Pi_{9a} - (\Pi_{13b} + \Pi_{13d} + \Pi_{16l}) + \Pi_{18a} + \Pi_{M1L6}$$

Each subscript in these expressions stands for line items of the Schedule K and Schedule M1—line 6 in the U.S. tax return. Each line item is associated with tax preference or attractiveness to pass-through U.S. taxable limited partners based on the likelihood of resulting in reducing the partner's overall tax payment.

## More Attractive Tax Items to U.S. Investors

Subscript 9a: net long term capital gain. As of now, the long-term capital gains rate is at the lowest point in decades, at 15 percent. If the gain is negative for the year, that is, a long-term capital loss, it is available only to combine with accumulated carry-forward capital losses to offset future (or current) capital gains. Thus, a net positive gain for the year is extremely attractive to a U.S. partner. This could be dampened in future years if the long-term capital gains rate is increased to, say, 28 percent.

Subscript 13b: investment interest expense. This item of pass-through, always negative investment interest tax allocation is extremely valuable to a U.S. taxable investor, provided that this investor makes investment gains over some period of time. This is because investment interest expense is allowed as a deduction against any kind of investment income in the current and future years. In any given year, the investor has some discretion on how much investment interest to count as a tax deduction in a given year and how much to carry to future years. Thus a prudent U.S. taxpayer may elect to pay 15 percent tax on long-term capital gains and apply investment interest expense deduction against the least preferred/least attractive tax items, which otherwise would be taxed at the maximum marginal tax rate, on the order of 36 percent, that is applicable.

It is extremely important for a U.S. hedge fund that engages in short sales to establish a proper dividend-tracking database system relating to dividends claimed on short sales positions. The IRS permits the counting of dividends claimed on short sale positions held for more than 45 days as investment interest expense and includes it in the reported number for total investment interest expense under subscript 13b. As described in the previous paragraph, investment interest expense is a highly attractive tax preference item, since it is available to offset practically every form of investment income. If the U.S. hedge fund does not bother to track whether the short positions were held for more than 45 days, the dividends claimed (always a negative number, an outflow) on short positions would simply net out and reduce reported capital gains. When capital gains are negative, that is, losses, dividends claimed on short positions would increase the accumulated carry-forward capital loss. The flexibility to offset and reduce other categories of immediately taxable investment income is lost.

Subscript 16: foreign taxes paid. This item of allocation to a U.S. partner is extremely attractive due to providing not just a deduction, but a dollar-for-dollar tax credit, provided the partner has had some form of foreign source income during any tax year. To the extent that foreign taxes paid exceed the maximum foreign tax credit allowed during your year, the excess could be carried forward indefinitely to the subsequent years. Of course, such carry-forward of disallowed foreign tax credits would be entirely worthless if the U.S. partner/investor never has foreign source income. Generally, foreign taxes paid are associated with the foreign source dividend subset of total dividends allocated to the investor, reported under subscript 16d: foreign gross dividends included in total ordinary dividends (subscript 6a).

Subscript 6b: qualified dividends included in total ordinary dividends (subscript 6a). Qualified dividends are those dividends received from U.S. companies held for more than 60 days. In order to mitigate double taxation of dividends, once at the level of 34 percent U.S. corporate tax, and next at the level of personal tax at the U.S. maximum marginal tax rate of about 36 percent, the second Bush administration passed a regulation to tax qualified dividends at a 15 percent flat tax rate. Like the current 15 percent long-term capital gains tax rate, it is the lowest possible tax rate that could conceivably be available to a U.S. investor. Just as is the case with tax-exempt interest income, it might be considered downright imprudent and irrational for a U.S. investor to pay the full 36 percent tax on qualified dividends, when the tax due is only at a rate of 15 percent.

## Less Attractive Tax Items to U.S. Investors

Subscript 5: taxable interest income invites tax at the maximum marginal tax rate that applies to the U.S. investor.

Subscript 6a: total ordinary dividends, including foreign source dividends, but excluding U.S. source qualified dividends, also invites tax at the maximum marginal tax rate to the U.S. investor.

Subscript 8: net short-term capital gain. This item is also taxed at the maximum marginal rate to the U.S. investor.

Subscript 13d: other investment expense deductions. This item represents management (fixed) fees and any other items of investment expense (other than investment interest, dividends claimed on short sales, and foreign taxes withheld). This is as an itemized deduction to U.S. individual investors for the amount in excess of 2 percent of their aggregate gross income. Generally, the aggregate gross income (AGI) of highly net-worth U.S. individual investors is sufficiently high so that the 2 percent of AGI threshold is sufficiently high. Even if the investment expense deduction (in excess of the 2 percent AGI threshold) were meaningful, rules of phase-out of itemized deductions and alternative minimum tax become binding for high net-worth, high-AGI U.S. individual investors such that this item no longer has any tax benefit.

Subscript 4: guaranteed payments. This item applies to the general partner, whose fixed fees collected according to the partnership agreement from limited partners is deemed to be a "guaranteed payment" that is considered to be ordinary income to the general partner. The general partner is almost always a business entity and not a U.S. individual, so it is able to deduct business expenses to arrive at a taxable net business profit.

# An Exception: Special Tax Preference for Gains from U.S. Exchange-Traded Futures Contracts

Capital gains arising from "Section 1256 contracts" qualify for special treatment under the U.S. tax code.[2] These include futures contracts that are traded on U.S. commodity exchanges, currency contracts, non-equity options, and dealer-market equity options and futures. Irrespective of whether futures contracts are closed in less than one year or in more than one year, capital gains (or losses) associated with them are classified as 60 percent long term and 40 percent short term.

# Ambiguities in Tax Preference

Swaps, or notional principal contacts, may have ambiguity with regard to classifying their features according to tax preferences. This is where tax experts, accountants, and lawyers offer advice and counsel. Often, there are entire hedge funds and U.S. partnerships set up for limited partners to obtain tax-preferred pass-through items of income based on ambiguities in the tax classification of items of income. Though such funds may seem to have a genuine business purpose and be absorbing risks to pursue profits, it is often the case that the tax benefits associated with allocations of tax-preferred items of pass-through income are significant in magnitude.

# Tax Efficiency Steps for U.S. Hedge Funds

Aim for Long-Term Capital Gains.    Taxable U.S. investors would always prefer that most of their investment income from a hedge fund should come from long-term capital gains. Unfortunately, most hedge fund strategies are geared to generating returns on a pretax basis by holding securities that are not restricted by a holding horizon of one year. To the extent possible, some part of the hedge fund strategy may be substitutable by exchange-traded futures contracts in fixed income and equities. As noted earlier, all capital gains from exchange-traded futures contracts are counted as 60 percent long-term capital gain and 40 percent short-term capital gain, without regard to the holding period. The recent rise in crude oil prices to historical highs in 2007 and 2008 is partly attributable to intense speculative fever and the exchange-traded crude oil futures market, which not only

---

[2]Section 1256 contracts and their tax treatment are defined in Title 26 of the U.S. Code, Section 1256. This is accessible at www.law.cornell.edu/uscode/html/uscode26/usc_sec_26_00001256----000-.html.

made it easy to acquire large exposures to crude oil, but also are tax preferred to U.S. investors.

Given that hedge funds have enormous flexibility and access to counterparties to arrange customized notional principal contracts, it should be possible to legitimately overlay swaps on a portfolio of securities containing short-term gains so as to extend the holding period to the threshold of one year while hedging away the economic exposure though swaps.

Silicon Valley venture funds produce almost all of their investment return in the form of long-term capital gain. This is because the underlying companies in their venture portfolio rarely mature or exit over short-term horizons of less than one year.

**Foreign Tax Credit for Taxable U.S. Limited Partners.** Taxable U.S. investors are permitted to recover all or part of distributive foreign tax expense payments against their own U.S. taxes. However, for smooth release of foreign tax credit by the IRS, the taxpayers are required to report a breakdown of foreign source income earned and foreign taxes paid by country on Form 1116. The maximum foreign tax credit allowed is calculated on Form 1116 by multiplying the average overall tax rate of the investor by the foreign source income. Foreign tax payments disallowed for credit against U.S. taxes in one given year can be indefinitely carried forward to subsequent years. Thus, foreign tax payments are an item of tax preference. General partners ought to place strict requirements on their bookkeeping accountants to produce the necessary data calculate aggregate amounts (at the level of the partnership), as well as distributive allocations (to partners), of both foreign income and foreign taxes by country. While it is irrelevant to hedge funds that do not have any kind of foreign tax withholding imposed upon them, practically every fund that invests in foreign equities is subjected to foreign withholding taxes on dividends attributable to these foreign equities. Even fixed-income funds might be subjected to withholding taxes on interest payments by various countries. While generally capital gains taxes are not subject to withholding in most countries, they should not be taken for granted and should be examined country by country. Many emerging market countries insist on imposing withholding taxes on capital gains from domestic market trades.

**Excise Taxes and Stamp Duty.** Some taxes are simply not recoverable and not even treated as taxes. For example, several countries in Europe, including the United Kingdom, have had a long tradition of imposing excise taxes on purchases of securities. Some emerging market countries impose excise taxes on exchange-traded derivatives contracts. It is a matter of tradition in the investment management industry to treat the stamp duties and excise taxes as part of the sale price or purchase price of the securities. These are certainly not taxes on income, but simply a form of transaction cost that varies across countries. Even the United States has excise taxes, labeled "exchange fees" and "SEC fee" on every securities trade, but it is minimal, at one-eighth basis point, so small that everybody considers the United States as being a country with no transactions costs from taxes and excise duties. This is indeed a major contributor in making U.S. securities heavily traded and highly liquid.

One of the reasons why equity derivatives trading has blossomed and taken off in Europe is that it enables the attainment of equity index exposure without the accompanying cost of stamp duty that would apply if the underlying equity portfolio were purchased. Stamp duties can be as high as 25 basis points. To the extent that European exchange-traded index futures markets have tight bid-ask spreads and low transactions costs, they offer an attractive lower transaction cost alternative to trading in underlying equity. For investors with long time horizons and no pressing need for interim illiquidity or mark-to-market valuation, the over-the-counter swaps market offers a mechanism to obtain equity exposure without stamp duties.

Several European companies have issued American depository receipts (ADRs), which trade in the U.S. stock markets without any meaningful stamp duty like transactions costs (other than the SEC fee of one-eighth basis point). The trading volume of several of these ADRs is phenomenal, on the order of several million shares per day, for various European companies in the pharmaceutical, oil, and telecom industries. It is cheaper for any fund to trade in ADRs than the underlying share in the home markets requiring a payment of stamp duty.

**Nonrecoverable Foreign Taxes Paid by Tax-Exempt U.S. Investors.** Consider the hedge fund that engages in an investment strategy that results in payment of foreign taxes, such as withholding taxes on foreign source dividends or foreign-source fixed-income securities. Also consider that it has a significant holding by limited partners who are tax-exempt U.S. investors. Since these tax-exempt investors do not pay any taxes, the issue of recovery of foreign taxes paid does not arise. Most tax-exempt U.S. investors simply treat this as a transaction cost or a deadweight loss, simply the cost of doing business and extending the reach of investment diversification. Some or all of such foreign taxes might be recovererable, depending on the circumstances. Suppose a particular hedge fund produces attractive returns, and also pays out significant foreign taxes. These foreign taxes are potentially recoverable in the form of credit to taxable U.S. investors, but not to tax-exempt U.S. investors. In such a situation, a captive solution or commingled holding structure may be constructed for various tax-exempt investors, similar to the idea of the offshore blocker entity that deflects and shields against UBTI for tax-exempt investors. When billions of dollars of investment capital are at stake, a hundred basis points or 1 percent in foreign taxes is significant. At a minimum, if recovered, it can pay for all or some part of the fixed fees charged to limited partners by the general partner, which, of course, is not recoverable from taxes by tax-exempt partners and rarely recoverable from taxes in the form of a tax deduction by limited partners due to the 2 percent aggregate gross income (AGI) threshold and further limitation to itemized deductions by overriding the alternative minimum tax and phase-out of itemized deductions according to income.

## A Structure for Tax-Exempt U.S. Entities to Recover Foreign Taxes

A structure for recovery of foreign taxes by a tax-exempt U.S. investor is presented here. A significant investment in U.S. hedge funds is by ERISA[3] accounts, that is, employee retirement plans. The ERISA assets are established as a holding of the tax-exempt entity as a separate account of a taxable U.S. multinational insurance company. The same insurance company invests for the benefit of the tax-exempt entity into the hedge fund. Distributive allocations of foreign taxes are recovered against from the U.S. corporate tax payments by the U.S.-domiciled insurance company.

A private letter ruling is sought by the same U.S. insurance company from the IRS, seeking permission to collect foreign tax credit against foreign taxes withheld from its separate account. Subsequently, the insurance company would pass through to the tax-exempt entity all or part of the foreign tax credit it has obtained. The IRS would have to rule on whether the foreign tax credit is a legitimate credit considered to be applicable to the taxable insurance company, including its separate accounts that are established for tax-exempt beneficial owners. The source capital in the separate account is ERISA protected, and the taxable insurance company would earn profits in the form of reduced U.S. corporate tax payments that are not attributable to any business activity. In all likelihood, the IRS would issue a private letter ruling to permit the taxable U.S. insurance company to pass through the foreign tax credit it has obtained against its U.S. taxes, less a legitimate administrative or management fee for expenses.

This could be a beneficial situation for the tax-exempt U.S. ERISA entity as well as for the U.S. insurance company. A separate account of an insurance company is well protected against bankruptcy and default by U.S.

---

[3]The Employee Retirement Income Security Act of 1974 (ERISA) is a federal statute that establishes standards for pension plans and protects retirement assets from being claimed by a creditor under the U.S. Bankruptcy Code.

insurance regulation. The assets contained in it are sequestered and protected from external claimants. There is a second round of protection from
potential claimants in a bankruptcy court in the form of ERISA beneficiaries
to the insurance company separate account. Generally, ERISA assets are
seriously protected from seizure by claimants to corporate liabilities under
bankruptcy. If there is risk, it is due to the chance that a given U.S. insurance company may unexpectedly start making losses and be unable to
recover foreign taxes against its own U.S. taxes, given that it owes no U.S.
taxes. The complex nature of this arrangement requires scale economies
on the order of billions of dollars and sufficient incentive for the U.S. insurance company to facilitate this structure.

The same logic might be extended to seeking recovery of foreign taxes
for other U.S. tax-exempt entities, such as a foundation or nonprofit corporation. The taxable insurance company establishes a separate account
and seeks a private letter ruling from the IRS to pass through some or part
of the foreign tax credit arising from the hedge fund asset holding in the
separate account.

# CHAPTER 10

# Hedge Fund Performance and Risk Presentation

## Performance Presentation: CFA Institute GIPS Verification

The CFA Institute in the United States is a nonprofit association of investment professionals that awards the designations Chartered Financial Analyst (CFA) and Certificate in Investment Performance Measurement (CIPM). The latter designation is relatively recent, while the CFA designation has had a very long and respected standing among investment professionals worldwide. The CFA Institute created the Global Investment Performance Standards (GIPS) to remove ambiguities and sleight-of-hand in the presentation of investment performance by fund managers to both preexisting investors as well as prospective new investors.

With hedge funds and investment partnerships, there isn't a gold standard net asset value (NAV) that is required to be calculated according to some rigorous standard and submitted periodically to a regulatory agency. This is where the CFA Institute has stepped in for the benefit of investors, not just in U.S. funds, but also in any other offshore or global hedge fund, to provide rigorous standards for calculating investment performance.[1]

The unambiguous calculation of investment performance over any time period is straightforward for an SEC-regulated mutual fund, which is obliged to publish its NAV and distributions (if any) at the close of every business day. Deposits and withdrawals occur at this published NAV at the close of business. Based on this publicly available data, investors can readily

---

[1]The CFA Institute's GIPS portal is at www.gipsstandards.org. The publication *Global Investment Performance Standards (GIPS) Handbook* (2nd ed., 2006) is offered for sale on this Web site.

calculate total returns over any time period and compare them with other benchmarks or investment alternatives. U.S. mutual funds typically deduct annual fees on a daily basis, so a given day's NAV is already net of all fees. The daily total return over one business day is simply the ratio of NAV, plus the percentage distribution that might have occurred on that business day, if any. Chain multiplication of these daily total returns would give us an accurate measure of cumulative total returns for any subperiod of interest. The GIPS standards do not provide any specific guidelines for U.S. mutual funds. This is because they are already in compliance with the requirements of GIPS. The exacting accounting procedures laid down by the SEC and exact standards for performance presentation in mutual fund prospectuses do not provide much latitude for GIPS to become a higher standard.

GIPS is an evolution, effective 2006, of previous performance presentation standards known as AIMR-PPS (at that time, the CFA Institute was named AIMR, the Association for Investment Management and Research; PPS stood for Performance Presentation Standards). GIPS extends the previous AIMR-PPS to a wider set of member countries. While there is no drastic change relative to the previous AIMR-PPS standards, its main achievement has been to morph beyond the U.S. investment management industry into the global investment world by seeking the participation and membership of different constituent country associations of professional investment managers and analysts into endorsing GIPS as a global standard.

Hedge funds and investment partnerships were not the focus of the previous AIMR-PPS and are still not the focus of the successor, GIPS. This is for one simple reason: GIPS primarily addresses the lack of uniformity and loose standards that prevail in the individual investment advisory industry, of investment managers who manage multiple individual accounts under a common or similar strategy, and investment firms that manage multiple funds and investment advisory services. The most important achievement of GIPS (and its predecessor) is that an investment advisory firm can pool multiple noncommingled individually managed accounts into one single theoretical performance measurement composite. The imposition of GIPS reduces the arbitrariness and wide latitude that is otherwise available to investment managers in making presentations about their performance capabilities to potential investors. GIPS permits investment firms to proclaim that their performance presentation is in compliance with GIPS, and also add further credibility to their proclamation by seeking verification by an independent verifier, who is usually an independent accountant.

Hedge funds do not need the endorsement of GIPS to the same degree as an investment adviser who manages multiple independent separate accounts and wants to present a composite. A hedge fund is in this sense like a mutual fund: It has one account, though commingled, representing investors with common objectives. What's more, the tracking of each partner's economic interest requires audit-quality accounting procedures to be in force. A monthly return calculation that is required by GIPS is a trivial by-product of hedge fund accounting based on mark-to-market values. That is why we did not have to perform any special calculations earlier for hedge fund return calculations for GIPS. Our return calculation formulas are automatically consistent with GIPS.

GIPS reveals wrinkles as an attempt to impose procedures and methodologies that might be infeasible or impossible. For instance, for private equity, it states:

"7.A.1: Private Equity MUST be valued according to the GIPS PRIVATE EQUITY valuation principle provided in Appendix D."

Appendix D referenced above states:

"4. The basis of valuation MUST be logically cohesive and applied rigorously. Although a FAIR VALUE basis is RECOMMENDED, all valuations MUST, at a minimum, recognize when assets have suffered a diminution in value."

In this context, consider the case of a Silicon Valley venture fund that is holding a number of venture portfolio companies. Venture funds have consistently taken the view that interim valuation of their venture portfolio holdings cannot be measured accurately. Further, accounting standards and principles already require any business entity to recognize write-offs as they occur, as against holding them on their books at acquisition cost indefinitely. As soon as such write-offs are made, they are recognized as realized losses and are allocated to their pass-through investors. The mandate provided to private equity funds by GIPS lacks substance, and is largely a warning that write-offs should not be concealed. Given that the fair value valuation of venture portfolio holdings is optional, a private equity fund need not implement this and still be in compliance with GIPS. The actual portfolio venture holdings of a private equity venture fund are by their very nature hard to value, and therefore are not amenable to any accurate assessment of diminution value. We have provided this example to demonstrate that GIPS does not provide value to investors of a venture fund. Such a venture fund could easily obtain an independent accountant's verification letter that it is in compliance with GIPS.

The post-2006 GIPS has made efforts to attract the hedge fund industry. The predecessor AIMR-PPS standards seem to be mostly written from the perspective of tightening performance presentation standards in the context of unleveraged institutional managed accounts. A requirement that the performance be presented before and after leverage in instances where leverage is applied in the fund or an investment management strategy was clearly outdated. Such a decomposition and projection of theoretical unleveraged returns of an essentially leveraged hedge fund would be possible only in simple instances of direct borrowing. It becomes practically impossible to make such a projection of unleveraged returns when a hedge fund portfolio holds complex internally leveraged securities such as forwards, futures, swaps, and options. GIPS does not require a leveraged fund to present two sets of projected returns: before and after leverage.

The hedge fund industry as well as the venture fund industry has largely ignored GIPS or its predecessor. Instead, they look upon GIPS verification as a by-product to be obtained in their fund's audit process and made available to investors and limited partners to signal quality and accuracy. Hedge funds present written information memoranda to their investors that look like surrogate prospectuses without the accompanying prospect as legal language. A critical part of the information memoranda are the historical returns before and after fees. It helps to add a footnote to these numbers that they are GIPS-compliant.

GIPS does not require that the verifier who writes a letter attesting that the return calculations are consistent with GIPS be an accounting firm. Most of the established large accounting firms are familiar with GIPS and provide GIPS verification service. The final GIPS verification letter usually encloses a table containing monthly rates and annual rates of return.

GIPS is liberal in permitting investment firms and funds to present performance numbers before fees and after fees. In the case of hedge funds, there are typically two fees: the periodic monthly fixed fee similar to that in a mutual fund, and the annual performance fee that is contingent upon performance and also depends on special terms negotiated with each limited partner (i.e., the performance fees may be individually negotiated and may deviate in their agreement for admission into the partnership from the general category of performance fee that is stated in the limited partnership agreement). Thus, it is typical for a hedge fund to calculate a sequence of monthly returns before all fees and present that separately. Subsequently, one other series of pro forma monthly returns after fixed fees are created, and finally, the pro forma annual return after fixed fees and performance fees is calculated based on the standard performance fee schedule that is provided for in the limited partnership agreement. Hedge funds like to show interim returns that give present profile of risk and volatility measured over shorter time intervals (such as monthly) to their investors, even though performance fees are not applied.

It should be noted that all of the return formulas shown in the earlier chapters for a hedge fund, whether U.S. or offshore, are entirely consistent with GIPS. Similarly, the calculation of return and performance by SEC-regulated mutual funds is also entirely consistent with GIPS. A hedge fund that adopts tax reporting, capital account tracking and return calculation according to the formulas provided in the earlier chapters would be GIPS-compliant.

Based on the time series of GIPS-compliant total return, the hedge funds themselves, as well as investors and a community of hedge fund consultants, proceeds to calculate risk-adjusted returns according to various methodologies, and compare those returns to those of other funds or relevant benchmarks. Such analysis becomes part of continually updated performance presentations that are made by the general partner of the hedge fund to existing and prospective investors.

Should hedge funds and venture funds become overly concerned about GIPS compliance and verification? As we have seen, GIPS does not place any new requirements that a hedge fund or venture fund does not already meet. It is a relatively minor hygiene function that scores points with investors conducting due diligence review of their prospective investment. The GIPS verification letter should be seen more appropriately as a light engagement of an independent verification firm. Such a GIPS verification letter provides comfort to existing and prospective investors that the return and performance numbers presented to them are calculated according to the rigorous GIPS methodology that leaves almost no room for ambiguity and sleight-of-hand.

## Calculation of Hedge Fund Returns for Performance Presentation

Every hedge fund is continuously calculating its performance and returns for the purpose of investor reporting as well as for marketing to potential new investors. All of the effort that went into formulating the linear algebra framework earlier is put to good use, since that is completely consistent with the highest performance presentation standards in the hedge fund industry: the CFA Institute's Global Investment Performance Standards (GIPS). The CFA Institute is a U.S.-based professional organization of investment professionals.

A previous chapter explicitly defined the rate of return before all fees for the hedge fund during the investment period $[t - 1, t]$ as:

$$r_t = \frac{\pi_t}{V_{t-1}} = \frac{W_t - V_{t-1}}{V_{t-1}} \text{ for } t = 1, 2, 3, \ldots$$

where $V_{t-1}$ is the opening fund value at time point $t - 1$, $W_t$ is the closing fund value before all fees at time point $t + 1$, and $\pi_t = W_t - V_{t-1}$, is the economic gain during the period $[t - 1, t]$.

We may also derive $r_t$ from the series $\{X_t\}$ according to the identity $X_t = V_t - D_t$. Thus, we have the more familiar-looking identity for calculating the period's return involving deposit at the instant beginning of that period, as:

$$r_t = \frac{\pi_t}{X_{t-1} + D_{t-1}} = \frac{W_t - (X_{t-1} + D_{t-1})}{X_{t-1} + D_{t-1}} \text{ for } t = 1, 2, 3, \ldots$$

Recall that $X_t$ is the net fund value after fees but before deposits $D_t$ at time point $t$, and that the convention of reporting $\{X_t\}$ is followed by many hedge funds and their accountants.

The above expression is identical to what GIPS calls the "true time-weighted return formula," only that we have not deducted fees. The GIPS standards require the calculation of fund returns after all fees. As we have discussed before, limited partners could have different fee rates both for fixed fees and performance fees, and further, the general partner is exempt from all fees. GIPS permits the presentation of the returns that would have been on a pro forma or hypothetical capital account that stayed in the fund for the entire period (say, one year) and was assessed the standard fixed fees and performance fees described in the master limited partnership agreement.

It is customary to calculate the three series of returns: returns before all fees, returns after fixed fees, and returns after both fixed fees and performance fees. The first two series are time-spaced according to $t = 1, 2, 3 \ldots$ whereas the last series are time-spaced according to $t = 12, 24, 36, \ldots$. This is because fixed fees are assessed at every month- or quarter-end, at which time draws and deposits are permitted, whereas performance fees are assessed and charged to limited partners at calendar year-ends.

From tracking the series $\{W_t\}$ and $\{V_t\}$ for $t = 0, 1, 2, 3, \ldots$, our definition for the fund's investment return before fees generates the series $\{r_t\}$ for $t = 1, 2, 3, \ldots$. Note that the return series always have one less element than the fund value series.

We then factor in the periodic (monthly) fixed fee rate $f$ to calculate the return series after fixed fees. There is no superscript to $f$ since for the purpose of GIPS, the entire fund is assumed to be paying the same homogenous pro forma fixed fee. Under this working assumption for GIPS, the fund's return after fixed fees is denoted by the series $\{r_t'\}$ as:

$$r_t' = \frac{\pi_t' - V_{t-1}}{V_{t-1}} \text{ for } t = 1, 2, 3, \ldots \text{ when } t - 1 \text{ is not a multiple of 12}$$

$$r_t' = \frac{\pi_t' - U_{t-1}}{U_{t-1}} \text{ for } t = 1, 2, 3, \ldots \text{ when } t - 1 \text{ is a multiple of 12}$$

Note that the above returns are expressed in terms of $V_{t-1}$ and could be easily restated in terms of $X_{t-1} = V_{t-1} - D_{t-1}$.

Here $\pi'_t$ is the hedge fund's absolute dollar profit after fixed fees earned in the time interval $[t-1, t]$, earned on the base of the aggregate fund value *after all fees* (i.e., after applying fixed fees and then applying performance fees when $t-1$ is a multiple of 12) at the beginning time point of this time interval. The fund's profit before all fees is derived as $\pi'_t = (1-f)\pi_t$. This is the calculation of pro forma or hypothetical return of the fund after fixed fees for GIPS purposes based on the assumption that all investors pay the same periodic fixed fee rate $f$. The formula for the return series $\{r'_t\}$ is identical to the GIPS definition of "true time-weighted return formula," with the qualification that it is after fixed fees but before performance fees.

The return calculation at calendar year anniversaries $t = 12, 24, 36, \ldots$ also resolves into a simpler form for GIPS purposes since the performance fee rate assumed to be applicable for the fee-paying limited partners in the fund is as one single aggregate who pay a performance fee at one common rate denoted by $\delta$ without any superscript required. However, as described earlier, it requires the tracking of the high-water mark. At time $t = 0$, $H$ is the first component of the highwater mark pair $= (H,0) = (V_0,0)$, so $H = V_0$.

$$P_{12} = \begin{cases} 0, V_{12} \le H \\ 0, V_{12} > H \text{ and } V_{12} - V_0(1+r_{0,12}) \le 0 \\ = \delta[V_{12} - V_0(1+r_{0,12})], V_{12} > H \text{ and } V_{12} - V_0(1+r_{0,12}) > 0 \end{cases}$$

The above is the same expression as that for a performance fee for individual capital accounts, the superscript $i$ for each capital account omitted.

Recall that $r_{0,12}$ represents the riskless Treasury bill rate that is applicable in the time interval $[0,12]$, that is, the time interval starting at time point $t = 0$ and ending at time point $t = 12$. The high-water mark is reset at time point $t = 12$ if the condition $V_{12} > H$ is satisfied, thus $H = (1-\delta)V_{12}$ if $V_{12} > H$, but remains unchanged at $H = V_0$ if $V_{12} < H$.

Having calculated the performance fee in absolute dollars, we calculate the profit in absolute dollars after performance fees at time point $t = 12$ and subsequently at $t = 24, 36, \ldots$ as follows:

$$\pi''_{12} = (1 - f_{annual})W_{12} - U_0 - P_{12}$$

and similarly, for subsequent years,

$$\pi''_t = (1 - f_{annual})W_t - U_{t-12} - P_t$$

which is defined only for $t = 12, 24, 36, \ldots$.

$\pi''_t$ is undefined when $t$ is not a multiple of 12, and similarly, since this series is only at 12-monthly intervals, interim deposits at time points that are not multiples of 12 are undefined.

We derive the return after fixed and performance fees at $t = 12$ under the GIPS assumption where $f$ and $\delta$ are the same for all partners as:

$$r_t'' = \frac{\pi_t'' - U_{t-12}}{U_{t-12}} \text{ for } t = 12, 24, 26, 48, \ldots .$$

Strictly, the return series $\{r_t''\}$ is defined only as an annual series, with $t = 12, 24, 36, 48, \ldots$ . Neither $r_t''$ nor $\pi_t''$ are defined for time points that are not multiples of 12 that coincide with the calculation of the performance fee for limited partners, that is, the return series after annual performance fees are defined as an annual series only. In contrast, the return series before all fees and the return series after fixed fees but before performance fees are defined at monthly time points.

Thus, for monthly reporting purposes, a hedge fund may report the series $\{r_t'\}$ for $t = 1, 2, 3, \ldots$ with the qualification that these monthly return numbers are based on deducting the fixed fees only, and not the performance fees. For annual reporting purposes, a hedge fund may report the series $\{r_t''\}$ for $t = 12, 24, 36, \ldots$ with the qualification that these are annual return numbers based on deducting the monthly fixed fees and annual performance fees.

For a traditional investment fund such as a mutual fund that does not charge performance fees, the return series $\{r_t'\}$ is the only relevant return series for $t = 1, 2, 3, \ldots$ and the series $\{r_t''\}$ does not apply, since there are no adjustments at year-end for performance fee. The monthly series $\{r_t'\}$ for $t = 1, 2, 3, \ldots$ is GIPS-compliant, since it represents total returns after all fees.

For the typical hedge fund whose *raison d'etre* is performance fees, the series $\{r_t'\}$ for $t = 1, 2, 3, \ldots$ is *not* GIPS-compliant since it does not include all fees, notably the annual performance fees. For the typical hedge fund, the series $\{r_t''\}$, which is defined only as an annual series for $t = 12, 24, 36, 48, \ldots$ is GIPS-compliant since it includes all fees, provided there is no claw-back provision in the limited partnership agreement of the hedge fund.

Based on setting up a framework for representing periodic cash flows and returns for partners in a hedge fund in the special case of a tax-exempt regime, we have derived a very useful by-product: a robust, well-defined framework for presenting the hedge fund's pretax and postfee returns that are compliant with GIPS standards for a hedge fund in any regime, whether taxable or not. Whatever accounting standards or methodology a hedge fund might choose to practice, the above procedures have to be implemented by every hedge fund for correctly calculating the fund's GIPS-compliant returns. We cannot call these procedures linear algebra, since the calculation of the performance fee involves evaluating the contingency related to the high-water mark and the hurdle rate. Of course, all the steps until the calculation of returns after fixed fees but before performance fees are strictly linear algebra since they do not involve contingencies.

# Facilitating Historical Risk and Return Review for Investors Using GIPS Guidelines

Hedge funds that trade in liquid securities are under peer pressure to self-report returns and assets under management to hedge fund performance–reporting database agencies such as Lipper-TASS. The legal profession debates whether such voluntary dissemination of performance constitutes solicitation of investors and holding out to the public as defined by the SEC for the purposes of requiring registration as an investment adviser with the SEC. Fortunately, the SEC has not taken a tough stance on this matter to corral the 8,000 to 10,000 hedge funds that self-report their performance to private hedge fund database organizers. Indeed, the comprehensive current and historical data are targeted at potential investors who are searching for hedge fund managers. They also attract a flock of fund of funds (FoF) organizers, who hold a portfolio of hedge funds in a separate investment partnership or offshore fund and admit limited partners who pay them an additional set of fees.

Hedge funds would achieve enormous appreciation from their limited partner investors, both existing investors as well as prospective new investors, by following the GIPS recommendation that:

5.B.2. It is RECOMMENDED that FIRMS present relevant COMPOSITE-level risk measures, such as beta, tracking error, modified duration, information ratio, Sharpe ratio, Treynor ratio, credit ratings, value at risk (VaR), and volatility, over time of the COMPOSITE and the BENCHMARK.

Most hedge funds indeed provide such analysis of risk along with their historical track record data series in some form or other. Investors could themselves take the historical track record data series for a hedge fund and calculate the GIPS-recommended risk analysis measures for the hedge fund.

The *GIPS Handbook* (2006) from which the above recommendation is reproduced does not provide an explanation to these measures of risk. Practically every finance textbook[2] provides the background and details ofeach of these measures, and every CFA is supposed to have these at their fingertips. We shall provide a simple explanation of these risk terms largely to address the ambiguities faced by hedge funds due to year-end fixed fees.

---

[2]Among several finance textbooks that cater to MBA finance course curricula, we recommend the co-authored work of the originator of the Sharpe ratio and 1990 Nobel Prize winner—Gordon J. Alexander, William F. Sharpe, and Jeffrey V. Bailey, *Fundamentals of Investments*, 3rd ed., (Prentice Hall, 2000).

A clean GIPS-compliant time series of monthly returns (after fixed fees but before annual performance fees) is the starting point for preparing a historical risk-return review of the hedge fund's performance. Ideally, all of the risk analysis should be conducted after all fees, including performance fees. That would give us an annual series, and even hedge funds that have held strong through a decade would barely have 10 observations, which is a barely sufficient sample to calculate risk.

Thus, a good starting point is to confine all the risk and return analysis to the monthly time series of returns after fixed fees (but before performance fees). The annual performance fee that is imposed upon the fund is not taken into account. This is because such imposition of an annual performance fee in the 12th month on a monthly time series would distort the measure of underlying economic risk. The monthly return after performance fees at the 12th month would show a large variation relative to the previous months and thus distort the measure of risk.

Recall that we had earlier defined the rate of return *before any fees* earned by the fund during the investment time period $[t,\ t-1]$ as:

$$r_t = \frac{\pi_t}{V_{t-1}} = \frac{W_t - V_{t-1}}{V_{t-1}} \text{ for } t = 1, 2, 3. \dots$$

where the $t$ subscripts are month-end time points. This is the return earned by the fund as an aggregate, which also is the return earned by each capital account before fees. Thus, $r_t$ is not subscripted for each capital account. We thus have the before-fee return series $\{r_t\}$ for the fund as a whole and as our starting point.

Since each capital account may have imposed different fixed fees and performance fees according to privately negotiated clauses in their agreement for admission to the limited partnership, we construct a *hypothetical or pro forma or representative or indicative* limited partner account, which pays the stated (undiscounted) fixed fees and performance fees in the limited partnership agreement.

The fixed fee is usually specified in the limited partnership agreement as an annual fee rate, which is denoted as $f_{annual}$. This annual fixed fee rate is transformed into a monthly rate $f$ according to the formula of continuous compounding:

$$f = (1 + f_{annual})^{1/12} - 1$$

We then transform before-fee return series $\{r_t\}$ into the pro forma return series *after fixed fees* for our hypothetical limited partner account according to: $r_t' = (1 - f)r_t$.

The annualized volatility, denoted by $\sigma$, of monthly returns (after fixed fees only and no performance fees) is simply the standard deviation of the monthly returns, multiplied by a scaling constant $\sqrt{12}$. Strictly speaking, it is the standard deviation of the log of the monthly return multiple, scaled by $\sqrt{12}$. That is, $\sigma$ is the standard deviation of the series $\{\log(1 + r'_t)\}$ times $\sqrt{12}$, where $t$ represents the month.

GIPS wants every hedge fund to have a compatible benchmark, and it is eminently appropriate to designate not just one benchmark, but several of them, such as various hedge fund indexes (or subindexes according to hedge fund strategy) that are in the public domain. We shall take just one benchmark return series that is contemporaneous with our target hedge fund, such as the Lipper-TASS hedge fund index monthly return series, which we shall denote as $\{r^m_t\}$. The superscript $m$ represents the market or benchmark.

The beta, denoted by $\beta$, is a measure of systematic risk of the hedge fund relative to the benchmark. It is the slope of the linear regression line of the series $\{r'_t\}$ as dependent variable versus $\{r^m_t\}$ as independent variable. It measures the sensitivity of returns to the hedge fund in response to returns to the market or benchmark, and is directly calculated $\beta = \dfrac{Cov\left(r'_t, r^m_t\right)}{Var\left(r^m_t\right)}$. In words, beta is the covariance of the returns of the hedge fund with the returns on the benchmark, divided by the variance of the benchmark.

To calculate the Sharpe ratio, we need the contemporaneous series of the riskless rate $\{r^f_t\}$. Suppose our time series runs as $t = 1, 2, 3, \ldots T$. We calculate the annualized return on the hedge fund and of the riskless asset over the time span. Thus, $r' = \left\{\prod_{t=1}^{T}(1 + r'_t)\right\}^{\left(\frac{12}{T}\right)} - 1$ is the annualized return of the hedge fund. Though this formula appears complex, it is simply chain multiplying monthly returns to determine the cumulative return, and then computing the *annualized* return from the cumulative return. Next, we calculate $r^f$, the *annualized* risk-free rate across the same time horizon, in a similar manner. The Sharpe ratio is simply $SR = \dfrac{r' - r^f}{\sigma\sqrt{12}}$, representing the excess *annual* return over the risk-free rate earned by the hedge fund (after fixed fees), divided by the *annualized* volatility of the returns of the hedge fund.

The Treynor ratio is simply $TR = \dfrac{r' - r^f}{\beta}$, representing the excess *annual* return over the risk-free rate earned by the hedge fund (after fixed fees), divided by the beta of the hedge fund relative to the benchmark index of choice.

Having come this far, it is simple to implement another risk measure that is not mentioned in the GIPS recommendations called the Sortino ratio,[3] which requires recalculation of the annualized volatility, taking into account only those observations where the hedge fund produces a monthly return that is below the riskless rate. Thus, we calculate a monthly series $\{r_t' - r_t^f\}$ and exclude those observations where $r_t' - r_t^f$ is positive. The remaining subset of monthly observations are used to calculate the "semi-" standard deviation denoted as $\sigma_s$. The Sortino ratio is simply $\dfrac{r' - r^f}{\sigma_s \sqrt{12}}$. It is an analog of the Sharpe ratio, with the denominator a risk measure, of the "semi-" standard deviation of underperforming monthly returns.

Another risk measure that is not mentioned in the GIPS recommendations, but almost mandatory in hedge fund presentations, is the drawdown, sometimes also called the maximum drawdown. The maximum drawdown is based on a look-back horizon $T$, say $T = 36$ months. We take monthly series $\{r_t'\}$ for $t = 1 \ldots T$. We then calculate all possible cumulative percentage returns, based on all starting points in all ending points. Of course, ending points have to be after starting points. We obtain a set of $T(T - 1)/2$ cumulative percentage returns. The lowest of these is called the maximum drawdown, and would likely be a negative number. It represents the worst possible cumulative return that would have been earned by investors, varying their entry and exit time points. The risk-return measure associated with maximum drawdown is called the Calmar ratio.[4] The numerator is the same as that used for calculating the Sharpe Ratio, the mean return in excess of the riskless rate, except that it is calculated over the same horizon T as the drawdown. The denominator is the maximum drawdown, expressed as a positive number. The original Calmar ratio envisaged $T = 36$ months and ignored the riskless rate, though it could be calculated for any other return look-back time series sequence, with or without reduction by the riskless rate in the numerator. The Calmar ratio is based on the postulate that risk is measured by the maximum drawdown calculated for a return time series sequence.

The calculation of the information ratio requires some additional setup. We calculate annualized average return produced by the index benchmark as $r^m$. Then we calculate the "tracking error," which is the standard deviation of the difference between the target hedge fund and the benchmark,

[3]F.N. Sortino and T.N. Price, "Performance Measurement in a Downside Risk Framework," *The Journal of Investing,* Fall 1994, 59–64.

[4]Young, Terry W., "Calmar Ratio: A Smoother Tool," *Futures*, October 1, 1991. The author named his risk-return ratio for his newsletter Calmar, an acronym for California Managed Accounts Reports.

that is, the standard deviation of the monthly series $\{r'_t - r^m_t\}$, denoted by $\sigma_t$. The information ratio is simply $IR = \dfrac{r' - r^m}{\sigma_t \sqrt{12}}$.

The value at risk measure can be defined in many ways. One common way is to represent the value at risk as the one-day probability of a certain level of decline in the hedge fund, usually an absolute number like $1 million. It is, however, more practical to designate this decline threshold in percentage units and state the value at risk as the probability of a one-day decline in the hedge fund by $X$ percent. The hedge fund managers have to be guarded and careful in presenting a number that is difficult to calculate with any degree of deep precision and might diverge with the other risk measures based on annualized volatility and beta. To begin with, we need a statistical model to represent the one-day return distribution of the portfolio of the hedge fund. Further, that should not contradict or be inconsistent with the annualized volatility of monthly returns. The general statistical assumption behind volatility and beta as a risk measure is that the distribution of monthly returns is normally distributed. The scaling factor that is applied in the investment management industry of calculating annualized volatility by multiplying by $\sqrt{12}$ implicitly reflects the statistical assumption that the square of volatility, that is, the variance, is proportional to time. In order to maintain consistency with this statistical assumption, it would be appropriate to project one-day volatility from annualized one-year volatility through multiplying it by a scaling factor of $\sqrt{\dfrac{1}{250}}$, assuming that there are 250 business days in a year. Thus, one-day volatility is simply $\sqrt{\dfrac{12}{250}}$, where $\sigma$ is the volatility of monthly returns as defined earlier. The one-day average return of the hedge fund is $s' = \left[ (r')^{\left(\frac{1}{250}\right)} - 1 \right]$. Though this term seems complex, all that is being done here is that the annualized return of the fund is being converted to an equivalent daily compounded return. Since all of the scaling is under the assumption of a normal distribution, we calculate the normal distribution $z$-score corresponding to a one-day return of $X$ percent or lower as $z = \dfrac{X - s'}{\sigma \sqrt{\dfrac{12}{250}}}$. We look up the normal probability tables to determine the value at risk as VaR $= N(z)$ where $N(.)$ is the cumulative standard normal probability function.

Modified duration is a risk measure that is applicable only to fixed-income portfolios containing securities that are straight bonds. It is simply the elasticity of the bond portfolio value to changes in interest rates. Hedge funds are rarely amenable to risk measurement according to bond portfolio analytics methodologies due to the relatively complex securities that they hold, so we shall not pursue bond portfolio risk analytics further.

Having thus far described all the GIPS *recommended* risk measures, we proceed to make adjustments to reflect the annual performance fee. The overriding assumption that we shall make is that the monthly return series net of fixed fees but before performance fees constitute the foundation to measure risk.

A hedge fund with sufficient performance history, say, of three years, could measure risk-adjusted performance according to annualized return net of performance fees. Recall the construction of $P_{12}^i$ earlier, which we defined as the *dollar amount of performance fees* charged to a limited partner indexed as $i$ at annual anniversary time point $t = 12$. We shall extend this construction to define the return after performance fees at time point $t = 12$ for the *hypothetical or pro forma or representative or indicative* limited partner account under consideration for the purposes of performance presentation. We denote $r_{1,12}'$ as the return over one calendar year, from time point $t = 0$ to time point $t = 12$, which is derived by chain multiplying the sequence of monthly returns after fixed fees $\{r_t'\}$. Similarly, $r_{0,12}^f$ is the riskless rate over the same period, and is the high-water mark expressed in percentage return terms relative to an initial investment at the beginning of the year. Recall that we associated each limited partner investor superscripted as $I$ with a high-water mark $(H^i, T)$. No performance fees apply if the investor's account value (after fixed fees) falls below the absolute dollar high-water mark $H^i$ at calendar year-end time point $T$. We convert the high-water mark into percentage terms, as $b_T = \dfrac{(H^i, T)}{V_{T-12}^i}$.

$V_{T-12}^i$ is the value of the limited partner capital account at the beginning of the calendar year. For the purposes of performance presentation, we are considering a single pro forma limited partner investor, so the superscript $i$ is dropped.

The pro forma return after performance fees at time point $t = 12$, denoted by $r_{0,12}''$, is derived as follows:

$$r_{0,12}'' = \begin{cases} r_{12}^1, & r_{0,12}' \leq b_{T=12} \\ r_{12}^1, & r_{0,12}' > b_{T=12} \text{ and } r_{0,12}' - r_{0,12}^f \leq 0 \\ r_{0,12}' - \delta\left(r_{0,12}' - r_{0,12}^f\right), & r_{0,12}' > b_{T=12} \text{ and } r_{0,12}' - r_{0,12}^f > 0 \end{cases}$$

The return after fixed and performance fees is calculated after testing three contingencies. If the return after fixed fees *falls at or below* the high-water mark for the calendar year expressed in percentage terms, there is no performance fee. Next, if the return after fixed fees *is above* the high-water mark, *and is at or below* the riskless rate for the calendar year period, there is no performance fee either. Only when the third contingency is met, that is, the return after fixed fees *is above* the high-water mark, *and is above* the riskless rate for the calendar year period, a performance fee of $\delta = 20$ percent applies on the excess return above the riskless rate. The return after performance fees earned by the pro forma limited partner is the return after fixed fees, $r'_{0,12}$, reduced by the performance fee per dollar of initial investment at time point $t = 1$, which is $\delta\left(r'_{0,12} - r^f_{0,12}\right)$.

It is important to recognize that the high-water mark (represented as a percentage increase to year-beginning account value) for purposes of calculation of the return after performance fees and the next calendar year-end time point $T = 24$ is reset to zero when the third contingency is met, that is,

$$b_{T=24} = \begin{cases} b_{T=12}, & r'_{0,12} \leq b_{T=12} \\ 0, & r'_{0,12} > b_{T=12} \end{cases}$$

Note that the high-water mark expressed as a percentage return for the year relative to the year-beginning account value is defined only at calendar year-end time points and is required only for the calculation of the year-end performance fee.

After providing a suitable disclaimer, the risk-adjusted performance measures are presented based on chain linking discrete calendar year-end time points $t = 12, 24, 36, \ldots$ . Suppose we have three calendar years of return numbers after performance fees. We calculate the *monthly* average return of the pro forma limited partner as $r'' = \left\{\prod_{t=12,24,36}(1 + r'_{t-12,t})\right\}^{(1/36)} - 1$, where $\Pi(\ )$ is the product operator, to be distinguished from the symbol $\Pi$ that we have used for denoting profit or income, that is, in expanded form, $r'' = [(1 + r'_{0,12})(1 + r'_{12,24})(1 + r'_{24,36})]^{1/36} - 1$. Once again, though this formula seems complex, all that we are doing is chain multiplying three annual return numbers to calculate the cumulative three-year return, and then applying the compound interest formula to determine the continuously compounded monthly equivalent return.

The beta risk measure is unchanged, because it is driven by the monthly series of returns of the fund. As a result, the Treynor ratio is unchanged. The Sharpe ratio is altered as $SR = \dfrac{r'' - r^f}{\sigma\sqrt{12}}$, where $r''$ replaces $r'$ in the numerator. Similarly, the Sortino ratio is altered to $\dfrac{r'' - r^f}{\sigma_s\sqrt{12}}$, and the information ratio is altered to $IR = \dfrac{r'' - r^m}{\sigma_t\sqrt{12}}$. The value at risk measure (VaR) will change, if at all only slightly, due to replacing $s'$ by $s''$.

An appropriate disclaimer is required to qualify why performance fees are deducted in the numerator of these various risk-adjusted performance measures, but the denominator is based on a monthly series without the lumpy imposition of year-end performance fees, which would cause an aberration to the true volatility of the fund. We need to provide an appropriate disclaimer, which might read something like the following:

> The measures of return factored into both pro forma fixed fees and performance fees applicable to a representative capital account are based on accurately calculating the return after all fees, that is, after deducting both fixed fees and performance fees. However, the risk measures like beta, volatility, tracking error, etc. are based on monthly return series after fixed fees, but before performance fees applied at every calendar year-end. This is because a lumpy one-time reduction in the monthly return at every calendar year anniversary would distort the resulting estimate of the volatility and systematic risk of the underlying portfolio.

Hedge funds live and die by their performance, or more appropriately, risk-adjusted performance. When the absolute returns earned by the hedge fund are stellar, such as 30 percent average annual returns consistently for 10 years, risk measurement becomes less important. The hedge fund manager becomes extremely popular with the media and is eagerly sought by investors. With every other hedge fund, risk-adjusted performance is important. A Sharpe ratio of 1.0 or less is considered to be prosaic. Under normal market conditions, equity market indexes easily achieve this ratio. A Sharpe ratio of 2.0 or more is considered outstanding. A hedge fund manager who produces 12 percent excess annual return over the riskless Treasury bill rate with a 6 percent annualized volatility is considered a genius. The convicted managed brokerage account advisor Madoff operated a pyramid scheme that essentially presented fictitious steady returns with very little volatility, resulting in a Sharpe ratio that was a rank outlier. This should have alerted investors and regulators that capital markets do not generally offer consistently easy arbitrage opportunities to extract profits with virtually no risk. Instead, investors looked at paper trails of auditor reports as a mark of authenticity of their managed securities trading accounts at the Madoff brokerage firm.

# CHAPTER 11

# Mutual Funds and Venture Funds Compared to Hedge Funds

## Tax Return Filing of U.S. Partnerships Is an Involved Task

It is not surprising that there are about 10,000 funds that are domiciled in the Cayman Islands. The pass-through taxation of U.S. partnerships is complex, even though it is derived from simple principles of combining capital and sharing income according to its nature. U.S. partnerships have to devote significant effort to translate the simpler task of economic bookkeeping (to track partners' economic interests) into correctly allocating taxable pass-through items of income and filing partnership tax returns with the IRS. Even the smallest U.S. partnership has to incur the fixed costs of establishing a CFO (chief financial officer) function and engaging accountants for accounting bookkeeping, and audit. A Cayman Islands fund dispenses with this distracting tax filing activity and focuses on maintaining the same economic books required of any hedge fund and having them audited under Cayman Islands or U.K. accounting standards.

## Comparison with Tax Allocations Made by Mutual Funds

SEC-regulated mutual funds targeted to small retail investors also face this issue of allocating taxable items of income to their shareholders every year. However, we do not observe any fuss made in the mutual fund industry about different methodologies for tax allocations. That is because over the decades, the IRS has established a set of procedures for mutual funds to report tax allocations to their investors and shareholders. Mutual fund companies, also called regulated investment companies, are governed by Sections 851–855 of the Internal Revenue Code.[1] Nearly all mutual funds, especially equity mutual funds, make their distribution of cash flows and record the associated tax allocations once a year. There are bond mutual funds that make their distributions and associated tax allocations at the end of every month. For now, we shall focus on the typical equity mutual fund, which makes its distributions once a year. Upon cursory examination, we immediately determine that there is no procedure that parallels tax allocations for partnerships governed by Section 704(b) of the Internal Revenue Code. The distributions that occur once a year from a mutual fund are subdivided into three types: interest, dividends, and net capital gains. A shareholder who owns the mutual fund shares starting just one day before the ex-dividend date gets the entire distribution and associated tax allocation that is calculated for a full year (relative to the previous year's ex-dividend date).

In this sense, mutual funds behave like stocks. Mutual fund dividends and distributions are lumpy, as is the case with stocks. The principle that governs tax allocations in partnerships, Section 704(b), of tax allocations following economic participation are disregarded, since we can have a situation where a shareholder who purchases shares in a mutual fund prior to the distribution date and redeems them immediately after the distribution occurs is allocated taxable dividends and capital gains calculated for a full year.

However, the most egregious procedure that is approved for mutual funds is that they *cannot allocate any net capital losses*. A mutual fund may go down in value due to sharp declines in the value of its holdings of securities and incur large realized losses upon sale of these securities. The net asset value (NAV) of the mutual fund would go down due to this reduction in value of the securities and associated realized capital losses. The mutual funds are required to carry forward these realized net capital losses and only offset them against future net realized capital gains. Only when the mutual fund emerges by offsetting all of its carry-forward realized capital losses against realized capital gains would it be required to make annual distributions of the resulting net positive capital gains.

---

[1]U.S. Code, Title 26, Subtitle A, Chapter 1, Subchapter M, Part I—Regulated Investment Companies, Sections 851–855. This is mirrored at the Cornell law library at www.law.cornell.edu/uscode/26/usc_sup_01_26_10_A_20_1_30_M_40_I.html.

If mutual fund shareholders who have suffered a loss in the NAV of their holdings decide to sell, they make a realized capital loss calculated according to the liquidation NAV, less the cost basis.

The mutual fund industry encourages its shareholders to check a box agreeing to reinvest all their distributions back into the mutual fund. While this is extremely convenient for tax-deferred retirement accounts, it places an unintended challenge upon the taxable small mutual fund investor. That is because at every occasion of automatic reinvestment of distributions, as far as the IRS is concerned, it is tantamount to having purchased a new tax lot of shares in the mutual fund. Upon liquidation of the holdings, the taxable investor is required to report capital gains on his or her personal tax return. The mutual fund provides Form 1099 that reports the proceeds of the sale to the IRS. Strictly speaking, the mutual fund investor is required to calculate the cost basis of the tax lots of mutual fund shares that were redeemed or sold. Imagine a situation where the small shareholder was smart to have decided not to reinvest dividends and distributions back into purchasing new shares of the mutual fund, but electing to receive cash payment of the distributions. The cost basis of the mutual fund shares redeemed is their original purchase price, plus capital gains distributions that were made in the years prior to their redemption. That is because the mutual fund investor was given tax allocations of net realized capital gains in the interim years prior to redemption. If these net realized capital gains were not added to the cost basis, then the investor would be paying double taxation on their capital gains: once taxed as interim distributions, and once again taxed at time of redemption. The tracking of cost basis of mutual fund shares redeemed becomes exceedingly complex in the situation where the taxable mutual fund investor elects to reinvest all distributions back into the mutual fund. It requires a sophisticated spreadsheet implementation of identifying every tax lot and then distributing interim realized capital gain allocations to every tax lot.

Not all individual taxable mutual fund investors are aware of this necessary adjustment to be made to their cost basis in order to prevent self-imposed double taxation of capital gains. The IRS and SEC ought to initiate an investigation to study the extent to which retail mutual fund investors failed to step up their cost basis according to interim capital gain distributions and hence subjected themselves to double taxation. It would be an easy fix to issue a mandate upon the mutual fund industry to track the correct cost basis corresponding to the mandatory 1099 reporting of proceeds of sale of mutual fund shares.

Suppose a U.S. investment partnership were to write clauses into the partnership agreement that mirror the tax allocation methodology that is approved for regulated U.S. mutual funds (i.e., companies regulated under the Investment Company Act). They declare a distribution date, an arbitrary date in November or December, like mutual funds. The partnership allocates all of its aggregated taxable items of income according to partnership ownership percentages that exist on that specific date of distribution, without regard to the history of participation in the partnership. For now, we take it that if there are any net realized capital losses for the year, the same would be allocated on that snapshot distribution date, unlike mutual funds, which never make tax allocations of net realized capital losses. This is indeed a simple mechanism. Mutual funds follow this mechanism with an added twist that net realized capital losses are never allocated. Would Section 704(b) be violated and call for an overriding procedure for making tax allocations to partners that follow economic allocations? This can be considered an extreme case of aggregation with full netting, where the history of partners' participation is disregarded and ignored. All taxable cash flows are aggregated for the year and allocated to partners according to their ownership percentages at one snapshot point in time, which is the calculation and distribution date.

Even if the IRS were to ignore the broad-brush requirement of Section 704(b) of the Internal Revenue Code that tax allocations to partners should be in line with the economic participation of partners in a partnership, and were to allow the snapshot aggregation method for tax allocation that is approved for the mutual fund industry, would taxable U.S. partners find it undesirable? Unlike small retail mutual fund investors, hedge fund investors are generally more sophisticated, and further, the large hedge funds admit only "qualified purchasers" as defined by the SEC. The taxable limited partner clientele in a hedge fund would strongly oppose snapshot tax allocations that could present huge tax bills to them that might be unrecoverable. It creates a perverse incentive for taxable investors to seek redemption of their holdings prior to the snapshot distribution and tax allocation date, saddling those investors who remain in the hedge fund with their tax bills. Since the investors redeeming just prior to the distribution and tax allocation date still collect their full economic value in the partnership, they would be reporting the tax allocations bearing higher tax rates of 35 percent that they just avoided and passed on to other continuing investors as long-term capital gain that is taxed at 15 percent.

Clearly, taxable investors in hedge funds have a strong incentive to seek tax allocations that are in line with Section 704(b) of the Internal Revenue Code. A perverse hypothetical example will make this lucid. Suppose a U.S. hedge fund has a large constituency of taxable U.S. investors. It persuades just one tax-exempt investor to make a relatively small investment in the fund. The fund then emulates the U.S. mutual fund industry's tax allocation procedure of aggregation and distribution based on snapshot partner ownership on December 15. The entire U.S. taxable investor constituency departs on December 1, leaving only the general partner and the tax-exempt investor in the partnership on December 1. The tax-exempt investor's holding in the U.S. hedge fund becomes 99 percent as of December 1 and is allocated 99 percent of the full year's taxable items of income on December 15. The tax-exempt investor has no tax consequence and does not pay any taxes. The taxable investor constituency, which bolted on December 1, collects its economic value upon redemption and potentially pays the lowest tax rate of 15 percent on capital gains calculated based on the redemption value less the cost basis of their investment in the partnership.

Instances parallel to this hypothetical example probably occur all the time in the mutual fund industry. The mutual fund industry is widely known for its high portfolio turnover rate, which is in excess of 100 percent for actively managed funds. As a result, practically all of the gain is short-term in nature. Suppose in Year 1, there was no capital gain distribution due to carry-forward realized losses from past years. In Year 2, there are net positive realized gains, and as a consequence, there is distribution and tax allocation of realized capital gains. Suppose an investor were to buy this mutual fund in the early part of Year 1 and sell it slightly more than one year later just on the eve of the capital gain distribution in Year 2. This mutual fund investor would report long-term capital gain on the redemption. Another mutual fund investor who holds the same mutual fund through the distribution date would get a tax allocation of short-term gains and would be required to pay short-term capital gains tax at a much higher rate.

The arbitrariness of the prevailing IRS-approved procedure of tax allocations in U.S. mutual funds is more starkly displayed in this hypothetical example. Consider a fund with 100 shares having a NAV of $10 per share. The fund owns a peculiar security that pays a one-time taxable distribution of $9 to investors on record just prior to the ex-dividend date. On the ex-dividend date, the NAV of the mutual fund falls to $1. The taxable distribution and corresponding tax allocation to the shareholders is $9. The value of the mutual fund is conserved. A tax-exempt investor would make no gains from purchasing the mutual fund shares at $10, holding them through the ex-dividend date, collecting $9 of distribution, and redeeming the shares for $1 just after the ex-dividend date. However, for a taxable investor, the consequences are disastrous. The taxable distribution and corresponding tax allocation is $9. The tax due is about $3 (at 33 percent tax rate). The taxable investor sells the holding for $1, reporting a capital gain of −9 (which is a loss). This example shows a nonrecoverable tax liability of $3 on the distribution, offset only by the benefit of carry-forward capital gain of −9 (a loss) that can be recovered only in the future by offsetting against future capital gains. This example demonstrates that taxable investors should not enter a mutual fund immediately prior to the ex-dividend date.

Perhaps the best feature of the procedure of aggregation by full netting and tax allocation according to snapshot ownership at one point in time that is followed by the mutual fund industry is its stark simplicity. U.S. hedge fund organizers who are focused on the clientele of taxable U.S. investors might consider introducing this into the partnership agreement and seeking advanced approval from the IRS. Subsequently, by encouraging a U.S. tax-exempt partner to join the hedge fund, those taxable U.S. investors who redeem prior to the snapshot tax allocation date might get the benefit of paying the taxes according to the lowest long-term capital gains tax rate of 15 percent. Alternately, a foreign investor domiciled in a nontaxable regime would be equally eminently suitable, provided that the particular U.S. hedge fund does not earn dividends that are subject to 30 percent U.S. withholding tax for the foreign partner.

At some point in time, U.S. legislators and the IRS should examine this issue, deem U.S. investment partnerships to be mutual funds, and consider permitting investment partnerships and hedge funds to adopt the substantially simpler standards and practices of tax allocation methods that are permitted to the mutual fund industry. Alas, this is wishful thinking. The wedge between the egregious practice of tax allocation according to a once-a-year snapshot that is permitted for the mutual fund industry, and the high standards of Section 704(b) of the Internal Revenue Code that persuades U.S. hedge funds to make tax allocations according to economic participation, is likely to prevail. A hedge fund sponsor aspiring to exploit the weaknesses of the tax allocation procedure approved for the U.S. mutual fund industry by incorporating the same into the partnership agreement might face serious challenges from the IRS.

In conclusion, we should note that Section 704(b) of the Internal Revenue Code, despite its broad-brush and loose wording, is the only thing that prevents taxable partners in a U.S. partnership from timing the tax allocation system and paying lower taxes by transferring tax allocations that attract higher tax rates to tax-exempt partners.

# U.S. Venture Partnerships (Silicon Valley Venture Funds)

Our focus in this section is to identify how taxation issues differ between investment partnerships holding traded financial securities (hedge funds, which we abbreviate in this section as HF) and those holding real projects (the Silicon Valley partnerships, which we abbreviate in this section as SV).

HF have the ability to permit withdrawals and deposits at quarterly or annual intervals based on a mark-to-market valuation of the financial securities. Of course, we now know that such interim valuation can be fickle when the HF holds complex illiquid securities or "troubled assets," and thus entry and exit of partners based on mark-to-market valuation may result in serious wealth transfers, not counting current and future tax allocations that could be sensitive to the interim valuations (and thus result in more arbitrary wealth transfers). SV do not have the luxury of interim valuation and hence are frozen until liquidation.

How do SV deal with this interim illiquidity? SV portfolio investments in private equity mostly either go down to zero, or provide an occasional stellar outburst of profit. SV typically have clauses in their partnership agreement relating to liquidation and transfer of partnership interests by private arrangement prior to liquidation. A typical SV venture partnership has a stated life of 10 years. Generally, there are clauses to extend its life automatically by up to two years at the discretion of the general partner. Further extension beyond two years usually requires the consent of all limited partners, which is rarely denied. This is because SV distribute all or part of the capital gain from successful "exits" from their portfolio of private equity investments, and those left behind after 10 to 15 years are the residue, venture portfolio holdings that the general partners could not liquidate and distribute, but that still have future potential and likely payoff. In contrast, HF provide clauses for termination only as required by a tax law, and almost never a relatively short-fuse time horizon of 10–12 years. The forced liquidation of SV at the end of, say, 10 years signals to the limited partners that the partnership is obliged to hold a portfolio of venture investments through a time horizon of at most 10 years, and subsequently declare a venture as either having failed and write it down to zero, or liquidate the venture company holding at whatever residue and value it can fetch.

What do the SV do with residual venture companies in their portfolio that are not liquidated or written off by the expected termination date (10 years?) There are rare instances where SV still retain residual portfolio venture companies beyond the stated life of 10 years, with the explicit permission of limited partners and appropriate amendments to the partnership agreement. These are cases when the SV general partners consider the illiquid portfolio companies to likely have value if managed and continued for a few more years.

For tax-exempt investors in SV, UBTI may get triggered in unanticipated and unexpected ways. SV partnership agreements usually have clauses and provisions that explicitly state that the general partners would not permit investments that trigger UBTI. However, this is a statement of intentions and best efforts, mostly addressed to tax-exempt U.S. limited partners who might be alarmed at the prospect of receiving tax allocations during the life of the SV that are subject to UBTI. Indeed most of the concerns regarding UBTI could be effectively put to rest by establishing an offshore feeder entity that effectively acts as a blocker corporation to virtually eliminate the risk that some unanticipated future event might trigger UBTI to tax-exempt U.S. limited partners.

Even though the risk of unexpected UBTI treatment can be reduced if the SV is established as an offshore UBTI-blocker entity, or as a feeder to a master SV that is a U.S. entity, we rarely see SV structuring offshore arms. In contrast, nearly all HF have offshore master-feeder structures. This could be for several reasons. SV have had sufficient capital raised from U.S. investors, including a significant amount from tax-exempt U.S. institutional investors. The latter are likely concerned about directly or indirectly having their ownership and participation in the SV through an offshore structure. Practically, the risk of unexpected UBTI is small, since SV hold their portfolio venture investments that are organized in turn as insulated subchapter C entities that are positioned for sale or expansion by issuance of new shares in an initial public offering (IPO). Once the shares of an SV portfolio company become public, the SV has an exit opportunity to realize gains for its limited partners by selling its shares in the public stock market.

HF are able to scale and expand elastically according to capital flows coming in from limited partners. They invest in traded financial securities whose supplies are vast. In contrast, SV invest in venture companies that are extremely limited in supply, so limited that they rarely can accommodate large flows of capital. SV have had a steady flow of capital from tax-exempt U.S. institutional investors. Indeed, SV take capital from their limited partners according to their capacity to find and invest in venture projects. SV have provisions in their limited partnership agreements that permit the general partner to make "capital calls" to limited partners. Partners initially contribute capital according to the capacity of the SV to make initial investments, and they provide additional capital according to pre-specified agreement language based on capital calls by the general partner.

Why is it that we rarely hear of many tax-exempt U.S. institutional investors creating a captive foreign blocker entity that likely skips UBTI, and then have that captive foreign corporation invest in one or more SV or HF, without fear of triggering UBTI? This is for two likely reasons. First, SV companies realize their returns and cash flows by sale and exit of their venture portfolio and private equity investments, which mostly spawn capital gain. Rarely is there any meaningful form of income that could be classified as UBTI. Second, those large U.S. institutional investors are public entities, whose trustees may be concerned about becoming subject to public censure and scrutiny.

It is generally believed that unlike HF, for whom leverage is like oxygen, SV are unleveraged. It is indeed true that SV generally do not take on debt and loans in the partnership. For one thing, it would trigger UBTI. But the more accurate reason is that the venture portfolio of college dorm-room and university lab ideas is not appropriate collateral for lenders. In contrast, financial securities that are purchased by HF are the collateral upon which HF are able to seek debt financing and leverage. However, SV have indirect leverage through any borrowing that their venture portfolio companies are able to achieve. These subchapter C companies in turn present a list of whatever they own to lending banks and obtain loans against whatever the banks would accept as collateral. That includes small items like furniture, computing equipment, machinery, any form of building and real estate, or practically anything that a bank would accept as collateral. Generally, for every dollar of capital invested by the SV into a venture portfolio company, only a small part is translated into hard assets that can service bank collateral. Most of the capital goes toward paying salaries and leases to sustain the development of a venture idea to a fully functional company. Thus, SV are indeed indirectly leveraged through the collateralized loans on hardware and equipment purchases by their venture portfolio companies. On aggregate, the overall leverage in SV after counting collateralized loans to their underlying portfolio companies would likely be small, on the order of 25 percent or less of the equity investment in the master SV. In contrast, HF are able to seek leverage of 3–10 times their equity, depending on the nature of their financial securities. This includes indirect leverage obtained by HF through internally leveraged forwards and futures contracts. Another way to look at SV versus HF is that the underlying holdings of SV are in the form of extremely risky private equity that is inadequate collateral for obtaining loans. HF, on the other hand, invest in securities that are considered adequate collateral for obtaining margin loans or are available in the form of internally leveraged forwards and futures contracts.

Suppose a portfolio company is shut down and defaults on its collateralized loans. Is the SV (venture partnership) a guarantor that has to make whole the outstanding bank loan claims? What kind of collateralized loans and leverage do SV permit their portfolio companies to take on? (In the case of HF, the lending banks seize assets of the HF and effectively bankrupt the HF.) What kind of bankruptcy risk does an SV venture partnership have, if any?

What is the approximate proportion of taxable versus tax-exempt investors in an SV? There does not seem to be any hard and fast rule, other than that SV cater to both taxable and tax-exempt investors. Both are significantly important clienteles to them. Taxable partners in an SV tend to be individuals who are subject to the personal tax rate schedule and are themselves reinvesting cash flows from previous successful venture investments.

It is rare that subchapter C taxable companies, which face the flat corporate tax rate of 35 percent on net income, invest in SV. The exceptions are large technological research-based companies like Cisco and Intel, who have their own captive venture funds that are divisions, affiliates, or subsidiaries of the parent subchapter C entity. The company sets aside capital to invest in a portfolio of venture companies, perhaps concerned that not doing so would result in being at a competitive disadvantage from nascent companies that are being hatched by SV venture partnerships and venture capital firms. The primary motive of such subchapter C firms is to extend in-house R&D and farm extramural ideas and inventions. Taxation of likely future profits from successful venture investments at the corporate tax rate of 35 percent is rarely a consideration.

HF have varying ownership percentages (by partners) according to entry and exit as well as general partner allocations over time. SV ownership percentages are relatively stable, except for general partner allocations contingent upon positive profits. SV partners may sell and transfer interests privately, since the SV partnership agreement does not provide for interim redemption. In the interest of fairness, the general partner cannot get meaningfully involved in interim valuation to support the transfer and sale of limited partnership interests. HF have to deal with the various tax allocation methodologies that were described in detail earlier. SV do not have to deal with nuances of different accounting methodologies for allocating partner's share of items of income. HF most commonly use the method of aggregation, and likewise, it is equally appropriate for SV to adopt the same method of aggregation as HF. (The aggregation method provides for allocating HF taxable and tax-exempt line items of income by aggregating for the full year and according to some fixed discipline of calculating partner's share.) The illiquidity and the lack of interim valuation in an SV makes the complex methodology of layering as used by some HF intractable and infeasible.

Other than capital gains or losses attributable to exit from venture portfolio companies, SV make other allocations of other taxable items of income such as ordinary business income, royalties, portfolio dividends, and interest. After having examined the structural and economic nature of SV versus HF, we may now pose the question: What taxable cash flows arise in SV and how are they allocated? The primary economic outcome of SV is net capital gains from the sale, liquidation, or exit from venture portfolio companies. As a result, the primary taxable item of income to taxable U.S. investors is capital gains. Within that, it is tax-preferred long-term capital gains, since each of these venture portfolio companies are held for more than one year, and they are tax preferred since long-term capital gains are taxed at the federal long-term capital gains tax rate of 15 percent. (We ignore state taxes on net income, which can be as high as about 9 percent in California, sufficient to prompt private individual investors in other lightly taxed states. Multiple homes owned by wealthy U.S. investors to seek residency and more than six months a year occupancy in these homes has been a popular mechanism of reducing the burden of state income taxes in high-tax states such as California and New York.) All other distributive items of income and expenses are inconsequential and incidental. It would be good if SV, along with all other HF, were to adopt a rigorous methodology for allocation of distributive items of income to partners, such as a methodology presented in earlier chapters of this book. In actual practice, we are likely to find that most SV, as well as most HF, delegate the apportionment of taxable distributive items of income according to arbitrary methods that could vary widely. We need to emphasize that in the case of SV that have not established blocker entities as feeder funds for tax-exempt U.S. partners, the general partners have to keep a watchful eye out for potential unanticipated income, which could become classified as UBTI and hence be taxed at the corporate tax rate (35 percent) to tax-exempt investors.

# CHAPTER 12

# Epilogue

## Economic Accounting Is a Common Denominator for U.S. and Offshore Funds

Apart from the benefit of anonymity to non-U.S. partners of an offshore fund, whether master or feeder, or the "blocker" corporation role provided by an offshore entity to tax-exempt U.S. investors, the economic accounting to be conducted for both U.S. onshore and offshore funds is the same. The *raison d'être* for an investment partnership, regardless of its domicile, is that partners share common investment objectives. Both U.S. and offshore partnership entities have to conduct economic accounting to track partners' capital accounts and economic sharing of profits according to the prespecified partnership agreement.

For a U.S. partnership entity, an independent audit of a partnership is not mandated by the U.S. government. Yet, for all practical purposes, U.S. entities hold themselves out to independent audit to appease limited partner investors. In most cases, the limited partnership agreement of a U.S. partnership specifies an annual independent audit to be conducted.

Despite loose regulations in the British crown colonies like the Cayman Islands that attract droves of offshore hedge funds, offshore funds are required to provide an independent (Cayman) audit for annual renewal of their permit.

Thus, whether onshore or offshore, partnerships are obliged to implement an economic accounting system, entirely independent of taxation, and hold it to audit-quality standards. Offshore entities greatly benefit from not having to deal with taxation, whether direct or pass-through. The tracking of partners' economic contributions, distributions, and profit sharing is all that is expected of their accounting system.

# Tax Return Filing of U.S. Partnerships Is an Involved Task

For U.S. partnerships, the economic accounting system is the starting point, labeled "book capital accounts" in the U.S. Treasury Regulations. U.S. partnerships have to engage in a second layer of involved, intensive tax accounting activity to prepare and file their annual tax returns and assign pass-through U.S. tax liabilities to all their partners. The tax return filing of U.S. partnerships requires significant effort by accountants who are well versed in U.S. partnership tax filings. Offshore entities are not required to make any kind of tax return filing and do not have to conduct the tax accounting that is required for U.S. partnerships.

# Calculating Partner Allocations Is Most of a U.S. Partnership's Tax Accounting Effort

This book provides a starting point of mapping the language of the U.S. partnership agreement to an economic accounting system, and describes both the economic accounting and the tax accounting methodology for it that follows. U.S. partnerships struggle with the method of "layering," which increases data-tracking complexity in direct proportion to the number of tax lots traded and the number of partners. Even though modern information technology (IT) offers elaborate ERP (enterprise resource planning) software systems such as SAP, which are capable of tracking physical miniscule nuts and bolts in an industrial enterprise, it might be a struggle to adapt to layering. This layering computation process itself is not computer processor intensive, and it might easily be performed on a standard desktop computer that is running customized database software. Instead, the primary burden of the layering methodology is to feed enormous quantities of input data on market values of securities and manage input data errors that arise even if input data are automated. It is further clouded by having to value securities that are not openly traded on any exchange and have to be manually input.

The economic accounting system indeed requires input data on the mark-to-market of private securities whenever there is even the slightest change in partnership ownership percentages. However, the method of layering places unusual burdens of tracking realized and unrealized gains for every tax lot, for every time subperiod, for every partner. The slightest input data error causes cascading errors in the tax accounting process and requires accountants to struggle with reconciliation.

## Layering and Netting Methodologies for Tax Allocation of Capital Gains

This book penetrates the fog of the tax allocation methodologies of layering, full netting, and partial netting, on which there appears to be no consensus. We have provided insights into how to make them work. Many U.S. partnerships allocate capital gains by the partial or full netting methodology, which provides relief from the intensely burdensome alternative methodology of layering. However, no two partnerships appear to adopt the same procedure, and the exact mechanism of layering and full/partial netting remains a matter of much debate and conjecture, supported by numerical examples. This book provides the method to accurately implement the methodology of layering and full/partial netting as provided in the U.S. Treasury Regulations.

## Example of Tax Allocation of Capital Gains by Full and Partial Netting in a 100-Partner Setting

Chapter 7 of this book introduces the relevant U.S. Treasury Regulations for full and partial netting, and described how the tax allocation of capital gains is represented as a convex optimization problem. Appendixes 2 and 3 elaborate upon it further, and provide concrete industrial-strength implementation examples of tax allocation of realized capital gains according to the full netting and partial netting methodologies. Appendixes 2 and 3 do not address the allocation of other items of income and assume that they are allocated to partners according to the layering methodology.

Layering is the predominant method adopted by U.S. partnerships for the tax allocation of items of income other than capital gains. This is because such items, like dividends and interest, are fungible single items and do not involve the tracking of thousands of tax lots. Yet the tax allocation of dividends, interest, and other items by layering require an equally elaborate setup, tracking and allocating to partners every month, resulting in a sea of spreadsheets and reconciliations with accounting source data such as monthly brokerage and bank statements. The automated procedures in Appendixes 2 to 5, which implement the U.S. Treasury Regulations on full and partial netting, offer permanent relief to U.S. partnerships from this burden.

## Tilting Tax Allocations According to Tax Preferences

The subject of tilting tax allocations according to tax preferences of partners is a matter of ongoing debate and conjecture, even though the U.S. Treasury Regulations (of full and partial netting) forbid abusive tax allocations that are designed to reduce the present value of partner tax liabilities.

Appendixes 2 and 3 produce a unique, robust, and seriously tax-neutral optimal solution to tax allocation of realized capital gains. This is elaborated further in Appendix 4, to create a single framework for making tax allocations according to tax preferences, and demonstrating abusive versus equitable tilts in the resulting tax allocations. The methodology presented in Appendix 4, along with an example with 100 partners, provides a resilient framework for making small, nonabusive, tax-preference-driven deviations from the tax-neutral "gold standard" that is presented in Appendixes 2 and 3.

## The Crown Jewel: Automated Tax Allocation of All Items of Income

Appendix 5 presents a methodology and a solution to a 100-partner example that offers permanent relief to U.S. partnerships from the burden of tax accounting. This methodology is based on careful reading of the relevant U.S. Treasury Regulations on full and partial netting, recognizing that the regulations are not confined to the allocation of realized capital gains only and permit extension to allocation of all other items of income without requiring any further official clarification or new regulations.

The method provided in Appendix 5 generalizes the tax allocation of capital gains only to all items of income. The adaptation of this method, which is entirely compliant with the U.S. Treasury Regulations on full and partial netting, eliminates the layering entirely, producing a robust unique solution that allocates all distributed (pass-through) items of taxable income to partners, that is, dividends, interest, capital gains, and investment expenses. This robust solution is also tax neutral, according to the methodology that was developed in Appendixes 2 and 3 and further analyzed for nonabusive allocation according to tax preferences in Appendix 4.

Some experts may be concerned that the simultaneous allocation of dividends and interest along with capital gains might become distorted by shifting the multiple subitems across partners according to tax preferences. This concern is fully eliminated in the methodology provided in Appendix 5. The robust optimal tax allocation solution provided is entirely tax neutral, and any significant deviation from the proposed optimum solution might be interpreted as tax tilting according to tax preferences.

# The End of an Era of Layering

Chapter 7, together with Appendixes 2 to 5, has provided a clear and succinct method to U.S. partnerships to eliminate layering entirely. The data input required by the method of Appendix 5 is minimal, requiring partners' (1) "book capital value" (i.e., economic capital account value) from the economic accounting system, and the aggregate partnership-level year-end quantities of dividends, interest, short term and long-term realized capital gains, investment expenses, and foreign taxes and (2) "tax capital value," which comes from the history of deposits and past tax allocations.

The solution to the tax allocation problem is provided in seconds, usually less than a second, running on a standard 2007-vintage desktop personal computer, by efficient open-source convex optimization algorithms. U.S. tax accountants who struggled with spreadsheets and never-ending reconciliations may henceforth devote their time and attention to other pressing accounting issues.

The economic cost of U.S. tax return filing to a U.S. partnership is reduced to nearly the bare minimum, because all the effort required to elaborately calculate tax allocations to partners is eliminated and replaced by an instant year-end automated tax allocation solution for *all* items of income, for all partners. The automated solution emerges from a computer algorithm that implements the relevant U.S. Treasury Regulations for full and partial netting.

U.S. partnerships are no longer at a disadvantage relative to offshore entities by having to perform involved calculations of tax allocations to partners. The new era relies upon automated convex optimization implementation of the relevant U.S. Treasury Regulations of partial and full netting to make tax allocations that are robust and also tax neutral. The annual tax allocation solution is calculated in an instant. This marks the end of the era of layering. U.S. partnerships that adopt the methodology of Appendix 5 would metaphorically cast aside their buggy-whips of layering and enter a modern era of automated year-end tax allocations of *all* items of income by full or partial netting.

# APPENDIX 1

# Excerpts of Key U.S. Statutes Discussed in Chapter 1 That Govern U.S. and Offshore Hedge Funds and Venture Funds

## Exemption from Registration of Securities with the SEC under Rule 506 of Regulation D of the Securities Act of 1933

### Actual Text of Rule 506 of Regulation D

Source: U.S. GPO, Electronic Code of Federal Regulations, Title 17. Part 230, section 506 (17 CFR § 230.506) at http://ecfr.gpoaccess.gov/cgi/t/text/text-idx?c=ecfr&sid=e05034cf336685566ed293f4846221ac&rgn=div8&view=text&node=17:2.0.1.1.12.0.43.179&idno=17

### Title 17: Commodity and Securities Exchanges

**PART 230—GENERAL RULES AND REGULATIONS, SECURITIES ACT OF 1933**

**§ 230.506 Exemption for Limited Offers and Sales without Regard to Dollar Amount of Offering**

(a) Exemption. Offers and sales of securities by an issuer that satisfy the conditions in paragraph (b) of this section shall be deemed to be transactions not involving any public offering within the meaning of section 4(2) of the Act.

(b) Conditions to be met—(1) General conditions. To qualify for an exemption under this section, offers and sales must satisfy all the terms and conditions of §§230.501 and 230.502.

(2) Specific conditions—(i) Limitation on number of purchasers. There are no more than or the issuer reasonably believes that there are no more than 35 purchasers of securities from the issuer in any offering under this section.

Note: See §230.501(e) for the calculation of the number of purchasers and §230.502(a) for what may or may not constitute an offering under this section.

(ii) Nature of purchasers. Each purchaser who is not an accredited investor either alone or with his purchaser representative(s) has such knowledge and experience in financial and business matters that he is capable of evaluating the merits and risks of the prospective investment, or the issuer reasonably believes immediately prior to making any sale that such purchaser comes within this description.

## SEC Discussion and Interpretation of Rule 506 of Regulation D

Source: www.sec.gov/answers/rule506.htm

Rule 506 of Regulation D is considered a "safe harbor" for the private offering exemption of Section 4(2) of the Securities Act. Companies using the Rule 506 exemption can raise an unlimited amount of money. A company can be assured it is within the Section 4(2) exemption by satisfying the following standards:

- The company cannot use general solicitation or advertising to market the securities;
- The company may sell its securities to an unlimited number of "accredited investors" and up to 35 other purchases. Unlike Rule 505, all non-accredited investors, either alone or with a purchaser representative, must be sophisticated—that is, they must have sufficient knowledge and experience in financial and business matters to make them capable of evaluating the merits and risks of the prospective investment;
- Companies must decide what information to give to accredited investors, so long as it does not violate the antifraud prohibitions of the federal securities laws. But companies must give non-accredited investors disclosure documents that are generally the same as those used in registered offerings. If a company provides information to

accredited investors, it must make this information available to non-accredited investors as well;

- Financial statement requirements are the same as for Rule 505; and
- Purchasers receive "restricted" securities, meaning that the securities cannot be sold for at least a year without registering them.

While companies using the Rule 506 exemption do not have to register their securities and usually do not have to file reports with the SEC, they must file what is known as a "Form D" after they first sell their securities. Form D is a brief notice that includes the names and addresses of the company's owners and stock promoters, but contains little other information about the company.

## SEC Discussion Paragraph on Accredited Investors

Source: www.sec.gov/answers/accred.htm

Under the Securities Act of 1933, a company that offers or sells its securities must register the securities with the SEC or find an exemption from the registration requirements. The Act provides companies with a number of exemptions. For some of the exemptions, such as rules 505 and 506 of Regulation D, a company may sell its securities to what are known as "accredited investors."

## Actual Text of Definition of Accredited Investor in Rule 501 of Regulation D

Source: U.S. GPO, Electronic Code of Federal Regulations, Title 17. Part 230, section 501 (17 CFR § 230.501) at http://ecfr.gpoaccess.gov/cgi/t/text/text-idx?c=ecfr;sid=3 b0e556c2ee447218d262a909a80edc5;rgn=div8;view=text;node=17%3A2.0.1.1.12.0.43 .174;idno=17;cc=ecfr

### Title 17: Commodity and Securities Exchanges

#### PART 230—GENERAL RULES AND REGULATIONS, SECURITIES ACT OF 1933

#### § 230.501 Definitions and Terms Used in Regulation D

As used in Regulation D (§§230.501–230.508), the following terms shall have the meaning indicated:

    (a) Accredited investor. Accredited investor shall mean any person who comes within any of the following categories, or who the issuer reasonably believes comes within any of the following categories, at the time of the sale of the securities to that person:

(1) Any bank as defined in section 3(a)(2) of the Act, or any savings and loan association or other institution as defined in section 3(a)(5)(A) of the Act whether acting in its individual or fiduciary capacity; any broker or dealer registered pursuant to section 15 of the Securities Exchange Act of 1934; any insurance company as defined in section 2(13) of the Act; any investment company registered under the Investment Company Act of 1940 or a business development company as defined in section 2(a)(48) of that Act; any Small Business Investment Company licensed by the U.S. Small Business Administration under section 301(c) or (d) of the Small Business Investment Act of 1958; any plan established and maintained by a state, its political subdivisions, or any agency or instrumentality of a state or its political subdivisions, for the benefit of its employees, if such plan has total assets in excess of $5,000,000; any employee benefit plan within the meaning of the Employee Retirement Income Security Act of 1974 if the investment decision is made by a plan fiduciary, as defined in section 3(21) of such act, which is either a bank, savings and loan association, insurance company, or registered investment adviser, or if the employee benefit plan has total assets in excess of $5,000,000 or, if a self-directed plan, with investment decisions made solely by persons that are accredited investors;

(2) Any private business development company as defined in section 202(a)(22) of the Investment Advisers Act of 1940;

(3) Any organization described in section 501(c)(3) of the Internal Revenue Code, corporation, Massachusetts or similar business trust, or partnership, not formed for the specific purpose of acquiring the securities offered, with total assets in excess of $5,000,000;

(4) Any director, executive officer, or general partner of the issuer of the securities being offered or sold, or any director, executive officer, or general partner of a general partner of that issuer;

(5) Any natural person whose individual net worth, or joint net worth with that person's spouse, at the time of his purchase exceeds $1,000,000;

(6) Any natural person who had an individual income in excess of $200,000 in each of the two most recent years or joint income with that person's spouse in excess of $300,000 in each

of those years and has a reasonable expectation of reaching the same income level in the current year;

(7) Any trust, with total assets in excess of $5,000,000, not formed for the specific purpose of acquiring the securities offered, whose purchase is directed by a sophisticated person as described in §230.506(b)(2)(ii); and

(8) Any entity in which all of the equity owners are accredited investors.

(b) Affiliate. An affiliate of, or person affiliated with, a specified person shall mean a person that directly, or indirectly through one or more intermediaries, controls or is controlled by, or is under common control with, the person specified.

(c) Aggregate offering price. Aggregate offering price shall mean the sum of all cash, services, property, notes, cancellation of debt, or other consideration to be received by an issuer for issuance of its securities. Where securities are being offered for both cash and non-cash consideration, the aggregate offering price shall be based on the price at which the securities are offered for cash. Any portion of the aggregate offering price attributable to cash received in a foreign currency shall be translated into United States currency at the currency exchange rate in effect at a reasonable time prior to or on the date of the sale of the securities. If securities are not offered for cash, the aggregate offering price shall be based on the value of the consideration as established by bona fide sales of that consideration made within a reasonable time, or, in the absence of sales, on the fair value as determined by an accepted standard. Such valuations of non-cash consideration must be reasonable at the time made.

(d) Business combination. Business combination shall mean any transaction of the type specified in paragraph (a) of Rule 145 under the Act (17 CFR 230.145) and any transaction involving the acquisition by one issuer, in exchange for all or a part of its own or its parent's stock, of stock of another issuer if, immediately after the acquisition, the acquiring issuer has control of the other issuer (whether or not it had control before the acquisition).

(e) Calculation of number of purchasers. For purposes of calculating the number of purchasers under §§230.505(b) and 230.506(b) only, the following shall apply:

(1) The following purchasers shall be excluded:

(i) Any relative, spouse or relative of the spouse of a purchaser who has the same principal residence as the purchaser;

(ii) Any trust or estate in which a purchaser and any of the persons related to him as specified in paragraph (e)(1)(i) or (e)(1)(iii) of this section collectively have more than 50 percent of the beneficial interest (excluding contingent interests);

(iii) Any corporation or other organization of which a purchaser and any of the persons related to him as specified in paragraph (e)(1)(i) or (e)(1)(ii) of this section collectively are beneficial owners of more than 50 percent of the equity securities (excluding directors' qualifying shares) or equity interests; and

(iv) Any accredited investor.

(2) A corporation, partnership or other entity shall be counted as one purchaser. If, however, that entity is organized for the specific purpose of acquiring the securities offered and is not an accredited investor under paragraph (a)(8) of this section, then each beneficial owner of equity securities or equity interests in the entity shall count as a separate purchaser for all provisions of Regulation D (§§230.501–230.508), except to the extent provided in paragraph (e)(1) of this section.

(3) A non-contributory employee benefit plan within the meaning of Title I of the Employee Retirement Income Security Act of 1974 shall be counted as one purchaser where the trustee makes all investment decisions for the plan.

(f) Executive officer. Executive officer shall mean the president, any vice president in charge of a principal business unit, division or function (such as sales, administration or finance), any other officer who performs a policy making function, or any other person who performs similar policy making functions for the issuer. Executive officers of subsidiaries may be deemed executive officers of the issuer if they perform such policy making functions for the issuer.

(g) Issuer. The definition of the term issuer in section 2(4) of the Act shall apply, except that in the case of a proceeding under the Federal Bankruptcy Code (11 U.S.C. 101 et seq. ), the trustee or debtor in possession shall be considered the issuer in an offering under a plan or reorganization, if the securities are to be issued under the plan.

(h) Purchaser representative. Purchaser representative shall mean any person who satisfies all of the following conditions or who the issuer reasonably believes satisfies all of the following conditions:

(1) Is not an affiliate, director, officer or other employee of the issuer, or beneficial owner of 10 percent or more of any class

of the equity securities or 10 percent or more of the equity interest in the issuer, except where the purchaser is:

(i)   A relative of the purchaser representative by blood, marriage or adoption and not more remote than a first cousin;

(ii)   A trust or estate in which the purchaser representative and any persons related to him as specified in paragraph (h)(1)(i) or (h)(1)(iii) of this section collectively have more than 50 percent of the beneficial interest (excluding contingent interest) or of which the purchaser representative serves as trustee, executor, or in any similar capacity; or

(iii)   A corporation or other organization of which the purchaser representative and any persons related to him as specified in paragraph (h)(1)(i) or (h)(1)(ii) of this section collectively are the beneficial owners of more than 50 percent of the equity securities (excluding directors' qualifying shares) or equity interests;

(2)   Has such knowledge and experience in financial and business matters that he is capable of evaluating, alone, or together with other purchaser representatives of the purchaser, or together with the purchaser, the merits and risks of the prospective investment;

(3)   Is acknowledged by the purchaser in writing, during the course of the transaction, to be his purchaser representative in connection with evaluating the merits and risks of the prospective investment; and

(4)   Discloses to the purchaser in writing a reasonable time prior to the sale of securities to that purchaser any material relationship between himself or his affiliates and the issuer or its affiliates that then exists, that is mutually understood to be contemplated, or that has existed at any time during the previous two years, and any compensation received or to be received as a result of such relationship.

Note 1: A person acting as a purchaser representative should consider the applicability of the registration and antifraud provisions relating to brokers and dealers under the Securities Exchange Act of 1934 (Exchange Act) (15 U.S.C. 78a et seq., as amended) and relating to investment advisers under the Investment Advisers Act of 1940.

Note 2: The acknowledgment required by paragraph (h)(3) and the disclosure required by paragraph (h)(4) of this section must be made with specific reference to each prospective investment. Advance blanket acknowledgment, such as for all securities transactions or all private placements, is not sufficient.

Note 3: Disclosure of any material relationships between the purchaser representative or his affiliates and the issuer or its affiliates does not relieve the purchaser representative of his obligation to act in the interest of the purchaser.

## Investment Company Act of 1940, Exemption for Qualified Purchasers, Chapter 2D, Subchapter I, Section 80a–3, Paragraph (c)(7)

Source: 15 U.S.C. § 80a–3 at www.law.cornell.edu/uscode/15/usc_sec_15_00000080---a003-.html

### Title 15 U.S. Code, Chapter 2D, Subchapter I, § 80a–3 (c) (1)

#### § 80a–3

#### (c) Further Exemptions

Notwithstanding subsection (a) of this section, none of the following persons is an investment company within the meaning of this subchapter:

(1) Any issuer whose outstanding securities (other than short-term paper) are beneficially owned by not more than one hundred persons and which is not making and does not presently propose to make a public offering of its securities. Such issuer shall be deemed to be an investment company for purposes of the limitations set forth in subparagraphs (A)(i) and (B)(i) of section 80a–12 (d)(1) of this title governing the purchase or other acquisition by such issuer of any security issued by any registered investment company and the sale of any security issued by any registered open-end investment company to any such issuer. For purposes of this paragraph:

(A) Beneficial ownership by a company shall be deemed to be beneficial ownership by one person, except that, if the company owns 10 per centum or more of the outstanding voting securities of the issuer, and is or, but for the exception provided for in this paragraph or paragraph (7), would be an investment company, the beneficial ownership shall be deemed to be that of the holders of such company's outstanding securities (other than short-term paper).

(B) Beneficial ownership by any person who acquires securities or interests in securities of an issuer described in the first sentence of this paragraph shall be deemed to be beneficial ownership by the person from whom such transfer was made, pursuant to such rules and regulations as the Commission shall prescribe as necessary or appropriate in the public interest and consistent with the protection of investors and the purposes fairly intended by the policy and provisions of this subchapter, where the transfer was caused by legal separation, divorce, death, or other involuntary event.

## Investment Company Act of 1940, Exemption for Accredited Investors, Chapter 2D, Subchapter I, Section 80a–3, Paragraph (c)(7)

Source: 15 U.S.C. § 80a–3 at www.law.cornell.edu/uscode/15/usc_sec_15_00000080---a003-.html

### Title 15 U.S. Code, Chapter 2D, Subchapter I, § 80a–3 (c) (7)

### § 80a–3

### (c) Further Exemptions

Notwithstanding subsection (a) of this section, none of the following persons is an investment company within the meaning of this subchapter:

(7)

    (A) Any issuer, the outstanding securities of which are owned exclusively by persons who, at the time of acquisition of such securities, are qualified purchasers, and which is not making and does not at that time propose to make a public offering of such securities. Securities that are owned by persons who received the securities from a qualified purchaser as a gift or bequest, or in a case in which the transfer was caused by legal separation, divorce, death, or other involuntary event, shall be deemed to be owned by a qualified purchaser, subject to such rules, regulations, and orders as the Commission may prescribe as necessary or appropriate in the public interest or for the protection of investors.

    (B) Notwithstanding subparagraph (A), an issuer is within the exception provided by this paragraph if—

        (i) in addition to qualified purchasers, outstanding securities of that issuer are beneficially owned by not more than 100 persons who are not qualified purchasers, if—

            (I) such persons acquired any portion of the securities of such issuer on or before September 1, 1996; and

            (II) at the time at which such persons initially acquired the securities of such issuer, the issuer was excepted by paragraph (1); and

(ii)  prior to availing itself of the exception provided by this paragraph—

   (I)  such issuer has disclosed to each beneficial owner, as determined under paragraph (1), that future investors will be limited to qualified purchasers, and that ownership in such issuer is no longer limited to not more than 100 persons; and

   (II)  concurrently with or after such disclosure, such issuer has provided each beneficial owner, as determined under paragraph (1), with a reasonable opportunity to redeem any part or all of their interests in the issuer, notwithstanding any agreement to the contrary between the issuer and such persons, for that person's proportionate share of the issuer's net assets.

## Definition of Qualified Purchaser Provided in Investment Company Act of 1940, Exemption for Accredited Investors, Chapter 2D, Subchapter I, Section 80a–2, Paragraph (a)(51)

Source: 15 U.S.C. § 80a–2 at www.law.cornell.edu/uscode/15/usc_sec_15_00000080---a002-.html

### Title 15 U.S. Code, Chapter 2D, Subchapter I, § 80a–2

### § 80a–2

**(a) Definitions**

When used in this subchapter, unless the context otherwise requires—

*(51)*

(A)  "Qualified purchaser" means—

   (i)  any natural person (including any person who holds a joint, community property, or other similar shared ownership interest in an issuer that is excepted under section 80a–3 (c)(7) of this title with that person's qualified purchaser spouse) who owns not less than $5,000,000 in investments, as defined by the Commission;

   (ii)  any company that owns not less than $5,000,000 in investments and that is owned directly or indirectly by or for 2 or more natural persons who are related as siblings or spouse (including former spouses), or direct lineal descendants by birth or adoption, spouses of such persons, the estates of such persons, or foundations, charitable organizations, or trusts established by or for the benefit of such persons;

(iii) any trust that is not covered by clause (ii) and that was not formed for the specific purpose of acquiring the securities offered, as to which the trustee or other person authorized to make decisions with respect to the trust, and each settlor or other person who has contributed assets to the trust, is a person described in clause (i), (ii), or (iv); or

(iv) any person, acting for its own account or the accounts of other qualified purchasers, who in the aggregate owns and invests on a discretionary basis, not less than $25,000,000 in investments.

## Regulation S of the Securities Act of 1933 Exempts Sales of U.S. Securities Outside the United States

Source: 17 C.F.R § 230.901 http://ecfr.gpoaccess.gov/cgi/t/text/text-idx?c=ecfr&sid =d3c29c6cfed07e8ad6144b1aee5c2f87&tpl=/ecfrbrowse/Title17/17cfr230_main _02.tpl.

### Title 17: Commodity and Securities Exchanges

#### PART 230—GENERAL RULES AND REGULATIONS, SECURITIES ACT OF 1933

#### § 230.901

GENERAL STATEMENT.
For the purposes only of section 5 of the Act (15 U.S.C. §77e), the terms offer, offer to sell, sell, sale, and offer to buy shall be deemed to include offers and sales that occur within the United States and shall be deemed not to include offers and sales that occur outside the United States.

## A Foreign Partnership or Association Is Not a Corporation, U.S. Code of Federal Regulations on IRS Procedures, 26 C.F.R. § 301.7701-3 (a) and (b)

Source: 26 C.F.R. § 301.7701-3 http://ecfr.gpoaccess.gov/cgi/t/text/text-idx?c=ecfr;s id=8e539d6874946fe0cbb319e1b3701e8c;rgn=div8;view=text;node=26%3A18.0.1.1.2. 20.69.4;idno=26;cc=ecfr

# Title 26: Internal Revenue

## PART 301—PROCEDURE AND ADMINISTRATION—DEFINITIONS

## § 301.7701-3

CLASSIFICATION OF CERTAIN BUSINESS ENTITIES

§ 301.7701-3 (a) In general. A business entity that is not classified as a corporation under §301.7701–2(b) (1), (3), (4), (5), (6), (7), or (8) (an eligible entity ) can elect its classification for federal tax purposes as provided in this section. An eligible entity with at least two members can elect to be classified as either an association (and thus a corporation under §301.7701–2(b)(2)) or a partnership, and an eligible entity with a single owner can elect to be classified as an association or to be disregarded as an entity separate from its owner. Paragraph (b) of this section provides a default classification for an eligible entity that does not make an election. Thus, elections are necessary only when an eligible entity chooses to be classified initially as other than the default classification or when an eligible entity chooses to change its classification. An entity whose classification is determined under the default classification retains that classification (regardless of any changes in the members' liability that occurs at any time during the time that the entity's classification is relevant as defined in paragraph (d) of this section) until the entity makes an election to change that classification under paragraph (c)(1) of this section. Paragraph (c) of this section provides rules for making express elections. Paragraph (d) of this section provides special rules for foreign eligible entities. Paragraph (e) of this section provides special rules for classifying entities resulting from partnership terminations and divisions under section 708(b). Paragraph (f) of this section sets forth the effective date of this section and a special rule relating to prior periods.

(b) Classification of eligible entities that do not file an election —(1) Domestic eligible entities. Except as provided in paragraph (b)(3) of this section, unless the entity elects otherwise, a domestic eligible entity is—

(i) A partnership if it has two or more members; or

(ii) Disregarded as an entity separate from its owner if it has a single owner.

(2) Foreign eligible entities —(i) In general. Except as provided in paragraph (b)(3) of this section, unless the entity elects otherwise, a foreign eligible entity is—

(A) A partnership if it has two or more members and at least one member does not have limited liability;

(B) An association if all members have limited liability; or

(C) Disregarded as an entity separate from its owner if it has a single owner that does not have limited liability.

## Special Rules for Foreign Entities, 26 C.F.R. § 301.7701-3 (d)

## 26 C.F.R. § 301.7701-3

(d) Special rules for foreign eligible entities—

(1) Definition of relevance—(i) General rule. For purposes of this section, a foreign eligible entity's classification is relevant when its classification affects the liability of any person for federal tax or information purposes. For example, a foreign entity's classification would be relevant if U.S. income was paid to the entity and the determination by the withholding agent of the amount to be withheld under chapter 3 of the Internal Revenue Code (if any) would vary depending upon whether the entity is classified as a partnership or as an association. Thus, the classification might affect the documentation that the withholding agent must receive from the entity, the type of tax or information return to file, or how the return must be prepared. The date that the classification of a foreign eligible entity is relevant is the date an event occurs that creates an obligation to file a federal tax return, information return, or statement for which the classification of the entity must be determined. Thus, the classification of a foreign entity is relevant, for example, on the date that an interest in the entity is acquired which will require a U.S. person to file an information return on Form 5471.

(ii) Deemed relevance—(A) General rule. For purposes of this section, except as provided in paragraph (d)(1)(ii)(B) of this section, the classification for Federal tax purposes of a foreign eligible entity that files Form 8832, "Entity Classification Election", shall be deemed to be relevant only on the date the entity classification election is effective.

(B) Exception. If the classification of a foreign eligible entity is relevant within the meaning of paragraph (d)(1)(i) of this section, then the rule in paragraph (d)(1)(ii)(A) of this section shall not apply.

(2) Entities the classification of which has never been relevant. If the classification of a foreign eligible entity has never been relevant (as defined in paragraph (d)(1) of this section), then the entity's classification will initially be determined pursuant to the provisions of paragraph (b)(2) of this section when the classification of the entity first becomes relevant (as defined in paragraph (d)(1)(i) of this section).

(3) Special rule when classification is no longer relevant. If the classification of a foreign eligible entity is not relevant (as defined in

paragraph (d)(1) of this section) for 60 consecutive months, then the entity's classification will initially be determined pursuant to the provisions of paragraph (b)(2) of this section when the classification of the foreign eligible entity becomes relevant (as defined in paragraph (d)(1)(i) of this section). The date that the classification of a foreign entity is not relevant is the date an event occurs that causes the classification to no longer be relevant, or, if no event occurs in a taxable year that causes the classification to be relevant, then the date is the first day of that taxable year.

(4) Effective date. Paragraphs (d)(1)(ii), (d)(2), and (d)(3) of this section apply on or after October 22, 2003.

## U.S. Internal Revenue Code Section 704(b) Requires Partnership Distributive Share Not Have "Substantial Economic Effect"

Source: 26 U.S.C. § 704 (b) at www.law.cornell.edu/uscode/html/uscode26/usc _sec_26_00000704----000-.html

### Title 26 U.S. Code—Internal Revenue Code

#### SUBTITLE A—INCOME TAXES

#### Chapter 1—Normal Taxes and Surtaxes

SUBCHAPTER K—PARTNERS AND PARTNERSHIPS

§ 704. Partner's distributive share

§ 704 (b) Determination of distributive share

A partner's distributive share of income, gain, loss, deduction, or credit (or item thereof) shall be determined in accordance with the partner's interest in the partnership (determined by taking into account all facts and circumstances), if—

(1) the partnership agreement does not provide as to the partner's distributive share of income, gain, loss, deduction, or credit (or item thereof), or

(2) the allocation to a partner under the agreement of income, gain, loss, deduction, or credit (or item thereof) does not have substantial economic effect.

## Demonstration of the Method of Layering in Treasury Regulations, 26 C.F.R Section 1.704-1(b)(5), Example 13(iv)

Source: 26 C.F.R § 1.704-1 at http://ecfr.gpoaccess.gov/cgi/t/text/text-idx?c=ecfr &sid=7d4fdcdbd76337ff73a4d0cfeecd9c92&rgn=div8&view=text&node=26:8.0.1.1.1 .0.13.235&idno=26

# Title 26: Internal Revenue

## PART 1—INCOME TAXES

### Partners and Partnerships

§ 1.704-1 Partner's distributive share.

§ 1.704-1(b)(5) Examples

Example 13(iv) demonstrates layering and requires the previous examples 13(i) to 13(iii).

Example 13. (i) Y and Z form a brokerage general partnership for the purpose of investing and trading in marketable securities. Y contributes cash of $10,000, and Z contributes securities of P corporation, which have an adjusted basis of $3,000 and a fair market value of $10,000. The partnership would not be an investment company under section 351(e) if it were incorporated. The partnership agreement provides that the partners' capital accounts will be determined and maintained in accordance with paragraph (b)(2)(iv) of this section, distributions in liquidation of the partnership (or any partner's interest) will be made in accordance with the partners' positive capital account balances, and any partner with a deficit balance in his capital account following the liquidation of his interest must restore that deficit to the partnership (as set forth in paragraphs (b)(2)(ii)(b) (2) and (3) of this section). The partnership uses the interim closing of the books method for purposes of section 706. The initial capital accounts of Y and Z are fixed at $10,000 each. The agreement further provides that all partnership distributions, income, gain, loss, deduction, and credit will be shared equally between Y and Z, except that the taxable gain attributable to the precontribution appreciation in the value of the securities of P corporation will be allocated to Z in accordance with section 704(c). During the partnership's first taxable year, it sells the securities of P corporation for $12,000, resulting in a $2,000 book gain ($12,000 less $10,000 book value) and a $9,000 taxable gain ($12,000 less $3,000 adjusted tax basis). The partnership has no other income, gain, loss, or deductions for the taxable year. The gain from the sale of the securities gain is allocated as follows:

|  | Y Tax | Y Book | Z Tax | Z Book |
|---|---|---|---|---|
| Capital account upon formation | $10,000 | $10,000 | $10,000 | $10,000 |
| Plus: gain | 1,000 | 1,000 | 8,000 | 1,000 |
| Capital account at end of year 1 | $11,000 | $11,000 | $11,000 | $11,000 |

The allocation of the $2,000 book gain, $1,000 each to Y and Z, has substantial economic effect. Furthermore, under section 704(c) the partners' distributive shares of the $9,000 taxable gain are $1,000 to Y and $8,000 to Z.

(ii) Assume the same facts as in (i) and that at the beginning of the partnership's second taxable year, it invests its $22,000 of cash in securities of G Corp. The G Corp. securities increase in value to $40,000, at which time Y sells 50 percent of his partnership interest (i.e., a 25 percent interest in the partnership) to LK for $10,000. The partnership does not have a section 754 election in effect for the partnership taxable year during which such sale occurs. In accordance with paragraph (b)(2)(iv)( l ) of this section, the partnership agreement provides that LK inherits 50 percent of Y's $11,000 capital account balance. Thus, following the sale, LK and Y each have a capital account of $5,500, and Z's capital account remains at $11,000. Prior to the end of the partnership's second taxable year, the securities are sold for their $40,000 fair market value, resulting in an $18,000 taxable gain ($40,000 less $22,000 adjusted tax basis). The partnership has no other income, gain, loss, or deduction in such taxable year. Under the partnership agreement the $18,000 taxable gain is allocated as follows:

|                                          | Y       | Z        | LK      |
| ---------------------------------------- | ------- | -------- | ------- |
| Capital account before sale of securities | $5,500  | $11,000  | $5,500  |
| Plus: gain                               | 4,500   | 9,000    | 4,500   |
| Capital account at end of the year 2     | $10,000 | $20,000  | $10,000 |

The allocation of the $18,000 taxable gain has substantial economic effect.

(iii) Assume the same facts as in (ii) except that the partnership has a section 754 election in effect for the partnership taxable year during which Y sells 50 percent of his interest to LK. Accordingly, under §1.743–1 there is a $4,500 basis increase to the G Corp. securities with respect to LK. Notwithstanding this basis adjustment, as a result of the sale of the G Corp. securities, LK's capital account is, as in (ii), increased by $4,500. The fact that LK recognizes no taxable gain from such sale (due to his $4,500 section 743 basis adjustment) is irrelevant for capital accounting purposes since, in accordance with paragraph (b)(2)(iv)( m )( 2 ) of this section, that basis adjustment is disregarded in the maintenance and computation of the partners' capital accounts.

|                                          | Y       | Z        | LK      |
| ---------------------------------------- | ------- | -------- | ------- |
| Capital account before sale of securities | $5,500  | $11,000  | $5,500  |
| Plus: gain                               | 2,500   | 5,000    | 2,500   |
| Capital account at end of the year 2     | $8,000  | $16,000  | $8,000  |

(iv) Assume the same facts as in (iii) except that immediately following Y's sale of 50 percent of this interest to LK, the G Corp. securities decrease in value to $32,000 and are sold. The $10,000 taxable gain ($32,000 less $22,000 adjusted tax basis) is allocated as follows:

|  | Y | Z | LK |
| --- | --- | --- | --- |
| Capital account before sale of securities | $5,500 | $11,000 | $5,500 |
| Plus: gain | 2,500 | 5,000 | 2,500 |
| Capital account at end of the year 2 | $8,000 | $16,000 | $8,000 |

The fact that LK recognizes a $2,000 taxable loss from the sale of the G Corp. securities (due to his $4,500 section 743 basis adjustment) is irrelevant for capital accounting purposes since, in accordance with paragraph (b)(2)(iv)( m )( 2 ) of this section, that basis adjustment is disregarded in the maintenance and computation of the partners' capital accounts.

## Partial Netting Methodology Defined and Approved under Treasury Regulations

Source: 26 C.F.R. § 1.704-3 (e)(3)(iv) at http://ecfr.gpoaccess.gov/cgi/t/text/text-idx ?c=ecfr&sid=7d4fdcdbd76337ff73a4d0cfeecd9c92&rgn=div8&view=text&node=26:8 .0.1.1.1.0.13.238&idno=26

## Title 26: Internal Revenue

### PART 1—INCOME TAXES

### Partners and Partnerships

§ 1.704-3 Contributed property.

(e)(3)(iv) Partial netting approach. This paragraph (e)(3)(iv) describes the partial netting approach of making reverse section 704(c) allocations. See Example 1 of paragraph (e)(3)(ix) of this section for an illustration of the partial netting approach. To use the partial netting approach, the partnership must establish appropriate accounts for each partner for the purpose of taking into account each partner's share of the book gains and losses and determining each partner's share of the tax gains and losses. Under the partial netting approach, on the date of each capital account restatement, the partnership:

(A) Nets its book gains and book losses from qualified financial assets since the last capital account restatement and allocates the net amount to its partners;

(B) Separately aggregates all tax gains and all tax losses from qualified financial assets since the last capital account restatement; and

(C) Separately allocates the aggregate tax gain and aggregate tax loss to the partners in a manner that reduces the disparity between the book capital account balances and the tax capital account balances (book-tax disparities) of the individual partners.

## Full Netting Methodology Defined and Approved under Treasury Regulations

Source: 26 C.F.R. § 1.704-3 (e)(3)(v).

### Title 26: Internal Revenue

#### PART 1—INCOME TAXES

#### Partners and Partnerships

§ 1.704-3 Contributed property.

(e)(3)(v) Full netting approach. This paragraph (e)(3)(v) describes the full netting approach of making reverse section 704(c) allocations on an aggregate basis. See Example 2 of paragraph (e)(3)(ix) of this section for an illustration of the full netting approach. To use the full netting approach, the partnership must establish appropriate accounts for each partner for the purpose of taking into account each partner's share of the book gains and losses and determining each partner's share of the tax gains and losses. Under the full netting approach, on the date of each capital account restatement, the partnership:

(A) Nets its book gains and book losses from qualified financial assets since the last capital account restatement and allocates the net amount to its partners;

(B) Nets tax gains and tax losses from qualified financial assets since the last capital account restatement; and

(C) Allocates the net tax gain (or net tax loss) to the partners in a manner that reduces the book-tax disparities of the individual partners.

## The Type of Gains or Loss Allocated under Full and Partial Netting Methodologies Must Be Preserved

Source: 26 C.F.R. § 1.704-3 (e)(3)(vi).

# Title 26: Internal Revenue

**PART 1—INCOME TAXES**

**Partners and Partnerships**

§ 1.704-3 Contributed property.

(e)(3)(vi) Type of tax gain or loss. The character and other tax attributes of gain or loss allocated to the partners under this paragraph (e)(3) must:

(A) Preserve the tax attributes of each item of gain or loss realized by the partnership;

(B) Be determined under an approach that is consistently applied; and

(C) Not be determined with a view to reducing substantially the present value of the partners' aggregate tax liability.

# APPENDIX 2

# Methodology and Implementation Example of Full Netting

## Full Netting Objective Stated Verbally in the Treasury Regulations

We described the relevant Treasury Regulation that verbally establishes the logic and objective of the full netting methodology as envisioned by the U.S. Treasury in Chapter 7. The full citation of 26 C.F.R. § 1.704-3 (e)(3)(v), which defines full netting and the perspective of the U.S. Treasury, was provided in Appendix 1.

The Treasury Regulations require explicitly in 26 C.F.R. § 1.704-3 (e)(3)(vi) that type of gains or loss allocated under full and partial netting methodologies must preserved. This dispels any ambiguity that short-term and long-term gains might be combined. It sets the stage to verbally define and set explicit constraints to the realized capital gains tax allocation problem.

## Mathematical Translation of the Treasury Regulations

We represent a mathematical formulation of the verbal guidelines in definitions provided in the Treasury Regulations for full netting. Our objective is to allocate two categories of full-year realized capital gains at the partnership level: short term realized capital gains, $\Pi_8$, and long-term realized capital gains, $\Pi_{9a}$, to each of the $M$ partners. Each partner's tax allocations are represented with superscripts, as $\Pi_8^j$ and $\Pi_{9a}^j$. Our analysis is focused on at year-end time point $T$. In this and subsequent appendixes, we omit the year-end time point subscript $T$ that was used throughout in Chapter 7, implicitly recognizing that the tax allocation problem in this appendix is only for the year-end time point $T$.

Tax allocations of other items of gains and losses, such as dividends and interest, are made to partners according to the method of layering described in Chapter 6. At the relevant year-end time point, we know each partner's capital account value $U^j$. We also know $\kappa^j$, which for each partner represents the tax basis before the allocation of current-year realized capital gains. It includes all deposits and tax allocations, *including* that of realized capital gains, made to partners in prior years, and all tax allocations *excluding* realized capital gains for the current year, $\Pi_8^j$ and $\Pi_{9a}^j$, which are to be determined.

At year-end time point $T$, no deposits or withdrawals are counted and are treated as not having occurred. This is consistent with Section 704(b) of the Internal Revenue Code, where economic allocations are first made, then corresponding tax allocations that follow the economics are to be made, and withdrawals or deposits occur only after tax allocations. We make it eminently clear that neither $U^j$ nor $\kappa^j$ take into consideration withdrawals or deposits that might occur at year-end time point $T$. We assume that if such withdrawals or deposits take place, they occur one nanosecond after the tax allocations for realized capital gains are made at year-end time point $T$.

## Translating the Treasury Term "Book-Tax Disparities"

The term "book" in the Treasury Regulations is IRS terminology for $U^j$, the partner's economic capital account value in the partnership. We calculate the book-tax difference *before* realized capital gains allocations for each partner as $\rho^j = U^j - \kappa^j$. $U^j$ and $\kappa^j$ are fixed constants known for the relevant year-end time point $T$, and hence $\rho^j$ is a known constant, or a parameter, for our tax allocation problem. In the notation used in Chapter 7, we wrote $\Pi_{M1L6}^j = \rho^j - \left(\Pi_8^j + \Pi_9^j\right)$. $\Pi_{M1L6}^j$ is interpreted as the cumulative unrealized gains of a partner. It is the economic income allocated (on books) but not matched with corresponding tax allocations. This quantity could be a negative or positive number, reported in Schedule M, Line 6 of the partnership tax return, and hence with subscript $M1L6$.

The book-tax difference for each partner *after* realized capital gains allocations $\Pi_8^j$ and $\Pi_{9a}^j$, is $\left[\rho^j - \left(\Pi_8^j + \Pi_9^j\right)\right]$. The Treasury Regulations on full netting only provide a verbal guideline on what the objective function should be. We are expected to implement a procedure that, according to 26 C.F.R. § 1.704-3 (e)(3)(v) (C), "allocates the net tax gain (or net tax loss) to the partners in a manner that reduces the book-tax disparities of the individual partners."

We are presented with the plural "disparities of the individual partners" as the objective function, which we are asked to reduce. We shall go one step further. We shall attempt to construct a mathematical objective function that not only meets the requirement of the Treasury Regulations to reduce the book-tax disparities of the individual partners, but would indeed give us an optimal minimum that cannot be beaten. We wish to uncover a capital gains tax allocation solution that would produce the rock-bottom of book-tax disparities. The Treasury Regulations do not require the tax allocations to be made such that they are optimal. The discovery of a rock-bottom minimum of book-tax disparities of partners would serve as a benchmark for the best possible equitable tax allocation that can be achieved, and a partnership could choose another that would have higher book-tax disparities.

The rock-bottom minimum could also serve as an automatically calculated benchmark in IRS computerized examination of partnership tax returns by investigating how significantly worse the tax allocations in a partnership's filed tax returns are, relative to the minimum. Significant deviation from the rock-bottom minimum would suggest that Section 704(b) of the Internal Revenue Code has been tripped, and that a "substantial economic effect" in the language of section 704(b) might have occurred.

The same rock-bottom minimum might also be extremely helpful for the general partner of the partnership, who might be under pressure from various limited partners with different tax preferences seeking favorable tax allocations. The general partner could communicate to such limited partners that tax allocations are made according to the Treasury Regulations.

# Relating the Treasury Regulations on Full Netting to a Mathematical Problem

What is not obvious is how we relate the Treasury Regulations to a mathematical optimization problem to which a unique rock-bottom minimum exists and can be uncovered by well-known preexisting procedures. This is achieved by mapping the requirement of the Treasury Regulations to a convex programming problem that is not degenerate and indeed has known feasible solutions, and belongs to the subclass of convex programming problems that have a guaranteed optimal (minimum) solution.

# Choice of Convex Objective Function

Our set of $2M$ tax allocation variables $\{\Pi_8^j, \Pi_{9a}^j\}$ for $j = 1 \ldots M$ partners is written in vector notation as a $2M$ row vector: $x = \left[(\Pi_8^1, \Pi_{9a}^1), (\Pi_8^2, \Pi_{9a}^2), \ldots, (\Pi_8^M, \Pi_{9a}^M)\right]$. This is a column vector, whose elements are ordered pairs of the short-term gain allocation $\Pi_8^j$ and the long-term gain allocation $\Pi_9^j$. We place this allocation outcome vector into a *convex* objective function, for which there are plenty of choices. The simplest and most familiar is the quadratic objective function, which evaluates to one single quantity, the sum of squared book-tax disparities, $f(x) = \sum_{j=1}^{M} \left[\rho^j - \left(\Pi_8^j + \Pi_9^j\right)\right]^2$. $f(x)$ maps tax allocations in a hyperspace of real numbers of dimension $2M$, $R^{2M}$, to a real number of dimension 1, $R^1$. This function is the square of the Euclidean norm, that is, it is the square of a measure of distance between the target economic holdings $\rho^j$ and the tax allocations $(\Pi_8^j + \Pi_9^j)$. There are many other candidate convex objective functions, but none as simple and tractable as the quadratic function. Some examples of convex functions are:

Sum of powers of absolute value: $f(x) = \sum_{j=1}^{M} \left|\rho^j - \left(\Pi_8^j + \Pi_9^j\right)\right|^p, p \geq 1$

p-Norm: $f(x) = \left[\sum_{j=1}^{M} \left|\rho^j - \left(\Pi_8^j + \Pi_9^j\right)\right|^p\right]^{\frac{1}{p}}, p \geq 1$

Log sum of exponentials: $f(x) = \log\left[\sum_{j=1}^{M} e^{\left[\rho^j - \left(\Pi_8^j + \Pi_9^j\right)\right]}\right]$

Maximum function: $f(x) = \max\{\rho^1 - \left(\Pi_8^1 + \Pi_9^1\right), \ldots, \rho^M - \left(\Pi_8^M + \Pi_9^M\right)\}$

Since any of the elements $\rho^j - \Pi_8^j - \Pi_9^j$ could be negative, we are obliged to find convex functions that can take negative arguments. We have to exclude many convex functions that take positive arguments only, such as the logarithm, because the logarithm of a negative quantity is undefined.

The sum of powers of absolute value is a generalized version of the quadratic objective function, with $p = 2$. The absolute value is not relevant for even powers. We could create similar even-powered extensions of the p-Norm function, with $p = 2, 4, 6, \ldots$ and these functions would apply stronger bias toward reducing large deviations.

A convex objective function that is to be minimized under linear inequality and linear equality constraints indeed has an optimum solution, and there exist well-documented and tested algorithms that derive such optimal solutions in polynomial time (i.e., in a number of calculation steps that is proportional to a polynomial function of the number of variables). Generally, convex objective functions subject to linear inequality and equality constraints are efficiently solved in polynomial time proportional to the cube of the number of variables. With a 10-fold number of variables, the number of calculations would be about 1,000-fold.

We have not provided an exhaustive list of candidate convex objective functions that are defined over negative elements. Neither have we explored the realm of quasi-convex functions (i.e., convex functions with the linear segments), or convex functions that are continuous but not differentiable everywhere. We focus on our choice of the robust, continuous, and differentiable convex function primarily for reasons of tractability and its intuitive geometric meaning. The nature of the problem does not suggest that other choices of convex objective functions would be either more tractable or preferable in terms of relating better to the verbal Treasury Regulations. On the contrary, the extended and broader class of convex objective functions has more parameters and restrictions imposed within them, introducing a degree of arbitrariness that we wish to avoid.

# Constraints That Follow from the Treasury Regulations on Full Netting

We now have our convex objective function, which even though it is one among many, has nice intuitive properties, being the sum of squared deviations from a fixed target.

We start with $2M + 2$ parameters of fixed data. We have $2M$ parameters of the $\{\rho_T^j\}$, for partners $j = 1$ to $M$, and the 2 given quantities of aggregate partnership level short-term and long-term realized capital gains calculated by full netting, $\Pi_8$, $\Pi_{9a}$ as input data.

We seek to minimize, by choice of tax allocations $\{\Pi_8^j, \Pi_{9a}^j\}$, one of the many possible measures of "book-tax disparities across partners," the sum of their squared disparities: $\sum_j \left[\Pi_{M1L6}^j\right]^2 = \sum_j \left[\rho^j - \left(\Pi_8^j + \Pi_9^j\right)\right]^2$.

Let us examine the constraints that our tax allocation elements in $x = \left[\left\{\Pi_8^j, \Pi_9^j\right\}\right]$ are subjected to. These tax allocations are subject to the *feasibility constraints* that are described below.

# Magnitude Constraints

All partner allocations $\Pi_8^j$ and $\Pi_{9a}^j$, for $j = 1 \ldots M$, must satisfy one of the following two constraints, depending on whether aggregate realized short-term gains $\Pi_s$ are negative or positive:

$\Pi_8 \leq \Pi_8^j \leq 0$ when $\Pi_8 \leq 0$, or
$\Pi_8 \geq \Pi_8^j > 0$ when $\Pi_8 > 0$.

Similarly, they must satisfy one of the following two constraints, depending on whether aggregate realized long-term gains $\Pi_9$ are negative or positive:

$$\Pi_{9a} \leq \Pi_{9a}^j \leq 0 \text{ when } \Pi_{9a} \leq 0, \text{ or}$$
$$\Pi_{9a} \geq \Pi_{9a}^j > 0 \text{ when } \Pi_{9a} > 0.$$

It should be noted that even though there are *four* sets of equations, there are only *two* sets of effective constraints. Only one of the first two equations becomes an operative constraint, and only one of the next two constraints becomes active, depending on the signs of known parameter values of $\Pi_8$ and $\Pi_{9a}$. We shall call these two the *magnitude* constraints. Also note that each equation has two inequalities.

What the two magnitude constraints mean is that:

1. When there are aggregate realized losses at the partnership level, no partner may be allocated gains, and vice versa, when there are aggregate realized gains at the partnership level, no partner may be allocated losses.
2. The absolute value of the aggregate realized losses or gains have to exceed the partner allocations. Thus, when the partnership makes aggregate losses, no partner may be allocated losses that exceed the aggregate losses.

## Additivity Constraints

Further, the realized gain tax allocations are subject to the two constraints that represent the meaning of the word "allocation":

$$\sum_{j=1}^M \Pi_8^j = \Pi_8 \text{ and}$$
$$\sum_{j=1}^M \Pi_{9a}^j = \Pi_9$$

These two constraints ensure that the short-term realized gain tax allocations must add up to the total short-term gains for the partnership, and likewise for long-term gains. These two constraints reflect the requirement in the Treasury Regulations to preserve the nature of gains when making allocations under full or partial netting.

## Additivity Constraints Simplify Magnitude Constraints

The two additivity constraints simplify the two magnitude constraints as previously stated. They eliminate the need for an upper bound to realized capital gain allocations and a lower bound to loss allocations constraints.

Consider the case of allocation of realized long-term gains that must add up to $\Pi_{9a}$. The feasibility constraints require that each partner allocation should be non-negative, that is, $\Pi_{9a}^j > 0$. This forces each partner allocation to be less than the overall gain but the partnership level, so that the constraint $\Pi_{9a} \geq \Pi_{9a}^j$ becomes implicit and we can eliminate it from formal consideration. Similarly, the lower bound, $\Pi_{9a} \leq \Pi_{9a}^j$, becomes implicit when $\Pi_{9a} < 0$. Our magnitude constraints, after factoring the additivity contraints into them, become much simpler:

$\Pi_8^j \leq 0$ when $\Pi_8 \leq 0$, or $\Pi_8^j > 0$ when $\Pi_8 > 0$ (we have $M$ such constraints applying on allocation of realized short-term capital gains)

$\Pi_{9a}^j \leq 0$ when $\Pi_{9a} \leq 0$, or $\Pi_{9a}^j > 0$ when $\Pi_{9a} > 0$ (we have $M$ such constraints applying on allocation of realized long-term capital gains)

## The Constrained Optimization Problem of Full Netting

We state our optimization problem for full netting as:

$$\min_{\{\Pi_8^j, \Pi_{9a}^j\}} \sum_{j=1}^{M} \left[ \rho^j - \left( \Pi_8^j + \Pi_9^j \right) \right]^2$$

subject to feasibility constraints that:

$\Pi_8^j \leq 0$ when $\Pi_8 \leq 0$, or $\Pi_8^j > 0$ when $\Pi_8 > 0$ ($M$ such magnitude constraints)

$\Pi_{9a}^j \leq 0$ when $\Pi_{9a} \leq 0$, or $\Pi_{9a}^j > 0$ when $\Pi_{9a} > 0$ ($M$ such magnitude constraints)

$\sum_{j=1}^{M} \Pi_8^j = \Pi_8$, and $\sum_{j=1}^{M} \Pi_{9a}^j = \Pi_9$ (2 such additivity constraints)

We have $2M$ unknowns, $\{\Pi_8^j, \Pi_{9a}^j\}$ for $j = 1 \ldots M$, that we have to solve for, subject to $2M + 2$ constraints. This is a classic convex optimization problem, to which there is no closed form direct formula solution.

## Verifying Convexity

The domain of a convex optimization, that is, the $2M$ choice variables $\{\Pi_8^j, \Pi_{9a}^j\}$, must be a convex set. We indeed verify that the domain is a convex set, for which we switch to vector notation of $x = [(\Pi_8^1, \Pi_{9a}^1), (\Pi_8^2, \Pi_{9a}^2), \ldots, (\Pi_8^M, \Pi_{9a}^M)]$. If the vectors $x_1$ and $x_2$ are two tax allocation vectors, then any linear combination $\theta x_1 + (1 - \theta)x_2$, where $0 \leq \theta \leq 1$, must also be an allowable tax allocation. The domain of the tax allocation is the real number hyperspace in $2M$ dimensions, $\mathbf{R}^{2M}$, a convex set. It may be verified that if we pick two feasible tax allocations, then a linear combination of the two defined in this way is also feasible.

The objective function $\sum_{j=1}^{M}[\rho^j - (\Pi_8^j + \Pi_9^j)]^2$ should be strictly convex. It is a quadratic function, interpreted geometrically as the graph of the objective function $\sum_{j=1}^{M}[\rho^j - \Pi_8^j - \Pi_{9a}^j]^2$ always having upward positive curvature, shaped like a U, at any given tax allocation $\{\Pi_8^j, \Pi_{9a}^j\}$.

The tax allocation vector of length $2M$ is $x = [(\Pi_8^1, \Pi_{9a}^1), (\Pi_8^2, \Pi_{9a}^2), \ldots, (\Pi_8^M, \Pi_{9a}^M)]$ and the objective function that is to be minimized by choice of $x$ is $f(x) = \sum_{j=1}^{M}[\rho^j - (\Pi_8^j + \Pi_{9a}^j)]^2$. Convexity requires that the domain of $f(x)$, that is, the tax allocation set $x$, should be convex, which we have shown above, and that the Hessian matrix associated with $f(x)$ should be positive semidefinite for all $x$ in its domain, that is, $\nabla^2 f(x) \geq 0$. Geometrically, what convexity means is that if $x_1$ and $x_2$ are two tax allocation vectors, then $f(\theta x_1 + (1 - \theta)x_2) \leq \theta f(x_1) + (1 - \theta) f(x_2)$, where $0 \leq \theta \leq 1$. This is also called Jensen's inequality, which holds for convex functions.

Our objective function, being the sum of squares, is strictly convex. Its Hessian is positive definite, that is, $\nabla^2 f(x) > 0$. This portends well for solving with standard quadratic programming software.

## The Hessian Matrix That Establishes Convexity Is a By-Product for Practical Computer Implementation

We verified that our specific objective function $f(x)$ is convex. In the process, we obtained a useful by-product for practical implementation, which is the Hessian matrix associated with our convex objective function. Without this Hessian matrix, our practical implementation would be stymied.

The Hessian matrix associated with our specific choice of quadratic objective function $f(x)$ turns out to be a positive semidefinite square matrix with $2M$ with a sparse structure of the form: $H = 2\begin{bmatrix} E & \cdots & Z \\ \vdots & \ddots & \vdots \\ Z & \cdots & E \end{bmatrix}$ where $E$ is a $2 \times 2$ matrix of ones along the diagonal, and $Z$ is a $2 \times 2$ matrix of zeros at all other off-diagonal positions. Thus, $E = \begin{pmatrix} 1 & 1 \\ 1 & 1 \end{pmatrix}$ and $Z = \begin{pmatrix} 0 & 0 \\ 0 & 0 \end{pmatrix}$.

We can show that our particular Hessian matrix is positive semidefinite, that is, $H = \nabla^2 f(x) \geq 0$. A square matrix $H$ with $2M$ rows is positive semidefinite, that is, for any nonzero real vector $z$ with $2M$ rows, $z^T H z \geq 0$. ($z^T$ is the transpose of $z$.) Our Hessian matrix $H$ satisfies this definition.

Our particular Hessian goes beyond: It is positive definite, that is, $H = \nabla^2 f(x) > 0$, for any nonzero real vector $z$ with $2M$ rows, $z^T H z > 0$. This means that the objective function $f(x) = \sum_{j=1}^{M} \left[\rho^j - \left(\Pi_8^j + \Pi_{9a}^j\right)\right]^2$ is *strictly* convex. Geometrically the graph of the objective function $\sum_{j=1}^{M} \left[\rho^j - \left(\Pi_8^j + \Pi_{9a}^j\right)\right]^2$ always has upward positive curvature, shaped like a U, at any given tax allocation $\{\Pi_8^j, \Pi_{9a}^j\}$.

The constraint set of $2M$ linear inequalities and 2 linear equalities is also convex, because all linear functions are convex.

We have established that our convex quadratic programming problem is indeed strictly convex, and therefore has a unique optimum. The solution provided by the quadratic programming algorithm comes with a certificate of optimality, the solution to the Lagrange dual of the original problem. A user may verify that the optimal value of the objective function for the original (primal) problem must coincide with that for the dual problem according to the Karush-Kuhn-Tucker conditions. When an optimal solution is accompanied by a mathematical certificate of optimality, as users, we need not be particularly concerned about which specific algorithm or procedure was used to obtain the solution.

We are guaranteed that there is a solution to achieve the global minimum for this convex optimization problem, and it can be that it can be solved in polynomial time. We therefore have assurance that the solution provided would be global optimal, and that the software packages would deliver a proposed optimum solution along with a certificate of optimality.

Had the Hessian matrix not been sparse, algorithms would struggle to converge to the minimum requiring significantly greater computation. Sparseness of the Hessian is a key to obtaining tractable polynomial time convergence to the optimal solution of a convex programming problem. We are indeed fortunate that our Hessian is nicely sparse, so we may expect tractable and fast computer implementation in polynomial time.

The Hessian matrix associated with our convex quadratic optimization problem subject to linear inequality and equality constraints is helpful for practical implementation. Algorithms and software to solve quadratic programming problem are formulated and implemented in a *canonical form* that involve the Hessian matrix.

## Solving the Full Netting Problem with 3 Alternate Solvers

Strict convexity permits us to use the convex programming and quadratic programming packages. We solved a test problem on a standard PC

with 100 partners using the quadratic programming modules of (1) R and
(2) Matlab, and with (3) CVX using SDPT3; (3) is an add-in to Matlab.

*Standard desktop PC hardware:* We ran the 100-partner test problem on a standard, somewhat dated desktop personal computer, a 2007
vintage AMD dual-core 2.8 GHz with 2 GB of memory running Windows 7.
This unremarkable piece of computer hardware would correspond to about
1 "computing unit" in Amazon's cloud computing product offerings.

## Open-Source R Solved 100-Partner Problem in 40 Milliseconds

The free open-source statistical software R (the R Project) available under
the GNU General Public License is a language and environment for statistical
computing in Linux or Windows. R is good as a general analytical and basic
statistical analysis tool. It has a contributed open-source module named
quadprog that solves quadratic programming problems supplied in canonical form, based on the Goldfarb-Idani[1] algorithm published in 1983.

The quadprog module of R requires the (convex) quadratic objective function to be specified as input in a canonical matrix form as
$f(x) = \frac{1}{2}x^T D x - d^T x$, where $D$ is a matrix and $d$ is a vector. (Note that $x^T$
is the the notation for the transpose of the vector $x$, and $d^T$ is the transpose of the vector $d$.) We are required by R to provide the matrix $D$ and
vector $d$ as input, in addition to the linear inequality and equality constraints in matrix form. Our next challenge is to transform our quadratic
objective function $f(x) = \sum_{j=1}^{M} [\rho^j - (\Pi_8^j + \Pi_9^j)]^2$ into the canonical form
$\frac{1}{2}x^T D x - d^T x$. What $D$ matrix and $d^T$ vector must we provide to R?

By longhand expansion of $f(x) = \sum_{j=1}^{M} [\rho^j - (\Pi_8^j + \Pi_9^j)]^2$, then
collecting terms and expressing them in matrix form, our objective function
transforms to:

$$f(x) = \frac{1}{2}x^T H x - g^T x + K$$

where $H$ is the same exact Hessian matrix corresponding to our objective
function, that was identified earlier. $H = 2\begin{bmatrix} E & \cdots & Z \\ \vdots & \ddots & \vdots \\ Z & \cdots & E \end{bmatrix}$ is a sparse block

---

[1] *Op. cit.*, Chapter 7.

diagonal matrix of size $2M \times 2M$, where $E$ is a $2 \times 2$ matrix of ones along the diagonal, and $Z$ is a $2 \times 2$ matrix of zeros at all other off-diagonal positions.

$$g^T = 2[(\rho^1, \rho^1), (\rho^2, \rho^2), \ldots, (\rho^M, \rho^M)]$$

$$K = \sum_{j=1}^{M} (\rho^j)^2$$

The vector $g$ with $2M$ elements contains a sequence of $M$ pairs of duplicates $\{\rho^j, \rho^j\}$. It consists of 2 repeated elements corresponding to each partner, $M$ times over, making it of length $2M$. The entire sequence is multiplied by the constant 2. We populate the vector $g$ with the tax-book disparities of partners. This is a starting point for our test problem. We arbitrarily fix the vector $g^T$ for our test example according to:

$\rho^1 = 10$
$\rho^2 = 2.05$
$\rho^2$ to $\rho^{51}$ increment by 0.05 until the 51st partner, starting at $\rho^2 = 2.05$
    until $\rho^{51} = 4.50$
$\rho^{52}$ to $\rho^{100}$ decrement by 0.05 until the 100th partner, starting at
    $\rho^{52} = -2.05$ until $\rho^{100} = -4.45$

These are arbitrary choices of input data. We have selected the first partner to have the largest single book-tax disparity as a positive number, then the next 50 partners having positive book-tax disparity, and the next 49 partners having negative tax-book disparity.

$K$ evaluates to a constant, and may be dropped out. Our longhand expansion of $f(x)$ includes the constant term $\Sigma_j(\rho^j)^2$ which is omitted from the canonical form of the quadratic objective function in R and Matlab. This is because the addition of a constant has no impact on the optimal solution. The optimal solution is invariant to the addition of a constant term to the objective function. R would provide the optimal solution $x$ and the value of $f(x) - K$ evaluated at the optimal $x$. To recover $f(x)$, we simply add back a constant $K$ to the value of $f(x) - K$.

Thus, for the objective function of the quadprog module of R which requires $D$ and $d$ as input data, we supply $D = H$ and $d = g$. $D$ is just our Hessian matrix, and $d$ is the negative of our vector $g$, without its negative sign. The quadprog module of R already has provided for a negative sign in its canonical form. By supplying a negative of $g$, we're converting it into a positive vector, and let the negative sign that is present in the canonical form restore its negative sign. These are minor inconveniences of mapping a given problem to the hard-wired canonical form of a software model.

Now all we need are the equality and inequality constraints. The quadprog module of R requires us to provide the combined set of constraints in the form of $A^T x \geq b$ along with a positive integer $m$ representing that the first $m$ rows of $A^T$ contain the equality constraints, and the remainder contain the inequality constraints. In our test example of full netting tax allocation, we have to have quality constraints, one for short-term gains and one for long-term gains, and hence we supply the parameter $m = 2$ to the quadprog module of R.

In our specific test example of allocating realized gains to 100 partners under full netting, we consider the case where $\Pi_8 = -20$ (million), a net short-term loss to be allocated, and $\Pi_9 = +130$ (million), a net long-term gain to be allocated. We construct our matrix $A^T$ and vector $b$ to represent our presenting constraints:

$\sum_{j=1}^{M} \Pi_8^j = \Pi_8$ and $\sum_{j=1}^{M} \Pi_{9a}^j = \Pi_9$ (2 such additivity constraints)

$\Pi_8^j \leq 0$ because, in our example, $\Pi_8 \leq 0$ ($M$ such magnitude constraints)

$\Pi_{9a}^j \geq 0$ when $\Pi_{9a} > 0$ ($M$ such magnitude constraints). We have written this as an inequality $\Pi_{9a}^j \geq 0$ without any loss of generality, even though we had represented them as $\Pi_{9a}^j > 0$ earlier.

The first two rows of $b$ are $beq = \begin{bmatrix} \Pi_8 \\ \Pi_{9a} \end{bmatrix} = \begin{bmatrix} -20 \\ 130 \end{bmatrix}$. The remaining $2M$ rows of $b$ are $bineq = [0, 0, \ldots, 0]$ (simply, a column of zeros). By stacking $beq$ and $bineq$ we get $b = [beq, bineq]$ with $2M + 2$ rows (and 1 column).

The first two rows of $A$ would look like $Aeq = [I, I, \ldots .I]$ where $I = \begin{bmatrix} 1 & 0 \\ 0 & 1 \end{bmatrix}$, a $2 \times 2$ identity matrix. The remaining $2M$ rows of $A^T$ would be a sparse matrix that looks like $Aineq = \begin{bmatrix} L & \cdots & Z \\ \vdots & \ddots & \vdots \\ Z & \cdots & L \end{bmatrix}$ where $L = \begin{bmatrix} -1 & 0 \\ 0 & 1 \end{bmatrix}$, a $2 \times 2$ matrix along the diagonal, and $Z$ is a $2 \times 2$ matrix of zeros at all other off-diagonal positions. We get $A^T$ by stacking $Aeq$ and $Aeq$, so that $A = \begin{bmatrix} Aeq \\ Aineq \end{bmatrix}$, which has $2M + 2$ rows and $2M$ columns. Note that the canonical form of the constraint that is required as problem structure input by the quadprog module of R is $A^T$. So we set up $A$, but proceed to supply its transpose $A^T$ to the quadprog module of R.

Now all our problem structure and data parameter matrices are ready for feeding to the quadprog module of R. We obtain the optimal solution to partner tax allocations by placing the function call in R code to the solve.QP function of the quadprog module of R, as follows:

```
x <- solve.QP(H, g, t(A), b, m)
```

Since the documentation of the quadprog module of R is written in the form solve.QP(Dmat, dvec, Amat, bvec, meq = 0), and error messages (if any) refer to these matrix names, we could also deliver the function call to the quadprog module of R as:

```
x <- solve.QP(Dmat=H, dvec=g, Amat=t(A),
  bvec=b, meq=m)
```

The solution x is returned as a data structure.

Unfortunately, to our disappointment, the quadprog module of R instantly returned an error message stating that the problem is not convex and cannot be solved. One does not give up quickly on well-tested open-source software, even though there is nobody to provide support. If that were the case, the open-source Linux operating system would have gone nowhere. We had gone to great lengths to establish that our problem was not just convex, but strictly convex. Clearly, the complaint of nonconvexity by the quadprog module of R is not valid. Instead of abandoning R and its quadprog module, we forged ahead by identifying its quirks and tweaking the input data.

The quadprog module of R for quadratic programming requires the Hessian matrix to be nonsingular, that is, it should have an inverse and have a nonzero determinant. It is based on an algorithm that requires the Hessian matrix to be invertible. Our Hessian is positive definite, but singular with a zero determinant, and hence not invertible. We could eventually get the quadprog module of R to work and produce an optimal solution, but only after "doping" the diagonal elements of our Hessian matrix by adding a tiny positive number $+10^{-12}$. This made the Hessian matrix acceptable to the quadprog module of R. Our Hessian has a zero determinant. In its given form, it is unacceptable to the quadprog module of R, which stops instantly with a complaint that the problem is not convex. However, upon "doping" the diagonal elements off our Hessian by adding $+10^{-12}$, the quadprog module of R accepted our problem, and presented a solution for this 100-partner problem along with a verifiable certificate of optimality (which we indeed verified).

We were concerned that our Hessian input data matrix had to be "doped," so any results provided by the quadprog module of R might be unreliable. Yet, we had to reject the notion of unreliability because the proposed solution provided by the quadprog module of R came with a certificate of optimality that we verified. When such a certificate is on hand, it is immaterial what algorithm or solution procedure was deployed. The solution provided is unequivocally a global minimum to our strictly convex optimization problem. Further, in the subsequent section, we ran the same exact test problem in Matlab, which produced the same exact solution.

Since the solve.QP function of the quadprog module of R does not produce a direct estimate of time taken by the procedure, we timed the above operation running on our standard PC hardware by embedding our function call as above within the elapsed system time function of the R programming language as:

```
system.time(x <- solve.QP(H, g, t(A), b, m))
```

This system time tracker, which is accurate to 0.01 second or 10 milliseconds, gave us a reading of elapsed time as 0.04 second or 40 milliseconds. This is an amazing feat, considering that we're using unremarkable standard 2007 vintage desktop PC hardware. A convex programming problem with 100 partners, to determine 200 tax allocations subject to 202 constraints, is solved within 40 milliseconds by the Goldfarb-Idani algorithm provided in R, converging in 124 iterations. In a few repeated runs, we timed the solution at 30 milliseconds.

## Matlab Solved the 100-Partner Problem in 6.60 Seconds

We proceeded in our subsequent numerical implementation with the commercial software Matlab. The suggested retail price of Matlab on its Web site is $2,000, with an additional $1,000 for the Optimization Toolbox, which contains its module that is also named quadprog. We used the recent version, R2009b, of Matlab. We presented the same 100-partner test problem to the quadprog module of commercially available software Matlab, and we were provided the same exact solution as that obtained from the quadprog module R. The tax allocation solution vector, the minimized value of the convex objective function, and the certificate of optimality were identical. The quadprog module of Matlab recorded 6.60 seconds taken and 494 iterations to solve the same exact problem. While 6.60 seconds is indeed fast, it is notable that this time taken is 160- to 220-fold the time and 4-fold the number of iterations taken by the quadprog module of R. This is despite the fact that the solution from the quadprog module of R provided to 6 significant digits, as compared to 4 significant digits by the quadprog module of Matlab. Error tolerance and significant digits did not seem to explain the time taken, and it is most likely due to the relative efficiency of the underlying algorithms and the relative computational overheads of the software environments.

Matlab has two algorithm choices within its quadprog module. The first choice is a "medium-scale" algorithm, which is the default choice, and the only choice available to us. This is because the second choice, its "large-scale" algorithm, requires us to provide a "trust-region" for it to conduct its search, and further, does not permit inequality constraints at all. It permits either equality constraints or upper/lower bound constraints, but not both simultaneously. The medium-scale procedure of Matlab is based on the 1981 algorithm of Gill, Murray, and Wright.[2] The large-scale procedure, though not directly relevant for us, is based on the 1994 algorithm of Coleman and Li.[3]

Matlab's quadprog module accepts only quadratic programming problems that are presented to it in strictly canonical form and solved according to algorithms that appear to be less robust. Matlab's canonical form of the objective function differs from that of .the quadprog module of R only by a minus sign. The quadprog module of Matlab requires the objective function to be provided in matrix form as $f(x) = \frac{1}{2} x^T D x + d^T x$, where $D$ is a matrix and $d$ is a vector. We provide our Hessian $H$ to Matlab, setting $D = H$, just as we did for the quadprog module of R. Our $g$ vector of book-tax disparities of partners was defined without a negative sign. Thus, instead of providing $d = g$ to the quadprog module of R, due to a negative sign already included in that canonical form, we supply our $d = -g$ to the quadprog module of Matlab, the negative of $g$ as we defined it.

The Hessian matrix $H$ that we identified earlier becomes the problem structure input into the solution process. The quadprog module of Matlab accepts our Hessian without hesitation, complaints, or rejection, effectively recognizing that the problem that we are presenting is (strictly) convex, despite our Hessian being singular (i.e., having a zero determinant). We did not have to "dope" by adding $+10^{-12}$ to the diagonal elements of the Hessian matrix as we had to in R. We now have to provide the linear inequality and equality constraints to the quadprog module of Matlab in matrix form to complete our problem specification.

The quadprog module of Matlab requires the inequality and equality constraints to be provided as separate matrix questions, unlike one single stacked matrix equation as required by the quadprog module of R. The underlying matrices are nearly identical except for the sign. The quadprog module of Matlab requires the inequality constraints to be represented as $(Aineq)x \leq bineq$ and the equality constraints as $(Aeq)x = beq$. In addition, the quadprog module of Matlab permits upper and lower bound constraints, which our problem structure already captures in the equality and inequality constraints, so we may ignore this feature.

---

[2] *Op. cit.*, Chapter 7.
[3] *Op. cit.*, Chapter 7.

R and Matlab constraint structures differ only by sign. The quadprog module of Matlab specifies the inequality constraints as "less than," while the quadprog module of R specifies them as "greater-than." For the two equality constraints $(Aeq)x = beq$, $Aeq$ and $beq$ are identical under both R and Matlab. For the $2M$ inequality constraints, $Aeq$ that is to be supplied to Matlab is simply $-1$ times $Aeq$ supplied for R.

Thus, the structure of the constraint matrices to be supplied to the quadprog module of Matlab is as follows:

$$beq = \begin{bmatrix} \Pi_8 \\ \Pi_{9a} \end{bmatrix} = \begin{bmatrix} -20 \\ 130 \end{bmatrix}$$

$Aeq = [I, I, \dots .I]$ where $I = \begin{bmatrix} 1 & 0 \\ 0 & 1 \end{bmatrix}$, a $2 \times 2$ identity matrix repeated $M$ times.

$Aineq$ for Matlab would be a sign-changed mirror of the inequality coefficient structure we created for R, so it would be a sparse matrix that looks like $Aineq = \begin{bmatrix} M & \cdots & Z \\ \vdots & \ddots & \vdots \\ Z & \cdots & M \end{bmatrix}$ where $M = \begin{bmatrix} 1 & 0 \\ 0 & -1 \end{bmatrix}$, a $2 \times 2$ matrix along the diagonal, and $Z$ is a $2 \times 2$ matrix of zeros at all other off-diagonal positions.

We're now ready to feed our matrices to the quadprog function of Matlab as follows:

```
tic
[x, fval, exitflag, output, lambda] =
quadprog(H, -g, Aineq, bineq, Aeq, beq,
   [], [], [], optimset('MaxIter',1000))
toc
```

The tic and toc statements track elapsed time. The default function call provides for a maximum of 200 iterations, which resulted in failure to converge. We had to set the optional parameter to permit 1,000 iterations. We obtained convergence after 494 iterations in 6.60 seconds.

We provided alternate parameters for book-tax differencs of partners, the $g$ vector, and found instances where the quadprog module of Matlab would not converge even after allowing for 100,000 iterations. The same exact problem that failed to converge under the quadprog module of Matlab did indeed converge under other algorithms. For this reason, we would recommend the quadprog module of Matlab only as a starting point or a demonstration benchmark for the purposes of determining tax allocations. Fortunately, we have a repository of robust algorithms that unquestionably determines the global minimum when a convex optimization problem is presented. The next section describes such an available robust algorithm.

## Open-Source CVX Solved the 100-Partner Problem in 0.78 Seconds

It would be appreciated by practitioners that transformation of a given convex optimization problem on hand into the canonical form of hard-wired algorithms that are provided in the form of old-school function calls is tedious and cumbersome. Minor errors in sign, or worse, failure to strictly conform to the canonical form, result in frustrating error messages. Even though a successful run in R takes barely 40 milliseconds, it may take days and weeks before a successful run takes place.

To overcome these wasteful efforts in transforming a given problem to suit hardwired algorithms in their canonical form, a small community of engineers centered around Stanford University have created an open-source add-in to Matlab named CVX[4]. This front-end scientific "middleware" accepts convex optimization problems in human-readable form according to simple disciplined mathematical structures. Function calls to convex programming algorithms take place behind the scenes. The output solution is produced directly by the algorithm.

The advantage of using the CVX package (as an add-in to Matlab) is that it does not require presentation of the convex optimization problem in canonical form, to be further adapted to the module's format for passing data parameters, but in a simple user-friendly representation of the convex programming problem within Matlab. Further, CVX does not use older quadratic programming algorithms, but more recent algorithms called "interior point methods." It does not expect the problem presented to be strictly convex quadratic as R and Matlab require, and also handles convex (but not strictly convex) problems. For us, strict convexity is not an issue, because our presenting problem is indeed strictly convex, which enables us to use R or Matlab to derive the global optimal solution.

CVX is effectively a user-friendly front-end for its default solver SDPT3.[5] CVX uses the SDPT3 add-in package under Matlab as its default

---

[4]Instructions, manuals and downloads are provided at www.stanford.edu/~boyd/cvx/.

[5]R.H Tutuncu, K.C. Toh, and M.J. Todd, "Solving semidefinite-quadratic-linear programs using SDPT3," *Mathematical Programming* Ser. B, 95 (2003), pp. 189–217. The SDPT3 algorithm was originally described in K.C. Toh, M.J. Todd, and R.H. Tutuncu, "SDPT3—A Matlab Software Package for Semidefinite Programming,"

solver. The open-source SDPT3 algorithm itself is a Matlab add-in package. The SDPT3 Matlab package is complex and is not particularly user-friendly. Fortunately, the open-source front-end Matlab package CVX comes with SDPT3 built in. We are still using the Matlab software environment, only we're not using Matlab's own quadprog module, but instead using the open-source package CVX for Matlab, which comes with embedded open-source SDPT3 for Matlab. CVX offers a second convex programming solver named SeDuMi[6] as an alternative to SDPT3.

CVX solves the convex programming problem presented to it by second-order cone programming (SOCP) algorithms in SDPT3 instead of using the quadratic programming algorithms of Matlab and R. The acronym SDPT3 represents SDP for semidefinite programming, and T3 for its three authors, Tutuncu, Toh, and Todd. The main advantage of using the more modern SDPT3 algorithm of 2003 relying on interior point methods is that it is highly efficient and converges fast in polynomial-time. The same exact test problem with 100 partners takes 0.78 seconds of elapsed computer time to converge in 24 iterations. This clearly demonstrates that SDPT3 has a better algorithm for making rapid strides to reach the target optimum that is guaranteed to exist.

Our experience suggests that CVX with its embedded SDPT3 algorithm running in Matlab is by far the dominant and preferred choice. This is not based on our look-and-feel, nor on time taken, but on the number of iterations. CVX with SDPT3 took only 23 iterations to reach the same exact optimal as the quadratic programming modules of R and Matlab. This was one-fifth of the iterations of the Goldfarb-Idani algorithm in R, and one-twentieth of the iterations of the Gill, Murray, and Wright algorithm in Matlab.

Our objective function $f(x) = \sum_{j=1}^{M} [\rho^j - (\Pi_8^j + \Pi_9^j)]^2$ can be rewritten in more compact form as $(\|H_1 x - g_1\|_2)^2$, where $H_1$ and $g_1$ look like a collapsed version of the Hessian matrix $H$ and book capital account values vector $g$ without the constant coefficients of 2. $H$ along with its constant coefficient 2 came from investigating convexity, and $g$ with its coefficient of 2, with repeated elements, was manufactured to achieve conformity with the canonical forms of the quadprog modules of R and Matlab.

---

*Optimization Methods and Software*, 11 (1999), pp. 545–581. This is downloadable from various mirrors, and from the Web site of its first author, K.C. Toh, at his server at the National University of Singapore, at www.math.nus.edu.sg/~mattohkc/sdpt3.html, or from the third author, R.H. Tutuncu, at Carnegie Mellon University, at www.math.cmu.edu/~reha/sdpt3.html.
[6]SeDuMi is documented and downloadable at http://sedumi.ie.lehigh.edu/.

The $M \times 2M$ coefficient matrix $H_1 = \begin{bmatrix} E_1 & \cdots & Z_1 \\ \vdots & \ddots & \vdots \\ Z_1 & \cdots & E_1 \end{bmatrix}$ has the vector $E_1 = [1 \quad 1]$ along its diagonals, and $Z_1 = [0 \quad 0]$ at all off-diagonal places. $g_1 = [\rho^1, \rho^2, \ldots, \rho^M]$ is a vector of length $M$. We may now proceed to minimize $(\|H_1 x - g_1\|_2)^2$. CVX also accepts this representation as the definition of the objective function, as squaring of a norm. We use an alternative objective function, the positive square root of our objective function, as $f_{alt}(x) = \|H_1 x - g_1\|_2$. The 2-norm is simply the Euclidean distance between $H_1 x$ and $g_1$. By convention, the subscript 2 is dropped for a 2-norm, so we may write the alternate objective function as $f_{alt}(x) = \|H_1 x - g_1\|$. This is convex, and any vector $x$ that minimizes $f(x)$ also minimizes $f_{alt}(x)$. In the process, we obtain an intuitive interpretation of our objective function, as one single number representing a geometric distance between book and tax capital accounts of partners.

It is not necessary to create $H_1$ and $g_1$ afresh if $H$ and $g$ were already created for R or Matlab. If $H$ and $g$ are already on hand, we may proceed to minimize $\|Hx - g\|$ because it is a scale multiple of $\|H_1 x - g_1\|$. Both would result in the same optimum. The only reason the vector $g$ was created with repeated elements and a coefficient of 2 was for conformity with the canonical forms of R and Matlab, and it is good to dispense with it when it is no longer needed.

We provide our CVX code here, using the same matrices $H$, $g$, *Aeq*, *beq*, *Aineq*, and *bineq* that we had defined for Matlab. $M = 100$ is the number of partners defined earlier in Matlab.

```
cvx_begin
 variable x(2*M);
 minimize ( norm( H1*x - g1) )
    subject to
      Aeq*x == beq ;
      Aineq*x <= bineq ;
cvx_end
```

The output solution is the tax allocation vector x with 200 elements. SDPT3 automatically provides a detailed readout of its inner workings and iterations, along with its certificate of optimality. CVX understands all of Matlab's functions, and norm(z) is the Matlab function for the 2-norm of a vector z. We also obtained the same solution by minimizing the square of the norm, which is the form of the objective function in Chapter 7, coded in CVX as:

```
minimize ( square_pos(norm( H1*x - g1)) )
```

CVX extends our reach to alternate convex functions beyond the 2-norm. We could define some other appropriate convex objective function, so that we are not confined with the narrow scope of a 2-norm. All we require is that we should know well in advance that it is convex, preferably strictly convex. For instance, we could now try the $p$-norm, as the sum of $p$th power of the book-tax differences, scaled back to the $(1/p)$ power, as $f_{alt}(x) = \|H_1 x - g_1\|_p$ (provided $p > 1$) and represent it in CVX according to the Matlab function for a $p$-norm, which is norm(x, p). Thus, if we replace the objective function in the previous code with norm( H1*x - g1, 4), our objective function would be the sum of the fourth powers of book-tax disparities, subsequently fourth-rooted.

Higher $p$-norms are interpreted as severe penalties to egregious deviations in book-tax disparities. We can take this to an extreme, to minimize the infinity norm, which is the highest absolute book-tax disparity number. It is defined in Matlab as norm(x,inf). We took this opportunity and indeed obtained a rapid convergence solution to our same problem by coding it in CVX as:

```
minimize ( norm( H1*x - g1, inf) )
```

SDPT3 did not take any more time or significantly more iterations to solve for tax allocations under norms other than the 2-norm.

This is another reason for recommending CVX, that we are no longer restricted to the objective function being selected as the 2-norm of book-tax disparities among the partners. CVX permits us to solve for tax allocations under a larger set of a convex objective functions. The only conditions are that we should know in advance that they are convex, and that CVX should accept them. Stated differently, the quadratic programming algorithms apply only to one case of a specific objective function: the square of the 2-norm of book-tax disparities among partners. No other objective function works with them. CVX with SDPT3 is one of the few practical modern tools, forged only in this past decade, to examine other convex objective functions.

Despite the discovery of CVX with SDPT3 as a highly efficient general-purpose convex programming tool that optimizes a large variety of convex functions, the 2-norm as an objective function is robust and resilient. It constitutes the backbone of regression analysis in statistics. It has an intuitive interpretation, as a measure of Euclidean distance between the book and the tax capital accounts of partners, albeit in a 100-dimension hyperspace that represents 100 partners, which is difficult to visualize.

# Multiple Solutions to the Global Optimum

We are guaranteed that there exists a global optimum, and that the solution to achieve this global optimum can be obtained by quadratic programming and other convex programming algorithms. However, our particular problem has a peculiarity, that there are multiple solutions, each of which satisfies the feasibility constraints, which evaluate to the same global minimum of book-tax disparities of the partners.

To see why this happens, let us examine the first-order conditions of optimality, disregarding the feasibility constraints. Our tax allocation solution vector $x$ has $2M$ elements. We take the derivative of $f(x)$ with respect to each of the $2M$ elements and set it to equal zero, which is the condition for an unconstrained optimum. We should have $2M$ such first-order conditions. However, only $M$ of them are unique. Take, for instance, the derivative of $f(x)$ with respect to $\Pi_8^j$, which is $-2\left[\rho^j - \left(\Pi_8^j + \Pi_{9a}^j\right)\right]$. This is identical to the derivative of $f(x)$ with respect to $\Pi_{9a}^j$, which is also $-2\left[\rho^j - \left(\Pi_8^j + \Pi_{9a}^j\right)\right]$.

At the global minimum for $f(x)$, which we denote as $f(x^*)$, all of the optimal solutions $x^*$ have the property that $(\Pi_8^{*j} + \Pi_{9a}^{*j}) = \Pi_{8+9a}^{**j}$. The elements $(\Pi_8^{*j}, \Pi_{9a}^{*j})$ may vary across the different solutions to produce the same global optimum $f(x^*)$, but the sum of this pair adds up to a unique number $\Pi_{8+9a}^{**j}$ across all solutions. Thus, $f(x^*)$ evaluates to the same global minimum value for all the optimal solutions with varying elements $(\Pi_8^{*j}, \Pi_{9a}^{*j})$ adding up to the unique number $\Pi_{8+9a}^{**j}$ across all solutions.

Despite a problem with a large number of partners (say, 100) having so many constraints (202 constraints, 100 partners), the solution is not likely to be unique. A smaller problem with 2–6 partners is also likely to contain multiple solutions. In the next section, we provide a simple and robust procedure for narrowing down multiple solutions to a single unique optimum solution. This is one of many similar methods that might be deployed.

# Second-Pass Procedure to Derive a Unique, Robust, and Efficient Solution

Let us consider the case where all partners are in identical tax preference situations. Thus, they are either all taxable subject to the same tax structure, or all tax exempt. This eliminates the consideration of tax preferences, which we shall address in Appendix 4.

The procedure to determine the "best" allocation is simple. We consider this an optional second-pass procedure. Having gone far enough to establish an optimal solution and the first pass, the incremental computer coding and implementation effort is minimal.

We solve the optimization problem of full netting using R, Matlab, or CVX in Matlab, as described in the previous sections. There might be other tax allocation solutions that achieve the same global minimum. We describe a simple procedure here that would achieve two purposes. First, we would ascertain whether the first-pass optimal solution obtained is indeed the better one, or ideally the best, among other possible solutions that achieve the same global minimum value of the objective function subject to the feasibility constraints. In most cases, the solution obtained in the first step is indeed the "best." Next, if the first-pass optimal solution is not the "best," we would have on hand the "best" solution to replace it.

We propose a simple criterion that the "best" solution should meet. Here is a numerical example. Suppose the first-pass optimal solution allocated $\{\Pi_8^{*j}, \Pi_{9a}^{*j}\} = \{-22, 24\}$ to a given partner so that $(\Pi_8^{*j} + \Pi_{9a}^{*j}) = \Pi_{8+9a}^{**j} = +2$. Suppose another optimal solution allocates $\{\Pi_8^{@j}, \Pi_{9a}^{@j}\} = \{-2, 4\}$ to the same partner so that the total is also +2. We would prefer the second allocation and would consider the first allocation to be exaggerated, even tilted according to tax preferences.

We want the *scaled* values of partner tax allocations, each scaled by their (unique) optimal total allocation $\Pi_{8+9a}^{**j}$, to be the lowest across partners. Mathematically, we would like the 2-norm of the *scaled* optimal solution to be the lowest. This is our standard for establishing the "best" tax allocation solution.

In the (primary) first-pass problem structure, the vector $x$ represented the tax allocations of partners. For the second-pass process, we representing the tax allocation vector by $z$, only to distinguish it from $x$. We now need to *scale* $z$, by dividing each element by the respective partner's optimal tax allocation $\Pi_{8+9a}^{**j}$ that was derived from the optimal solution $x^*$ in the first pass. Recall our ubiquitous Hessian matrix $H$. $Hx^*$ is a vector, which we shall call *xopt2*. It is of size $2M$, and looks like $Hx^* = xopt2 = \{(\Pi_{8+9a}^{**1}, \Pi_{8+9a}^{**1}), (\Pi_{8+9a}^{**1}, \Pi_{8+9a}^{**1}), \dots, (\Pi_{8+9a}^{***M}, \Pi_{8+9a}^{**M})\}$. We scale our decision vector $z$ by dividing each element of $z$ by the corresponding element of *xopt2*. Consistent with Matlab code for scaling vector elements, we shall denote $(z)./(xopt2)$. (In Matlab, the ./ operator divides the first element of $z$ by the first element of *xopt2*, and so on.) Our second-pass objective function is to choose $z$ so as to minimize $f_2(z) = \|(z)./(xopt2)\|$, that is, we wish to find $z$ with the smallest scaled 2-norm that belongs to the envelope or set of first-pass optimal solutions. Note that the vector *xopt2*, which was obtained from the first-pass solution $x^*$, is a fixed parameter for the second pass.

We extend the original feasibility constraint set by placing additional constraints that define the envelope or set of all optimal solutions. For $M$ partners, we establish the vector $xopt1 = \{\Pi_{8+9a}^{**j}\}$ with $j = 1...M-1$ elements. Note that $xopt1$ collapses the repeated elements in $xopt2$, but skips the last partner. Each element of $xopt1$ is $\Pi_{8+9a}^{**j}$, which is determined from the first-pass optimal solution as $\Pi_{8+9a}^{**j} = (\Pi_8^{*j} + \Pi_{9a}^{*j})$.

The additional constraints that define an envelope or set that must be satisfied by any optimal solution $\{\Pi_8^j, \Pi_{9a}^j\}$ are:

$\Pi_8^j + \Pi_{9a}^j = \Pi_{8+9a}^{**j}$ for $j = 1...(M-1)$ (there are $(M-1)$ such constraints).

We need to provide only the first $(M-1)$ constraints, because the optimal allocation for the last partner $\Pi_{8+9a}^{**M}$ is known from the additivity constraint and is therefore implicit. The quadratic programming algorithms of both R and Matlab become alarmed when the constraint set has dependencies. However, CVX is tolerant of dependent constraints being thrown in by eliminating them from consideration. We may provide all the $M$ such constraints and CVX would continue to perform. We shall, however, avoid redundancies and dependencies, so we shall apply only $(M-1)$ equality constraints.

The new set of $(M-1)$ constraints that define the envelope of optimality are expressed in matrix form as for use by CVX as:

$$(Aeq2)z = xopt1$$

The sparse coefficient matrix with $(M-1)$ rows and $2M$ columns looks like this:

$$Aeq2 = \begin{bmatrix} 1 & 1 & 0 & 0 & 0 & 0 & ... \\ 0 & 0 & 1 & 1 & 0 & 0 & ... \\ 0 & 0 & 0 & 0 & 1 & 1 & ... \\ \vdots & \vdots & \vdots & \vdots & \vdots & \vdots & \ddots \end{bmatrix}$$

We have $3M + 1$ constraints in matrix form as:

$(Aeq)z = beq$  [2 original feasibility constraints]
$(Aineq)x \leq bineq$  [$2M$ original feasibility constraints]
$(Aeq2)z = xopt1$  [additional $(M - 1)$ envelope of optimality constraints]

Following is our CVX code, using the same matrices *Aeq*, *beq*, *Aineq*, and *bineq* that we had defined for Matlab, and the new matrices *Aeq2* and *xopt*. $M = 100$ is the number of partners defined earlier in Matlab.

```
cvx_begin
 variable z(2*M);
 minimize ( norm( (z)./(xopt2) ) )
    subject to
      Aeq*z == beq ;
      Aineq*z <= bineq ;
      Aeq2*z == xopt2 ;
cvx_end
```

The output solution is the tax allocation vector $z$ with 200 elements for our test problem of full netting with 100 partners. CVX with SDPT3 solved this in 0.82 second with 12 iterations.

The second-pass optimal solution $z^*$ improved upon the first-pass optimal solution $x^*$ when measured by its *scaled* norm. Thus, we obtained the optimal solution $x^*$ in the first pass and improved upon it in the second pass, according to its *scaled* minimal norm, that is, $\|(x^*)./xopt2\| > \|(z^*)./xopt2\|$. (Recall that in Matlab, the ./ operator divides the first element of $z$ by the first element of *xopt2*, and so on.)

The same procedure may be implemented in R and Matlab, with the added burden of stacking the constraints in R. In both R and Matlab, the Hessian matrix $H$ would be a diagonal matrix with $2M$ rows, whose diagonal elements are divided twice by the elements of *xopt2*. Thus, for the quadprog module of Matlab, $H$ would be $H = 2I./(xopt2 * xopt2')$. The vector $g$ would be a zero vector with $2M$ elements. That is because the norm of scaled $z$ squared represented to conform to the canonical form of R and Matlab would be: $\|z./xopt2\|^2 = \frac{1}{2}z^T[2I./(xopt2*xopt2')]z$. This is the circuitous way to force R and Matlab's hard-coded quadratic programming algorithms to minimize the squared norm of a scaled vector. The nature of our problem is becoming sufficiently complex, to a point where the added burdens of conforming to hard-coded canonical forms is tiresome. CVX dominates these hardwired software tools.

# Methodology and Implementation Example of Partial Netting

## Partial Netting Implementation Example

The matrices and vectors for partial netting in canonical form have a similar structure. Under full netting with $M$ partners, we have $2M$ tax allocation numbers to be determined. Under partial netting for the same $M$ partners, we have $4M$ tax allocation numbers that are to be solved.

This appendix will be much shorter than the previous one for full netting, because we do not have to elaborate upon the problem formulation and convexity with the same degree of detail. Further, we will use only one solver: CVX using SDPT3 in Matlab. Recall that the full netting convex optimization problem is stated in Chapter 7 as:

$$\min_{\Pi_{8,L}^j, \Pi_{9a,L}^j, \Pi_{8,G}^j, \Pi_{9a,G}^j} \sum_{j=1}^{M} \left[ \rho^j - \left( \Pi_{8,L}^j + \Pi_{9a,L}^j + \Pi_{8,G}^j + \Pi_{9a,G}^j \right) \right]^2$$

subject to the feasibility constraints that:

$\Pi_{8,G}^j \geq 0$ ($M$ such constraints)
$\Pi_{8,L}^j \leq 0$ ($M$ such constraints)
$\Pi_{9a,G}^j \geq 0$ ($M$ such constraints)
$\Pi_{9a,L}^j \leq 0$ ($M$ such constraints)

and subject to the four aggregation constraints that:

$$\sum_{j=1}^{M} \Pi_{8,G}^{j} = \Pi_{8,G}$$

$$\sum_{j=1}^{M} \Pi_{8,L}^{j} = \Pi_{8,L}$$

$$\sum_{j=1}^{M} \Pi_{9a,G}^{j} = \Pi_{9a,G}$$

$$\sum_{j=1}^{M} \Pi_{9a,L}^{j} = \Pi_{9a,L}$$

The subscript $T$ used to denote the calendar year-end time point in Chapter 7 is dropped. The subscripts $L$ and $G$ denote loss-making tax lots and gain-making tax lots, each partially aggregated, respectively. The subscripts 8 and $9a$, which appear practically everywhere in this book, represent short-term and long-term realized capital gains, respectively.

We have $4M$ unknowns to be solved for, subject to $4M + 4$ constraints.

We denote our vector of $4M$ tax allocations to be solved for as $x = \left\{ \Pi_{8,L}^{j}, \Pi_{9a,L}^{j}, \Pi_{8,G}^{j}, \Pi_{9a,G}^{j} \right\}$ for $M$ partners $j = 1 \ldots M$. Our tax allocation decision vector $x$ has $4M$ elements, 4 for each partner.

We rewrite our alternate objective function, which is the positive square root of the above expanded form as: $f_{alt}(x) = \| H_1 x - g_1 \|$, where

$H_1 = \begin{bmatrix} E_1 & \cdots & Z_1 \\ \vdots & \ddots & \vdots \\ Z_1 & \cdots & E_1 \end{bmatrix}$ is an $M \times 4M$ coefficient matrix containing the length

4 row vectors $E_1 = [1\ 1\ 1\ 1]$ along its diagonals, and $Z_1 = [1\ 1\ 1\ 1]$ at all off-diagonal locations.

We are given the column vector $g_1$ in advance, with $M$ elements, representing each partner's economic or book allocations. This is an input data parameter. The elements of our vector $g_1$ of length $M$ are: $g_1^T = [\rho^1\ \rho^2 \ldots \rho^M]$.

We may also choose to minimize the function $\| Hx - g \|$, which is a scale multiple of $f_{alt}(x) = \| H_1 x - g_1 \|$, to obtain the same optimal solution. $H$ is

our familiar Hessian, which for partial netting looks like $H = 2 \begin{bmatrix} E & \cdots & Z \\ \vdots & \ddots & \vdots \\ Z & \cdots & E \end{bmatrix}$

where the vector $g$, with 4 repeated $M$ times, would be required to conform to the canonical form of R and Matlab as:

$$g^T = 2[(\rho^1, \rho^1, \rho^1, \rho^1), (\rho^2, \rho^2, \rho^2, \rho^2), \ldots, (\rho^M, \rho^M, \rho^M, \rho^M)]$$

We follow the same notation as we did with full netting. The inequality constraints are to be represented as $(Aineq)x \leq bineq$ and equality constraints as $(Aeq)x = beq$.

Thus, the structure of the constraint matrices to be supplied to the quadprog module of Matlab is as follows:

$$beq = \begin{bmatrix} \Pi_{8,G} \\ \Pi_{8,L} \\ \Pi_{9a,G} \\ \Pi_{9a,L} \end{bmatrix} = \begin{bmatrix} 50 \\ -70 \\ 220 \\ -90 \end{bmatrix}$$

*Aeq* = [*I,I, ... . I*] where *I* is a 4 × 4 identity matrix repeated *M* times. *Aineq* would be a sparse 4*M* × 4*M* matrix that looks like:

$$Aineq = \begin{bmatrix} M & \cdots & Z \\ \vdots & \ddots & \vdots \\ Z & \cdots & M \end{bmatrix}$$

where $M = \begin{bmatrix} -1 & 0 & 0 & 0 \\ 0 & 1 & 0 & 0 \\ 0 & 0 & -1 & 0 \\ 0 & 0 & 0 & 1 \end{bmatrix}$, a 4 × 4 matrix along the diagonal, and *Z* is a

4 × 4 matrix of zeros at all other off-diagonal positions. The vector *bineq* is simply a zero vector of length 4*M*.

We're now ready to run the first pass in CVX code (running within Matlab) as follows:

```
cvx_begin
 variable x(4*M);
 minimize ( norm( H1*x - g1) )
    subject to
      Aeq*x == beq ;
      Aineq*x <= bineq ;
cvx_end
```

## CVX Solved the 100-Partner Partial Netting Problem in 0.88 Second

The output solution is the tax allocation vector *x** with 400 elements. Our test problem has 400 variables and 404 constraints. CVX running the SDPT3 algorithm converged for our 100-partner test problem on our unremarkable standard desktop PC after 15 iterations in 0.70 seconds.

# Second Pass to Derive a Unique Solution for Partial Netting

Having obtained an optimal tax allocation vector $x^*$ in the first pass, we create $(M-1)$ additional constraints that any optimal solution should meet.

Applying our ubiquitous Hessian matrix $H$, we obtain $xopt2 = Hx^*$. We *scale* our new decision vector $z$ by dividing each element of $z$ by the corresponding element of $xopt2$, denoted as $(z)./(xopt2)$. Our second-pass objective function is to choose $z$ so as to minimize $f_2(z) = \|(z)./(xopt2)\|$, that is, an optimal solution that has the smallest *scaled* Euclidean length, where the scaling factor for each partner is their optimal tax allocation contained in the first-pass solution vector $x^*$.

The feasibility constraint set is extended by placing additional constraints that define the envelope or set of all optimal solutions. For $M$ partners, we also establish the vector $xopt1 = \{\Pi_{8+9a}^{**j}\}$ with $j = 1 \dots (M-1)$ elements. $xopt1$ collapses the repeated elements in $xopt2$.

The additional constraints that define an envelope or set that must be satisfied by any optimal solution $\{\Pi_{8,G}^{j}, \Pi_{8,L}^{j}, \Pi_{9a,G}^{j}, \Pi_{9a,L}^{j}\}$ are: $\Pi_8^{j} + \Pi_{9a}^{j} = \Pi_{8+9a}^{**j}$ for $j = 1 \dots (M-1)$ (there are $(M-1)$ such constraints).

We need to provide only the first $(M-1)$ constraints, because the optimal allocation for the last partner $\Pi_{8+9a}^{**M}$ is known from the additivity constraint and is therefore implicit.

The new set of $(M-1)$ constraints that define the envelope of optimality are expressed in matrix form as for use by CVX as:

$$(Aeq2)z = xopt1$$

The sparse coefficient matrix with $(M-1)$ rows and $4M$ columns looks like this:

$$Aeq2 = \begin{bmatrix} 1 & 1 & 1 & 1 & 0 & 0 & 0 & 0 & 0 & \dots \\ 0 & 0 & 0 & 0 & 1 & 1 & 1 & 1 & 0 & \dots \\ 0 & 0 & 0 & 0 & 0 & 0 & 0 & 0 & 1 & \dots \\ \vdots & \vdots & \vdots & \vdots & \vdots & \vdots & \vdots & \vdots & \vdots & \ddots \end{bmatrix}$$

$Aeq2$ is simply the matrix $H_1$ with its last row omitted.
We have $5M + 3$ constraints in matrix form as:

$(Aeq)z = beq$ [4 original feasibility constraints]
$(Aineq)x \le bineq$ [$4M$ original feasibility constraints]
$(Aeq2)z = xopt1$ [additional $(M - 1)$ envelope of optimality constraints]

Following is our CVX code, using the same matrices *Aeq*, *beq*, *Aineq*, and *bineq* that we had defined for Matlab, and the new matrices *Aeq2* and *xopt*. $M = 100$ is the number of partners defined earlier in Matlab.

```
cvx_begin
 variable z(4*M);
 minimize ( norm( (z)./(xopt2) ) )
    subject to
      Aeq*z == beq ;
      Aineq*z <= bineq ;
      Aeq2*z == xopt1 ;
cvx_end
```

The output solution is the tax allocation vector $z^*$ with 400 elements for our test problem of partial netting with 100 partners. The second-pass optimal solution $z^*$ had a lower *scaled* norm when compared to the first-pass optimal solution $x^*$.

CVX invoked the SDPT3 algorithm and solved the second-pass problem, which had 400 variables and 503 constraints in 2.0 seconds after 27 iterations.

# Nonabusive Tilting of Tax Allocations According to Tax Preferences

## Tax Preference Option

A tax preference option arises when a partnership has both tax-exempt and taxable partners, and has net long-term gains that are being allocated to partners. The tax-exempt partners are indifferent to the nature of the tax allocations of short-term and long-term gains. Taxable partners would always have a preference for an increased proportion of long-term gain allocations.

## Treasury Regulations Forbid Outright Tax Preference Tilting

Following is the relevant subsection from the Treasury Regulations that describes full and partial netting. The language in paragraph (C) clearly forbids making tax allocations that significantly shift partners' aggregate tax liability.

**The Type of Gains or Loss Allocated under Full and Partial Netting Methodologies Must Be Preserved**

Source: 26 C.F.R. § 1.704-3 (e)(3)(vi).

**Title 26: Internal Revenue**

**PART 1—INCOME TAXES**
**PARTNERS AND PARTNERSHIPS**

**§ 1.704-3 Contributed Property**
(e)(3)(vi) Type of tax gain or loss. The character and other tax attributes of gain or loss allocated to the partners under this paragraph (e)(3) must:

**(A)** Preserve the tax attributes of each item of gain or loss realized by the partnership;
**(B)** Be determined under an approach that is consistently applied; and
**(C)** Not be determined with a view to reducing substantially the present value of the partners' aggregate tax liability.

# A Simple 2-Partner Example of Abusive Tax Preference Tilt

Consider a partnership with just two partners, one taxable and another tax exempt. The partnership makes short-term and long-term gains that are both net positive. The total gains to be allocated to each partner to minimize book-tax disparities are easily determined because of the simplicity of this to the partner case. Suppose most of the short-term gains are allocated to the tax-exempt partner, so that allocation of most of the long-term gains to the taxable partner. This is a situation that is prohibited by paragraph (C) above of the Treasury Regulations on full and partial netting.

# The Unique Optimum Scaled Solutions in Appendixes 2 and 3 Also Minimize Tax Preference Tilts across Partners

Recall that the second-pass procedure in Appendixes 2 and 3 for full netting and partial netting, respectively, was based on minimizing *scaled* tax allocations. Each partner's tax allocations are scaled according to dividing by their total (invariant) optimum tax allocation derived from the first-pass procedure. This provided a robust unique optimal tax allocation solution that minimizes the *scaled* book-tax disparities without regard to the tax preferences of the partners.

When we divide the individual components by the total, we obtain a fraction that is interpreted as a percentage of each component. By minimizing the norm of such percentages across all partners, we are effectively flattening out egregious percentage allocations, such as long-term capital gain being 20 times the net total allocation. It is precisely such outliers that may be considered as sensitive to tax preferences.

Even though we did not directly model tax preferences, the objective function $f_2(z) = \|(z)./(xopt2)\|$, implicitly weighed in tax preference distortions across partners. A large *scaled* allocation (disregarding the sign, because the norm is the positive square root of the sum of squares) to a given partner is penalized, and the emergent optimal solution $z^*$ is "flattened" so as to minimize partners' collective *scaled* allocations. Given this robust nature of our unique second-pass optimal solution, which also simultaneously reduces potential tax shifting or tilting across partners, we do not want to introduce additional complexity in modeling tax preferences and proceeding to optimize according to tax preference shifting or tilting across partners.

## The Scaled Tax-Neutral Allocations in Appendixes 2 and 3 Are a Gold Standard for Tax-Neutral Allocations

The Treasury Regulations in the relevant paragraph (C) above forbid abusive tax preference–driven allocations, but do not provide any standard against which allocations in a large partnership may be evaluated for tax neutrality. Our optimal solution $z^*$ for partial netting, which was achieved by minimizing $f_2(z) = \|(z)./(xopt2)\|$, subject to its constraints in Appendix 3, presents itself as a gold standard for tax-neutral allocations.

Abusive tilting of tax allocations could be considered as being made without regard to any standard that constitutes equitable tax neutral allocations. Allocating zero long-term capital gains to tax-exempt partners would constitute such an abusive shift that it would likely be contrary to the requirements of paragraph (C) of the relevant Treasury Regulations previously.

However, by making tax allocations that penalize any excessive tilting away from a gold standard of tax-neutral allocations, we would likely not be contravening the requirements of paragraph (C) of the relevant Treasury Regulations.

# Nonabusive Allocations That Consider Tax Preferences

Consider a large partnership that is following the partial netting methodology, which has loss items being allocated to all partners in order to achieve the lowest book-tax disparities. This is not a situation of allocating only gains, as in the simple example above. The sum total of all allocations, negative and positive, add up to the total optimal gain allocation for a given partner, which we have saved in the column vector that we named $xopt1$.

Can we reduce minimized allocations of long-term gains to tax-exempt partners, while still maintaining the rock-bottom minimum of book-tax disparities of the partners, and not abusively shift the allocations according to tax preferences? This is a generalized case of the simple two-partner example of extreme tax shifting provided earlier.

We have followed the Treasury Regulations to achieve the lowest possible book-tax disparities. It turns out that there are multiple solutions that achieve the same global minimum of book-tax disparities. From that set of multiple optimal solutions, we look for those that reduce or minimize the allocation of long-term gains to tax-exempt partners.

The first-pass optimal solution $x^*$ to partial netting led to the sum total of total optimal allocations to partners, which we labeled as $xopt1$. We subsequently obtained the second-pass optimal solution $z^*$ by minimizing the *scaled* optimal allocations obtained in the first pass, without regard to tax preferences. We consider $z^*$ as the gold standard of a tax-neutral allocation. Let us denote the tax-preference tilted allocation as $z_1$. We maintain the optimal *total* allocations $xopt1$ so that we are assured that the objective function of book-tax disparities, $f_{all}(z_1) = \|H_1 z_1 - g_1\|$, remains at its global minimum value. We impose the constraint that we encountered in Appendix 3, $(Aeq2)z_1 = xopt1$.

For the partial netting problem, our objective function that is yet to be specified must contain the tax-preferred items that are allocated to tax-exempt partners $\sum_{j \in TE} \Pi_{9a,L}^j$, where the subscript $j \in TE$ stands for partners who are tax exempt. To represent this in matrix form, we create a row vector $d$ with $4M$ elements that describes whether a partner is tax exempt or taxable. The vector $d$ is initialized to zero and is rewritten as $d = [d_1 \ d_2 \ ... \ d_M]$, where for a given partner $j$, $d_j = [0 \ 0 \ 0 \ 0]$ if the partner is taxable, and $d_j = [0 \ 0 \ 1 \ 0]$ if the partner is non-taxable. The third element of $d_j$ maps to the ordered sequence of tax allocations, whose third item is realized long-term gains. The inner product of $d$ and $z_1$, denoted as $(d).^*(z_1)$, results in $\sum_{j \in TE} \Pi_{9a,L}^j$. The operator .* is Matlab code for inner product. In our test problem of partial netting with $M = 100$ partners, we assume that the first $M1 = 10$ partners are tax exempt.

We now define the objective function as the sum of two parts, written as $f_{tax}(z_1) = \|(d).*(z_1)\| + \omega\|(d).*(z_1 - z^*)\|$, and that has a number $\omega \geq 0$ provided as an external parameter. This objective function, due to inner product of $z_1$ with our vector $d$, considers only tax-exempt partners and disregards all other taxable partners.

The first part of our objective function $\|(d).*(z_1)\|$ is the allocation of long-term gains to tax-exempt partners, which we would like to be as small as possible. The parameter $\omega \geq 0$ is such that that makes $\omega = 0$ permits the objective function $f_{tax}(z_1)$ to completely ignore with the gold standard tax neutral allocation $z^*$ that is solved in Appendixes 2 and 3. Thus, $\omega = 0$ may produce an abusive tax allocation that disregards the tax-neutral gold standard $z^*$.

The second part of our objective function $\omega\|(d).*(z_1 - z^*)\|$ is a penalty for deviation from the tax-neutral gold standard $z^*$, whose magnitude increases as $z_1$ deviates further from $z^*$, the deviation measured as a Euclidean distance between the two. The two parts when added together constitute a trade-off that is represented as a convex function. We may reduce the allocation of long-term gains to tax-exempt partners, but doing so would invoke a penalty of deviating from the tax-neutral gold standard. The parameter $\omega$ is interpreted as a penalty weight. When $\omega$ is large, the second part of the objective function dominates and applies an overwhelming penalty to any deviation from the tax-neutral gold standard $z^*$, forcing $z_1$ to coincide with $z^*$.

Our constraints are the same as in Appendix 3:

$(Aeq)z = beq$   [4 original feasibility constraints]
$(Aineq)x \leq bineq$   [4M original feasibility constraints]
$(Aeq2)z_1 = xopt1$   [M − 1 constraints that ensure $z_1$ belongs to the envelope of optimal solutions]

We provide our CVX code below, using the same matrices *Aeq*, *beq*, *Aineq*, and *bineq* that we had defined for Matlab, and the new matrices *Aeq2* and *xopt*. $M = 100$ is the number of partners defined earlier in Matlab.

```
w=1
cvx_begin
 variable z1(4*M);
 minimize ( norm( (d).*(z1) ) + w*norm(d.*(z2-z1)) )
    subject to
      Aeq*z == beq ;
      Aineq*z <= bineq ;
      Aeq2*z == xopt1 ;
cvx_end
```

The output solution is the tax allocation vector $z_1$ with 400 elements for our test problem of full netting with $M = 100$ partners. This is based on $\omega = 1$. The second-pass tax preference–based optimal solution $z_1$ had a lower norm of long-term gains allocated to tax-exempt partners when compared to the first-pass optimal solution $x^*$. Both optimal solutions $z_1^*$ and $x^*$ produced the same global minimum of book-tax disparities, that is, $\|H_1 z_1^* - g_1\| = \|H_1 x^* - g_1\|$.

CVX invoked the SDPT3 algorithm and solved this tax preference tilt problem, which had $4M = 400$ variables and $5M + 3 = 503$ constraints, in 0.52 second after 12 iterations, with the parameter $\omega$ set to 1. The optimal solution $z_1^*$ allocated about 5 percent lower total of long-term gains to tax-exempt partners compared to the tax-neutral gold standard $z^*$. This is well within the realm of an equitable tax allocation consistent with paragraph (C) of the relevant Treasury Regulations.

To pursue this matter in further detail, the sensitivity of the solutions to the parameter may be further explored by creating a graph or table of versus $(d).*(z_1^*)$. There is no strong basis for determining what $\omega$ should be, and this is where some degree of subjectivity would enter.

## Further Minimizing the Dispersion of All Partner Tax Allocations from the Target Optimum

Effectively, what we have achieved is that from the envelope of multiple solutions that achieve the minimized book-tax disparities of partners, we have found the one that has the lowest allocation of long-term capital gains to tax-exempt partners, adjusted for a penalty for deviation from a tax-neutral gold standard.

Having determined the minimized long-term gain allocations to tax-exempt partners reflecting penalty-adjusted tax-preferences, we run a final pass, a third pass in this case, as we did before in Appendixes 2 and 3. This final pass identifies an allocation that (1) belongs to the envelope of optimal tax allocations that minimize book-tax disparities, and (2) contains the minimal allocation of long-term gains to tax-exempt partners.

The first pass produced the optimal solutions $x^*$, which became the basis of establishing the envelope of multiple solutions that achieve the same minimal book-tax disparities, which we named the vector $xopt1$. We have then identified another optimal solution $z_1^*$ within the envelope of optimal solutions, which had minimal allocations of penalty-adjusted long-term gains to tax-exempt partners. We now determine the final (third) pass optimal solution $z_2$, also within the envelope of optimal solutions, which has the lowest *scaled* norm, that is, deviates the least from the target total allocations $z_1^*$.

The additional constraints that we impose in this third pass are:

$$\Pi_{9a,L}^{j} = z_1^{*j}$$

where $j \in TE$, that is, the allocation of long-term gains to tax-exempt partners are fixed according to the second-pass optimal solution $z_1^*$. To represent these constraints, we create a coefficient matrix $Aeq3$ and $xopt3$ as follows. Suppose the set of tax-exempt partners is of size $M1 < M$. In our test example of 100 partners, we arbitrarily classified the first 10 partners as being tax exempt, so $M1 = 10$. The matrix $Aeq3$ has $M1$ rows and $4M$

columns and looks like $Aeq3 = \begin{bmatrix} E_3 & Z_1 & Z_1 & ... & Z_1 \\ Z_1 & E_3 & Z_1 & ... & Z_1 \\ \vdots & \vdots & \vdots & \ddots & Z_1 \end{bmatrix}$, where the length 4

row vectors $E_3 = [0\ 0\ 1\ 0]$ along the diagonal for M1 rows, and $Z_1 = [0\ 0\ 0\ 0]$ everywhere else. This is because the third element in a partner's tax allocation represents long-term capital gains. The column vector $xopt3$ has $M1$ elements, which are the minimized long-term gain allocations for the tax-exempt partners contained in the solution $z_1^*$. The quality constraint $(Aeq3)z_2 = xopt3$ in matrix form corresponds to our additional constraints for the third pass $\Pi_{9a,L}^{j} = z_1^{*j}$ where $j \in TE$, the set of tax-exempt partners.

Following is our CVX code, using the same matrices $Aeq$, $beq$, $Aineq$, and $bineq$ $Aeq2$ and $xopt$ that we had defined earlier, and the new tax-preference coefficient and allocation matrices $Aeq3$ and $xopt3$. $M = 100$ is the number of partners defined earlier in Matlab.

```
cvx_begin
 variable z2(4*M);
 minimize ( norm( (z2)./(xopt2) ) )
    subject to
      Aeq*z2 == beq ;
      Aineq*z2 <= bineq ;
      Aeq2*z2 == xopt1 ;
      Aeq3*z2 == xopt3 ;
cvx_end
```

The output solution is the tax allocation vector $z_2^*$ with 400 elements for our test problem of full netting with 100 partners, with the first 10 partners being tax exempt. The second-pass tax preference–based optimal solution $z_1$ had a lower norm of long-term gains allocated to tax-exempt partners when compared to the first-pass optimal solution $x^*$. All optimal solutions $z_2^*$, $z_1^*$ and $x^*$ produced the same global minimum of book-tax disparities, that is, $\|H_1 z_2^* - g_1\| = \|H_1 z_1^* - g_1\| = \|H_1 x^* - g_1\|$.

CVX running SDPT3 in Matlab solved this third-pass minimization and produced the *scaled* optimal solution $z_2^*$ in 24 iterations taking 1.64 seconds. We had imposed an additional $M1 = 10$ constraints, so this was a convex optimization problem with $4M = 400$ variables and $5M + 3 + 10 = 513$ constraints.

# Eliminating Layering Entirely, by Allocating Dividends, Interest, Capital Gains, and Expenses in One Step

## Making All Allocations, Including Dividends and Interest, by Using Netting Methodology

Upon close reading of the language of the full and partial netting methodologies in the relevant U.S. Treasury Regulations that are reproduced at the end of Appendix 1, we observe that there is no mention that the Treasury methodology is confined to allocation of realized capital gains only. U.S. partnerships have typically applied the full and partial netting approaches to the allocation of realized capital gains to partners. Items of income and expense of other than realized capital gains, namely dividends, interest, investment expense, and foreign taxes, are allocated based on the layering methodology, which requires intensive bookkeeping to track dividends, interest, and expenses on a monthly basis and allocate them to partners according to their corresponding ever-shifting ownership percentages.

We have demonstrated that the tax accounting operation of a U.S. hedge fund or investment partnership can be greatly simplified by making one-time year-end allocations of taxable realized short-term and long-term capital gains according to the methodology and guidance for implementing full and partial netting in the relevant U.S. Treasury Regulations. The relevant input data are partners' economic capital account values, which come from the economic accounting system of the partnership, and the few input numbers for fully or partially aggregated realized gains for the full year. Minor effort expended in setting up computer code to solve the tax allocation problem results in an automated tax allocation solution within about 1 to 2 seconds of desktop computer time.

The same methodology of full and partial netting may be extended to allocate dividends, interest and expenses simultaneously. The incremental time and effort is negligible, and perhaps almost zero. The efficient convex programming algorithms are eminently able to handle additional variables being introduced into the problem formulation, without getting swamped.

## Dispelling Fears about Simultaneously Allocating Dividends/Interest and Capital Gains

Some experts might believe that by combining dividends and interest with capital gains, tax allocations may be skewed according to tax preferences. Further, there might be undesirable shifts and trade-offs between dividends/interest and capital gains allocations among the partners.

Our methodology has already resolved this source of concern by producing a unique, robust second-pass tax allocation that also serves as a gold standard for tax neutrality. We may therefore dispense with this fear and declare it to be unfounded, on the grounds that our methodology efficiently addresses this concern and produces a robust tax-neutral allocation among the partners. The second-pass procedure resulting in *scaled* optimal tax allocations results in tax neutrality, and also prevents shifts and trade-offs between dividends, interest, expenses and capital gains allocations.

We have separately shown that small nonabusive tax tilts may be achieved, taking into account partner tax preferences relative to this tax-neutral gold standard.

## Generalizing the Partial Netting Methodology to Include Allocations of Dividends, Interest, Investment Expense, and Foreign Taxes

We noted in Chapter 5 that a U.S. partnership is required to report a breakdown of its annual income on its U.S. partnership tax return as:

$$\Pi = \Pi_4 + \Pi_5 + \Pi_{6a} + \Pi_8 + \Pi_{9a} - (\Pi_{13b} + \Pi_{13d} + \Pi_{16l}) + \Pi_{18a} + \Pi_{M1L6}$$

Chapter 7 and subsequently Appendixes 1, 2, and 3 focused on allocating realized short-term and long-term gains, $\Pi_8$ and $\Pi_{9a}$, respectively, to the partners. This allocation is conducted on an annual basis at year-end and also reported on the U.S. partnership tax return.

The first item, $\Pi_4$, is the guaranteed payment to the general partner, which is the sum of all fixed fees paid by the limited partners. $\Pi_{13d}$ is the sum total of all fixed fees paid by the limited partners to the general partner, and the relationship $\Pi_4 = \Pi_{13d}$ must hold.

Recall that we defined $\rho^j$ in Chapter 7 and later in Appendix 1 as the book-tax difference *before* realized capital gains allocations for each partner. All economic allocations are factored into $\rho^j$, and so also all tax allocations *except* current year realized long-term and short-term capital gains. We followed the U.S. Treasury Regulations on full and partial netting and made allocations of *current year* realized long-term and short-term capital gains so as to minimize or reduce the resulting collective book-tax disparities of the partners after the current year allocation.

We now wish to extend the current year allocation procedure to partners not only to long-term and short-term realized capital gains, but also to other items of partnership income and expense, notably dividends, interest, investment expense, and foreign taxes. Since the calculation of fixed fees is already conducted according to the limited partnership agreement, by methodology that is the same as layering, we cannot redistribute them or change them across partners.

We alter the definition of book-tax disparity $\rho^j$ for a given partner indexed by the superscript $j$ to *exclude* allocations of current year taxable items of dividends, interest, investment expense, and foreign tax, *include* all nontaxable items of unrealized capital gains and tax-exempt interest, and *include* the taxable item of fixed fees. We will continue to denote this as $\rho^j$, and from here onward in this appendix, $\rho^j$ would means the book-tax disparity of a given partner *before* current year realized capital gains and *before* current year dividends, interest, investment expense, and foreign tax.

The expanded objective is to allocate aggregate partnership taxable items of income $\Pi_5 + \Pi_{6a} + \Pi_8 + \Pi_{9a} - (\Pi_{13b} + \Pi_{16l})$ to partners, given as input their individual book-tax disparities $\{\rho^j\}$.

The above expression is written according to the IRS convention on the U.S. partnership tax return. Realized capital gains $\Pi_8$ and $\Pi_{9a}$ are expressed as positive quantities. Realized capital losses are expressed as negative quantities that are to be added. However, investment expense and foreign tax payment $\Pi_{13b}$ and $\Pi_{16l}$ are reported as positive quantities that are to be subtracted.

## Formulating the Grand Problem of Simultaneously Allocating Dividends, Interest, and Capital Gains under Netting Methodology

We extend the formulation that we created for allocating realized short-term and long-term gains under partial netting to include four more items: dividends, interest, investment expense, and foreign tax paid. We also do not deviate from the IRS partnership tax return convention that investment expense and foreign tax paid are represented as positive numbers.

Our grand full netting convex optimization takes the form:

$$f_{alt}(x) = min.\left\{ \sum_{j=1}^{M} \left[ \rho^j - \left( \Pi_5^j + \Pi_{6a}^j + \Pi_{8,L}^j + \Pi_{9a,L}^j \right. \right. \right.$$
$$\left. \left. \left. + \Pi_{8,G}^j + \Pi_{9a,G}^j - \Pi_{13b}^j - \Pi_{16l}^j \right) \right]^2 \right\}^{\frac{1}{2}}$$

by choice of partner allocations $x = \left\{ \Pi_5^j, \Pi_{6a}^j \Pi_{8,L}^j, \Pi_{9a,L}^j, \Pi_{8,G}^j, \Pi_{9a,G}^j, \Pi_{13b}^j, \Pi_{16l}^j \right\}$.

Our tax allocation decision vector $x$ has $8M$ elements, 8 for each partner.

Note that we have taken a shortcut and defined our objective function directly as a 2-norm by taking the square root of a sum-of-squares.

Our choice is subject to the *feasibility constraints* that:

$\Pi_5^j \geq 0$ ($M$ such constraints: interest allocations must be positive)

$\Pi_{6a}^j \geq 0$ ($M$ such constraints: dividend allocations must be positive)

$\Pi_{8,G}^j \geq 0$ ($M$ such constraints: gain-making realized short-term gain tax lots must be positive)

$\Pi_{8,L}^j \leq 0$ ($M$ such constraints: loss-making realized short-term gain tax lots must be negative)

$\Pi_{9a,L}^j \leq 0$ ($M$ such constraints: loss-making realized long-term gain tax lots must be negative)

$\Pi_{9a,G}^j \geq 0$ ($M$ such constraints: gain-making realized long-term gain tax lots must be positive)

$\Pi_{13b}^j \geq 0$ ($M$ such constraints: investment expense allocations must be positive, because these are expressed as a positive number)

$\Pi_{16l}^j \geq 0$ ($M$ such constraints: foreign tax paid allocations must be positive, because these are also expressed as a positive number)

and subject to the eight aggregation constraints that:

$$\sum_{j=1}^{M} \Pi_5^j = \Pi_5$$

$$\sum_{j=1}^{M} \Pi_{6a}^j = \Pi_{6a}$$

$$\sum_{j=1}^{M} \Pi_{8,G}^j = \Pi_{8,G}$$

$$\sum_{j=1}^{M} \Pi_{8,L}^j = \Pi_{8,L}$$

$$\sum_{j=1}^{M} \Pi_{9a,G}^j = \Pi_{9a,G}$$

$$\sum_{j=1}^{M} \Pi_{9a,L}^j = \Pi_{9a,L}$$

$$\sum_{j=1}^{M} \Pi_{13b}^{j} = \Pi_{13b}$$

$$\sum_{j=1}^{M} \Pi_{16l}^{j} = \Pi_{16l}$$

For hedge funds, it is realistic to impose a ninth set of $M$ additional equality constraints, that foreign tax should be a fixed proportion of dividends, equal to $\dfrac{\Pi_{16l}}{\Pi_5} = k$. This makes the $\left\{\Pi_{16l}^{j}\right\}$ redundant. This constraint ensures that foreign taxes cannot be allocated to partners out of proportion to their dividends. The problem specification could be simplified by eliminating $\Pi_{16l}$ entirely. Instead, we shall keep $\Pi_{16l}$ independent in the formulation thus far, and introduce the new equality constrained to make $\Pi_{16l}$ redundant:

$$k\Pi_5 - \Pi_{16l} = 0 \quad (M \text{ such equality constraints})$$

We have $8M$ unknowns to be solved for, subject to $8M + 8 + M$ constraints.

We set up the appropriate coefficient matrices and express our convex optimization problem in matrix form, so as to facilitate solution by the computer algorithms of CVX running SDPT3 in Matlab. The preceding formulation is rewritten as:

We rewrite our objective function, which is the positive square root of the preceding expanded form as: $f_{alt}(x) = \|H_1 x - g_1\|$, where $H_1 = \begin{bmatrix} E_2 & \cdots & Z_1 \\ \vdots & \ddots & \vdots \\ Z_1 & \cdots & E_2 \end{bmatrix}$ is an $M \times 8M$ coefficient matrix containing the length 8 row vectors $E_2 = [1\ 1\ 1\ 1\ 1\ 1\ -1\ -1]$ along diagonals, and $Z_1 = [0\ 0\ 0\ 0\ 0\ 0\ 0\ 0]$ at all off-diagonal locations. Note that the last two elements of $E_1$ have a negative sign, due to representing $\Pi_{13b}$ and $\Pi_{16l}$ as positive numbers on the U.S. partnership tax return. Note that our objective function is still convex, and if we calculate our $8M \times 8M$ Hessian matrix $H$, this would have the same structure as our earlier $4M \times 4M$ Hessian after taking into account that two items, investment expense and foreign tax, are negative and act to reduce economic profit, but are expressed as positive numbers on the U.S. partnership tax return.

We are given the column vector $g_1$ in advance, with $M$ elements, representing each partner's economic or book allocations. This is an input data parameter. The elements of our vector $g_1$ of length $M$ are: $g_1^T = [\rho^1 \rho^2 \dots \rho^M]$.

The inequality constraints are to be represented as $(Aineq)x \leq bineq$ and the first 8 equality constraints as $(Aeq)x = beq$. The ninth set of $M$

equality constraints that tie foreign taxes as a fixed proportion of dividends are represented as as $(Aeq9)x = beq9$.

The structure of the constraint matrices to be supplied is as follows:

$$
beq = \begin{bmatrix} \Pi_5 \\ \Pi_6 \\ \Pi_{8,G} \\ \Pi_{8,L} \\ \Pi_{9a,G} \\ \Pi_{9a,L} \\ \Pi_{13b} \\ \Pi_{16l} \end{bmatrix} = \begin{bmatrix} 10 \\ 30 \\ 50 \\ -70 \\ 220 \\ -90 \\ 20 \\ 2 \end{bmatrix}
$$

$Aeq = [I,I, \ldots . I]$ where $I$ is a $4 \times 4$ identity matrix repeated $M$ times. $beq9$ is simply a zero vector of length $M$. $beq9$ is an $M \times 8M$ matrix, which looks like $Aeq9 = \begin{bmatrix} E_9 & \cdots & Z_1 \\ \vdots & \ddots & \vdots \\ Z_1 & \cdots & E_9 \end{bmatrix}$, with vectors $E_9 = [k\ 0\ 0\ 0\ 0\ 0\ 0\ -1]$ along diagonals, and $z_1$ is a zero vector of length 8 at all off-diagonal locations. Based on our input data, $= \dfrac{\Pi_{16l}}{\Pi_5} = 0.2$, which ensures that foreign tax allocations are always 20 percent of dividend allocations.

$Aineq$ would be a sparse $8M \times 8M$ matrix that looks like:

$$
Aineq = \begin{bmatrix} M & \cdots & Z \\ \vdots & \ddots & \vdots \\ Z & \cdots & M \end{bmatrix}
$$

where $Z$ is an $8 \times 8$ matrix of zeros at all other off-diagonal positions. $M$ is a $8 \times 8$ matrix with either $-1$ or $+1$ along its diagonal, according to the direction of the inequality of the 8 sets of constraints, and zero elsewhere. The eight diagonal elements of $M$ are $\{-1, -1, -1, 1, -1, 1, -1, -1\}$. The vector $bineq$ is simply a zero vector of length 8M.

We're now ready to run the first pass in CVX code (running within Matlab) as follows:

```
cvx_begin
 variable x(8*M);
 minimize ( norm( H1*x — g1) )
    subject to
      Aeq*x == beq ;
      Aeq9*x == beq9 ;
      Aineq*x <= bineq ;
cvx_end
```

# CVX Solved the 100-Partner Grand Allocation Problem in 0.78 Seconds

The output solution is the tax allocation vector $x^*$ with 400 elements. Our test problem has 800 variables and 907 constraints. CVX running the SDPT3 algorithm converged for our 100-partner test problem on our unremarkable standard desktop PC after 17 iterations in 0.78 seconds.

# Second Pass to Derive a Unique, Robust, and Tax-Neutral Solution

Having obtained an optimal tax allocation vector $x^*$ in the first pass, we create $(M - 1)$ additional constraints that any optimal solution should meet.

The feasibility constraint set is extended by placing additional constraints that define the envelope or set of all optimal solutions. For each of the partners, we calculate the total optimal allocation expressed in matrix form as $[\Pi^{**j}] = H_1 x^*$. For $M$ partners, we also establish the vector $xopt1$ as the first $(M - 1)$ elements of $H_1 x^*$, $xopt1$ is expanded with repeated elements $xopt2$, only that $xopt2$ is for all $M$ partners and has $8M$ elements. The first eight elements of $xopt2$ are the first element of $xopt1$ repeated eight times. The next eight elements of $xopt2$ are the second element of $xopt1$ repeated, and so on. The last element of $xopt2$ would simply be $\Pi^{**j}$ for the last partner $j = M$.

We *scale* our new decision vector $z$ by dividing each element of $z$ by the corresponding element of $xopt2$, denoted as $(z)./(xopt2)$. Our second-pass objective function is to choose $z$ so as to minimize $f_2(z) = \|(z)./(xopt2)\|$, that is, an optimal solution that has the smallest *scaled* Euclidean length, where the scaling factor for each partner is their optimal tax allocation contained in the first-pass solution vector $x^*$.

The additional constraints that define an envelope or set that must be satisfied by any optimal solution are expressed in matrix form as $H_1 z = H_1 x^*$ (there are $M - 1$ such constraints).

We need to provide only the first $(M - 1)$ constraints, because the optimal allocation for the last partner $\Pi^{**M}$ is known from the additivity constraint and is therefore implicit.

The new set of $(M - 1)$ constraints that define the envelope of optimality are expressed in matrix form as for use by CVX as:

$$(Aeq2)z = xopt1$$

The sparse coefficient matrix $Aeq2$ with $(M-1)$ rows and $8M$ columns is obtained by taking the M by $8M$ matrix $H_1$ and eliminating its last row (which corresponds to the last partner). $Aeq2$ is the matrix $H_1$ with its last row omitted.

We have $10M + 7$ constraints in matrix form as:

$(Aeq)z = beq$ [8 original feasibility constraints]
$(Aeq3)z = beq3$ [$M$ constraints to tie down foreign tax to dividends]
$(Aineq)x \leq bineq$ [$8M$ original feasibility constraints]
$(Aeq2)z = xopt1$ [additional $(M-1)$ envelope of optimality constraints]

Following is our CVX code, using the same matrices $Aeq$, $beq$, $Aineq$, and $bineq$ that we had defined for Matlab, and the new matrices $Aeq2$ and $xopt$. $M = 100$ is the number of partners.

```
cvx_begin
 variable z(8*M);
 minimize ( norm( (z)./(xopt2) ) )
    subject to
      Aeq*z == beq ;
      Aeq3*z == beq3 ;
      Aineq*z <= bineq ;
      Aeq2*z == xopt1 ;
cvx_end
```

The output solution is the tax allocation vector $z^*$ with 400 elements for our test problem netting with 100 partners. The second-pass optimal solution $z^*$ had a lower *scaled* norm when compared to the first-pass optimal solution $x^*$.

CVX invoked the SDPT3 algorithm and solved the second-pass problem, which had 800 variables and 1,007 constraints in 5.42 seconds after 35 iterations. It is likely that if the problem were reformulated by eliminating the variable for foreign tax, which would eliminate 100 tie-down equality constraints, the problem might have been solved faster.

## The End of the Era of Layering

We have demonstrated that modern open-source convex programming algorithms can be deployed to eliminate the use of layering methodology entirely. The key lies in formulating the convex optimization problem,

recognizing that it indeed has a guaranteed minimum of book-tax disparities, but there exist multiple solutions that achieve the same optimum. The
envelope of optimal solutions contains a "flattened" robust and unique
solution that *simultaneously* allocates dividends, interest, capital gains, and
investment expense, and also is unique, robust, and a gold standard for
tax-neutral allocations.

U.S. partnerships no longer have to struggle with endless tax accounting spreadsheets to allocate dividends, interest, and investment expense
according to the layering methodology. The U.S. Treasury Regulations
define the methodology of full and partial netting that offers relief from
the cumbersome data-intensive methodology of layering. Many U.S. partnerships continue to adopt the methodology of layering for all tax
allocations. There are a significant number of U.S. partnerships that adopt
some form of full or partial netting for the allocation of capital gains,
but continue to adopt layering to allocate dividends, interest, and investment expense.

Few U.S. partnerships follow through the U.S. Treasury Regulations to
formulate a convex optimization problem according to the guidance provided in the regulations and solve for robust, unique, and tax-neutral
allocations of not just capital gains, but also dividends, interest, and investment expense *simultaneously*.

U.S. partnerships greatly reduce the tax accounting burden by implementing full or partial netting in a systematic manner as a 2-pass convex
optimization problem. This appendix has provided such a methodology,
building upon the previous appendixes that focused on capital gains allocations only.

## Summary of the Results in Appendixes 2, 3, 4, and 5

Appendixes 2 and 3 provide U.S. partnerships with a roadmap to accurately
implement full or partial netting, respectively, for allocating realized capital
gains, under the assumption that tax allocations of other items of income
such as dividends, interest, and investment expense are made according
to the layering methodology. Appendix 4 provides U.S. partnerships the
means to make nonabusive tax allocation tilts according to tax preferences.
Finally, Appendix 5 enables U.S. partnerships to dispel with layering per-
manently, replacing it with an automated convex optimization methodology
for full or partial netting to *simultaneously* make tax allocations of *all* items
of taxable pass-through income, not just realized capital gains, but also
dividends, interest, and investment expense.

## Acknowledging the Originators of the Front-End Convex Optimization Software CVX and Its Back-End Algorithm SDPT3

Computer hardware and pioneering convex programming algorithms have come a long way. A standard desktop computer has enormous computing power today. CVX using the SDPT3 algorithm running within the Matlab software environment produces shockingly fast convergence, usually in fractions of a second. The mathematical programming community has innovated algorithms called "interior point methods" that intelligently know the best direction for iterations, as a result of which they require very few iterations for large industrial-scale problems. The ability of CVX using SDPT3 to digest a test problem that was presented, consisting of 100 partners, that led to 800 tax allocation decision variables with 1,007 constraints solved in barely a few seconds, is impressive.

We conclude by acknowledging the authors of the developing opensource front-end software engine CVX for convex optimization, particularly its chief architect Michael Grant and its co-architect Stephen Boyd, who host its download and manual at his Stanford University Web page.[1] CVX is inspired by the idea of "disciplined convex programming," which greatly reduces the human effort required to persuade hard-wired computer algorithms to recognize problem and data inputs that are human-readable.[2] CVX enabled us to take the abstract formulation of the convex optimization problem in Chapter 7 to the efficient and practical industrial-strength problems presented in Appendixes 2, 3, 4, and 5. CVX proverbially "stands on the shoulders of giants," since it passes on the problem to the open-source SDPT3 algorithm, for which we give due credit to the trio T3 (Toh, Todd, and Tutuncu[3]), who originated their semidefinite programming (SDP) algorithm named SDPT3 as an efficient large-scale general-purpose code based on a polynomial-time interior-point method.

---

[1] *op. cit.*, Appendix 2.
[2] Michael Grant, Stephen Boyd, and Yinyu Ye, "Disciplined Convex Programming," in Leo Liberti and Nelson Maculan (ed.), *Global Optimization: From Theory to Implementation*, Springer US, 2006, pages 155–200.
[3] *op. cit.*, Appendix 2.

# Index